Second Edition

Engaging Diversity

Multiculturalism in Canada

Bruce Plcombs
April 2000 (?) 2002
Dook Copy.

Augie Fleras
University of Waterloo

Jean Leonard Elliott

NELSON
™
THOMSON LEARNING

Australia • Canada • Mexico • Singapore • Spain • United Kingdom • United States

NELSON

THOMSON LEARNING ™

Engaging Diversity:
Multiculturalism in Canada
Second Edition

by Augie Fleras and
Jean Leonard Elliott

Editorial Director and Publisher:
Evelyn Veitch

Executive Editor:
Joanna Cotton

Marketing Manager:
Cara Yarzab

Developmental Editor:
Su Mei Ku

Production Editors:
Susan Calvert/Wendy Yano

Production Coordinator:
Hedy Sellers

Copy Editor:
Matthew Kudelka

Proofreader:
Wayne Herrington

Creative Director:
Angela Cluer

Cover Design:
Ken Phipps

Cover Image:
Always Returning by Cameron
Sharpe

Compositor:
Janet Zanette

Printer:
Transcontinental Printing Inc.

**National Library of Canada
Cataloguing in Publication Data**

Fleras, Augie, 1947–
    Engaging diversity :
multiculturalism in Canada

2nd ed.
Previous ed. published under title:
Multiculturalism in Canada.
Includes bibliographical references
and index.
ISBN 0-17-616857-5

1. Multiculturalism—Canada.
I. Elliott, Jean Leonard, 1941- .
II. Multiculturalism in Canada.
III. Title.

FC104.F54 2001   305.8'00971
C2001-902779-6
F1035.A1F54 2001

To Jocelyn

Table of Contents

Preface

People abroad conjure up a variety of images about Canada. Foremost among these is that Canadians are a resilient people with unlimited resourcefulness in meeting the demands of a harsh and often unforgiving environment. People also marvel at Canada's ability to withstand being absorbed into the United States while continuing to benefit from that relationship in economic terms. Yet another perception of Canada has taken root in recent years. Canada is widely admired as an ethnically diverse and remarkably cohesive society of aboriginal peoples, English- and French-speaking charter groups, and immigrants and refugees. Canada's engagement with diversity is praised as enlightened, especially when compared with global norms. Survey after survey confirms a solid core of political and public support for the principles of diversity. Initiatives for engaging diversity are routinely perceived as legitimate and worthwhile, despite disagreements over pace and scope. Not surprisingly, Canada's reputation as a pioneer in "building bridges" has attracted the attention of governments elsewhere, many of whom are stumbling with minority dynamics and ethnic nationalisms.

Appearances are deceiving, however. Canada may not be as diversity-minded as many would like to believe. Its endorsement of diversity is conditional, generally lacks passion, and is often devoid of commitment. Support is forthcoming, but is also easily revoked when costs escalate or "national interests" are threatened. Furthermore, Canada's lofty reputation has dimmed in recent years because of social breakdowns. Of particular note are conflicts involving the following: police–minority youth relations in metropolitan areas; government repression of aboriginal civil disobedience; racially inspired hate crimes; media misrepresentations of minority women and men; the proliferation of Internet hate sites; and the continuing politics of brinkmanship that distort Quebec–Ottawa relations. No less disruptive to the diversity agenda is continuing prejudice and discrimination, the cumulative impact of which has been to deny and exclude.

But while the gravity of these threats to Canada's social fabric should not be soft-pedalled, the obverse is no less true. Canada is still among the most successful of the world's societies at accepting diversity. Few initiatives in this country have garnered as much prominence—and notoriety—as official multiculturalism. Canada declared itself the world's first officially multicultural nation in 1971—a move as unprecedented as it turned out to be provocative. A fact of Canadian demographics was repackaged into a society-building virtue that declared the then-preposterous goal of multicultural coexistence around a unifying vision. Three decades of official multiculturalism seemed to have confirmed the obvious: never underestimate the power of an idea whose timing is right.

Official multiculturalism is still renowned as a bold if imperfect experiment in forging unity from diversity. Both legislation and constitutional changes have secured a Canadian model of multiculturalism that has proven to be a "beacon of enlightenment" in a world of ethnic cleansing and final solutions. Multiculturalism as a blueprint for living together is widely extolled. Its popularity in contemporary intellectual discourses has further cemented the status of official multiculturalism as Canada's quintessential invention (Glazer, 1997; Weisman, 2000). This accolade was nicely captured by the Australian Advisory Council on Languages and Multicultural Education (VOX, 1988: 20) when it proclaimed:

> Indeed, the term "multiculturalism" is a Canadian creation. Canadians are to enter the 21st century as the world's best prepared country, enjoying an important advantage over her friends and competitors. (cited in Cummins and Danesi, 1990: 99)

To be sure, blemishes exist. Debates over multiculturalism continue to challenge Canada's diversity agenda in many ways. Its legitimacy is based on the as yet unproven assumption that differences can be integrated without chaos or confusion. But its perceived shortcomings should not obscure advantages. Multiculturalism deserves credit for grappling with the age-old conundrum of how to balance "culture" with "equality" and "inclusion." The blending of national interests with international goodwill ensures its value as an ideological export. As Europe confronts the possibility of massive immigration to offset population declines and bolster economic growth, many European countries are looking to Canada's multicultural project as a blueprint for survival (Isajiw, 1997; Rex, 1997; Crossette, 2000).

However wide and deserved the acclaim, not all is well in "multicultureland." Multiculturalism is under siege (Magsino, 2000). A crisis of confidence is eroding those certainties which once made multiculturalism the centrepiece of Canadian identity building. The concern is mounting in the debate over how Canadians should live together. Some Canadians concur with the principles of multiculturalism but have grave doubts about its relevance in this postmodern world of nationalisms and human rights agendas. Others are growing increasingly indifferent or apathetic to multiculturalism, to the extent that political and public support for it is dwindling (Sugunasiri, 1999). Multiculturalism is criticized for distracting minorities from concerns over equality (Bolaria and Li, 1988). Others feel that multiculturalism as many

Canadians practise it damages national unity (Bibby, 1990; Bissoondath, 1994). It is often seen as a problem rather than as a solution, and this has polarized critical opinion (Li, 1999). For some, the timidity of official multiculturalism reinforces its status as little more than a "sheep" in "wolf's" clothing. For others, official multiculturalism is a "wolf" in "sheep's" clothing in the sense that it has the potency to disrupt or destroy Canadian society. Which appraisal is more accurate? Will it make any difference? Does anyone care?

In short, not everyone has hopped aboard the multicultural bandwagon. Some see multiculturalism as nothing less than an impertinent affront to the principles of equality and justice. Others believe that only multiculturalism can overcome the disfiguring legacy of racism and its discrimination. Still others are bewildered by what official multiculturalism is trying to do, and why (Fleras and Kunz, 2001). Yet approve or disapprove, like or dislike, a recontouring of Canada along multiculturalism lines is no longer an option or a luxury. At a time when many sacred cows are under scrutiny, pressure is mounting to analyze and assess multiculturalism without capitulating to cynicism or despair. A rethinking of conventional wisdom is overdue. Official multiculturalism may have originated in people's desire to make Canada safe *for* diversity, yet safe *from* the excesses of diversity. At present, however, the challenge may lie in inverting this equation: that is, in finding ways to make diversity safe *from* Canada yet safe *for* Canadian society. If we fail to navigate the tricky shoals between "diversified unity" and "unified diversity," Canada will be in trouble.

It is in this context of criticism and concern, admiration and confusion, that this book addresses the sometimes murky realm of Canadian multiculturalism. In *Engaging Diversity* I grapple with the paradoxes and politics of multiculturalism as a blueprint for living together with differences. After thirty years, has official multiculturalism lived up to its expectations? Does multiculturalism contribute to a vision of Canada as a "just society"? Have Canadians truly embraced multiculturalism? Has official multiculturalism made any difference? In this book I try to answer these questions. I contend that multiculturalism has proven a formidable challenge to Canada. Multiculturalism embraces diversity; yet at the same time, it defends the dominant ideology. Overall, official multiculturalism remains a flawed though workable social experiment that remains compromised by its own inconsistencies.

In *Engaging Diversity* I consider multiculturalism as both a formal doctrine and a system of practices. I explore official multiculturalism as fact, as ideology, as policy, as practice, and as critique. I consider public attitudes, regional responses, and critical reactions to it. To these ends, I use various frames of reference, including interpersonal, institutional, national, and international. I discuss attempts to integrate multicultural principles into Canada's mainstream institutions. I expose the inherent ambiguities in official multiculturalism and debunk the myths that erode its potential for building bridges. In sum, I expose official multiculturalism for what it really is: a model for inclusiveness that is both progressive and doable, yet at the same time superficial and regressive.

I hope this book will provide a forum for enlightened debate over official multiculturalism. My central argument is fairly straightforward, even if the supporting evidence is conflicting and contested. Like it or not, approve or disapprove, Canada has little choice but to embrace multiculturalism. Multiculturalism is the only option Canadians have for living together. But that doesn't make it easy.

I have divided this book into two parts. Part 1 (Chapters 1 to 4) offers an overview of multiculturalism. Chapter 1 broadly introduces the politics of diversity, and shows that multiculturalism is a site of complicated debates about diversity. Chapter 2 looks at multiculturalism's various meanings—at multiculturalism as fact, ideology, policy, practice, and critique. Chapter 3 discusses multiculturalism as something politicians "invented." Chapter 4 appraises official multiculturalism in terms of public attitudes.

Part 2 addresses the politics of putting multicultural principles into practice. Chapter 5 considers how multicultural principles have been applied in the criminal justice system. In Chapter 6 the mainstream media are put to the multicultural test. Chapter 7 discusses multicultural education. Chapter 8 explores how multiculturalism is put to work at interpersonal levels.

Like any author, I have had to leave out a great deal. For example, I have largely ignored the "folkloric" aspects of multiculturalism. In any case, by including such "examples," I would have been veering toward stereotyping. Capsulized commentaries of Canada's cultural mosaic can easily reinforce the very problems that multiculturalism attempts to address. My effort is on the big picture: on the implications of multiculturalism for Canadian society building. Many Canadians are looking for ways to live together by building bridges; I hope this book provides some insight.

In the process of rethinking this book, I lost my co-author. Jean Leonard Elliott was a remarkable talent whose dislike of injustice informed much of her work. To say that her passion for equality infused all our work together would surely qualify as an understatement. Her untimely death in 1995 left a gaping hole that I have yet to fill. May *Engaging Diversity* stand as lasting testimony to a treasured friend and pioneering colleague whose courage of conviction propelled Canada to the forefront of societies for living together, multiculturally.

Acknowledgments

Many people have helped put this book together. I would like to acknowledge the contribution of the reviewers of this book: Alan Anderson (University of Saskatchewan), Paul Baxter (Georgian College), Jerome Black (McGill University), Parrin Dossa (Simon Fraser University), Leo de Jourdan (Canadore College), Karen Moreau-Petti (Niagara College), Ruth Rees (Queen's University), and Lloyd Wong (University of Calgary).

PART 1 | The Idea of Multiculturalism

The world over, diversity is now a common and also controversial feature of the political landscape (Frederickson, 1999). As the new millennium begins, significant change is taking place in the political and cultural outlooks that shape debates about diversity. The twentieth century was consumed by two overarching cultural trends: Marxism and liberalism. Both Marxism (which includes communism and socialism) and liberal pluralism emphasized the universal qualities of humankind and refused to take differences between peoples seriously. At one end of the continuum was liberal pluralism, which claimed, at its centre, that what individuals had in common mattered more than any differences arising from their membership in a group. Any differences that existed didn't really matter, and were to be tolerated only if everyone differed in the same kind of way.

At the other end of this continuum were Marxist models, which also endorsed a "pretend pluralism." In Marxist thought, people could only secure equality through collective action and universal progress. Oppression was the result of one basic contradiction—class relations, which were more important than any ethnic differences in explaining who got what. Though they defined an ideal society in very different ways, both Marxists and liberals were strongly committed to universality. True equality could only be based on treating everyone the same, whatever their differences. In a world divided sharply into classes and segregated by race, this type of enlightened universalism was a considerable advance. But in denying that differences between groups mattered when it came to understanding who got what, both Marxists and liberal pluralists badly miscalculated world history.

For most of the modern era, Western societies embraced the universal and the uniform as a basis for living together. But we have since entered the postmodern era, in which differences between people are recognized and rewarded simply because they exist. Postmodernism challenges conventional notions of order, universality, and hierarchy on the grounds these try to impose a contrived uniformity on a fragmented and contradictory world (Li, 1999). It proposes instead a multiculturalism that truly reflects social realities. This new cultural politics has a number of important features, including the following (see West, 1996):

- Rejection of the monolithic and fixed in favour of diversity, heterogeneity, and multiplicity.
- Rejection of the abstract and universal in favour of the customized, concrete, and specific.
- Rejection of the rigid and doctrinaire in favour of the contingent, changing, and provisional.
- Rejection of the uniform and conformity in favour of the distinctive in defining who gets what.
- Rejection of an objective reality in favour of "realities" as all surfaces, hybrids, and discourses.

This rise of the distinctive is hardly unprecedented. A similar struggle consumed the nineteenth century, during which Enlightenment thinkers squared off with the Romantics over such issues. The Enlightenment view was that what people had in common mattered more than any differences between them; the Romanticist view was the reverse. The same debate is taking place in (post) modern Canada.

To be sure, Canadians do not seem to be especially in love with diversity as something to which people are "entitled." We tend to prefer a "pretend pluralism"—to tolerate rather than embrace differences. That being said, changes are clearly taking place in the social climate: struggles for recognition and demands for redistribution are rapidly becoming the focus of political conflict (see Fraser, 1998). Diversity as one mechanism for ordering society is no longer dismissed or ignored; instead, it is being increasingly accepted as grounds for recognizing and rewarding people and as the basis of social relationships. In this world of shifting boundaries and contested nationalities, the politics of diversity are here to stay.

A commitment to diversity has profoundly altered the society-building process in Canada (Samuel and Schachhuber, 2000). Diversity in this country is proving to be highly controversial, with the arguments for and against it hinging on the related issue of disadvantage. Wherever the debate flares, confusion and hostility are rampant. Differences are perceived in a number of ways: (a) as superficial and irrelevant, or as fundamental and worthy of recognition; (b) as a threat and challenge, or as an opportunity and asset; (c) as empowering, or as having the potential to deny, exclude, or stereotype; and (d) as contrary to society building, or as consistent with an inclusive society. Disparities in opinion like this should come as no surprise: in societies historically organized around the principles of conformity, rationality, consensus, and control, appeals for diversity tend to be dismissed as disorderly or disruptive (Eisenstein, 1996). When diversity is dismissed as superficial—as "exceptions to the rule" of an essentially universal humanity—any commitment to taking differences seriously is undermined (Fish, 1997). Diversity may be tolerated, and even encouraged as a positive contribution to society. But its acceptance hinges on the simultaneous acceptance of a common institutional framework that diminishes differences to a one-size-fits-all sameness.

Multiculturalism policies are subject to the same debates, doubts, and pressures. The politics of diversity rarely result in consensus; in the same way, debates about multiculturalism are racked with contention over objectives, premises, processes, and outcomes. Multiculturalism has been criticized as a paternalistic solution to the "problem" of minorities. It has also been endorsed as progressive in that it extends recognition and authenticity to those who lack either or both. Its perception as the political outcome of power struggles both ongoing and negotiated is no less controversial (Modood, 1997; Samad, 1997).

Contradictions abound in this climate. Multiculturalism may encourage, without meaning to, the very divisiveness it sets out to control. Or it may just as unwittingly reinforce the very assimilation it sets out to discourage. One side of the multiculturalism debate (the "modern" one) favours an egalitarian rhetoric and a commitment to social equality. The other (the "postmodern" one) accepts that cultural differences are authentic but rejects government efforts to "interfere" as little more than a power grab (Joppke, 1996; also Bulmer and Solomos, 1998). Regarding Canadians at large, multiculturalism has been seen as highly beneficial for some but a detriment to others; and as a source of solace for some but of confusion for others. For others still, it has constituted proof that society is indifferent to them.

Multiculturalism is an "article of faith" in Canada and a "norm of Canadian social policy," yet no one has ever succeeded in defining it. Canada has suffered from this failure to resolve the ambiguities and paradoxes attached to the term; this in itself more than justifies the effort in the next section to explore what it actually means.

Any close examination of multiculturalism must go beyond the factual or descriptive. There are tensions within multiculturalism arising from different levels of meaning. Multiculturalism can be seen as any or all of the following:

- a description (i.e., an empirical fact)
- a prescription (i.e., an ideology)
- a political slant (i.e., a policy)
- a set of intergroup dynamics (i.e., a practice)
- a challenge to conventional patterns of power and privilege (i.e., a critique)

To complicate all this, multiculturalism can be interpreted from various perspectives: political, economic, cultural, social, and ideological. Moreover, any attempt to theorize about multiculturalism must acknowledge variations in the following:

- What people think multiculturalism is *doing*.
- What people think it *should* do.
- What multiculturalism was *intended* to do.
- What it *really is* doing.
- What it *can* do in the circumstances.
- What it *should* do in balancing competing interests.

Having considered all of the above, we will have established a solid framework for studying multiculturalism. The following questions provide a window of opportunity for discussing and debating multiculturalism:

- What are the preconditions for "living together with differences"? Does "official" multiculturalism provide an appropriate blueprint for achieving this goal?
- Is multiculturalism about creating a society in which differences are minimized? Or is it about creating a society in which those differences are taken seriously as a basis for rewards and recognition?
- Does official multiculturalism help or hinder Canada-building? And how can we tell?
- Is multiculturalism about justice? about recognition? about redistribution? Or is it mainly a power-grabbing strategy devised by the government?
- Is official multiculturalism culture *blind* or culture *conscious*? In other words, is it about promoting diversity, or is it about eliminating disadvantage by taking differences into account in defining who gets what?
- Is official multiculturalism capable of taking differences seriously? Or is it doomed to a "pretend pluralism" by simultaneously affirming and denying differences as a basis for living together?
- Multiculturalism in some of its forms can exclude and silence people even while including and empowering them. So how, then, can we assess it in this regard? As good *or* bad depending on the criteria? As good *and* bad because of its double-edged nature? Or as *neither* good *nor* bad but rather something that just "is"?
- Does multiculturalism increase the risk of ethnic conflict by encouraging diversity at the expense of national unity? Or do multicultural policies establish a framework for living together by depoliticizing the threat of ethnicity?

- How much diversity can be "tolerated," and what kinds, before multiculturalism explodes? Conversely, how much conformity can Canada tolerate before imploding? Who should be answering these questions, and what should the decisions be based on?
- Does one size really fit all? Can official (i.e., federal) multiculturalism be applied across Canada's multilayered diversity? And can the Canadian model be applied to other parts of the world?
- Is official multiculturalism little more than a political strategy for exerting social control? Is it merely a means for ruling by dividing a multiethnic society? Or is it an exercise in inclusiveness that challenges exclusion and inequality without disrupting the status quo?
- Regarding Canadian culture, to what extent is multiculturalism a "preservative" policy—a kind of assimilation in slow motion? And does multiculturalism have the potential to resist, challenge, and "reimagine" Canada along pluralistic lines?
- Does official multiculturalism accomplish what it sets out to do? Is it working? How can we tell?
- Do the various forms of multiculturalism have anything in common? Or does the term's meaning depend entirely on context?
- Where do we draw the line in terms of what is acceptable in a multicultural society? Should a liberal multiculturalism be tolerant of illiberal practices that are at odds with laws, rights, or core cultural values?
- Is Canada a multicultural society? Yes? No? Maybe? It depends…? What would a truly multicultural society look like?
- How relevant will official multiculturalism be in the twenty-first century? How will it cope with the demands of Canadian society, which is rapidly changing and increasingly interconnected with other societies in the broader context of globalization, human rights, and ethnic nationalism?

In this book we will not flinch from asking tough questions about Canada's commitment to multiculturalism. To be sure, the above questions and similar ones rarely yield simple answers. But we must arrive at some critically informed answers if official multiculturalism is to reclaim its potential to challenge racist discourses and social inequities, and if multiculturalism as a debate about diversity is to stay relevant. It is within this context of criticism and concern, coupled with admiration and confusion, that we justify the following excursion into the sometimes murky realm of Canadian multiculturalism.

CHAPTER
1

Multiculturalism and Diversity

CHAPTER OBJECTIVES

- To show how diversity and multiculturalism are linked and affect each other.
- To show that diversity can be both empowering and disempowering.
- To show that diversity is very much a matter of context and is socially constructed.
- To show that diversity per se is not the problem; rather, problems arise when diversity is perceived as inferior or irrelevant.
- To show that "living together with differences" is not as easy as it sounds, especially when "deep" diversities clash with the principles of liberal pluralism.
- To show how the interplay of the political with the social and demographic makes it difficult to map multicultural landscapes.
- To discuss how "pretend pluralism" differs from "taking differences seriously."
- To show how hard it is to define multiculturalism beyond a broad commitment to engage diversity as "different yet equal."
- To explain the distinction between generic multiculturalism and "official" multiculturalism.
- To convey how debates over diversity in a multicultural society always raise questions about where the line should be drawn.

CASE STUDY
Drawing the Multicultural Line

How should pluralistic societies that are tolerant of diversity respond to minority customs that conflict with mainstream values and beliefs? Where should the broader society draw the line? Consider the following issues:

- disciplinary techniques such as shaming and physical punishment
- parent–child sleeping arrangements
- group rituals and initiation ceremonies involving scarification or genital mutilation
- arranged marriage or polygamy
- the subordination and/or segregation of women
- deference to the powerful or elderly (Crossette, 1999)

Should these practices be dismissed as un-Canadian and punished accordingly? Or must we take them into account if multiculturalism is to mean anything? How should multicultural societies, which presumably are based on tolerance and pluralism, deal with cultural practices that suppress just those values? How should multiculturalism deal with religious or cultural groups whose values compromise the rights of other protected groups (Giese, 2000)? Minority women and men with drastically different cultures sometimes contend that they should not be held to a universal standard if justice is to be served—that the majority must take their differences seriously, if only to shield them from monocultural laws and ethnocentric standards (Clause, 1999).

Superficial differences are easy to tolerate. But mainstream acceptance stiffens visibly when cultural differences are perceived as contrary to fundamental principles such as gender equality and individual rights. Moreover, taking differences seriously can pose a problem when the rights of multicultural *groups* are considered. When minority groups are given special rights to protect them from the dominant group, discrimination within the protected group can be perpetuated, whether that was the purpose or not. As Susan Okin (1999) writes, most cultures are suffused with practices and ideologies that subjugate women to men, that restrict women's well-being and freedom of choice, and that privilege males as "normal."

Dilemmas like this force us to ask ourselves whether there are limits to what Canadian multiculturalism can tolerate. Who should decide what those limits are, and how should this be decided? Should minority groups be permitted to "import" into Canada violent animosities originating in their homeland? A good example of this problem is that Muslims are reluctant to embrace broadly accepted precepts of liberal-pluralist society when those are at odds with Islam, and prefer to follow practices that fall outside an openly secular and only nominally religious society. In fairness to Muslims, there are fundamentalist Christian sects that are just as uncomfortable with overtly secular domains and have taken steps to protect their interests.

Perhaps the very best example of this dilemma relates to female genital mutilation (FGM), a practice that affects perhaps as many as 120 million women and girls in Muslim Africa. In broad terms, the purpose of genital mutilation is to control the sexuality of women—to ensure their fidelity or virginity. The practice varies in severity. The "milder" procedures involve the removal of the clitoris. The more severe ones involve cutting away all external genitals ("infibulation") and amputating the clitoris; all of this leaves an aperture the circumference of a matchstick for urinary and menstrual functions (Dyer, 1999). As many as 10 percent of young women die soon after the procedure from shock or infections. Another 25 percent may succumb from long-term complications. Yet there is a paradox here: the victims of this practice often grow up to be its most vocal supporters.

There is growing concern that as a result of immigration, this practice is appearing in Canada, especially among conservative Muslims who fear that their daughters will not find husbands unless they are circumcised. Reactions to FGM in the non-Muslim world are extremely varied. Does criticism of it reflect an ethnocentric criticism of culturally specific practices? Or is FGM purely and simply a violation of universal human rights? Many people feel that there is no moral justification for such a seemingly cruel and discriminatory tradition, even in a multicultural society. The law and the medical profession agree, and condemn FGM as a coercive custom that does needless harm. Only a misguided multiculturalism would tolerate practices such as FGM; after all, respecting others' cultural customs is not the same as tolerating practices that are at odds with Canadian laws and values.

Yet some people are dismayed that Canadian society has failed to recognize the cultural (as opposed to the legal) dimensions of "female circumcision," and are questioning more and more whether it is proper or even practical to ban culturally entrenched customs that don't happen to be Western customs. If Canada takes itself seriously as a multicultural society, how can it banish a practice that is culturally embedded and widely condoned? Where does FGM stand in relation to human rights? Do universal human rights *always* transcend specific cultural norms? How does an official multiculturalism position itself on this issue? How would a thoughtful (multi)cultural relativism rule in this issue? In the continuation of this case study at the end of the chapter, I cast additional light on this conundrum.

THE MULTICULTURAL LANDSCAPE

Almost all contemporary nation-states must find ways to engage diversity without falling into chaos. Most states are multiethnic (Connor, 2000). Nearly 40 percent of states contain five or more significant ethnic groups; Nigeria and the ex–Soviet Union have over one hundred ethnic groups each. In 30 percent of states the largest national group is not even a majority. The challenges of diversity are especially evident in the white settler dominions, where the politics of indigeneity are challenging assumptions about governance, power sharing, and sovereignty (Stasiulis and Yuval-Davis, 1995; Havemann, 1999; Ivison et al., 2000). Recent large-scale immigration to Canada, Australia, the United States, and New Zealand has further disrupted the once monocultural landscape of these transplanted European societies (Hellsten, 1999). This strong demographic shift has intensified pressures to rethink the challenges of "living together with differences" (Fleras and Spoonley, 1999).

Multiethnic states have responded by adopting various accommodation policies and practices. Some endorse the separation or segregation of minorities; others support assimilation and integration; still others advocate pluralistic incorporation (Fleras and Elliott, 1999). Modern liberal-democratic societies such as Canada and Australia have embraced pluralism and are attempting to integrate immigrant minorities by removing exclusionary barriers (Pearson, 1996; Vasta and Castles, 1996; Jupp, 1997). The United States and New Zealand are taking a different approach; both seem anxious to reject the assimilationism of the past in favour of more inclusive overtures (Goldberg, 1994; Fleras, 1998). This commitment to diversity has a deceptively simple yet elusive objective—to create a culturally plural yet socially inclusive society without compromising national interests.

In their state-building activities, all pluralistic societies face the challenge of reconciling unity and diversity. They must establish political and cultural arrangements that foster national unity without suppressing cultural differences. Many of them have found that multiculturalism policies enable them to do this—that such policies promote a cohesive society, and incorporate diversity without destroying society's core values or damaging its constituent parts. Multiculturalism has often delivered at least some of what was hoped: a workable multiethnic society with a common vision. Multicultural policies have often had these goals (Hudson, 1987):

- to harmonize group relations through intercultural exchanges
- to eliminate discrimination, both personal and systemic
- to reduce minority disadvantage, both social and economic
- to expand minority opportunities
- to help individuals preserve their cultural identity
- to celebrate diversity as valuable in its own right and as advancing national interests
- to (re)educate the public about the virtues of tolerance and cultural diversity
- to establish a voice for neglected and historically disadvantaged minorities
- to challenge the existing balance of cultural power
- to transform society along pluralistic-friendly lines
- to create a society safe "for" diversity, yet safe "from" diversity
- conversely, to make diversity safe "from" society, yet safe "for" society
- to connect diversity with the demands and opportunities of a global market economy

It is clear from this list that multiculturalism has many dimensions. It directly strengthens cultural identity, social justice, citizenship, and national unity. It also offers an alternative way of viewing the world, thinking about society, experiencing reality, and relating to diversity. This is a significant departure from the past, when philosophies of denial and exclusion prevailed.

But multiculturalism is vulnerable to various criticisms. Michael Possner has observed (1997) that in recent years, few issues in Western culture have triggered as much controversy as official multiculturalism. The mere idea of it is a red flag waved at modern society's combatants. Depending on whom one asks, multiculturalism denies diversity or affirms it; involves either hurling criticism or building consensus; promotes either conformity or diversity, either control or freedom from control; increases the centre's power or encourages resistance to that power; encourages people to belong or excludes them from belonging; and helps them build both bridges and walls (see Vasta, 1996). Those on the political left dismiss multiculturalism as a capitalist ideology bent on dividing and distracting the disadvantaged; those on the political right condemn it for diluting core values and for compromising national unity and identity. Those in between often endorse the principles of pluralism, but only superficially and with strings attached. Or they dismiss multiculturalism as too indefinite a term to have any worth (Li, 1999).

Since it first appeared as an item on the social policy agenda, multiculturalism has never stopped shaking Canada's social foundations. For some, in a truly multicultural society differences wouldn't matter, since equality is really about emphasizing similarities. For others, multiculturalism is really about taking differences into account to ensure genuine equality. For still others, the issue is not differences but rather *disadvantage*, to the extent that differences deny others' rights or exclude them from participation. Ellie Vasta (1996: 48) captures the tensions surrounding multiculturalism:

> As public policy, multiculturalism is concerned with the management of cultural differences. It is this apparently innocuous objective that all the ambivalence of multiculturalism arises; it is simultaneously a discourse of pacification and emancipation; of control and participation; of the legitimation of the existing order and of innovation. Multiculturalism is part of a strategy of domination over minorities by the majority, but also points beyond this, to the possibility of new forms of social and cultural relations. As such, multiculturalism is a power relationship, and has something of the intrinsic ambivalence of power that Hegel demonstrated in his analysis of the master-slave relationship.

Multiculturalism is full of contradictions, both political and economic. Because it is, it has the potential to actually compromise minority rights and shore up vested interests, even when it is intended to do the opposite. Multiculturalism can have these seemingly "negative" consequences, some of them inadvertent and some not:

- securing social control
- cultivating social divisions
- encouraging ethnic conflict
- fostering "slow motion" assimilation
- entrenching inequality
- fomenting racism
- creating the illusion of progressive and planned change
- dismembering a country

The criticisms of multiculturalism are as compelling as the arguments in its favour. Predictably, then, there is ample room for applying different spins to what is essentially an innovative yet flawed social experiment. Ambiguity and conflict are likely to prevail, with politicians and minority groups capitalizing on multiculturalism by resorting to tactics that are both self-serving and mutually opposed. The paradoxes inherent in multiculturalism should not be lightly dismissed: unless there is an overarching multicultural vision, the same powers that transform diversity into a progressive force can inadvertently breed hatred. It is precisely this ambiguity regarding official multiculturalism as a blueprint for progressive change *and* as an instrument of social control that generates debate. These mixed signals also confirm the obvious: when it comes to theorizing about multiculturalism, clichés and slogans are no substitute for informed analysis.

DEFINING MULTICULTURALISM

> If the word multiculturalism is harder than ever to contain or pin down, it is because it has been very busy on many fronts and is now being changed, by its triumphs, by its failures, but also by changes occurring around it. (Longley, 1999: 79)

Multiculturalism has emerged as a "must use" word in modern cultural debates (Bharucha, 1999). According to Savard and Vigezzi (1999), it is the most widely discussed phenomenon in the modern world. Yet we cannot ignore its ambiguous and contradictory properties. Multiculturalism has an uncanny knack for arousing both high hopes and profound fears. The term is now deeply embedded in Western cultural debates, and from that unassailable position has proven to be a source of both enlightenment and disempowerment. It is championed as a fountainhead of cultural ideals, and at the same time criticized for allowing Western democracies to pervert those ideals. All of this confusion and ambiguity should come as no surprise: the word "culture" is generally regarded as one of the most complex in the English language (Eagleton, 2000). Imagine then the complexities associated with the concept of *many* ("multi") cultures.

Multiculturalism has been busy on many fronts and doing many jobs that are widely if not enthusiastically supported. Yet all of this staunch support for multiculturalism has not helped anyone define what it is. Also, no unifying and consistent theory has been developed for multiculturalism; the term embraces too many things for one theory to address (Willett, 1997). Nor is there any agreement over how to apply it, or what its implications are (Bulmer and Solomos, 1998). Consider this partial list of definitions of multiculturalism:

only the first two of these definitions are serious.

- A "descriptive" definition—The existence of ethnically diverse groups who are culturally different and who wish to remain so at least in principle (if not always in practice).
- A "prescriptive" definition—A set of ideals that promote diversity as normal, necessary, and acceptable.
- A "political" definition—A framework for justifying government initiatives in diversity issues.
- A "practical" definition—Something to be used by minority groups to advance their interests, compete for scarce resources, or upbraid society for failing to abide by multicultural principles.

There is almost no limit to the definitions. Multiculturalism can mean everything, or nothing; it can empower and enable, or it can disable and disempower; it can describe a state of society, or it can describe what society must not be allowed to become; it can enlighten people, or it can conceal the truth from them; it can reassure them, or it can instill fear in them. Further complicating the cultural landscape are the different perceptions people hold regarding what multiculturalism is *supposed* to do, what it is *really* doing, what it *can* do, what people *think* it is doing, and what people think it *should* do. Finally, multiculturalism can focus on social equality (for individuals), cultural identity (for groups), or broader national interests. And all of the above overlap and intersect.

Multiculturalism has an uncanny knack for meaning different things to different people in different contexts. The British magazine *Melting Pot* is marketed as the "magazine for today's multi-cultural society." For some, multiculturalism is synonymous with Canada's official multiculturalism (Fleras, 1998). For others, the word amounts to a subversive challenge to the cultural status quo (Goldberg, 1994). For others still, it is an ambitious yet ambiguous social experiment in (mis)managing race and ethnic relations (Li, 1999). For yet others, multiculturalism is a "loaded" concept that means everything yet nothing. Multiculturalism, in sum, is an empty category that can absorb many things as contexts dictate (Gunew, 1999). Todd Gitlin (1995: 228) alludes to this:

> The word is baggy, a melange of fact and value, current precisely because it is vague enough to serve so many interests. Partisans may use the term to defend the recognition of difference, or to resist policies or ideas imposed by conquerors, or to defend cosmopolitanism—the interests and pleasures that each may take in the profusion of humanity. The purists of identity politics use it to defend endless fission, a heap of monocultures. On the other side, multiculturalism and its demonic twin, "political correctness," serves

conservatives as names for a potpourri of things they detest—including an irritating insistence on the rights of minorities.

Precision is further blunted by loose terminology. Terms like "mosaic," "celebrating differences," "inclusiveness," "moving over and making space," "living together," and "diversity" have been badly overused in modern Canadian society. At the same time, they are so deeply embedded in the cultural discourse that many people have stopped thinking about what they actually mean, or assume that other people share their definitions. Yet these definitions are anything but self-evident. All of the above concepts are loaded and misleading, and often conceal and distort as much as they reveal and explain. It follows that these terms can curtail debate as easily as they encourage it.

In short, multiculturalism is a victim of its own success. Multiculturalism, which is so central to modern Canadian discourse, has come to mean so many things that consensus about what it is may no longer be possible (Caws, 1994). For example, consider the notion that multiculturalism means a society comprising different cultures that interact in a wide variety of ways (Martiniello, 1998). This definition is so broad as to be unusable. Other definitions are much more specific but run the risk of excluding much that is valuable. For example, we could define multiculturalism in Canada as a set of government policies and practices that promote diversity, respect, and equality as integral to this country's political, social, cultural, and symbolic order (Wilson, 1995; Annual Report, 2000; Fleras and Elliott, 1999). This definition is useful to the extent that it highlights the political dimension, but it also has two drawbacks. First, it reduces multiculturalism to "no more than" a government policy, which is unacceptably restrictive (Longley, 1998). Second, it assumes that Canada's multicultural model is the only one that exists, and ignores different models found in other parts of the world (Fleras, 1998).

What we need, then, is a definition broad enough to be inclusive but specific enough to capture the reality we are studying. It would also be helpful if our definition did more than tell us what multiculturalism *is*, and included what it *ought to be*. Concepts that end in "ism" tend to require defending or advocating—that is, they are always debatable (Hiller, 2000). Thus, we can define multiculturalism as a debate about what diversity is and what its repercussions are. Multiculturalism involves a process of engaging diversity as different yet equal. This definition approaches multiculturalism as a social concept, and assumes two things: that diversity is valuable in its own right, and that minority women and men have the right to be part of society. Implicit in all this are two further assumptions. First, that individuals ought to be able to identify with their language or culture without relinquishing their right to social or economic parity (Wieviorka, 1998; Kymlicka, 1998). Second, that diversity ought to be engaged in a constructive and proactive manner. Constrast this inclusiveness with "diversity-unfriendly" frameworks such as separatism and assimilation.

Some argue that *multicultural* is not a good adjective for Canada's multilayered pluralism; they suggest instead that Canada is (a) a three-nation state, those three nations being the First Nations, francophone Québécois, and anglophone Canadians, and (b) a polyethnic society that includes immigrant groups from around the world—Chinese, Africans, Latin Americans, and so on (Kymlicka, 1998). Some argue that historically, multiculturalism in Canada has been more about preserving a monocultural agenda (i.e., keeping minorities in place) than about actively engaging diversity (Vasta and Castles, 1996; Copeman and Scollen, 1999). Still others point out that contemporary cultures do not fall into fixed and separate streams; they are better described as hybrids—as patchworks of intersecting differences and overlapping similarities (Dijkstra et al., 2001). Seen in this light, Canada is not a fixed and independent mosaic of incompatible world views (Tully, 1995).

It is best to view Canadian society as a kaleidoscope of overlapping and intersecting identities. In the present-day world, identities are "intercultural" rather than multicultural. They are also hybridized, fragmented, fluid, and provisional rather than fixed. *Interculturalism* has has been defined as cross-cultural interaction between two territories (e.g., nation-states), or more than two; in contrast, *intraculturalism* involves relations between cultures within a given territory (Bharucha, 1999). The Quebec government uses the term *interculturalism* to describe its version of multiculturalism. Most people use the term *multiculturalism* in all circumstances, if only because it is the easiest one to reach for, after decades of familiarity.

DIVERSITY: FOR WHAT ENDS, IN WHOSE INTERESTS, ON WHAT GROUNDS?

> Long live diversity as long as it conforms to my standards, to my mind set, to my view of life, to my sense of order.
>
> Arturo Madrid (1988)

Canada is praised around the world for its success in embracing diversity. Yet Canadians tend to be of two minds where diversity is concerned. On the one hand, we take considerable pride in our diversity and acknowledge that tolerance is our defining characteristic. On the other, we bristle at the prospect of moving over to make cultural space, especially if it will be expensive or inconvenient. We insist on drawing a line between what is culturally acceptable and

17

what is not. This ambivalence toward diversity is reflected in our popular reactions to multiculturalism. Some Canadians are strongly critical of this country's commitment to multiculturalism and strongly denounce any concessions to or compromises with it. Others are willing to go to the wall to support Canada's diversity initiatives. Within the extremes of this continuum are those who withhold their opinions on diversity for fear of stepping on cultural landmines.

The politics of diversity continue to baffle. Some Canadians perceive diversity as both a personal threat and a threat to society, and favour the status quo. Others are drawn to diversity as something that is both valid in its own right and a valuable resource for society as a whole. Still others are indifferent and couldn't care less; or they endorse diversity in principle, but fret over the costs and consequences of its practice. Many shy away from endorsing diversity, seeing the debate as inherently divisive. A few, however, see more danger in conformity, in a world becoming more and more interconnected both economically and culturally. So the real challenge may actually lie in determining just why some perceive diversity as disruptive to a society in which uniformity and universality are losing their appeal.

It is an inescapable fact that however Canadians feel about it, the diversification of Canada is inevitable. Unfortunately, there is no magic formula for living together with difference, even as pressure mounts for a way to be found. No one has any idea how to build a society around the principles of taking differences seriously. What kinds of differences are permissible? How much diversity is acceptable? How much conformity is required? Where do we draw the line? Who is to decide all these things, and on what grounds? These questions are always being raised, yet consensus is impossible. Only one conclusion seems certain: any distinctions between the mainstream and minorities are bound to collapse because of urban demographic trends. Minority women and men will no longer accept being relegated to the edges of society's mainstream. At some point, diversity is going to be *inseparable* from the mainstream, and the mainstream is going to be repositioned as merely a *part* of the multicultural kaleidoscope rather than its unquestioned centre.

The Problems of Diversity

Multiculturalism is now the central debate in Canadian society. Before it was, diversity was routinely disparaged as either irrelevant or even something to be stamped out. Yet as concepts, multiculturalism and diversity have not received rigorous attention and tend to be overromanticized (Li, 1999; Harvey, 1992). Some people perceive diversity as mainly about differences and similarities

(Thomas Jr., 1995). For others, diversity is a self-standing "thing" rather than a structure of relationships. Diversity as "thing" refers to the notion that cultures are both fixed and inherently separate. This is the metaphor of the cultural mosaic carried to its extreme: individuals are slotted into pre-existing cultural categories without much option or choice; society is seen as a panorama of culturally different tiles locked into place by mainstream grout.

References to diversity as a static "thing" are not incorrect per se—they are merely insufficient. When diversity is approached as a "thing," too much emphasis is placed on differences, with the end result that diversity is defined as basically whatever isn't mainstream (see Rigor, 1997). This approach to diversity flattens analysis by diverting attention away from relations within groups and from power distributions between groups. Diversity is in fact fluid and situational; when it is seen any other way—that is, as a matter of factions in conflict—one side tends to win and the other to lose. Put another way, one side ends up subordinate to the other, with minority women and men locked into hermetically sealed categories that are at odds with mainstream standards. There are other dangers besides this to disconnecting diversity from social dynamics, as Joan Wallach Scott points out in *The Campaign Against Political Correctness* (1996). When we promote diversity as a condition of separate existence, we end up ignoring history, power, and context (McLaren, 1994). We also turn diversity into something bounded and fixed around pre-existing categories. But diversity is not about categories, nor is it about foods, festivals, or culture per se. Rather, diversity is about relationships of interdependence between groups in the context of unequal power and domination (James, 2000).

Any approach we take to diversity must go beyond the cultural and descriptive. It is not enough merely to acknowledge diversity; we must also confront the broader social and political forces that construct it and consider who decides what diversity means, and what their motives are (Dei, 2000: 306). A "happy face" multiculturalism cannot possibly resolve society's deeper inequities. What is needed instead is an approach that defines diversity as a function of power relations in society (Bannerji, 2000; Dei, 2000).

In brief, diversity is about power relations and how individuals are categorized, and the tensions that arise from those relations and that categorization. There are three good reasons to approach diversity as a context rather than a "thing": it helps defuse "we against them" conflicts; it helps us perceive diversity as relative rather than fixed; and it serves as a reminder that diversity and inequality are more or less inseparable. In linking diversity to inequality, we can see how these inequities developed, how they are sustained, and how they can be challenged and transformed through government policies and minority resistance.

When we apply this notion that diversity in Canada is relational, we find a multilayered pluralism. Canadians comprise three major ethnic groups: aboriginal peoples, French- and English-speaking descendants of European colonists, and various multicultural minorities. Of course, these three are "big tent" categories. For example, aboriginal peoples are divided by statute into status Indians, non-status Indians, Métis, and Inuit. Other social and cultural differences reflect variations in location, age, gender, degree of urbanization, and level of development. Similarly, multicultural minorities encompass new and settled Canadians from all corners of the world (see Chapter 2). And each of these main "layers" in Canada is constantly realigning itself in relationship to the others in the competition for power and resources.

Yet Canada's diversity is not just about description or demographics; it is also about the inequalities confronting historically disadvantaged "minority groups." Both aboriginal peoples and visible minorities (whether native-born or foreign-born) have been relegated by poverty to the margins of Canadian society (Pendakur and Pendakur, 1995; Lian and Matthews, 1998; Kunz et al., 2001; Galabuzi, 2001). It takes wealth and/or assets to generate opportunities and secure status, and visible minorities tend to have less of both (Oliver and Shapiro, 1995). These patterns of inequality are not temporary; they do not reflect the costs of initial adjustment and settlement. Rather, they are predictable, enduring, and difficult to dislodge (Fleras, 2001).

Put bluntly, we must find a brand-new way of analyzing diversity, one that focuses on the long-standing power differentials faced by minority women and men in Canada. Talk of tolerance will do no good until we face up to the reality that diversity and power are closely linked, to the detriment of visible minorities. As George M. Sefa Dei reminds us (2000), a multiculturalism that emphasizes celebration, empathy, commonality, and goodwill is sharply detached from the realities faced by minority groups, to the extent that it glosses over entrenched inequities and power imbalances. We need to focus instead on how the poor have historically been excluded. A multiculturalism that celebrates differences instead of removing discriminatory barriers does not solve problems but *prevents* us from solving them.

Living Together with Differences: Perils and Promises

The expression "living together with differences" has a reassuring ring to it if repeated often enough. But this concept is laced with ambiguities and uncertainties. Living together is not easy, despite platitudes to the contrary: diversity brings new rhythms, new learning, and new excitement; it may also foster suspicion, uncertainty, and resentment (Iyer, 2001). Besides this, there are practical difficulties: because every country is diverse in its own way, all solutions will have to be somewhat local (Parekh, 1999).

There are different ways of conceptualizing minorities. An obvious one is how they came to be in Canada: some were in fact here before the Europeans (obviously, Canada's aboriginal peoples); some immigrated to Canada voluntarily, or their families did (e.g., Toronto's West Indian community); and some fall between these two groups (e.g., the descendants of slaves, such as the Blacks of Africville in Nova Scotia) (Fleras and Elliott, 1999). But there are other ways of conceptualizing minorities. Some minority societies are large enough to find "safety" in their own numbers; others are too small to be anything but marginalized. Some minority groups are tightly wedded to the cultures of their home countries; others find it much easier to embrace the Canadian mainstream. Some groups want to be left alone; others want to involve themselves actively in Canadian society. Some concentrate themselves in specific territories or neighbourhoods; others disperse themselves. Some are recent arrivals; others have old and deep roots. Some seek individual rights; others want collective rights. To fail to acknowledge these differences would be to oversimplify our analysis.

Underlying the entire multiculturalism debate are conflicting opinions about "human nature." Are people fundamentally the same or essentially different? If people are fundamentally alike, then differences are relatively unimportant, and should be immaterial in deciding who gets what. If people are essentially different, then their differences should be taken into account as a basis for living together. A corollary offers yet another spin: If people are the same, how much diversity should be tolerated? Conversely, if people are different, in what ways should they be treated the same anyway? There is no end to debates over these questions, which do, however, reveal some of the choices and challenges that confront Canadians' attempts to live together.

These debates highlight a deep ideological rift. On the one hand, we have the liberal-pluralist principle of universalism. An indifference toward differences is consistent with liberal pluralism, which assumes that all individuals are morally autonomous and freedom-loving, and thus more alike than their group membership makes them different. By this approach, people can only attain true equality when differences are ignored in passing out entitlements. On the other hand, there is the principle of particularism. Particularity stresses the importance of group membership as it relates to issues such as citizenship, belonging, recognition, and entitlements (Taylor, 1992; Kymlicka, 2001). For particularists, true equality and equal treatment depend on taking differences seriously; only when they are can people be protected from the tyranny of universal standards. Group membership and collective rights are defined as liberating and empowering, since most individuals construct their sense of identity and meaning through such membership.

It is quite easy to live together with differences when minorities endorse mainstream beliefs such as "family values," and a commitment to education and the work ethic, and are willing to live and let live. Multiculturalism is famed for acknowledging people's right to disagree as long as they play by the rules. A willingness to agree to disagree is simple enough when the differences are superficial and choices are easy. ("Shall we order Szechuan tonight? How about a falafel? Anyone care for perogies? Let's do the multicultural festival weekend! Caribana anyone? Aren't those the cutest costumes 'these' people are wearing?") Things get more complex when fundamentally different and mutually opposed values come into play. Difficulties arise when customary practices are perceived as repugnant, contrary to Canadian values, and an infringement of human rights.

A Canadian Conundrum

Should everyone be equal before the law regardless of culture or religion? Or should concessions be made to ensure full and equal participation for those who would otherwise be excluded because of their differences? The B.C. Human Rights Tribunal acknowledged that turban-wearing baptized Sikhs were suffering discrimination because of a law in that province requiring motorcyclists to wear helmets. According to the ruling, individuals' rights to full and equal participation are compromised by one-size-fits-all rulings that run contrary to cultural/religious practices over which they have no control. Others disagree, arguing that safety and potential medical costs should be mitigating factors. The ruling has done little to dampen debate over the primacy of multicultural rights versus "rational interests" (Matas, 1999).

As the above insert demonstrates, minor differences are easy to accommodate; substantive differences that challenge hegemony and resist being co-opted are much harder for the mainstream to accept (see Halka, 1996). This brings two different issues to the fore. First, should illiberal differences be permitted in a society committed to the principles of multiculturalism? Should tolerance be offered to those who are intolerant of others—who disagree with the principle of agreeing to disagree? Second, should cultural differences be acknowledged when it comes to parcelling out social entitlements? Assuming that these questions have no clear answers, how does society even begin to decide?

PARADOXES OF DIVERSITY

Let's rephrase the debate, with the help of the prominent American scholar Stanley Fish (1997). People have different perceptions of diversity. For some, diversity is largely about ethnic restaurants and brightly costumed weekend festivals. This "boutique" multiculturalism (or "pretend pluralism") does not take diversity very seriously. Human differences are simply a superficial overlay to a fundamentally rational and common humanity. Diversity is not on the agenda except as a dash of spice to an otherwise monocultural menu.

Others, at least in principle, tacitly approve of fundamentally different cultural practices that are at odds with mainstream norms and values. This "strong" approach (again Fish's terminology) tends to value differences for themselves, even to the point of allowing groups to nourish their own sense of what is rational and humane. Yet support for this strong version is revoked when other cultures insist on intolerance. Should people be tolerant of those who are intolerant in a society that espouses the principle of tolerance? Should those who reject the authority of tolerance be included in debates when tolerance is the norm? Approval for deep diversity is withheld when differences are seen as infringing on individual (or human) rights, as breaking the law, or as interfering with core values and institutions.

A third position goes to the wall for diversity. A really strong multiculturalist takes differences so seriously as a general principle that no exceptions are tolerated for fear of compromising the principle at large. Yet in cases where a really strong multiculturalist endorses a particular instance, Fish writes, that individual is not really a multiculturalist but a uniculturalist who privileges the primacy of one culture to the exclusion of others.

Each of these multiculturalisms poses problems for living together. Consider the options:

- A boutique multiculturalism endorses superficial differences.
- An abstracted multiculturalism supports differences but only in principle rather than in practice.
- A radical multiculturalism embraces a specific diversity regardless of cost to other groups or society.

The dilemma is obvious: too little diversity makes a mockery of multiculturalism; too much is an existential and unworkable nightmare. How, then, do we live together with differences in a liberal and multiculturally oriented society when these differences are divisive, or provocative, or reject tolerance toward others? Perhaps the question is all wrong—perhaps the conflicts of living together should not be couched as a problem to be solved, and their resolution should not be seen as a goal to be attained. The project of engaging diversity may in fact resemble more a journey to be travelled ... a tension to be accommodated ... an arrangement to be lived with ... a sense of community to be nurtured ... an opportunity to be seized upon ... an imperfect situation that must be tolerated ... (see Gwyn, 1998).

For multiculturalism, then, the challenge is to affirm diversity without holding back equality. Any multicultural "solution" must begin by creating conditions that are inclusive without being assimilationist—that neither eliminate differences nor exaggerate their importance. The challenge is to take differences seriously without resorting to a "pretend pluralism." Too much uniformity tends to treat everyone the same, regardless of their differences. Too much heterogeneity is also problematic, in that people end up being treated as slaves to their own distinctiveness. A multiculturalism based on the principle that we are fundamentally the same yet endlessly different—and that we must acknowledge our differences without compromising what we have in common—may provide a key to the challenge of living together without breaking apart.

CASE STUDY (Continued)
Drawing the Multicultural Line

MULTICULTURALISM AND MUTILATION

Official multiculturalism grapples with the placement of cultural differences that are at odds with commonly accepted values. It also provides a blueprint for drawing the line over how much and what kind. Under official multiculturalism, tolerance is extended to only those cultural practices that do not break the law, interfere with individual rights, or violate fundamental Canadian values such as gender equality. Practices are dismissed that infringe on people's rights, run afoul of the law, and are inconsistent with important values and institutions. Logically, then, official multiculturalism denies the legitimacy of FGM as an acceptable practice in Canada. This custom is multiculturally incorrect, since individual rights are violated, laws are broken, and core Canadian values pertaining to gender equity are sacrificed.

Yet issues are never quite so simple. First, multicultural diversity is relatively easy to accommodate when superficial differences are involved. Most multicultural minorities tend to be content with the existing social arrangements. Only a tweaking here and there is deemed necessary to ensure equality and participation. Many are willing to adjust accordingly, even if certain cultural practices need to be discarded or compartmentalized into the private. In contrast, multi (or bi) national diversity challenges the integrity of the state and citizenship. Multinational diversity is based on a people's (or nation's) claims to territorial base, demands for self-government, and possible secession. Not surprisingly, an accommodation-hugging official multiculturalism cannot cope with such transformative challenges to the status quo. Nor is it equipped to handle "deep" diversities. To date, Canada has struggled to install an institutional framework that meets the demands of its multinational and deep diversities (Cairns, 2000).

Second, problems continue to erode any consensus on where to draw the line when living together. An official multiculturalism may set limits by drawing lines. Nevertheless, any demarcation is subject to challenge and transformation. Laws are constantly being adjusted to reflect changes in reality. The content of individual rights is being contested in light of the collective rights and human rights agenda. Fundamental values and foundational principles are being challenged as little more than a "smokescreen" for the benefit of vested interests. In other words, the debate over drawing the line in a multicultural society is not about laws or policies. Rather, multiculturalism as a discourse about diversity as different yet equal is inseparable from the politics of power. It also is linked with the kind of Canada we want and the role of diversity in shaping this vision. And if diversity is to mean anything as part of Canada's vision of itself, a refusal to "take differences seriously" may prove a major stumbling block to living together.

Chapter Highlights

- Diversity as both a fact and a norm is a key dynamic in contemporary societies such as Canada. Its emergence as a challenge to society building has been subjected to debates, pressures, contradictions, and a wide range of responses.

- Jurisdictions around the world are turning to multiculturalism as a means of addressing the paradoxes of engaging diversity.
- Multiculturalism has many dimensions, which may account for its popularity as well as the disdain it generates. Multiculturalism is linked with society-building goals of benefit to minority women and men. But intentionally or not, it may also help the powerful to control and contain diversity.
- Multiculturalism is very hard to define. As a working definition, this book defines multiculturalism as a process of engaging diversity as "different yet equal."
- Debates over diversity invariably raise several basic questions: "For what ends?" "In whose interests?" "On what grounds?"
- Diversity is about integrating differences. Yet questions arise: "What kind of diversity?" "How much?" "Where do we draw the line?" "Who says?"
- There is a misconception that diversity involves slotting individuals into separate categories of existence.
- Diversity is relational, fluid, constructed, and relative, and is inseparable from patterns of inequality.
- References to living together with differences are problematic. No one can say exactly what is meant by "living together" and "with differences."
- Debates about diversity are basically ideological. The fundamental questions: For purposes of entitlement, should everyone be treated the same, or should differences be taken into account?
- A possible solution is to acknowledge that people are both different and the same. Differences must be taken seriously without compromising what we have in common.
- Different approaches to diversity—from the boutique to the really strong—do not seem to help us answer the key question of this chapter: How do we live together without succumbing to conformity or capitulating to chaos?
- To date, official multiculturalism has not taken differences seriously, preferring instead a "pretend pluralism" that does not interfere with national interests.

Review Questions

1. Why is so difficult to define multiculturalism? How would you define multiculturalism? Justify your answer.

2. Why is the idea of "living together with differences" so complicated?
3. Multiculturalism can be seen as a discourse about diversity. Discuss some of the issues and paradoxes associated with the concept of diversity. How do some of these issues and paradoxes apply to Canada as a multilayered multiculturalism?
4. Are there limits to Canada's tolerance for multiculturalism in terms of "drawing the line"? Explain, and provide examples.
5. Is it possible to construct a society based on the principle of taking differences seriously? Or are liberal-democratic societies such as Canada compelled to endorse a pretend pluralism as a basis for living together?

Recommended Reading

Zillah Eisenstein. 1996. *Hatreds: Racialized and Sexualized Conflicts in the Twenty-first Century*. New York: Routledge.

Stanley Fish. 1997. "Boutique Multiculturalism, or Why Liberals Are Incapable of Thinking About Hate Speech." *Critical Inquiry*. Winter. 378–94.

Carl E. James. 2000. *Experience Difference*. Halifax: Fernwood.

Stephen E. Nancoo, ed. 2000. *21st Century Canadian Diversity*. Mississauga: Canadian Scholars Press (especially the article by George M. Sefa Dei).

James Tully. 1995. *Strange Multiplicities: Constitutionalism in an Age of Diversity*. Cambridge: Cambridge University Press.

Cynthia Willett, ed. 1997. *Theorizing Multiculturalism: A Guide to the Current Debate*. Oxford: Blackwell.

Iris Marion Young. 1990. *Justice and the Politics of Difference*. Princeton: Princeton University Press.

CHAPTER 2

Multiculturalism: Fact, Ideology, Practice, and Critique

CHAPTER OBJECTIVES

- To determine whether Canada is a multicultural society or a society that tries to abide by the principles of multiculturalism.
- To demonstrate how the term multiculturalism is not self-explanatory, but must be interpreted in different ways: as fact, as ideology, as policy, as practice, and as critique.
- To show how Canada's ethnic diversity drives government policies and practices.
- To appreciate the magnitude of multicultural diversity in Canada.
- To expand on the ideals that define multiculturalism as a blueprint for living together with differences.
- To show how multiculturalism is practised by minority, political, and commercial interests in ways that are not necessarily consistent with multicultural principles.
- To reveal the gulf between "taking differences seriously" and "pretend pluralism."
- To show how the principles of multiculturalism differ from those of monoculturalism.
- To explore why and how Canada developed nonviolently from a predominantly white society to one of the world's most diverse and tolerant.

CASE STUDY

Is Canada a Multicultural Society?

Is Canada a multicultural society? "Of course it is," most Canadians would reply, and many would find the question annoyingly simple. Multiculturalism has been a keystone of government policy—including its immigration policy—since 1971, and this has had a profound impact on Canadian demographics. Canadians are generally tolerant of diversity, and many are proud of their country's record for embracing it. Multiculturalism is supported by Canadians' cultural values and is widely perceived as the norm for Canada. The proliferation of multicultural buzzwords—"celebrating differences," "living together," "cooperative coexistence," "mosaic," "building bridges," "constructive engagement," and so on—serves to underscore the obvious: Canada is indeed a multicultural society.

But appearances can be deceiving. Home truths aside, no one can really say what a multicultural society actually *means*. What does a multicultural society look like? Can it be defined or measured in concrete terms? Is it based on taking differences into account, or on treating everyone the same regardless of their differences? Is it about celebrating differences or achieving social equality or securing national interests? In sum, whether Canada is a multicultural society depends on how we define the term. Is multiculturalism a thing? a process? an outcome? an idea? a practice?

There are at least five possible approaches to defining a multicultural society, which were outlined in the introduction to Part 1. To review, they are:

- as a description (i.e., an empirical fact that recognizes the reality of Canada's human diversity)
- as a prescription (i.e., an ideology or statement of what ideals Canadians ought to embrace)
- as a political slant (i.e., a policy determined and followed by governments)
- as a set of intergroup dynamics (i.e., a practice or a tool that groups can use to further their own agendas)
- as a challenge to conventional patterns of power and privilege (i.e., a critique of Canada's founding principles, which are still basically white, Anglo-Saxon, and colonialist)

To put it bluntly, Canada may not after all be a multicultural society; much depends on how you define both "multicultural" and "society." Quite

possibly, Canada is actually a monocultural society with a few multiculturalism bits thrown in for good measure. Alternatively, Canada is genuinely
a multicultural society whose commitments are undermined by monocultural legacies. Perhaps the question is badly phrased. Instead of asking
whether Canada is a multicultural society, perhaps we should consider
instead whether Canada as a society abides by the principles of multiculturalism, however these are defined. In the conclusion of this case study at
the end of the chapter, I shed more light on Canadian society's real record
in multiculturalism.

CONCEPTUALIZING MULTICULTURALISM

Canadians' reactions to multiculturalism have been decidedly mixed. Canada
is widely praised around the world for its commitment to the principles of
multiculturalism. But this country has also been pilloried as a society that is
only nominally diverse and whose commitment to multiculturalism is provisional, superficial, and calculating. Some see multiculturalism as of only
minor importance, if it is relevant at all. Others acknowledge it but are
ambivalent about multiculturalism, perceiving it as reactionary or progressive
depending on the circumstances.

In the final analysis, there is nothing "natural" about multiculturalism as
either principle or practice. Essentially, it is a convention—something individuals construct within particular contexts. As with almost any social construct,
multiculturalism can be analyzed and reformed. But this in itself raises problems: without secure definitions of multiculturalism, there can be no consensus
about it; and without such a consensus, multiculturalism is little more than a
"floating signifier" (Gunew, 1999)—that is, it will always mean whatever different individuals want it to mean, with all the bitter divisions that entails.

We would gain little by assigning a fixed meaning to multiculturalism. We
would gain even less by analyzing it in isolation from its context. I propose
here instead to approach multiculturalism as a complex, even contradictory,
array of forces that are deeply affected by changing social, political, and
demographic realities. Audrey Kobayashi (1999: 33) deftly concedes that
multiculturalism has many dimensions:

> Canadian multiculturalism is an aspiration and an ideology, a national dis-
> course and a personal project, a way of life and a structural framework. It
> is contested, transformative and transforming, a product of collective imag-

ination and an ideal that fuels the imagination. The imaginative plane of multiculturalism is diverse, fragmented, complicated and extensive, and as a result often incoherent or incomprehensible. To a large extent this fragmented picture represents the contradictions that arise from a diverse society, in which ideological and cultural divisions, riven with unequal power relations, creates conflicts of interest and frustrates the postmodern dream of living harmoniously in our diversity.

In this chapter I break down multiculturalism to expose four of its various dimensions: as fact, ideology, practice, and critique. In doing so, I provide a comprehensive basis for analyzing Canada as a multicultural society. I begin by discussing multiculturalism as an empirical *fact* of Canadian society, and examine Canada's various demographic features: who Canadians are, where they live, how they came to live where they do, and how they perceive themselves in ethnic terms. Then I consider multiculturalism as an *ideology* for living together. As an ideology and cultural value, multiculturalism celebrates diversity in its own right and for its contribution to society. I then consider multiculturalism as *practice,* by exploring government responses to diversity. Official multiculturalism was embraced for political reasons, and is still useful for drawing votes and for securing economic advantages in this globally interconnected world. At the same time, minority women and men have been able to capitalize on official multiculturalism, in that it provides them with a platform for articulating their concerns about Canadian society. Finally, I consider multiculturalism as a means of *critiquing* Canadian society, which aspires to multicultural ideals but falls short in the practice of them. Multiculturalism as government *policy* will be discussed in the next chapter.

MULTICULTURALISM AS AN EMPIRICAL FACT

Canada's peoples are astonishingly diverse. People have lived in what is now Canada for perhaps 50,000 years. That is how long ago East Asians began crossing the Bering Strait, which was a land bridge at the time. Most academics (though not all aboriginal leaders) assume that the 1 million aboriginal peoples who currently live in Canada are the descendants of these migrants. The indigenous peoples of "Turtle Island" are themselves extremely diverse, varying in numbers, economic and social health, and cultural vigour.

Europeans, specifically the French and English, were the second wave to arrive. They came as traders, adventurers, and explorers, and eventually displaced the original inhabitants by unilaterally assuming official status for themselves as the "founders" of Canada. The descendants of these colonizers continue to set the agenda for Canadian society.

The <u>third</u> wave—which is also the present one—consists of the non-English- and non-French-speaking immigrants who have arrived in Canada since the late 19th century. The first of these people came from Europe and settled on the prairies and in northern Ontario, where they are still a major presence. Since the 1900s, immigration patterns have shifted greatly, with profound effects on Canada's demographic profile. Immigration is still a fact of Canadian life: recently, between 175,000 and 225,000 people have immigrated to Canada each year (the figure for 2000 was 226,861). The backgrounds of new Canadians have changed: as many as 75 percent now come from "nonconventional" sources, including Asia. Five million Canadians—around 17 percent of the population—were born somewhere else. This percentage has held steady since 1951, though the raw numbers have varied. Just under half of foreign-born Canadians have arrived from the United Kingdom and Europe.

Most Canadians are familiar with the expression "two solitudes," which was coined to describe the chasm separating English and French Canada. However, the Quebec–Canada gap is not the only solitude in town. New solitudes have arisen to complicate the idea that Canada is a multicultural society.

On one side of this emergent divide is what Richard Gwyn (2001) calls the Old Canada (see also Samuel and Schachhuber, 2000). Old Canada is profoundly *not* multicultural—it is even antimulticultural. The Old Canada is rural, homogeneous, European white, inward-looking, and opposed to change. It endorses the values of stability, uniformity, tradition, and acceptance of rules. In contrast, the New Canada is profoundly pro-multicultural in spirit and outlook. The New Canada is urban, and composed largely of immigrants with little connection to Old Canada. It is committed to a cosmopolitan society of flexibility, innovation, individualism, and heterogeneity. It also is outward-looking and globally involved in a post-industrial economy, and receptive to diversity and change.

These two Canadas represent the new two solitudes. Each occupies a distinctive universe and has a distinct set of values, outlooks, and concerns. Connecting these solitudes will prove as vexing as bridging the Quebec–Canada divide.

A DEMOGRAPHIC REVOLUTION

Canada is a remarkably diverse society. To start with, there are the country's 1.1 million aboriginal peoples, who include the Inuit, the Métis, and status and non-status Indians. Together the first peoples account for around 3 percent of Canada's population. Then there are the descendants of the original colonists. In the 1996 census, 17 percent reported British-only origins, 10 percent French-only, and 19 percent Canadian-only (most of these latter had indicated French or British in the previous census) (Canadian Heritage, Multiculturalism, 1998). Around 26 percent of Canada's 30 million people reported that they were not British, French, or Canadian in origin. Not quite half of all Canadians (44 percent) reported some non-British, non-French, or non-Canadian ancestry.

Canada's multicultural minorities are no less diverse (most of these data are from the 1996 census, Canadian Heritage, Multiculturalism, 1998). The most frequently reported origins other than French, British, or Canadian are German (2.7 million; both single and multiple responses) and Italian (1.1 million), followed by aboriginal, Ukrainian, Chinese, Scandinavian, Polish, and South Asian. Just over 11 percent of respondents identified themselves as visible minorities or people of colour (*visible minority* is an official government category that includes native- and foreign-born, nonwhite, non-Caucasoid individuals—Blacks, Chinese, Japanese, Koreans, Filipinos, Indo-Pakistanis, West Asians and Arabs, Southeast Asians, Latin Americans, and Pacific Islanders). Of the 3.2 million visible minority people in Canada, the Chinese are numerically the most prominent (860,000, or 26.9 percent), followed by the South Asians (671,000, or 21.0 percent), and Blacks (574,000, or 17.9 percent).

There are noticeable demographic differences between cities and also between regions. Ontario has the largest number of people with non-British, non-French origins—over 5 million. British Columbia and Alberta have just over 2 million each, and Quebec has 1 million. Over half of all immigrants (55 percent) live in Ontario; this means that one-quarter of Ontarians were born outside Canada (the percentage in British Columbia is the same). Canadian demography provides all sorts of interesting numbers. Almost 66 percent of Manitobans report aboriginal and "other" ethnic origins. Over half of all visible minorities live in Ontario, about 20 percent in B.C., and 14 percent in Quebec. Visible minorities make up 17.9 percent of B.C.'s population, 15.8 percent of Ontario's, and 10.1 percent of Alberta's, but only 1.1 percent of New Brunswick's and Prince Edward Island's, and 0.7 percent of Newfoundland's.

Urban regions are magnets for modern-day immigrants and refugees. The vast majority of postwar immigrants have settled in a handful of metropolitan areas. In terms of both absolute numbers and relative percentages, Montreal, Toronto, Calgary, and Vancouver are more diverse than the provincial or national averages (Hiebert, 2000). According to Statistics Canada, 85 percent of all immigrants—and 93 percent of those who arrived between 1991 and 1996—live in the major census metropolitan areas.

Access to opportunities, services, and social networks makes these centres attractive for them. Italian was the most frequently reported ethnic origin (other than French or English) in Toronto, Montreal, and Edmonton. In Vancouver it was Chinese, and in Calgary, Ottawa–Hull, and Halifax it was German. Canada's major cities are home to 86 percent of visible minorities, both native-born and foreign-born.

Almost half of all new Canadians settle in Toronto, whose population is 48 percent foreign born, and represents 169 different countries and about 100 different languages. Torontonians of non-European descent now out-number those of European descent. It may take another decade for this demographic revolution to transform the entire metropolitan region (Hiebert, 2000). In 1996 visible minorities accounted for 31.6 percent of the population of Toronto's census metropolitan area (CMA) (in 1971 the per-centage was only 1 percent). Put another way, the Toronto region is home to 42 percent of Canada's visible minorities. So it is proper to describe Canada as a moderately multicultural society, in which concentrated pockets of vis-ible diversity are separated by vast stretches of "white" ("European") ethnic-ities. References to this unequal distribution are not intended to belittle Canada's nonviolent transformation from a predominantly white society into one of the most spectacularly diverse countries in the world (Dyer, 2001).

MULTICULTURALISM AS IDEOLOGY

Demographics offer us empirical proof of Canada's ethnic diversity, and at least suggest that Canada's peoples belong to different cultures, which they want to maintain (see also Alba, 1999). But demographics only *describe* mul-ticulturalism, and we must do more than that. Practically any society can be described as multicultural on the basis of descriptive accounts. Few of the world's countries are *not* home to a broad array of ethnically diverse minori-ties. But there is little point in analyzing multiculturalism if we define every society as multicultural by virtue of its demographics. Purely descriptive accounts have other drawbacks besides this: they neglect to consider what *ought* to be, and they prevent us from seeing multiculturalism as a set of ideals for living together. Or as put by a leading British ethnologist:

> Multiculturalism doesn't simply mean numerical plurality of different cul-tures, but rather a community which is creating, guaranteeing, encouraging spaces within which different communities are able to grow at their own pace. At the same time it means creating a public space in which these new communities are able to interact, enrich the existing culture, and create a

new consensual culture in which they recognize reflections of their own identity. (Bhiku Parekh, cited in Giroux, 1994: 336)

The challenge, then, is clearly before us. Multiculturalism as an ideology considers "what ought to be" rather than describing "what is." Multiculturalism as an *ideal* has the capacity to influence behaviour, evaluate actions, and legitimize activity. Multicultural ideals help us understand the nature, benefits, and consequences of diversity; decide how much diversity a society can absorb; evaluate the status of minority women and men in Canadian society; and judge where to draw the cultural lines in an increasingly complex society. Many people contend that Canada has not lived up to its multicultural ideals; whether they are right or wrong depends on what those ideals are, and there is no consensus on this.

Ideology Defined

Ideology is pivotal to human existence. The world we inhabit is never neutral or normal; rather, it is loaded with ideas and ideals that draw attention to some aspects of reality at the expense of others. Ideology frames issues in ways that privilege some perspectives as natural, normal, and superior, and dismiss others as irrelevant or inferior. In sum, ideologies shape what we see, how we think, what we experience, and how we relate to the world at large.

Ideologies can be politicized or apolitical. Basically, an apolitical ideology is defined as a relatively coherent and deeply held system of ideas and ideals associated with a particular community. It aims to bind together diverse social elements in a coherent way by equipping people with understandable explanations for their physical, social, and cultural reality. Social stability and social order are enhanced in societies that are based on clearly articulated and widely accepted ideals. It also provides a medium for justifying patterns of behaviour within a community, while securing a basis for assessing the value and validity of other cultures' practices. Apolitical ideologies are socially constructed, but this does not mean they are "fake" or "fickle." Their integrity does not depend on either their truth or their empirical accuracy. Also, apolitical ideologies tend to confirm or reinforce beliefs rather than question them. In this sense, apolitical ideologies function mainly as a source of social regulation and group consensus.

Politicized ideologies exist to defend highly political ideas and ideals that privilege some points of view. Other points of view are dismissed accordingly. According to many social theorists from Karl Marx to Antonio Gramsci, political ideologies are instruments for shaping, perpetuating, camouflaging, and legitimizing the often harsh realities of social life. They serve primarily to maintain systems of dominance anchored around class, race, and gender. Compliance with such ideologies is secured by concealing the contradictions of social existence related to power, privilege, and wealth. In a given society, several ideologies may compete for supremacy. The dominant ideology maintains its privileged position through its capacity to dominate debates over what is acceptable or normal. The most powerful dominant ideologies are not necessarily articulated as comprehensive world-views. Instead, they derive their potency from commonsense assumptions ("false consciousness"), which are conveyed as "natural" and self-evident rather than socially constructed and reflective of group interests. Ideologies do not set out to control, but they may have a controlling effect ("hegemony") by forcing minorities into acquiescence.

Hegemony is a word that is often encountered in social science. Here it can simply be defined as control without physical force. It involves a process by which ideas and ideals are reproduced through consent and active involvement but without people being aware that their attitudes are being changed. As a result, certain ideals become taken for granted as natural, normal, and necessary. They also become an item of faith to be defended at all costs.

We are now ready to analyze multiculturalism as an ideology. At one level, multiculturalism is a fairly coherent set of ideas and ideals about the value and validity of diversity in society. But at another level, multiculturalism can be seen as a dominant ideology backed by vested interests. Official multiculturalism is more than a discourse about diversity; it also represents a defence of ruling class ideology. A hegemonic multiculturalism strengthens the interests of the ruling class by "normalizing" that class's view of the world as natural, universal, and superior (Povinelli, 1998). Canada faces strong pressure to conceal, evade, and distort; if it did not do these things—that is, if it did not write its own national myths to paper over its cultural contradictions—it might well dissolve as a nation, and multiculturalism serves as such a myth (Bannerji, 2000). The durability of these "ideals" does not depend on their accurate portrayal of truth or reality. It only matters that they advance vested interests without blatantly revoking minority concerns or disrupting the prevailing status quo.

In short, multiculturalism is *an ideological ploy*. It justifies the exclusion of minority women and men from full and equal access, and does so behind a façade of good intentions (Cummins and Danesi, 1990). In light of all this, it can only be expected that Canada will continue to be an unsettled and contested site in the ideological struggle to transform the basis for living together.

The Ideology of Multiculturalism: A Blueprint for Living Together

Ideologies for "managing" diversity have evolved over time and in different places. Like other white settler societies, Canada for a long time managed diversity by adopting ideologies of assimilation, segregation, and integration. In recent years, authorities have embraced an ideological climate that is receptive to diversity. This endorsement of an ideology of cultural pluralism represents a sharp divergence from earlier eras, when government policies and programs explicitly endorsed majority concerns, values, and institutions. Other cultures were sloughed off as contrary to Canada-building.

A commitment to cultural pluralism transforms into virtues those differences that once were perceived as working against national unity and identity. Cultural pluralism considers it a good thing for different cultures to coexist, with the proviso that society's foundational principles must not be challenged. This includes a commitment to secular tolerance, cosmopolitan worldliness, civic nationalism, and rational scientism (Ryan, 1997). Diversity is also endorsed as vital to egalitarian societies formed of loose confederations of cultural groups (Weisman, 2000). It goes without saying that explicit patterns of exploitation and abuses of human rights are inconsistent with the principles of cultural pluralism. This commitment to diversity and equality exerts pressure on the state to intervene to ensure equitable outcomes.

Multiculturalism is the height of cultural pluralism. Multiculturalism as an ideology offers a normative statement of "what ought to be"; it prescribes a preferred course of thought or action that is opposed to monoculturalism, fits well with the principles of cultural pluralism, and embraces ideals such as freedom, tolerance, acceptance, and respect. A number of prescriptions underpin this ideology: "Take differences seriously!" "Diversity within unity!" "(Multi)cultural relativism!" "Respect others!" "Active acceptance!" "Mosaic!" "Inclusiveness!" and so on. To capture the ideological dimensions of multiculturalism, we must examine each of these more carefully. However, these ideals embrace an idealized version of multiculturalism. They may not necessarily reflect the reality of multicultural practices in Canada or the United States.

1. *Taking differences seriously.* Multicultural ideals embrace a commitment to differences. A plurality of cultures is promoted as valuable: diversity is a good thing because living in a multicultural society makes for a richer and more rewarding life than under monoculturalism (Poole, 1999). No single cultural entity is perceived as taking precedence over others: all are equally valued and encouraged for the

contributions they make to society. These ideals assume that members of the ethnically diverse groups see themselves as different and collectively wish to remain so, for practical or personal reasons. Cultural diversity is seen as offering meaning and security to minority women and men in times of rapid social change and dislocation. A preference for select elements of an ancestral past is not a sign of mental inferiority, stubbornness, confusion, disloyalty, or lack of patriotism. Rather, people have a right to be different, provided their attachments to those differences fall within an acceptable range. At the same time, these differences must not be celebrated in an inward-looking sense. The objective, multiculturally speaking, is a sharing through intercultural exchanges within a common cultural framework (Alba, 1999).

2. *Diversity within unity*. A commitment to multiculturalism is consistent with the ideals of unity-within-diversity. Within limits, diversity is not automatically criticized and dismissed as incompatible with the national interest. The preference of minorities to be "with their own kind" does not make them any less committed to participating in the broader society as social and economic equals. On the contrary, cultural diversity is an important tile in the national "mosaic," a reflection of the Canadian ideal, and a source of enrichment and strength. Cultural pluralism is no longer feared for its political consequences; as an integrative ideology, multiculturalism makes a virtue of the very differences that at one time precluded a unifying national identity (Harles, 1998). Moreover, these differences can be forged into a workable national framework if individuals are permitted to affiliate voluntarily with the cultural tradition of their choice. Granted, affiliation must be first with the state. But minority women and men possess the option of secondary identification with a preferred cultural tradition so long as this does not interfere with core institutional values, the laws of the land, or the rights of individuals. In other words, it is both possible to be Canadian *and* accept multiculturalism. Conversely, it is possible to maintain an ethnic heritage without revoking a strong Canadian identity and attachment to Canada (Kalin and Berry, 1995).

3. *(Multi)cultural relativism*. The multicultural ideal is well suited to the principles of cultural relativism, in that both seem to tolerate a wide range of cultures and practices. In essence, cultural relativism sees the worth of cultural practices as arising from their context. It sees truth and knowledge as historically conditioned and socially constructed (as opposed to eternally fixed). In sum, cultural relativists claim that there

are no solid definitions of good or right or acceptable; these inevitably vary between cultures, and over time and space (Younkins, 2000).

Few would dispute all of this. But problems arise with the normative (or prescriptive) version of cultural relativism, which contends that in the absence of absolute standards of right and good, *all* cultural practices (and cultures) are *equally* right and good. It follows from this that no culture is superior to another, all cultural practices are equally valid. According to the relativists, you have your truths, and we have ours, and no one can determine the absolute truth, since we are all "trapped within our truths." And in a climate where what is right for you is not necessarily right for me, you should not impose your values on me (nor I on you), since my practices are justified by the world view within which they exist, just as yours are.

Most would agree that the tolerance implicit in cultural relativism is basic to a multicultural ideology. But a thoughtful relativism does not condone an "anything goes" attitude, since practices can really only be justified in the context in which they originated. Whether they are good and valid expressions of culture in the Canadian context has to depend on how well they fit with Canadian society. Also, cultural relativism does not automatically approve or endorse customary practices that deny rights, exploit or exclude others, or inflict pain. Customs that deny personal dignity or infringe on human rights may rightfully be denounced as violations of the very principles on which cultural relativism stands. Admittedly, difficulties are inevitable when it comes to sorting out what is right and acceptable, since no absolute or reliable means exist for assessment. Nevertheless, some standards must apply if people are to live together with their differences, and a good starting point is respect for fundamental human rights within the context of equality, diversity, and respect.

(Multi)cultural relativism is useful as a learning device, though not particularly as a principle for coexistence. It is most useful as a reminder that culture—including mainstream culture—is a relative thing, and that standards of right and normal are not necessarily universal. In this light, perhaps it also teaches us to approach diverse customs with respect, and remember that they must have been meaningful sometime and somewhere (even if no longer, in Canada), and that we should judge them only reluctantly, if we have to at all.

4. *Respecting others.* In complex and diverse societies, multiculturalism is advocated as an ideal for intergroup harmony. As an ideal,

multiculturalism rests on the conviction that cultural and linguistic minorities can find a satisfactory level of accommodation and mutual understanding if pluralistic principles are broadly applied. A commitment to multiculturalism reflects the premise that those who are secure in their cultural background will concede a similar right to others (Berry et al., 1977). Conversely, those who feel threatened are unlikely to act magnanimously toward others (Berry, 1991). It follows that multiculturalism promotes intergroup tolerance on the assumption that "the more someone experiences his own way of life as ... fulfilling, the more likely he is to welcome attainments by others" (Rawls, 1971, in Roberts and Clifton, 1990). Intergroup harmony can also come about through sustained and equitable interaction between individuals who are secure in their identities. As Prime Minister Pierre Trudeau stated in his speech to Parliament on October 8, 1971, when he introduced his government's new policy: "National unity, if it is to mean anything in the deeply personal sense, must be founded on confidence in one's own individual identity; out of this can grow respect for that of others and a willingness to share ideas, attitudes, and assumptions. A vigorous policy of multiculturalism will help to create this initial confidence."

5. *Active acceptance.* Accepting multiculturalism as an ideology involves more than a commitment to tolerance. It also involves accepting differences as valid and valuable expressions of the human experience. Tolerance in itself is not enough, since this implies politely putting up with intolerable things—a product of indifference or resignation. Paradoxically, tolerance can actually *reinforce* domination, in the sense that tolerance is a matter of choice, and those who make that choice have the power to revoke it (i.e., choose intolerance instead) (Mackey, 1999). In contrast, multiculturalism is about encouraging active acceptance, with the emphasis on *active*. Some have argued that Canada is already a multicultural society, so state policies that promote it are superfluous. But these people are naive about the politics of cultural diversity. If left unattended, racial and cultural differences can easily generate tension, frustration, and interethnic conflict. Managed correctly, diversity can become socially, politically, and economically productive. In short, it is not enough to recognize or tolerate diversity; it must be actively promoted as a desirable asset with vast social potential. Diversity can result in a stable and well-regulated society, provided there is an overarching vision anchored in the principles of tolerance of diversity, a diversity of tolerances.

6. *Mosaic.* Canadian society is often idealized as a multicultural mosaic. Susan Crean (1986: 9) notes that the mosaic image has become so ingrained in Canadian society that it is in danger of being crushed by its own hype:

> As a national cliché it is right up there with maple syrup and the Musical Ride, equally sugary and ceremonial. Politicians love to drop it into Canada Day speeches, decorating their blenderized prose with a little high sounding imagery. And it is an effective image ... the one feature which (finally) sets us apart from the great melting-pot to the south.

> Yet in Canadian terms, the mosaic metaphor is misleading. A mosaic is an arrangement of individual tiles with distinctive shapes, colours, and textures. These tiles are placed in such a way that from the right distance, the image looks unified and coherent. This overall image transcends the individual tiles, which when viewed from close up maintain their own integrity and distinctiveness. But when we focus on cultural tiles as colourful relics from the past, it is too easy to overlook the inequalities they reflect. The tiles in Canada's cultural mosaic are not equal: some are raised while others are lowered, reflecting differences in social status and unequal contributions to society (Tepper, 1988). The grout that fastens these tiles into place provides a sharp reminder of who is in control. Put simply, the mosaic metaphor promotes a far too simplistic and static view of cultural differences.

7. *Inclusiveness.* A commitment to equality, participation, and inclusiveness is yet another cornerstone of the multicultural ideal. After all, a commitment to "celebrating diversity" can't possibly mean anything if minority women and men are denied, excluded, or exploited. Only full and equal involvement can create an environment for multicultural ideas to flourish. Otherwise, cultural retention is not a choice but a default option for those seeking security from the outside world.

MULTICULTURALISM AS PRACTICE

Nowhere is the controversy over multiculturalism more obvious than at the level of practice. When it comes to practice, various groups—both the mainstream and the "minority-stream"—will try to use multicultural ideals to advance their own projects. The idea that multiculturalism is a renewable "resource" has gained prominence. Politicians and government institutions see multiculturalism as something that can be exploited economically or politically, at the national and international levels. For their part, minority women and men perceive multiculturalism as a political platform. In the gap between multicultural ideals and practices, there is plenty of space for the resulting grievances to be articulated. The governed and the governing draw on different readings of multiculturalism to pursue opposing interests. Not surprisingly, then, when multicultural principles are put into practice, ambiguities and tensions can prove awkward.

Political Interests

Official multiculturalism arose from the interplay between good intentions and political opportunism (Gwyn, 1994). Because of its unique history and demography, Canada was unable to adapt European models of nationhood, and had to find alternative models for living together, against the backdrop of aboriginal dispossession and competing ethnicities. The model chosen would have to be based on tolerance for cultural "others" (Mackey, 1999: 13). Official multiculturalism set out to formulate a new founding myth: Canada as land of opportunity and equality for all Canadians. The goal in this, at a time of political turmoil and emergent nationalism, was to unite all Canadians without actually redistributing power in any fundamental way (Helly, 1993). The role of multiculturalism in building Canada is widely acknowledged. Yet society building is not a straightforward process; in fact, it is relentlessly complicated and endlessly controversial, and takes very different forms at different times (Mackey, 1999: 18).

Multiculturalism was a response by Canada's elites to an unstable postwar situation created by external pressures and by the cultural politics of internal difference. As a policy, multiculturalism faced conflicting demands: to shore up electoral strength in urban immigrant Ontario; to counterbalance Western resentment over perceived favouritism toward the Québécois; to mollify the demands of certain ethnic groups such as Ukrainians, who rejected a two nations view of Canada; to block American cultural imperialism; and to thwart political unrest arising from changes in immigration patterns and from renewed demands by native people's groups (see Burnet and Palmer, 1988; Harles, 1998). Multiculturalism also had purely political objectives: to weaken opposition by dividing it; to appeal to popular sentiments and public instincts; to create the appearance of change (as opposed to actual change); to modify minority interests to suit the national agenda; and to secure the goodwill and admiration of the international community.

To put it bluntly, then, Canada's multiculturalism is mainly a political program for achieving political goals in a politically astute manner (Peter, 1978). At one level, multiculturalism as state-sanctioned cultural pluralism reinforces the dominance of Canada's elites by taming diversity so that it serves national interests (Dijkstra et al., 2001). At a more practical level, multiculturalism is a tool for attracting the votes of minority groups. The vast majority of Canada's multicultural minorities are concentrated in major urban centres such as Toronto, Montreal, and Vancouver. All of Canada's political parties are pursuing the multicultural vote by promising more funding, more representation, and more equity initiatives. They are also fielding more and more minority candidates (minorities are still underrepresented in Parliament) (Stasiulis and Abu-Laban, 2000). Politicians openly advocate multiculturalism in order to ensure a profile in ethnically diverse communities come voting time. Even immigration decisions reflect a degree of political pragmatism, given that immigrant quotas are widely perceived as a political grab for ethnic votes in urban ridings. Political parties may be open to charges of pandering to the ethnic vote, but at least their behaviour reflects a growing awareness among politicians of Canada's multicultural realities.

Commercial Interests

Both private and public interests are capitalizing on the commercial potential of multiculturalism. Multiculturalism is currently being promoted as a valuable "export," just as wood, minerals, and hydroelectricity were promoted in the past (Moodley, 1983; Abu-Laban, 2001). In 1986 the then–prime minister, Brian Mulroney, endorsed this strategy in his "Multiculturalism Means Business" speech at a Toronto conference. This perspective on multiculturalism—that it's a means of gaining advantage in the increasingly global economy—is still popular, judging by this statement from Hedy Fry, Secretary of State for Multiculturalism and the Status of Women (Annual Report, Introduction, 2000):

> In the knowledge based economy of the 21st century, where people are key to a nation's productivity and competitiveness, Canada's multiculturalism is its most valuable resource. It encourages new ways of thinking and stimulates innovation and creativity. It helps us forge links with the rest of the world at a time when jobs and growth depend more than ever on global trade and investment. These links also strengthen our international influence as we work for humanitarian reforms and to combat threats to human security.

The commercial strategy is clear enough: Canada hopes to enhance its international image and its competitive edge by exploiting its multicultural goodwill both at home and abroad (Hage, 1998). Multiculturalism is touted over and over as having the potential to increase trade, especially in the rapidly expanding Asian market (Multiculturalism/Secretary of State, 1993). The City of Toronto lobbied hard to land the 2008 Olympic Games (unsuccessfully) by endorsing multicultural diversity as a main plank of that effort (Carey, 2000). Canada must maintain good relations with its minorities if it is to meet the economic goals it has set for itself—goals that include opening new foreign markets, increasing the clout of Canadian-based transnational companies, and encouraging tourism.

According to Katharyne Mitchell in her 1993 article "Multiculturalism, or the United Colors of Capitalism?" multiculturalism is being used to attract members of the transnational elite associated with global capital. The emphasis is on promoting Canada as a welcoming country of many different cultures—"Hey, look at us, we're multicultural"—rather than a single, exclusive national culture. The reworking of multiculturalism as an ideology of racial harmony and cooperative coexistence, Mitchell (1993) says, provides a degree of reassurance for nervous investors and fidgety international capital. It also ensures Canada's integration into the international networks of global capitalism. In the increasingly globalized economy, in this increasingly borderless world, multiculturalism may well provide Canada with an advantage that the larger powers lack (see Woodley, 1997).

Minority Interests

Immigrants and visible minorities confront many problems once they enter Canada. Public reaction to their physical appearance and cultural differences accounts for many of these. Because they are so visible, many must endure racial abuse and discrimination in employment, education, housing, and government services (*Equality Now!* 1984; Henry et al., 2000; Kunz et al., 2001). Even when they aren't openly barred from certain occupations, many find themselves shunted into menial jobs that pay badly and offer little security or prospect for promotion. Schools have long been attacked for their insensitivity to minorities' needs and aspirations. Students of colour may perform poorly because of racial stereotyping, low teacher expectations, alienating curriculums and textbooks, and lack of positive role models among the teachers (Samuda et al., 1984). The criminal justice system is also under scrutiny. Evidence is mounting that certain minorities are arrested, sentenced, and incarcerated at rates greater than those for "mainstream" ethnic groups (Neugebauer, 2000). In large urban areas in recent years, the police have been criticized for failing to respond appropriately to demographic, political, and social trends (Cryderman et al., 1998). This criticism is especially vocal in Toronto, where perceptions of police brutality or indifference toward some minority youth have eroded public confidence in the ability of police to do their job in a multicultural society.

Refugees and immigrants must also contend with culture shock. Typically, Canada's values, expectations, and environment are radically different from what they have known. Cultural blueprints that they have always taken for granted are repeatedly dismissed in Canada as irrelevant, inferior, or illegal. Examples: children are disciplined differently here, women typically enjoy more social standing, authority figures demand different kinds of deference. Furthermore, refugees and immigrants lack the resources and networks that would help them adjust. Both immigrants and refugees must overcome isolation, discrimination, language barriers, and stress in a society that is at best ambivalent toward diversity. And all of these difficulties are compounded by various reality gaps: *generational* gaps, when parents perceive their children as drifting away from the old culture; *employment* gaps, when credentials earned overseas fail to meet Canadian standards; *gender* gaps, when women begin chafing over traditional roles and pervasive paternalism; and *credibility* gaps, when elites become estranged from those they allegedly represent. To help new immigrants adjust, agencies such as the Kitchener–Waterloo Multicultural Centre provide a host of services, including English classes, housing and employment services, women's support groups, and translation services.

Both new and native-born Canadians of colour embrace multiculturalism as a resource for attaining practical goals (Isajiw, 1997). Their needs are basic, practical, and survival oriented: they want to fit in, sink roots, establish themselves, expand economic opportunities for themselves and their children, eliminate discrimination and exploitation, and maintain their cultural heritage without losing their rights as citizens. Multicultural minorities are determined to partake of both worlds without forsaking the benefits of either. Culture, language, and identity are important to them, but so, equally, is fitting into the broader society. To be sure, some ethnic minorities prefer inclusion to integration; but for these, separatism is only a means to preserve separation and power in a hostile environment. Generally speaking, few new Canadians would willingly relinquish meaningful involvement in Canadian society. Rais Khan, a professor of political science at the University of Winnipeg, put it this way:

> I wish neither to be assimilated nor to be differentiated; I wish to be integrated. If I want to nurture my culture, speak my language, sing my songs, play my music, wear my traditional clothes, cook my traditional food and feed it to others, display the handicrafts from my former country, it is my

business. I should not expect government grants for that purpose, nor should I get them. But, at the same time, I should not be impeded from doing any or all of the above. (*Winnipeg Free Press*, June 25, 1989)

Requests that language, culture, or identity be protected must not be construed as demands for autonomy or separate homelands. Minorities want to be accepted as part of the national fabric without paying a penalty for being different (Cardozo and Musto, 1997). Whether they succeed in this depends to some extent on how multiculturalism is "resourced." Multiculturalism is endorsed by minority groups as a tool for opening up economic opportunities and for ending discrimination in employment, education, housing, and criminal justice. It provides a buffer for those who are trying to adjust to Canadian society; it also helps mediate relationships with the dominant sector in matters such as employment and the delivery of services. Minorities have also embraced multiculturalism as a resource for coping with the demands of a society that is secured around the agendas of the aboriginal peoples, the French, and the English. Multicultural minorities often find themselves unable to influence government policy, for various reasons: geographical dispersal, cultural heterogeneity, and poor negotiating skills. In relative terms, the charter groups are far more powerful, because their formal status and legal authority were long ago written into Canada's foundational principles. Members of multicultural communities have rights only as individual citizens; they cannot demand political changes the way that Canada's charter groups can (Mackey, 1999: 66).

Official multiculturalism has empowered an otherwise powerless sector. Minority women and men now possess the leverage to prod, embarrass, and provoke the central policy structures by holding them accountable for their failures to practise what they preach. In doing so it has turned minorities into legitimate contenders in the competition for power and resources. Appeals to multiculturalism are thus calculated to extract public support and global sympathy (in a similar way, Canada's aboriginal peoples have relied on the United Nations to embarrass the federal government into acting on their needs).

MULTICULTURALISM AS CRITIQUE

For thirty years the world's first and possibly only constitutional multiculturalism has earned praise (and scorn) as an innovative (yet flawed) experiment for engaging diversity without losing sight of national interests. Generally speaking, official references to multiculturalism tend to be couched in "bureaucratese": "celebrating diversity," "mosaic," "understanding, acceptance, exchanges, and sharing," "living together," and so on. But not everyone accepts that multiculturalism is what the government says it is. To the doubters, multiculturalism is more ambiguous than the government line suggests. Sneja Gunew (1999: 18) captures some of this ambiguity when she writes about colonial legacies:

> Multiculturalism can mean on the one hand simply a way of managing or controlling diversity. On the other hand it might signal more democratic participation by minority groups, and constitute, notionally, a utopian move. In popular populist discourse (exploited by politicians at strategic moments) it is perceived as running counter to the interests of the coherent nation-state with its allegiance to core values and many progressive political analysts perceive it as a sleight-of-hand by the state functioning to perpetuate dominant interests under the guise of extending political and cultural suffrage to minority groups.

Multiculturalism can be approached as a means of criticizing the government's policy toward minorities—supposedly so enlightened—as a form of disguised monoculturalism. Those who take this approach toward multiculturalism criticize society for failing to abide by its own stated principles, and in doing so express ways of thinking that are at odds with the mainstream (Burayidi, 1997). These critical approaches to multiculturalism present minority cultures as a challenge to the cultural power of the majority. They take a hard look at traditional, "universalizing" concepts such as truth, rationality, and citizenship; they question conventional assumptions about language and symbols; they ask where moral authority in society actually lies, and whether cultural differences are permanent (Li, 1999). Finally, critical perspectives approach multiculturalism as a means for rejecting Eurocentric (read *white*) supremacy. The goal of all this is to unmask the supposed neutrality of mainstream society by showing its rootedness in unequal power relations (Stam, 1997).

In this postmodern world, there is renewed interest in multiculturalism (Li, 1999), which is increasingly seen as a weapon for challenging the cultural dominance of free market societies. The assumption that reality is coherent, objective, and amenable to rational analysis no longer holds. In this world without a "centre," there is no ojective reality; there are only different discourses about reality. Because everything has its own location in time and space, and because no two people can ever share the same perspective, nothing can be neutral or impartial. Because everything is relative, and anything *could* be true or good, nothing is absolutely knowable. If reality

47

is a matter of perspective, there is nothing to be gained from searching for universal principles. Instead, we must analyze the world as an infinitely complex multiplicity of fragments. In terms of societies, all of this means that the closest we can come to truth will have to involve some form of pluralism (Adam and Allan, 1995). Once you understand all this, it is easy to see how a critical multiculturalism draws heavily from postmodern discourses to challenge society's cultural elites (Vertovec, 1996).

Some critics contend that multiculturalism, which is supposed to be liberating, has been co-opted by central authorities, who are using it to strengthen their dominance (Bharucha, 2000). A critical multiculturalism challenges traditional authority. It rejects any form of pluralism that is based on a hierarchy which merely tolerates minority cultures. It endorses instead a multiculturalism that involves rethinking society's power relations (Henry and Tator, 1999). This critique of conventional multiculturalism focuses on ideas such as empowerment and resistance, the politicization and mobilization of marginal groups, the transformation of institutions, the dismantling of cultural hierarchies and structures, and the promotion of diversity within the context of equity and justice. As bell hooks (1995: 201) writes:

> As more people of color raise our consciousness and refuse to be pitted against one another, the forces of neo-colonial white supremacist domination must work harder to divide and conquer. The most recent effort to undermine progressive bonding between people of color is the institutionalization of "multiculturalism." Positively, multiculturalism is presented as a corrective to a Eurocentric vision of model citizenship wherein white middle-class ideals are presented as the norm. Yet this positive intervention is then undermined by visions of multiculturalism that suggest everyone should live with and identify with their own self-contained cultural group. If white supremacist capitalist patriarchy is unchanged then multiculturalism within that context can only become a breeding ground for narrow nationalism, fundamentalism, identity politics, and cultural, racial, and ethnic separatism.

The critique of multiculturalism as monoculturalism in disguise acknowledges these ambiguities. The need to expose these contradictions makes it doubly important to reclaim multiculturalism as a tool for advancing empowerment and change.

CASE STUDY (Continued)

Is Canada a Multicultural Society? It Depends...

Multiculturalism has been affirmed by federal and provincial authorities as *the* fundamental characteristic of the Canadian identity (Harles, 1998). Does this mean that Canada is a multicultural society? Yes and no. *Yes*, to the extent that multiculturalism exists as fact, ideology, policy, and practice. But perhaps *no*, to the extent that Canadian society remains fundamentally monocultural, and that it merely tolerates diversity.

Consider the contrasts: in a monocultural society the population has basically one ethnic or racial origin. As an ideology, monoculturalism endorses uniformity, homogeneity, and conformity. Policies in a monocultural society are geared toward mainstream needs and concerns. Monocultural practices ensure that only those who conform are entitled to reward or recognition. In a monocultural society, people are criticized for failing to abide by the principles of "one size fits all."

Is Canada multicultural in principle or practice? The evidence suggests that Canadians have moved beyond monoculturalism by accepting multicultural principles, at least in rhetoric if not in practice. But it is hard to determine what these principles are. The concept of multiculturalism is too convoluted to capture except by resorting to simplistic reductions or rigid formulas. Consider these variations in multiculturalism:

- Multiculturalism as consensus, versus multiculturism as controlled from the centre, versus multiculturalism as a commitment to challenge, resist, and change society.
- Multiculturalism as a denial that diversity is relevant (i.e., "pretend pluralism"), versus multiculturalism that takes differences seriously as grounds for living together.
- Multiculturalism as minorities see it, versus multiculturalism as viewed by the majority.

Despite these difficulties, it may be possible to isolate the principles of multiculturalism. At minimum, a Canada that abides by multicultural principles should concede the following:

- A commitment to living together with differences in a spirit of partnership and power sharing.
- A commitment to taking differences seriously, including one's own culture.

- A commitment to ensuring full and equal participation in society for all Canadians.
- A commitment to closely and seriously consider other cultures.
- A commitment to flexibility and open-mindedness, and a willingness to compromise.
- A commitment to a thoughtful and critically informed (multi)cultural relativism.

Judged on this basis, it would be fair to say that Canada endorses the principles of a multicultural society. It would also be accurate to say that Canadians still have a long way to go before they put those principles into everyday practice in securing a truly multicultural society.

Chapter Highlights

- Whether Canada is a multicultural society depends on how we define multiculturalism.
- Multiculturalism can be analyzed at five different levels of meaning: as fact, ideology, policy, practice, or critique.
- In literal terms, a multicultural society is one in which many (ethno)cultures exist. In more normative terms, multiculturalism is an approach to talking about diversity.
- Canada is a "multicultural society" in the descriptive sense that more and more racial and ethnic minorities are settling here. Canada is also multicultural in the sense that these ethnic and racial minorities wish to retain their identity while participating as full equals in Canadian society.
- Multiculturalism is an ideology because it embraces certain ideas and ideals about diversity in Canada.
- Multiculturalism as practice is mainly about how the concept is "used" by political and minority interests. This approach to multiculturalism stresses its value as a resource for achieving desired outcomes.
- The state endorses multiculturalism in defence of its power—that is, to control and contain diversity without appearing to do so.
- Women and men of colour have capitalized on the moral authority implicit in official multiculturalism to hold the government accountable for any actions it takes that are inconsistent with statutory laws and constitutional guarantees.

- As a critique, multiculturalism is critical of multiculturalism itself, and especially of the consensus and control models espoused by government. As a critique, multiculturalism is also critical of society for failing to abide by the principles of multiculturalism.
- Canada can be defined as a multicultural society. It can also be defined as a society that no longer subscribes to monocultural principles but to multicultural principles—at least in theory.

Review Questions

1. Is Canada a multicultural society? Is Canada a society that abides by the principles of multiculturalism? Defend your answer.
2. Compare the different levels of meaning associated with the term multiculturalism in terms of what they say about multiculturalism in Canada.
3. Indicate some of the ideas and ideals associated with multiculturalism. Are Canadians inclined to uphold these ideals? Explain.
4. What is meant by the term "multiculturalism as a critique"? What are the two main lines pursued by a critique of multiculturalism?
5. Compare and contrast the principles of multiculturalism with those of monoculturalism.
6. Compare multiculturalism with alternative ideologies (or strategies) for managing diversity, including assimilation, integration, and segregation. You may need to consult outside sources.
7. Many have argued that Canada is multicultural in ideology. The practice of multiculturalism is something altogether different. Discuss.

Recommended Reading

Himani Bannerji. 2000. *The Dark Side of the Moon*. Toronto: Ontario Scholars Press.

John Berry, Rudolph Kalin, and Donald M. Taylor. 1977. *Multiculturalism and Ethnic Attitudes in Canada*. Ottawa: Minister of Supply and Services.

Stephen Castles and Mark J. Miller. 1998. *The Age of Migration*. London: MacMillan Press.

Dean A. Harris, ed. 1995. *Multiculturalism from the Margins*. Westport: Greenwood Press.

Wsevolod Isajiw. 1997. *Multiculturalism in North America and Europe: Comparative Perspectives on Interethnic Relations and Social Relations and Social Incorporation*. Toronto: Ontario Scholars Press.

CHAPTER 3

Official Multiculturalism: The Politics of Policy

CHAPTER OBJECTIVES

- To acknowledge Trudeau's contribution to advancing the principles, policies, and practices of Canada's official multiculturalism.
- To understand how multiculturalism has become institutionalized as government policy.
- To situate multiculturalism within the framework of the Canadian state.
- To appreciate the difference between a freewheeling, popular multiculturalism and multiculturalism as a state-sanctioned policy of containment.
- To assess the potentially revolutionary impacts of multiculturalism.
- To reveal how official multiculturalism has evolved through three phases: as ethnicity, as equity, and as civic.
- To point out how the *cultural* in multiculturalism is mainly about the *social*.
- To compare Canadian multiculturalism with multiculturalism in other places, including the United States, Australia, New Zealand, and Quebec.
- To show how the "pretend pluralism" of official multiculturalism cannot cope with the transformational challenges of taking differences seriously.
- To explain "the Canadian way" as a model for engaging with diversity.

CASE STUDY
Trudeau and Multiculturalism: Strange Bedfellows?

A country after all is not something you build as the pharoahs built the pyramids, and then leave standing there to defy eternity. A country is something that is built every day out of certain basic shared values. And so it is in the hands of every Canadian to determine how well and wisely we shall build this country of our future.

Pierre Elliott Trudeau, *Memoirs*

Pierre Elliott Trudeau's passing in October 2000 provides an excellent opportunity for us to reflect on his life and contributions. Many look on multiculturalism as one of Trudeau's great projects, and perceive that he did more than anyone to remake Canada into a multicultural society. Some are sorry he did, as Canadians spiral apart because of multicultural rifts. Still others are of two minds about his place in Canada's multicultural evolution. Put bluntly, Trudeau was not especially keen about multiculturalism in the conventional sense of the word. Yet his vision of Canada was profoundly multicultural. How can this be?

To answer this, we must consider Canada's history. Canada was not always a diverse society. In fact, it was predominantly white before 1965, when Trudeau entered federal politics. Canada's people were nearly 95 percent European, most of them of French or British stock, and immigration laws ensured that they stayed that way (Dyer, 2000). This very whiteness had led to bitter rivalry between the French and the English and was threatening to destroy Confederation, which had been a fragile agreement at best. Trudeau's initiatives to diversify Canada were an attempt to diffuse this binational rift into multicultural fragments.

TRUDEAU'S CONTRIBUTION: FROM WHITE DOMINION TO MULTICULTURAL MOSAIC

Official multiculturalism in 1971 turned out to be a watershed in Canadian history. For one thing, it filled a gap for English-speaking Canadians, many of whom were desperately seeking an alternative vision to replace their fading British identity (Conlogue, 2000). Official multiculturalism was also an attempt to appease Canadians who were neither anglophone nor francophone. Finally, the government had strong political reasons for trying to secure a "True North, Strong and Free."

For Trudeau, then, multiculturalism was not about promoting differ-ences; rather, it was about eliminating disadvantages by removing preju-dice and discrimination of all kinds. Official multiculturalism would make all cultures equal, and thus ensure the inclusion of minorities as full and equal participants in Canadian society. Trudeau's multiculturalism was also a sharp challenge to Canadian identity, in that it superimposed a *one Canada* perspective over the prevailing *deux nations* view. This *one Canada* perspective had a number of profound repercussions:

- It embraced a commitment to the principles of multiculturalism and bilingualism.
- It added moral heft to Canada's *Charter of Rights and Freedoms* (read: *individual* rights and freedoms).
- It strengthened the central government, or attempted to.
- It insisted on seeing individuals as Canadians (and vice versa) rather than as members of ethnic communities (Richards, 2000).

By and large, English-speaking Canadians have endorsed Canada's transformation into "one Canada." Quebec has not, and has come to see itself as the relatively autonomous homeland of a people in search of an appropriate political arrangement, within *or* without Canada. Paradoxically, Trudeau's plan to quash Quebec nationalism has had the opposite effect.

To be sure, Trudeau hardly transformed Canada all by himself. Canada was multicultural before he arrived on the political scene. For proof of this, consider the arrival before the First World War of Ukrainians and Germans, and the postwar waves of Italians and Hungarians (Stoffman, 2001). The liberalization of immigration policies in 1962 and 1967 further opened the door to multicultural diversity. Nor can we say that Trudeau invented multiculturalism. Canada had long accepted the principle of diversity as a basis for attracting immigrants to the West, and the Citizenship Act in 1947 and the Human Rights Bill in 1960 both strength-ened this principle. Trudeau's contribution was to institutionalize the prin-ciple of multiculturalism as a blueprint for an inclusive Canada.

TRUDEAU'S MULTICULTURALISM

It might seem that Trudeau and multiculturalism were not an especially good fit. Mistaken readings of multiculturalism have contributed to this perception. For many, multiculturalism is about celebrating diversity or promoting minorities—about abandoning reason for the charms of belonging to one's own kind. Multiculturalism, seen in this light, is also about placing ethnic diversity at the centre of society. Canadian society as seen from this perspective is a "cultural mosaic"—the sum of diverse yet static cultures (Rukszto, 2000).

Contrast this ethnic particularism with the humanistic universalism espoused by Trudeau. Trudeau believed deeply in individual freedoms and endorsed the equality of all people, whatever their language, ethnicity, or race. He also took the classic liberal-pluralistic position toward ethnic diversity. To review what that position is: (1) When it comes to portioning out rewards and recognition, what we have in common as freedom-loving and equality-seeking individuals overrides our differences as members of a group. (2) The content of a person's character is more important than the colour of his or her skin. (3) Equality before the law is more important than special treatment because of race or ethnicity. (4) Merit is preferred over birth or ascription as a basis for defining who gets what. To the extent that differences exist, they are best treated as private or personal.

Individuals were at the centre of Trudeau's Just Society; in other words, groups were not. Individuals were free to express their heritage in terms of contributing to the Canadian mosaic (see Breton, 2000), but an ethnicity-blind inclusiveness had to prevail. In the Just Society that Trudeau envisioned, all members would be able to participate fully and equally, and none would be prevented from doing so by messy ethnic entanglements (Nemni, 2000). The Official Languages Act, the Constitution, the *Charter of Rights and Freedoms*, and the Multiculturalism Act all contributed to the creation of this pan-Canadian solidarity. The idea that each individual should be fully involved in Canada as a self-defining agent is yet another legacy of Trudeau (Breton, 2000; Siddiqui, 2000).

MULTICULTURALISM, NOT MULTINATIONALISM

Is an official multiculturalism compatible with the principles of an ethnicity-blind just society? Was Trudeau's vision of Canada fundamentally at odds with his philosophical principles? A careful reading suggests it was not, although Trudeau's policies often contradicted one another. He had little tolerance for ethnicities that clashed with reason, tolerance, freedom, and equality. He detested any form of nationalism that was not based on reason and individual freedom. His distaste for Quebec nationalism was hardly a secret; neither was his annoyance with British-Canadian nationalism, with its refusal to concede even the smallest concessions to the French or to other minorities (Radwanski, 1997).

For Trudeau, in other words, the only good ethnicity was a multicultural ethnicity. Multiculturalism was acceptable only when it was rooted in personal experiences; when it involved appreciating different arts and crafts; when it did not make demands on the public sector; when it contributed to national unity and identity; and when it amounted to a transition on the path to a truly inclusive Canadian society. Other forms of ethnicity he saw as racist and as threats to individual freedom. Not surprisingly, Trudeau rejected the notion that Canada was a compact between two founding nations. Instead, he endorsed a vision of Canada that emphasized individual rights at the expense of nationalistic communities, especially when the latter asserted the right to restrict individuals' choices.

The irony is inescapable. Trudeau is still seen as the founder of official multiculturalism, yet he was clearly ambivalent about diversity. For him, pretend pluralism was tolerable, whereas taking differences seriously was not. And therein lay Trudeau's genius: by creating social and cultural space for minority women and men, he established an inclusive yet multicultural Canada, in which minorities enjoyed the same level playing field as the French and English (Siddiqui, 2000). At the same time, he established a Canada that endorsed diversity in principle without actually changing in any fundamental way how power and resources were distributed.

FRAMING MULTICULTURAL POLICIES

In the past thirty years, the white settler societies of Canada, New Zealand, Australia, and the United States have become more and more diverse as a result of immigration from "nonconventional" sources. Accompanying this, minorities have been growing more and more assertive over entitlements and recognition (Fleras and Spoonley, 1999). Central authorities have responded to this increasing political clout in a variety of ways, from indifference or rejection on the one hand, to an acceptance of diversity as a potential society-building asset on the other. Or they have simply been indecisive. Traditional initiatives such as assimilation and segregation are no longer morally acceptable as approaches to engaging diversity. Instead, debates over inclusion have been recast as debates over multiculturalism. Both governments and minorities are struggling to cope with an assortment of challenges, including the following: the "influx" of immigrants; the proliferation of identity politics; the rising importance of ethnicity as a mobilizing force; the tenacity of racism; and the ascendancy of ethnic nationalist movements. Not surprisingly, the challenge of building societies along multicultural lines is as formidable as ever (Smolicz, 1997). Consider the following questions, which must be addressed:

- Is it possible to forge unity from diversity in ways that are workable and fair?
- How can societies disengage from monoculturalism without jeopardizing national unity?
- How exactly can societies learn to live together with differences?
- Can any society survive by "taking differences seriously"? Or is "pretend pluralism" the only realistic goal?
- How can societies balance their national interests with social justice and ethnic identity?

All of these questions can be boiled down into one: Is it humanly possible to create a society that is safe *from* diversity as well as safe *for* diversity? Alternatively, is it possible to ensure that diversity is safe *from* society yet safe *for* society (Fleras, 1998)?

More and more countries are endorsing multiculturalism as official policy. Multiculturalism has emerged as the most obligatory word in modern-day cultural discourse. In Western democracies such as Australia and Britain, it is resorted to so routinely that it has become almost synonymous with the very idea of the nation (Bharucha, 2000). Nowhere is this more evident than in Canada, where thirty years of official multiculturalism have generated both delight and dismay. In a remarkably short time, Canada has transformed itself from a British colonial outpost into one of the world's most diverse societies; and it has done so without collapsing into ethnic strife. Canada has discarded its explicitly monocultural agenda—one in which people were judged and rewarded according to how close they were, racially and culturally, to the Anglo mainstream. In its place is a bold, albeit imperfect, strategy for "living together with differences." Official multiculturalism has also served well as a means for managing conflict, on the foundation principle that people can live together as long as there is a unifying vision to "harmonize" their differences. In this country, official multiculturalism is mainly about balancing the nation's interests with those of social justice and cultural diversity.

This point is increasingly clear: under Canada's multiculturalism banner, people are accepted as no less Canadian for whatever their differences, and enjoy the same citizenship rights, duties, and entitlements regardless of their origin, creed, or colour. This multicultural ethic goes beyond mere coexistence or the tolerance of others (see also Jelloun, 1999). Emphasis instead is on constructively engaging diversity in a way that is workable, necessary, and fair. To be sure, we Canadians are not nearly as multicultural as we proudly believe (Fleras, 1997). In some ways we may even be less diversity-minded than our melting pot neighbours to the south (Reitz and Breton, 1994; Simpson, 1998). Even so, we have promoted multiculturalism as a framework for living together, and have done so with a success that many other nations envy. Paradoxically, however, we ourselves have become blasé or even critical of our efforts (Kurthen 1997; Sugunasiri 1999).

Official multiculturalism is now a political force in itself, at the federal, provincial, and municipal levels. Once it was written into the Constitution Act (1982) and the Multiculturalism Act (1988), Canada became the world's first officially multicultural country. Moreover, official multiculturalism has evolved to the point where it is now central to Canada's national identity. Its strength at all levels of Canadian society—both personal and institutional— has profoundly changed how Canadians think about themselves and their relationship to the world. Canada's commitment to inclusiveness has fostered innovative approaches to integrating new Canadians into society (Harles, 1998; Kymlicka, 1998). Demographic upheavals and political developments have changed *how* diversity is engaged, but not the central commitment of forging unity from diversity.

As a complex new model for living together, official multiculturalism is both valued and condemned. It has not always delivered what it promises: principles that sound good in theory have regularly fallen short in practice because of hidden agendas and political expediencies. In this chapter I explore the politics of official multiculturalism as state policy with respect to its origins, development, underlying assumptions, hidden rationales, impacts, and implications for society building. This approach—the political economy approach—enables us to analyze official multiculturalism as essentially "a state apparatus designed to manage pluralistic demographies" (Gunew, 1999: 11). I show that multicultural policies developed in three phases, with each phase reflecting a change in focus rather than a change in objectives. I then compare Canada's efforts in multiculturalism with those of Quebec and of various other countries, including the United States, New Zealand, and Australia. I end the chapter by showing how official multiculturalism promises more than it can deliver.

THE POLITICAL ECONOMY OF MULTICULTURALISM AS POLICY

Multiculturalism as official government policy has done much—perhaps more than anything else—to reshape the cultural contours of Canadian society. Canada's multiculturalism policies since 1971 have advanced the ideal of a socially cohesive society without eroding either the interconnect-edness of the parts or the principles of liberal pluralism. They have also provided a means for regulating Canada's diversity, in the form of initiatives for enhancing both inclusiveness without compromising national interests.

In general terms, we can define a *policy* as three linked processes: a government's *goals*, that is, its explicit statement of intent to solve problems according to certain principles; the *actions* it chooses to take (or not take) to achieve those goals; and the ground-level *practices* that support those actions. (Of course, none of this means that policy rhetoric always matches program realities.) The goals, plans, and practices of a policy are always in flux. They are also open to different interpretations by competing interests.

Multiculturalism as State Policy

As policy, official multiculturalism is interventionist by definition. It was born as a means for the state to preserve the status quo, and it still serves that end. Put another way, it is an ideological framework whose purpose is to stifle dissent by cooling out potentially troublesome minorities. It attempts to depoliticize diversity in the hope of minimizing social disruptions and maximizing the orderly accumulation of capital. Seen in this light, "celebrating diversity" is largely about lulling the general population into compliance without challenging fundamental inequities.

Admittedly, official multiculturalism may not set out to control. Nevertheless, in practice it has a controlling effect, in that its outcomes reflect national or vested interests rather than minority concerns. The end result? Reforms under official multiculturalism may well address the superficial aspects of inequality by removing discriminatory practices, and leave the impression that "something" is being done when, in reality, substantive issues are rarely addressed. In other words, when it comes to multiculturalism, appearances are indeed deceiving.

Securing social control by endorsing diversity may sound like a paradox. We can explain it by referring to what Eva Mackey calls the "institutionalization of difference" (1999: 62). Institutionalizing cultural differences basically involves a process by which the government absorbs and neutralizes diversity. In doing this, the government has empowered itself to regulate potentially troublesome ethnic minorities and at the same time taken away their power. In effect, the state has built a symbolic order around a "pretend pluralism" instead of committing itself to taking differences seriously. Of course, this process is not completely exploitative, nor is it completely one-sided. Insofar as official multiculturalism is a means of regulating minorities, we are not denying that it is an enlightened experiment in living together. To the contrary, now that it has been established and put into practice, official multiculturalism is assuming a life of its own and evolving in unexpected directions.

We must not assume that minority women and men are passive actors in the political arena. The "dis-privileged," both as individuals and in groups, have long demonstrated they are capable of making official multiculturalism the focus of struggles over resources (Pearson, 1995). The powerless have learned how to turn the very tools that were designed to control them into means of resistance (Walker, 1998). The paradox of official multiculturalism should now be clear: the ambiguities inherent in official multiculturalism have improved conditions for some minorities even while defusing potential threats to the state's stability.

OFFICIAL MULTICULTURALISM: EVOLUTION OF A REVOLUTION

On October 8, 1971, in the House of Commons, the Prime Minister of Canada, Pierre Elliott Trudeau, announced his party's commitment to the principles of multiculturalism. Since then, official multiculturalism has been enshrined in statutory and constitutional law as a defining characteristic of Canada, and has generated both support and opposition at both ends of the political spectrum. The "content" of multiculturalism has evolved as well. Originally, the emphasis was on ethnicity; now it is on equity, and also on civic multiculturalism as a response to political, social, and intellectual trends.

Official multiculturalism has evolved slowly, yet its impact has been revolutionary: it has permanently altered Canada's politics and culture and infiltrated the very fabric of Canadian society. Official multiculturalism has changed the concept of who gets what, and how government is "done," and—even more fundamental—what society itself is *for*. Multicultural ideals such as diversity, equality, and respect are now seen as vital to upholding Canadian principles such as cultural identity, social justice, and civic participation (Annual Report, 2000). Multiculturalism as a formal policy is now used to assess Canada's commitment to inclusiveness. Various laws are now in place that justify a variety of government initiatives for diversifying Canada. Recent initiatives, such as the establishment of the Canadian Race Relations Foundation, have further bolstered the status of official multiculturalism as a beacon of enlightenment. Not surprisingly, Canadians increasingly see themselves as a tolerant and open people, and dismiss the American melting pot as inferior to "the mosaic."

Building Toward Multiculturalism

After thirty years of official multiculturalism, there is now a national consensus that diversity is necessary to a progressive and prosperous society. Yet diversity was never so popular in the past. Before the Second World War, governments in Canada routinely dismissed diversity as inferior, irrelevant, or subversive. Canadian society was anchored in the French and English agendas, and Canada's immigration policy was more or less "whites only," and the more British, the better.

Religious and cultural differences were tolerated as long as they were kept private; when these differences tried to "come out" in society, they were treated as divisive or dangerous. Governments saw assimilation as essential for society building. Sometimes governments were almost ruthless in their efforts to stamp out diversity. Other times, assimilationist philosophies were applied quite deliberately to achieve national goals. Still other times, government policies *amounted* to assimilation (i.e., in deed if not in word). This embrace of assimilation reflected a commitment to Anglo-Canadian conformity: any cultural attribute that wandered too far from the principles of God, King, and Empire was dismissed as incompatible with national identity or loyalty to the Dominion.

But national conformity and the commitment to Anglo ideals began to erode after the Second World War. Ethnic conflicts in Europe made it doubly important for the government to encourage new Canadians' loyalty to Canada (Annual Report, 2000). Also, pressure was mounting to find ways to accommodate postwar immigration without compromising national interests (Pearson, 1995; Wilson, 1995). If only to help immigrants settle and foster community harmony, successive governments began to modify the existing concept of Canada in line with new demographic realities.

The Citizenship Act in 1947 signalled Canada's intention to stop identifying so closely to its mother country, the United Kingdom. Once that act was passed, both foreign-born and native-born Canadians were no longer defined as British subjects who happened to live in Canada. Thereafter, Canada was to be a separate society with a distinct destiny. The shocking assumption here was that unity could be forged without suppressing diversity. Tolerance toward diversity was further bolstered by the following government moves:

- The Fair Practices Acts of the 1950s, which promised to abolish discriminatory practices in public venues such as theatres and bars.
- The Bill of Rights of 1960, which sought to ensure equal rights for all Canadians.

- Changes in procedures for selecting immigrants; skills now counted more than nationality.
- Confirmation in 1969 that Canada was officially bilingual.

Clearly, official multiculturalism did not appear out of nowhere. It was one of a string of events and trends that cumulatively broke down exclusionary barriers.

Official multiculturalism was introduced largely as a political exercise— as a pragmatic political program rather than an exercise in humanitarianism. It was a response to pressing political conundrums rather than a compassionate nod to social justice (see Ujimoto, 1999: 278; Harles, 1998; Peters, 1978). Canada in the late 1960s was swamped with political problems. There were growing fears of a crisis in race relations that could delegitimize the Canadian state. New immigrants were seen by many as a threat to Canadian ways, and the government was expected to do something about it. Aboriginal groups were protesting a White Paper that supported assimilation. Finally, a political response had to be made to the forces of Québécois separatism (Breton, 1989).

In short, official multiculturalism was originally envisioned as a strategy for bolstering national unity by a rethinking of Canada's social contract. Ethnic minorities were no longer junior partners; rather, they were a possible means of neutralizing Canada's French–English rift (Webber, 1994). There were also partisan politics at play: multiculturalism was intended to shore up Liberal strength in the West and in cities, to defuse Quebec nationalism, to thwart American cultural imperialism, and to transform immigrants and ethnic minorities into loyal and law-abiding citizens (Harles, 1998). Official multiculturalism made a virtue out of a necessity; it parlayed a potential weakness (diversity) into a strength (unity), and it did so without necessarily revoking a commitment to social cohesion, national identity, domestic peace, economic growth, and global respect (Kurthen, 1997).

Phase One: Ethnicity Multiculturalism

Multiculturalism arose in the aftermath of the Report of the Royal Commission on Bilingualism and Biculturalism in 1969. The B&B commission had found that Canada was not as dichotomous as the national mythology would have it, and that the interests and concerns of "other ethnic groups" would have to be taken into account to ensure social harmony (Kobayashi, 1999). Various ethnic minority groups, especially the Ukrainians and the Germans, had argued vigorously that their language and culture were as vital as Quebec's to Canadian society building (Wilson, 1993). A compromise was eventually struck that took into account the contributions that other ethnic groups made to the cultural enrichment of Canada (see Jaworsky, 1979). The prevailing image of Canada as a bicultural partnership between French and English was thus challenged by the notion that Canada was actually a multicultural mosaic of equality-seeking, rights-bearing individuals (McRoberts, 1997).

In the aftermath of this report, the Liberal government arrived at a policy of multiculturalism within a bilingual framework. Pierre Elliott Trudeau, then prime minister, articulated this new cultural policy:

> There cannot be one cultural policy for Canadians of British or French origins, another for the originals, and yet a third for all others. For although there are two official languages, there is no official culture. Nor does any cultural group take precedence over another ... We are free to be ourselves. But this cannot be left to chance ... It is the policy of this government to eliminate any such danger and to safeguard this freedom.

Endorsing the principle that all of Canada's cultures and ethnic groups were equal had profound implications. The Liberals' multicultural policy seemed to both affirm and deny the relevance of diversity as a basis for living together: "No matter who you are or where you came from," according to official multiculturalism, "you can become one of us by discarding your differences in public and playing by the rules. Entitlement is yours by rights as a Canadian and no one is to be excluded because of ethnicity or race."

All players were expected to adjust when it came to the integration of ethnic and new Canadians. Mainstream Canadians were to be encouraged to discard their prejudices; minorities were expected to dismantle their cultural jealousies and those cultural practices which inhibited adaptation and involvement. In the government's own words on the perils of exclusion, recourse to multiculturalism would "strengthen the solidarity of the Canadian people by enabling all Canadians to participate fully and without discrimination in defining and building the nation's future." The government outlined the anti-exclusionist objectives of its multiculturalism policy in the House of Commons (Debates 1971: 8581):

1. The Government of Canada will support all of Canada's cultures and will seek to assist, resources permitting, the development of those cultural groups that have demonstrated a desire and effort to continue to develop, a capacity to grow and contribute to Canada, as well as a clear need for assistance.

2. The Government will assist members of all cultural groups to overcome cultural barriers to full participation in Canadian society.
3. The Government will promote creative encounters and interchange among all Canadian cultural groups in the interests of national unity.
4. The Government will continue to assist immigrants to acquire at least one of Canada's official languages in order to become full participants in Canadian society.

Clearly, the intent of the government's multiculturalism policy was not to celebrate diversity per se. Rather, the government was committing itself to breaking down barriers by changing how ethnic Canadians were integrated (Kymlicka, 1998). The focus was shifting from cultural diversity to society building—to fostering an inclusive society in which ethnic minorities would be accorded both equal dignity and equal treatment. Pride in culture was perceived as critical to people's self-worth. Having gained confidence in their identity, people would strengthen their identification with Canada, accept the rights of other groups, and participate more fully in their community and in Canadian life. Five main principles prevailed in this commitment to reconfigure Canada along liberal-pluralist lines:

- Equality of status—No cultural group has special status over another; all cultures are equal to each other.
- Canadian identity—Diversity lies at the heart of the Canadian identity.
- Personal choice—The ability to choose lifestyles and cultural traits is a positive thing. Everyone in society has freedom of choice, that is, the freedom to be different within a set of Canadian values shared by all.
- Protection of individual rights—People have the right to be free of discrimination that precludes equality and participation. (Passage of the Human Rights Act in 1977 reinforced the right of all Canadians to equal opportunity and full participation without fear of discrimination.)
- Official languages—Canada does not have an official culture, but it has two official languages.

To put these principles into practice, the government proposed a set of initiatives, the aim of which was clearly integrative. Funds were set aside for specific initiatives in the following areas: securing language and culture, cultural sharing, the learning of official languages, and the removal of cultural barriers to equality. Government funding in these areas was positively received insofar as the groups that got it secured a degree of political legitimacy. The government also established various agencies. For example, in 1972 a multicultural directorate was formed within the Department of the Secretary of State with the mandate to promote multicultural ideals, social integration, and racial harmony (*Equality Now!* 1984). Efforts were made to consolidate human rights, strengthen Canadian identity, prevent discrimination, foster citizenship involvement, reinforce national unity, and promote cultural diversity.

To assist the federal authorities, the Canadian Consultative Council on Multiculturalism was established in 1973. In 1983 this council was restructured (and renamed the Canadian Ethnocultural Council) in the hope of improving its advisory and monitoring capacities. Still later, a Ministry of Multiculturalism was created to monitor government departments regarding their compliance to multicultural principles. This gave way in 1991 to a federal Department of Multiculturalism and Citizenship, established on the heels of the 1988 Multiculturalism Act. This last body was scrapped in 1993.

To sum up: Multiculturalism played well in English Canada. With its commitment to individual rights and to government intervention to ensure tolerance for others, official multiculturalism did not veer from a liberal-pluralist ethic. It seemed to be endorsing diversity yet also denying its relevance as grounds for entitlement. It was inclusive to the extent that it focused on neutralizing those disadvantages which prevented minority women and men from participating fully in society. Ethnicity was to be tolerated to the extent that it was shared with other Canadians, made a contribution to Canada, was consistent with core Canadian values, and was confined to the private or personal domain. Cultural differences were to be purged from the public domain; in this the hope was to ensure that everyone was treated alike. To be sure, the practice turned out to have less appeal than the theory: privatizing pluralism under a "no official culture" policy had the effect of "morphing" diversity into museum curiosities rather than integral components of Canada's cultural life (Brooks, 1998). This privatizing also prompted fears of an inward-looking ethnic tribalism—a kind of "cultural apartheid"—rather than an interaction based on sharing and exchange (Hutcheon, 2001).

Phase Two: Equity Multiculturalism

By the late 1970s official multiculturalism had shifted its focus (Jaworsky, 1979; Agocs and Boyd, 1993). At the outset it had protected yet also denied the distinct ethnic identities that immigrants brought with them. It had also increased the government's involvement in solving the social problems facing immigrant communities (Poole, 1996). Multiculturalism was directed almost exclusively at the European ethnic sector. It attempted to enhance the social status of ethnic minorities by symbolically affirming their language and culture; yet at the same time, it hoped to increase their acceptance in society by removing cultural barriers and countering the prejudicial attitudes of the mainstream. For those seeking inclusion, multiculturalism helped end the exclusions of the past. But official multiculturalism proved anathema for national minorities such as those Québécois who sought inclusion without integration.

Official multiculturalism had no choice but to shift its focus once non-European visible minorities began arriving in Canada in large numbers. As it turned out, older approaches to multiculturalism were insufficient to handle them. Pre-1970s immigrants from Europe shared a broad commitment to Anglocentric values and priorities, and this helped them join the mainstream quite quickly. In contrast, the immigrants of colour who followed them were not going to succeed in Canada without government intervention (Sajoo, 1994). The new view was that disadvantages were not the result of individual impairment or cultural differences. Rather, they were a result of circumstances beyond individual control, including political and economic forces that raised barriers and limited opportunities. For new immigrants from non-European sources, the need to dismantle racial barriers to opportunity and inclusion was more important than any celebration of cultural heritage (McRoberts, 1997).

Not surprisingly, this new emphasis on equity and disadvantage displaced the earlier one on tolerance and identity. Changing demographics led to a more inclusive policy and symbols for a diverse population (Abu-Laban, 2001). Social justice assumed far more importance in government policy; discriminatory barriers at "structural" (= institutional) levels were removed. The emphasis now was on combating racism and promoting inclusiveness. Government funds have followed this shift in mandate: relatively less money is now going to ethnocultural organizations and events, and relatively more toward spending on pragmatic goals. In the 1993–94 fiscal year, federal multiculturalism grants totalled $25.5 million: $13.3 million was earmarked for community support and participation (i.e., to help new Canadians settle); another $6.5 million for public education and antiracism campaigns; and $5.5 million for promoting heritage cultures and languages (Thompson, 1994). Multiculturalism continues to receive only a fraction of the $2 billion allocated to Heritage Canada (Brooks, 1998).

Later developments sharpened this new focus on equity-based multiculturalism. The Constitution Act (1982) and the *Charter of Rights and Freedoms* (which came into effect in 1985) enshrined multiculturalism as a distinguishing characteristic of Canadian life. Section 27 stated clearly that multiculturalism was now a prominent part of the national agenda at the highest levels: the "Charter shall be interpreted in a manner consistent with the preservation and enhancement of the multicultural heritage of Canadians." In 1988 Canada became the first country to give legal weight to multiculturalism, through the Multiculturalism Act. Among the specific objectives of this act were these:

- to improve understanding of the importance of multiculturalism to Canadians;
- to promote equality and the full and equal participation of individuals while acknowledging the legitimacy of those differences that contributed to Canada;
- to foster recognition of differences by way of exchanges and sharing; and
- to redesign institutional policies, programs, and practices for improving minority representation, access, and equity.

The Multiculturalism Act also required all federal institutions to assume a leadership role in actively promoting multiculturalism.

The Multiculturalism Act did not pass through Parliament without a fight (Parel, 1992). Critics on the left disliked how the act papered over fundamental inequities behind a raft of vague platitudes and unenforceable intentions. The act obligated the government to comply with Canada's multicultural character by submitting annual reports on progress toward inclusiveness; yet there were no specific guidelines, no penalties for lack of compliance, and no efforts to link multiculturalism with broader debates (Kobayashi, 1999). Those on the right continued to fear unnecessary social divisiveness and loss of national identity. They also criticized the act's requirement that federal institutions relate to Canadians on ethnic grounds rather than on geographical or functional ones (Srebrnik, 1997). Still, the Multiculturalism Act has proven pivotal. It reaffirmed in law what in the past had only been policy. And by giving multiculturalism the force of law, the act did much to protect it from party politics and electoral whims (*Multiculturalism*, 1987).

Phase Three: Civic Multiculturalism

With its commitment to accommodating diversity, official multiculturalism still attracts supporters. We see this in the commitments made by key institutions to ensure access, representation, and fair treatment for minorities. For a time, multiculturalism was also linked with citizenship under the Department of Multiculturalism and Citizenship. Multicultural policy is still overseen by the Citizenship and Canadian Identity portfolio, within the superministry of Heritage Canada.

This emphasis on good citizenship is the latest development in official multiculturalism (Abu-Laban, 2001). The guidelines for the multiculturalism program emphasize policy aims—to "foster a society that recognizes, respects, and reflects a diversity of cultures such that people of all backgrounds feel a sense of belonging and attachment to Canada" (Canadian Heritage, 1997: 1). Civic multiculturalism emphasizes core values such as equality, diversity, and mutual respect regardless of race, ethnicity, language, or culture. A commitment to inclusiveness is central to civic multiculturalism, according to the government's 2000 annual report on multiculturalism, *Strengthening Canada*. It sees Canada as a multicultural society that encourages citizen participation by supporting three fundamental goals:

- *Identity*—to foster a society in which all Canadians, whatever their background, feel a sense of belonging and attachment to Canada.
- *Civic participation*—to promote active citizenship, so that all citizens are able to participate in shaping Canadian society.
- *Social justice*—to build an inclusive society that ensures fair and equitable treatment.

In short, civic multiculturalism is about building a society based on citizenship, and fostering a sense of shared identity to enhance national unity. The focus is on what we have in common as rights-bearing and equality-seeking individuals, rather than on what divides us. Just as important is social cohesion and the absorption of shared core values. Also, civic multiculturalism concerns itself with society at large rather than with specific interests. As Hedy Frey, the Minister of Multiculturalism, put it, civic multiculturalism's goal is to "break down the ghettoization of multiculturalism" if Canadians are to "live together with their differences." Clearly, there is a consistent theme to civic multiculturalism: it must balance national interests with minority concerns without jeopardizing the vision of a single, unified Canada.

CONTINUITY IN CHANGE

Thirty years of official multiculturalism in Canada have resulted in a national consensus around the participation of minorities. The "ethnicity multiculturalism" of the 1970s seemed intent on neutralizing ethnicity to ensure minority involvement in society; the "equity multiculturalism" of the 1980s focused on eliminating racism and discrimination at the level of institutions; the "civic multiculturalism" of the 1990s/2000s promotes inclusiveness through a shared civic identity (Fleras and Elliott, 1999). Table 3.1 compares and contrasts these phases in Canada's multiculturalism policy according to the following criteria: focus, reference point, mandate, scope, problem source, problem solution, and key metaphor.

TABLE 3.1

Multiculturalism Policies

	Ethnicity Multiculturalism (1970s)	Equity Multiculturalism (1980s)	Civic Multiculturalism (1990s/2000s)
Focus	celebrating differences	managing diversity	belonging
Reference point	culture	institutional structure	society building
Mandate	ethnicity	race relations	citizenship
Scope	individual adjustment	accommodation	participation
Problem source	prejudice	systemic discrimination	exclusion
Problem solution	tolerance	employment equity	inclusion
Key metaphor	mosaic	level playing field	living together

While there have been changes in emphasis, content, and direction, the core of Canada's multiculturalism policy has not changed much over the decades. It has always been based on consensus, and on building society by promoting integration. It contains ethnicity by setting limits on what is acceptable in society. Only the *means* for achieving these ends have fluctuated, in response to demographic shifts and political developments.

The past decade has not been kind to official multiculturalism. Since the Liberals were returned to power in 1993, responsibility for it has been bounced around many departments (including Parks and Amateur Sport) within the superministry of Heritage Canada. It is significant that multiculturalism has been downgraded from a stand-alone federal department to merely one program among many in a much larger ministry. In this era of fiscal restraint, multiculturalism is being sacrificed on the altar of political expediency, to make way for issues perceived as more immediate and pressing (Kobayashi, 1999). This change in federal attitudes toward multiculturalism has weakened its support among the general public; it has also discouraged minorities from promoting their multicultural interests (Magsino, 2000). The Canadian government is still committed to multiculturalism, but its support is highly symbolic and increasingly muted, and it has not hesitated to axe some multicultural programs (see also Poole, 1996; Magsino, 2000).

Canada is not the only country to commit itself to multiculturalism. Australia, which has many similarities to Canada, has followed much the same path, as the following case study shows.

CASE STUDY
Multiculturalism Down Under: Australian Perspectives

Canada and Australia have much in common even though positioned at opposite "corners" of the globe. Both countries began as British colonies; both conquered indigenous peoples by taking away their land and authority; both saw themselves as "white" societies; and both must now face the challenges of living together with differences in a globally inter-connected world. The two countries have also had very similar experiences with immigration. Only in the past few decades has Australia allowed immigration from "nonconventional sources" (i.e., non–English-speaking backgrounds, or NESBs) such as Asia. Since the Second World War, immi-gration to Australia has increased to the point where the Commonwealth (central) government has been compelled to intervene in pursuing social cohesion and national unity (Jayasuriya, 1989). The Australian model of multiculturalism, like the Canadian one, has succeeded—though not totally—in managing the contradictions of living together by balancing national interests with a commitment to diversity and equality.

Official multiculturalism in Australia began as a response to postwar trends and events. The most notable of these was the end of the White Australia policy. In 1945, Australia's 7.5 million people were largely of British or Irish descent. There are now nearly 18 million Australians, and 40 percent of the increase is due to immigration. Today, 40 percent of Australians are either foreign born or have at least one immigrant parent. Asia is the most significant source of new immigrants (Poole, 1999). The main political parties, making a virtue of necessity, have adopted multicul-turalism as formal policy, in "appreciation of cultural diversity" and "[to] maintain the languages and cultural traditions of minority groups."

Australia's policy focused at first on racial tolerance and equal opportunity, with the goal of helping immigrants settle. It acknowledged that government programs were needed if distinct cultural identities were to be protected as part of the national identity (Manzo, 1996; Poole, 1999). Official multicultur-alism was further boosted when Australia signed the International

Convention on the Elimination of All Forms of Racial Discrimination. Later, it passed its own Racial Discrimination Act, which made it:

> unlawful for a person to do any act involving a distinction, exclusion, restriction, or preference based on race, colour, descent, or national or ethnic origin which has the purpose or effect of nullifying or impairing the recognition, enjoyment, or exercise, on an equal footing, of any human right or fundamental freedom in the political, economic, social, cultural or any other field of public life. (Racial Discrimination Act, 1975, in Hudson, 1987: 97)

In the wake of the 1978 Report on the Review of Post-Arrival Programs and Services for Migrants (the Galbally Report), the Australian Institute of Multicultural Affairs was established. This institute's goals included the following:

- To enhance public awareness of Australia's diverse cultures and an appreciation for their contributions to Australian society.
- To promote harmony and sharing between Australia's various ethnic groups.
- To foster social cohesion through understanding and tolerance of diversity.
- To promote an environment that encourages full and equal participation for all minorities by enhancing opportunities for minority women and men to achieve their own potential.

In response to another report, the government launched a multicultural television station, Special Broadcasting Services, to provide a variety of foreign-language programs (Manzo, 1996). The central government also began funding nearly nearly 1,300 part-time ethnic schools in forty-seven languages. This initiative was consistent with the National Language Policy of 1987, which advocated second-language learning as critical for social justice, cultural and intellectual enrichment, foreign trade and tourism, and foreign policy (Foster and Seitz, 1989). Australian children are now expected to acquire one or more languages besides their first language. Also, immigrant children are now offered English immersion classes (Fishman, 1989).

In July 1989, multiculturalism in Australia was given further impetus with the establishment of a National Agenda for Multicultural Australia. This agenda focused on three things:

- *Cultural identity*—the right of all Australians to express (within limits) their language and culture.

- *Social justice*—the right of all Australians to equal treatment and opportunity through the removal of all discriminatory barriers.
- *Economic efficiency*—the need for Australia to capitalize on the skills and resources of all its citizens.

This agenda also has eight basic goals:

- freedom from discrimination
- equality of life chances
- equality of access and resources
- equal participation in society
- development of potential for all
- sharing of cultural heritage
- institutional responsiveness
- acquisition of English and community languages (Foster and Seitz, 1989)

Australia has committed itself to ethnic pluralism and social justice, but the point of it is to advance Australia's national interests. Though diversity is acceptable, all Australians are expected to endorse certain basic institutions and core values (Richmond, 1991).

In sum, Australia has an active multicultural policy and has established a broad range of cultural and language programs that closely resemble ones in Canada. There are some differences, of course. Multiculturalism in Australia is government policy, but is not entrenched in law or the Constitution. Australia is much more strongly commited to community languages; in Canada, support for heritage languages is mainly passive. And Australia's commitment to multiculturalism is tied to debates over anti-British sentiments and the desire to become a republic (Manzo, 1996). Even so, the similarities are unmistakable. Australia's formal multiculturalism like that of Canada is meant to promote the national interest. Also, both focus on ending disadvantage by knocking down discriminatory barriers and bringing minorities into the mainstream. Furthermore, the crisis in multiculturalism is palpable in both countries. Multiculturalism in Australia is losing steam as the government looks for ways to reduce expenditures. Finally, multiculturalism programs in Australia are being pared back for plainly political reasons: the government doesn't want to be seen as catering to special interest groups such as Asian migrants (Poole, 1999).

Predictably, multiculturalism in both countries has received criticism from both ends of the political spectrum (Longley, 1999). Australians on the left point to multiculturalism's failure to end racism; those on the right see it as a threat to the white settler identity; and the Aborigines have stepped away from the debate on the grounds that their interests are quite different from those of immigrants. Critics in Australia have attacked multiculturalism for denying past racism and supporting a national monoculture (Povinelli, 1998), and for amounting to little more than a political pork barrel (i.e., a means of buying ethnic loyalties) (Hughes, 2000). It has also been claimed that multiculturalism is too contradictory an ideology to gain wide and enduring support; too limiting, because of its cultural approach to the structural problems of racism and inequality; and too reductionist, in that it fossilizes cultural differences in an imagined community of national cohesion (Vasta and Castles, 1996). To the extent that these criticisms are comparable to those voiced in Canada, we can glean much from that venerable slogan, "The more things change ..."

MULTICULTURALISM IN THE UNITED STATES: DUELLING DISCOURSES

Multicultural policy in Canada does not challenge the prevailing distribution of power; nor does it promise to transform society along pluralistic lines. On the contrary, Canada's official multiculturalism is about building society by affirming yet denying the importance of ethnicity as a basis for distributing social goods. It focuses on inclusiveness within a pre-existing institutional framework; in that sense it tends to be monocultural in content and conservative in orientation; it also tends to be controlling, assimilationist (albeit slowly), and preoccupied with national rather than minority interests.

But not all multiculturalisms are cut from the same cloth as Canada's consensus style. Some forms of multiculturalism—let's call them *critical* forms—openly challenge, resist, and transform existing social structures. Critical forms are found in some unlikely places, including the United States. Considering that Americans have long considered assimilation (i.e., the melting pot approach) as key to society building, the emergence of critical multiculturalism in the United States may come as a shock. That it is driving multicultural wars in education and the media is no less shocking.

"Isms" of Resistance, Challenge, and Transformation

Multiculturalism has attracted unprecedented attention in American society, which is better noted for its diversity "melt-down" (Buenker and Ratner, 1992; Bak, 1993). In just the past fifteen years, multiculturalism has become a hot issue (Glazer, 1997), and provoked strongly mixed reactions. It has been applauded for reasserting people's control over their lives, detested as political correctness gone mad, deplored for making a "fetish" of diversity at the expense of a national unity, and dismissed for generating excessive zeal (see Higham, 1993; Smelser and Alexander, 1999).

Multicultural discourses challenge the old liberal principle that individuals are endlessly variable yet fundamentally alike. They contest the liberal-pluralist credo at the core of America's melting pot ethos—namely, that what people have in common as rights-bearing individuals is much more important as a basis for entitlement than their membership in a group. Multiculturalism advocates the "un-American" notion that entitlement should be based on disadvantage or birthright rather than merit, on identity rather than conformity, and on diversity rather than universality (McLaren, 1994).

Of course, not all multicultural discourses in the United States are shaped by the same cookie cutter. "Happy face" multiculturalism continues to be underpinned by the notion that while diversity should be celebrated, differences should be scaled back to ensure control and containment (Eisenstein, 1996; Hesse, 1997). Some forms of liberal multiculturalism are no more than a retooling of liberal pluralism in defence of the status quo (Giroux 1994). Liberal-pluralist forms of multiculturalism seem to have three constants:

- Multiculturalism is unavoidable.
- Multiculturalism must focus on individuals within a framework of fluid and open-ended group relations.
- The priority must be to end the marginalizing of African Americans (Kymlicka, 2000).

Yet there is no mistaking that "subversive" forms of multiculturalism are posing strong questions to the culture of whiteness (D'Souza, 1996; Eller, 1997). Critical multiculturalism challenges, resists, and transforms other forms: it *challenges* social authority, *resists* white hegemony, and *transforms* society by creating space for other cultures. It refuses to treat European culture (i.e., white, capitalist, male-centred, exclusionist culture) as "normal" culture (Giroux, 1994; Eisenstein, 1996; Stam, 1997). It questions the right of Eurocentric culture to dominate other cultures in a way that flattens diversity, while privileging European norms as necessary and superior (Stam, 1997). And it questions cultural and political institutions that elevate "white" standards and values over those of other cultures (D'Souza, 1995). It sees old-style, consensus multiculturalism as a form of pluralism that denies the historical importance of power relations; in contrast, critical multiculturalism sets out to promote historical memory, national identity, and the politics of difference (Giroux, 1994: 336).

Critical multiculturalism calls for a profound transformation of power relations. It seeks to mobilize marginalized groups, transform institutions to create social and cultural space, and dismantle dominant institutional structures (see St. Lewis, 1996). Critical multiculturalism does not call for minorities to be incorporated into the existing institutional framework, where they would face containment and control. Instead, it endorses the concept of culturally safe spaces where minorities will not have to justify their existence, and where they will be able to challenge the system from a position of strength. This approach could hardly be more different from the consensus-seeking approach of Canadian multiculturalism.

To date, the media and the education system have been the main battlefield of critical multiculturalism (Frederickson, 1999). The Eurocentric notions that form the core of American cultural life are challenged, multicultural alternatives are promoted, and the superiority and neutrality of mainstream values are questioned (Stam, 1997). Critical multiculturalism emphasizes the principle that people are fundamentally equal, and makes this the basis for challenging how power and privilege are distributed and how history and literature are taught. To the extent that multicultural interests are beginning to demand the right to shape and define critical multiculturalism is fuelling the (multi)cultural wars in the United States.

A Continental Divide

Many have said that Canadians and Americans use the same words but speak different languages. Nowhere is this more evident than in the multiculturalism debate. Multiculturalism means something very different to Americans than it does to Canadians.

Canada's *official* multiculturalism is centred on consensus, conformity, and accommodation (Fleras, 1998). Canadians have generally preferred to deploy multiculturalism in a society-building sense. Americans tend to emphasize multiculturalism's capacity to challenge dominant power structures by attacking its foundational principles. Critical multiculturalism is not constrained by official policies, nor is it weakened by political manoeuvring; instead, it is a freewheeling process that subverts as it transforms.

Canada's consensus multiculturalism transforms cultural differences into debates about *social inequality*; the Americans' critical multiculturalism transforms social inequalities into debates about *public culture*. Critical multiculturalism radicalizes cultural politics; this appeals to minorities, who demand that their visions be recognized and that their concerns be made part of a multicultural agenda (Wieviorka, 1998).

Canadian multiculturalism endorses a form of citizenship in which social equality requires everyone to be different *in the same kind of way*. In contrast, the American multiculturalism is adversarial, and revolves around "victim" groups whose ancestors never asked to come there (e.g., the descendants of slaves). Canada's multiculturalism aims to transform the mainstream without straining the social fabric; American multiculturalism aims to empower minorities by pulling out the monocultural roots of society. Canada's multiculturalism amounts to a defence of the dominant ideology; the Americans' is about challenging existing power distributions. Canada's multiculturalism strives to make diversity irrelevant as a basis for entitlement or engagement; the Americans' highlights the importance of differences in shaping who gets what. Canada's is a quest for unity and universality; the Americans' embraces differences, and sees in these differences the opportunity to construct new social forms (Wrong, 2000).

In short, Canada's consensus multiculturalism tries to make *society* safe both *from* diversity and *for* diversity; in contrast, criticial multiculturalism seeks to make *diversity* safe both *from* society and *for* society.

INTERCULTURALISM IN QUEBEC

In Canada, official multiculturalism is not only a federal matter. Most Canadian provinces have formally endorsed the principles of multiculturalism as guidelines for defining majority–minority relations. In 1974 Saskatchewan became the first officially multicultural province when it established its Multicultural Council and Multicultural Directorate. The government of Ontario has acknowledged the reality of multiculturalism and has committed itself to recognize all citizens, whatever their racial or religious background, as equal before the law, with full political rights and equal access to government services. Many municipalities have implemented their own multiculturalism and equity initiatives.

Quebec is officially a multicultural province. Yet Quebec rejects federal multiculturalism as irrelevant because of the following reasons:

- It contravenes the special status of Quebec as one of the founding (charter) members of Canada.
- It undermines Quebec's right to manage its own diversity.
- It violates the bicultural vision on which Canadian federalism has been constructed.

- It intrudes into Quebec's internal affairs (McRoberts, 1997).
- It treats ethnic minorities as if they had fully the same rights as the Québécois, and thereby strengthens the domination of English-speaking Canada (Breton, 2000).

Quebec also criticizes the primacy of the individual under official multiculturalism. Such a liberal-pluralistic commitment runs roughshod over the notion that for some Canadians, membership in a community is critical and nonnegotiable. Eric Breton (2000: 158) puts this nicely: Quebeckers and aboriginal peoples "need to be recognized as strongly situated within their communities, and the distinctiveness of their communities needs to be recognized by others." By rejecting the centrality of community to the Québécois, official multiculturalism denies the legitimacy of their sense of "Canadianness." In this way it amounts to a ruse to outflank Quebec's collective rights as a founding nation.

In place of federal multiculturalism, Québécois authorities have developed their own ways to engage "allophones" (i.e., minorities whose first language is neither English nor French). "Interculturalism" policy concerns itself with integrating immigrants into French language and culture. Under interculturalism, Quebec asserts itself as unmistakably a *French-speaking* society, as a *democratic* society in which everyone is expected to contribute to public life, and as a *pluralistic* society that respects the diversity of various cultures. A social contract is clearly implied in all this. Quebec is promising to protect the reality of cultural communities, to sensitize Québécois to the value of ethnic diversity, to promote the integration of minorities into Quebec society, to remove discriminatory barriers and promote equal opportunity to historically excluded groups, and to help allophones acquire competence in French (Jantzen, 1992). In return, allophone immigrants are expected to accept Quebec's Charter of Rights, to contribute to Quebec-building alongside francophones, and to acknowledge the primacy of French in the public domain (Economic Council of Canada, 1991).

How different are multiculturalism and interculturalism? Official multiculturalism denies the existence of an official culture and argues that all cultures and ethnic groups are equal in status within a bilingual framework. Quebec's interculturalism openly endorses the primacy of French language and culture in Quebec society. It tolerates and encourages diversity, but within a framework that ensures the unquestioned supremacy of French as the language and culture of Quebec. Interculturalism proposes, instead of the federal mosaic, an "arboreal" model of multiculturalism. Multicultural branches are grafted onto an unmistakably Québécois trunk, whose roots must be nourished in francophone soil if the entire tree is to survive (see Webber, 1994). The focus is on affirming the principle of cultural plurality and equal participation, but in a way that does not threaten the primacy of French language and culture, the sovereignty of the National Assembly, the secular state, or the equality of men and women (Hudson, 1987; Helly, 1993; Webber, 1994).

Yet the differences between multiculturalism and interculturalism may be more apparent than real. Both strive to eliminate barriers to the full and equal involvement of ethnic minorities. Each takes measures to integrate immigrants and ethnic minorities into the broader society. And neither takes differences seriously, preferring, instead, a kind of "pretend pluralism" based on superficial symbols. Even a denial that an official culture exists may reflect semantics rather than substance or lifestyle. Federal multiculturalism tacitly endorses a orbit model in which multicultural satellites revolve around the long-established centre. Quebec's interculturalism is based on a tree-trunk model with off-shooting branches. Perhaps the only difference between interculturalism and multiculturalism is Quebec's openness and honesty about its objectives.

MULTICULTURALISM VERSUS MULTINATIONALISM

Canada's aboriginal peoples dismiss federal multiculturalism as a solution to their problems (Ignace and Ignace, 1998). They do not see themselves as a minority group that needs integrating into Canadian society. In the same way, aboriginal peoples resent any policy that compromises their status as a fundamentally autonomous political community. They disdain any arrangement that reduces their communities to yet one more "tile" in Canada's multicultural mosaic. They are suspicious of official policies that acknowledge diversity but deny their unique situation. Canada's aboriginal peoples do not see themselves as a special interest group with problems and needs that can be solved within the existing institutional framework. Rather, as peoples or nations, they claim the right to be treated as partners with Canada in setting agendas and challenging foundational principles (Fleras and Spoonley, 1999; Fleras, 1999, 2000).

Like the Québécois, then, aboriginal peoples prefer to negotiate from a bicultural—more accurately, multi-nation—framework that recognizes their collective right to special status and entitlements. They see their different communities as each a culture in its own right, and they reject the idea of a reductionist multicultural policy. Instead, they propose a multi-nation model that acknowledges a multilayered Canada (see Breton, 2000). Insofar as official multiculturalism is little more than "an old wolf in sheep's clothing," mainstream dominance may be more subtle than in the racist and assimilationist past, but the objective remains the same: to colonize "the nations within."

"THE CANADIAN WAY": UNIVERSAL MODEL OR ONE OF A KIND?

Canada's model of multiculturalism reflects the unique realities of Canadian society. Its consensus model for living together differs from the critical multiculturalism encountered in the United States. Quebec openly disagrees with the federal multiculturalism policy and follows its own—an intercultural model that in many important ways is little different from the federal model. Australia's multicultural policy is quite similar to Canada's: both have society building as a goal, and are meant to serve national interests. Neither is culturally based; instead, both are concerned with finding ways to include those who have been historically excluded. Both strive to depoliticize differences— that is, to make society safe *from* diversity and also safe *for* diversity. Each is committed to diversity that is only skin deep—to "pretend pluralism" rather than to taking differences seriously. This strong commitment to national interests rather than minority concerns perhaps tarnishes Canada's international reputation as a multicultural model worth emulating.

Is there a "Canadian way" when it comes to multiculturalism? Certain principles or patterns distinguish Canada's official policies from those of other countries. Four features in particular do this: a commitment to society building, disadvantage/inclusion, belonging, and pretend pluralism.

- *Society building.* Official multiculturalism has rarely wavered from its society-building commitments. It never set out to celebrate ethnic differences per se or to promote cultural diversity except in the most superficial manner. Nor did it ever endorse the creation of segregated ethnic communities with special collective rights. The intent of official multiculturalism is to strengthen Canadian society by restructuring relations within the existing framework. That is, to create a cohesive society in which differences are seen as legitimate and integral to the extent they do not compromise national interests (Fleras and Elliott, 1999).
- *Disadvantage, inclusion, and social equality.* Official multiculturalism is not about diversity per se. Nor is it concerned with fostering cultural differences that could possibly exclude Canadians from full and equal participation in society. Rather, it focuses most sharply on

eliminating disadvantage—on ending discrimination by combatting prejudice and removing institutional barriers.

- *Belonging*. The principle at work here is that only those who are full and equal participants in Canadian life will be loyal and committed to Canada. Multicultural policy was initially aimed at Canadians of European origin who felt excluded by the two official languages. In the 1980s, approaches were adjusted; discriminatory barriers would have to be broken down if visible minorities were to be accommodated. The most recent emphasis is on encouraging all Canadians to participate in society while maintaining their cultural identity. Clearly, the rationale for belonging may always be evolving, but the logic behind it never does: Canada is a community to nurture, not a treasure trove to plunder.
- *Pretend pluralism*. Official multiculturalism is not really concerned about celebrating cultural differences, for all the assurances that differences are not a problem but a strength (Dion, 2000). Under pretend pluralism, differences don't count in any substantive way; instead, they are depoliticized—that is, channelled into the personal or private domains. To the extent that differences are celebrated, it is in the context of sharing cultures. Any commitment to taking differences seriously is compromised by liberal pluralism, which acknowledges the primacy of each individual and his or her right to identify with the cultural tradition of his or her choice, as long as this affiliation does not interfere with the rights of others, violate the laws of the land, or infringe on core values or institutions.

With a colour-blind multiculturalism, diversity is relatively *un*important, since what we have in common as individuals overrides ethnic differences. Refusal to take differences seriously may advance the national interest, but it does so at the expense of those national minorities who seek inclusion without integration by mobilizing along nationalist lines and using the language of nationhood to advance their agendas (Kymlicka, 2000; 2001).

Is "the Canadian way" applicable to other places? Not all multiculturalisms are created equal, and not all of them are likely to work in other countries. Canada's multiculturalism is widely praised, but this is no guarantee that it can be copied. How applicable is our version in a world in which minorities are looking for inclusion without integration? In New Zealand, which like Canada is a white settler society, bicultural politics continue to challenge and provoke. The next case study considers what happens when the principles of multiculturalism clash with binational realities.

CASE STUDY
Contesting a Multicultural Agenda in Bicultural New Zealand

New Zealand, like Canada, has long enjoyed an international reputation for managing ethnic relations harmoniously. This assessment is accurate to some extent, even if outcomes have been tarnished in recent years and a result of accident rather than design. New Zealand, again like Canada, has found it a challenge to craft a new political order in which differences are recognized and rewarded. Many *pakeha* (non-Maori) New Zealanders reject an openly monocultural framework, but at the same time reject radical constitutional change. They vaguely endorse multiculturalism or biculturalism, in principle if not always in practice (Massey University, 1996).

New Zealand's official commitment to biculturalism is being contested as a result of an influx of Asian immigrants, which is creating new ethnic fault lines in New Zealand society (Vasil and Yoon, 1996). Some argue that the differences between multiculturalism and biculturalism are minor and unimportant. Others disagree, and see them as very different in terms of scope, objectives, underlying rationale, strategies, and outcomes. At the same time, the definitions of the two terms have bled together through imprecise use. The challenge, it seems, is to foster a binational society without forsaking commitments to multiculturalism (Fleras, 1997).

CONTESTING THE ISMS

In New Zealand, biculturalism has been widely accepted as the best framework for government policy and practice. As a concept, it attracted attention as far back as the 1960s (see Schwimmer, 1968), though it languished in political limbo until the mid-1980s. Eventually, however, the ideals of biculturalism displaced those of multiculturalism at governmental levels (Sharp, 1990). Biculturalism assumed the status of de facto government policy in 1986 with passage of the State Owned Enterprises Bill, which read: "Nothing in the Act shall permit the Crown to act in a manner that is inconsistent with the principles of the Treaty of Waitangi." (The Treaty of Waitangi, signed in 1840 between the British Crown and many Maori chiefs, is widely regarded as New Zealand's founding document.) A 1987 Court of Appeal ruling reaffirmed that the relationship between the Crown and the Maori was one of partnership, and that each partner was expected to act reasonably and in good faith toward the other. The State Services Act, passed in 1988, confirmed the "biculturality" of Aotearoa (the Maori name for New Zealand) by instructing state institutions to incorporate the treaty obligations of partnership, participation, and protection into the delivery of services (Ramsden, 1995; Kelsey, 1996).

New Zealand's cultural politics shifted dramatically in the mid-1990s with in-migration from Hong Kong, Taiwan, Korea, the Philippines, and Japan. As a result of this demographic shift, 5 percent of New Zealanders are now of Asian origins. Pacific Islanders constitute a further 5 percent of the population, and Maori around 16 percent. The remainder (74 percent) are of European descent. Advocates of multiculturalism consider it unfair and unjust to encourage immigration without a corresponding commitment to multiculturalism (see Greif, 1995). Demographic changes virtually require that multiculturalism be endorsed when it comes to allocating rights and responsibilities.

Others disagree, and consider the Treaty of Waitangi irrevocable. That treaty declares Aotearoa/New Zealand a bicultural partnership, and guarantees collective rights to the Maori that override the individual rights of recent immigrants. It follows that Maori bicultural rights as original inhabitants must take precedence over the multicultural rights of immigrants. If they don't, Maori concerns could end up being treated on the same footing as those of recent immigrants. As a result of that, Maori status as *tangata whenua* ("original occupants") would be diminished. In sum, it would be irresponsible to displace bicultural commitments with multicultural ones (Walker, 1995). Multiculturalism cannot work in New Zealand unless biculturalism is first securely entrenched (Shepard, 2000).

ISMS IN COLLISION

As an ideal, biculturalism differs from multiculturalism. Multiculturalism is concerned mainly with embracing diversity at the level of institutions. In contrast, biculturalism emphasizes some degree of exclusion between communities, each of which is more or less politically autonomous, though some jurisdictions are shared (Maaka and Fleras, 2000). To be sure, New Zealand's official biculturalism does not quite meet this ideal. At present, it barely addresses the possibility of Maori self-determination. It tends to focus instead on accommodating the Maori by incorporating a Maori dimension into institutional practices and national symbols. For example, Maori names have been adopted for government departments; Maori language and protocols are being resorted to more and more for ceremonial occasions; and official reports are available in both Maori and English (Spoonley, 1993; Durie, 1995; Poata-Smith, 1996).

Not surprisingly, Maori politics is becoming increasingly rooted in a binational agenda. Under this agenda the Maori are "nations within" with unique collective rights relating to land, culture, and political voice (Fleras and Elliott, 1992). Clearly, the Maori are strongly opposed to multiculturalism, which in New Zealand is seen essentially as a society-building exercise that seeks to depoliticize differences. Compare this with the ideal of binationalism with its politicization of differences.

The intrusion of the multicultural ideal has complicated an already complex balancing act in New Zealand (Race Relations Conciliator, 2000). To the extent that multiculturalism endorses a pretend pluralism, New Zealand is multicultural, in practice if not principle. To the extent that the Maori are trying to politicize their differences, they overwhelmingly prefer a bicultural (a "bi-national") approach. No workable compromise between these "isms" has yet been found, and this has prompted the country's race relations conciliator, Dr. Rajen Prasad (1997: A9), to plead for "another way of thinking about ourselves as a multi-ethnic society with an indigenous culture, and with a founding document that regulates the relationship between Maori and Crown."

Chapter Highlights

- Canada's official multiculturalism is expressed in three ways: as government policy (since 1971), as statutory law (with passage of the Multiculturalism Act in 1988), and as entrenched in the Constitution Act (in 1982).
- Multiculturalism in Canada cannot be understood apart from its relationship to the state; in the same way, it is inappropriate to divorce the state from its broader project of building society along multicultural lines.
- A *policy* is best defined as a formal initiative for putting principles into practices and programs. The objective of multiculturalism policy is to strike a working balance among cultural diversity, social equality, and the national interest.
- From the perspective of political economy, official multiculturalism is a means for the state to uphold the dominance of the ruling class. It is an apparatus for ensuring that diversity is controlled and contained through consensus.
- Under multiculturalism, the state encourages the full and equal participation of minorities by removing discriminatory barriers, both cultural and institutional. In the resulting social and political climate,

diversity can be introduced without provoking a backlash or social turmoil.

- Official multiculturalism has gone through three distinct but related phases. The initial focus was on *ethnicity*—that is, on ending exclusion by removing cultural jealousies. The focus then shifted to *equity*—that is, the removal of discriminatory barriers at the level of institutions. The focus now is on *civic multiculturalism*, which concerns itself with citizenship through belonging, with participation through inclusiveness.

- In multicultural policy, ethnicity is not about celebrating differences but rather about acknowledging that people's cultural differences impede full and equal participation. Policies that focus on ethnicity attempt to eliminate the cultural prejudices held by mainstream society; at the same time, minorities are expected to discard those cultural practices which foster divisiveness and work against integration.

- Equity multiculturalism emphasizes the need to remove discriminatory barriers at institutional levels, especially as those relate to women and men of colour.

- Both the *Charter of Rights and Freedoms* and the Multiculturalism Act have reaffirmed Canada's commitment to equity multiculturalism. The goal in this is to enhance Canadian identity, eliminate discriminatory and racist barriers, and promote full institutional participation for minorities.

- Civic multiculturalism seeks to create an open and tolerant society in which inclusiveness is the norm and all Canadians can participate fully and equally.

- Canada's consensus multiculturalism differs from the critical multiculturalism that predominates in the United States. Consensus multiculturalism is state-sanctioned and is mainly about control, containment, management, discipline, and uniformity. Critical multiculturalism is outside the state and is mainly about challenging, resisting, and transforming the state.

- Quebec has rejected federal multiculturalism as inconsistent with its political objectives. Quebec's policy of interculturalism attempts to integrate minorities without threatening the primacy of the French language and culture.

- New Zealand is both a binational state and a multicultural one, and faces enormous tensions in trying to balance the two.

- Australia's multiculturalism policy resembles Canada's official multiculturalism in terms of processes and outcomes. It is also subject to the same internal paradoxes, vulnerable to similar criticisms, and exposed to comparable outside influences.
- The "Canadian way"? Even if official multiculturalism works in this country, there is no guarantee that it will work in others. And it may not work for Canada forever—too many circumstances can change.

Review Questions

1. Official multiculturalism has been described as the "Canadian way" of living together with differences. Expand on this notion by demonstrating what characterizes official multiculturalism and makes it distinctive from other forms.
2. How does Canada's official multiculturalism contribute to a society that is safe *for* diversity and *from* diversity?
3. Official multiculturalism has been described as a state apparatus designed to manage multiple ethnicities. Explain.
4. "Official multiculturalism is a policy for containing ethnicity by modifying the rules of engagement and entitlement." Explain what is meant by this.
5. Official multiculturalism has evolved in three phases. Compare and contrast each of these phases in terms of how the problem is defined and what the proposed solutions are.
6. Compare and contrast Canada's consensus multiculturalism with the critical multiculturalisms that flourish in the United States.
7. Official multiculturalism has been described as a policy of inclusion that cannot deal with the politics of exclusion. Show how this is true with respect to Canada (the First Nations and Québécois) and New Zealand.

Recommended Reading

Canadian Heritage. 2000. *Annual Report on the Operation of Canada's Multiculturalism Act*. Ottawa: Minister of Public Works and Government Services.

Augie Fleras and Paul Spoonley. 1999. *Recalling Aotearoa: Indigenous Politics and Ethnic Relations in New Zealand*. Auckland: Oxford University Press.

David T. Goldberg, ed. 1994. *Multiculturalism: A Critical Reader*. Oxford: Blackwell.

John Harles. 1998. "Multiculturalism, National Identity, and National Integration: The Canadian Case." *International Journal of Canadian Studies.* 17 (Spring). 80–89.

Will Kymlicka. 2001. *Politics in the Vernacular: Nationalism, Multiculturalism, Citizenship.* Toronto: Oxford University Press.

Tariq Modood and Pnina Werbner. 1997. *The Politics of Multiculturalism in the New Europe: Racism, Identity, and Community.* London: Zed Books.

Ross Poole. 1999. *Nation and Identity.* London: Routledge.

Pierre Savard and Brunello Vigezzi, eds. 1999. *Multiculturalism and the History of International Relations from the 18th Century Up to the Present.* Ottawa: Carleton University Press.

Appraising Multicultural-ism: Attitudes, Criticisms, Benefits, and Costs

CHAPTER OBJECTIVES

- To debunk many of the myths and fallacies surrounding official multiculturalism.
- To determine whether people's expectations of official multiculturalism are consistent with what Canada's multicultural policies are designed to do.
- To show that even though survey polls reflect strong public support for multiculturalism, this support may be conditional.
- To demonstrate the wide range of attitudes toward official multiculturalism.
- To assess the validity of the most common criticisms of official multiculturalism.
- To show that official multiculturalism has both costs and benefits.
- To point out the paradoxes in multiculturalism—i.e., that it justifies minority empowerment yet serves as a political tool for domination.
- To point out the dissonances between multiculturalism's rhetoric ("celebrate differences"), processes ("inclusiveness"), and realities ("containment through consensus").
- To evaluate official multiculturalism in terms of its impact on Canadian society.

CASE STUDY
Multicultural Facts/Multicultural Fictions

Every society has its own shared delusions. This must be expected, given that societies are socially constructed and imaginary communities and depend on symbols and fictions for their survival. Canada is no different in this regard, and as an ideal, multiculturalism is cluttered with more than its share of myths and misconceptions. Some conceptions we hold are based on reality, and others on wishful thinking, yet somehow we must find a way to see multiculturalism realistically, for what it is and does. Canadians remain curiously misinformed about multiculturalism (Musto, 1997). What is it? What does it do, and what is it supposed to do? How does it work? Has it succeeded? What impact has it had on Canadian society? Indifference to these questions is regrettable, because unless answers to them are found, public understanding of official multiculturalism will continue to be distorted. Consider the following common perceptions:

Perception 1: Official multiculturalism is ineffective and not working.

Perception 2: Multicultural diversity is divisive and disruptive.

Perception 3: Multiculturalism is only for minority women and men.

Perception 4: Multiculturalism tolerates an "anything goes" mentality because of "cultural relativism."

Perception 5: Multiculturalism celebrates diversity at the expense of national unity.

Perception 6: Multiculturalism is about multiple cultures.

Perception 7: Multiculturalism is a problem.

Perception 8: Multiculturalism is irrelevant.

Perception 9: Multiculturalism is experiencing a public backlash.

Perception 10: Multiculturalism promotes collective rights over individual rights.

Perception 11: Multiculturalism is an expensive luxury in times of fiscal restraint.

Each of these perceptions is accurate to some extent. But each is also distorted in that it excludes alternative readings of multiculturalism. These perceptions are based on the assumption that multiculturalism is a problem rather than an opportunity. They also reflect a view of official multiculturalism that is somewhat outdated, that misreads the empirical evidence, that overestimates what can be accomplished under liberal-democratic capitalism, and that improperly links multiculturalism with immigration and employment equity. At the end of this chapter I test these perceptions. But first, how do these perceptions arise?

A CONTESTED DOMAIN

Canada is widely touted as a progressive and properous multicultural society. Multiculturalism in Canada has become the central discourse in nation building (see Giroux, 1994). Historically, of course, Canadians tended to demean minorities as irrelevant and inferior. Prejudice and discrimination reinforced the belief that diversity worked against the grain of a strong and cohesive Canada. Ethnic minorities were expected to fit into pre-existing institutional frameworks as the price of admission into Canada.

But attitudes toward diversity have mellowed under official multiculturalism. As a policy, it marked a fundamental shift in political and public attitudes toward minority women and men. Diversity is now being promoted as a vital and legitimate component of Canada's social fabric, and as having great potential for improving Canada's national wealth and international standing. Multicultural differences are no longer dismissed as bothersome anomalies with no redeeming value except personal or private. Instead, they are endorsed as a necessary part of living together with differences.

Because of its approach to diversity, Canada now enjoys a reputation as one of the world's most "enlightened" nations. A shortage of praise is not a problem here: Haroon Siddiqui, editor emeritus of the *Toronto Star*, refers to multiculturalism as the "defining feature of the late twentieth century that distinguishes us from Americans." Charles Taylor, a philosopher at McGill University, refers to multiculturalism as "one of our greatest successes." And Tom Axworthy, the high-ranking Ottawa mandarin who orchestrated the original policy for the late Pierre Elliott Trudeau, calls it "our Alamo, without the war"—a rallying cry for Canadians to regroup reminiscent of the battle cry used by the Texans against the Mexicans (cited in Siddiqui, 1999: A18).

International praise is no less effusive. The respected British magazine *The Economist* (June 19, 1991) lavishly praised Canada as a "rich," "peaceful," and "enviably successful" country whose racial difficulties are "pretty wholesome" compared to the atrocities in Africa and the Balkans. According to international scribes, European societies would benefit by applying Canada's "much maligned" multiculturalism policies to defuse ethnic conflict (Tu Thanh Ha, 2000). And in perhaps the most glowing praise of all, the American economist Tyler Cowan (1999: B1) has called Canada a marvel of the civilized world:

> Based on the dual ideals of peace and multiculturalism, Canada is one of mankind's greatest achievements. It is comparable to notable civilizations of the past, and indeed exceeds most of them in terms of stability, living standards, and civil liberties.

The accolades keep rolling in. Canada has been portrayed as a "humane," "civilized," and "tolerant" society with a generous welfare state, a welcome mat for immigrants and refugees, a dislike for inequality, and a benign, some-what "Scandinavian" outlook on the world. Racial problems exist, to be sure, but on a much smaller scale than might be expected, considering Canada's status as a colonizing country historically dependent on immigration. With crimes against humanity continuing to claim victims, Canada sparkles as a beacon for all multilayered societies whose borders were created by settle-ment rather than by history or geography.

But not everyone has hopped aboard the multicultural bandwagon. Canada's much ballyhooed multicultural mosaic is cracking under pressures from within and without. The multicultural rhetoric does not always reflect the realities of practice. Criticisms of official multiculturalism follow two intersecting tracks:

- Track #1: "Multiculturalism is the wasteful government funding of special interest projects that divide the nation more than they do to unite it."
- Track #2: "Multiculturalism 'essentializes' cultures by 'fossilizing' them into folklore or commodity—even when these cultures endorse practices that are considered barbaric or violations of human rights" (see Grillo, 1998; Partington, 2000; Gilroy, 2000).

Some critics have dismissed multiculturalism as an empty buzzword that means everything yet nothing, in the process concealing as much as it reveals (Gunew, 1999; Gilroy, 2000). Other critics see official multiculturalism as a recipe for disaster, even though it is Canada's defining characteristic and a key economic advantage in this increasingly global world. For all its advan-tages, critics contend, Canada is teetering on the brink of ruin, with no centre to unify the parts. Multiculturalism has the potential to fracture Canada; it also makes it enormously difficult to forge a united country and a distinct society. "Sooner or later," *The Economist* (June 19, 1991) opines, "Canadians are going to become Americans ... Too bad."

Official multiculturalism generates a broad spectrum of responses, from the positive and supportive, to the negative and critical, with the indifferent or ignorant in between. Critics can't decide whether multiculturalism is dangerous ("a wolf in sheep's clothing") or simple bluster ("a sheep in wolf's clothing"). Multiculturalism as an idea and ideal may be widely endorsed by Canadians, and even hoisted high as a symbol of pride and distinction, but many aren't certain what they are endorsing or why. Fissures continue to mar the multicultural façade: many Canadians are supportive of multiculturalism as a morally superior alternative to diversity-destroying alternatives such as assimilation. Even so, many are becoming more and more perplexed about its short-term impact and long-term implications. This confusion also reflects disarray regarding the *functions*, *goals*, and *outcomes* of official multiculturalism:

- *Functions*: What is official multiculturalism supposed to do? What do people *think* it is supposed to do? What is it *actually* doing? What do people *believe* it *should* be doing? What *can* it accomplish, in light of existing realities?
- *Goals*: What are the goals of official multiculturalism? What *should* be its goals? What are its *perceived* goals? Are these goals attainable? If multiculturalism is the solution, what exactly is the problem? If multiculturalism is a problem, what is the solution? Who says, and why?
- *Outcomes*: Should official multiculturalism be concerned with promoting social justice? or cultural diversity? or ethnic identities? or national interests? Whose interests should prevail? On what grounds? What roles does multiculturalism play in advancing a particular vision of Canada?

Controversies over official multiculturalism are inevitable in a society that sets out to balance unity and diversity. Questions are not the problem: What is too much unity and not enough diversity, and vice versa? Has Canada conceded too much to diversity or not enough? How can Canadians make society safe *for* and safe *from* diversity? Its answers may be the problem: too often, responses to these queries are driven by confusion, ignorance, or indifference rather than by principled debate and informed analysis. Official multiculturalism has lost support as a result.

Official multiculturalism has turned out to be one of the most complex policies ever instituted in this country. Its potential is limitless, yet its pitfalls are bottomless. At present, official multiculturalism is under scrutiny because of its perceived failures. It also is experiencing a crisis of identity with respect to "what it is," "where it fits," and "what it should be doing" (Subash, 1999).

To address this crisis in multiculturalism, in this chapter I appraise it in terms of public attitudes, standard criticisms, and costs and benefits. All the various reactions to official multiculturalism can be categorized as the "good," the "bad," the "really ugly," or the "in between." To one side, we must never discount the Canadian public's concerns and criticisms as unfounded or as over-reactions. To the other side, official multiculturalism has rarely met the many expectations placed on it except, perhaps, to advance national interests at the expense of minorities. Multiculturalism is so complex, and encounters so many hidden agendas, competing priorities, and conflicting powers, that it can't help but generate contradictions (Bannerji, 2000). Even so, I will argue in this chapter that criticisms of official multiculturalism often reflect a certain amount of miscalculation, ignorance, conceit, or double-dealing. Not surprisingly, paradox is at the heart of multicultural coexistence, as Manju Subash (1999: 420) concludes:

> Multiculturalism is controversial, mainly because it means different things to different people and it stirs up primitive fears and emotions. It serves as an interventionist strategy that ameliorates the conditions of life for various ethnocultural minorities. At the same time, multiculturalism enhances the legitimacy of the State by defusing potential threats to its stability. An ideological framework is established whose objectives are geared toward shifting dissent while cooling out potentially troublesome minorities. It also reinforces the privileged status of the ruling classes by innoculating them against lower-class threats to the status quo.

A sense of balance is required when we analyze official multiculturalism. Too much emphasis on its negatives is just as damaging as too strong a preoccupation with its positives. Too much emphasis on costs at the expense of benefits may prove unduly provocative. Too much emphasis on benefits is no less distorting. Official multiculturalism has benefited some, and it has cost others. It is both progressive and regressive, depending on how you assess it. So we have to step carefully in navigating our way through the labyrinth of multicultural issues.

GAUGING PUBLIC ATTITUDES

Official multiculturalism originated in an era of optimism, modernism, and progress, but it is being scrutinized in this more recent era of discontent, retrenchment, and disillusionment (Cardozo and Musto, 1997). What started out as a good idea with noble intentions—to assist newcomers to Canada—has evolved into a flashpoint between multiculturalists and those who recoil in horror at the prospect of yielding more ground to minorities or to the government. Some people can't get enough multiculturalism; others have had a gutful. Furthermore, indifference is competing with criticism for space. References to official multiculturalism are becoming more and more passé in a Canada consumed by debates over deficit reduction, the brain drain, illegal migrants, bank profits, and poverty and homelessness (Sugunasiri, 1999).

Not surprisingly, public attitudes toward official multiculturalism have varied (see Henry and Tator, 1999). Some Canadians are strongly supportive of a multicultural Canada; others totally reject the idea; still others are indifferent; and yet others are uninformed (see Musto, 1997). Most Canadians seem ambivalent about it to some degree, and accept it with qualifications. Younger, more affluent, better educated, and urban Canadians are more likely to approve of it. So are westerners and southern Ontarians. Quebeckers and aboriginal peoples tend either to be contemptuous of it or see it as irrelevant (Ignace and Ignace, 1998; Breton, 2000). Inasmuch as most Canadians aren't sure what official multiculturalism is meant to accomplish, and what it realistically can accomplish in a capitalist democracy, the situation is ripe for analysis and assessment.

Surveying Multiculturalism

Surveys and opinion polls have long sought to determine levels of support for official multiculturalism (Berry et al., 1977). This has been a difficult project. When it comes to words like "multiculturalism" and "tolerance," no one is quite sure what is being measured. Also, different research instruments often yield different answers depending on the kinds of questions asked and how they are asked (Poole, 1996). Until the most appropriate tools are found, any definitive statement will be dodgy at best.

All of that being said, national surveys on multiculturalism suggest that it enjoys a solid base of support (Berry et al., 1977; Angus Reid, 1991; Berry, 1993). Three studies from the 1990s confirm this (all of them cited in Musto, 1997). The first, conducted by Environics Research Group in 1995, found that 66 percent of Canadians knew there was a federal multiculturalism policy. Of these, 62 percent approved of federal multiculturalism. But support for tolerance seemed to have declined slightly between 1989 and 1995, presumably because of economic uncertainty. Another study, by Ekos Research Associates (also in 1995), found that almost half of Canadians (48 percent) were unfamiliar with federal multiculturalism policy. Only 2 percent were extremely familiar with it, while another 16 percent were quite familiar with it (Musto, 1997). Paradoxically, a 1996 Environics Research Group survey found that 71 percent of respondents defined multiculturalism as an important symbol of Canadian unity and identity—only the health care system and the *Charter of Rights and Freedoms* were more important. Venerable icons such as the CBC, bilingualism, and hockey were found to be less important.

Support for multiculturalism is selective. Respondents were asked which elements of a federal multiculturalism program they would support, and endorsed it when it meant helping new Canadians settle in Canada, removing discriminatory barriers, and/or promoting tolerance. Nearly three-quarters of respondents said they would support a multiculturalism policy that helped people integrate into society without having to give up their ethnic identity. Just over half (55 percent) approved of initiatives to help ethnic minorities preserve their culture. A third Environics study (cited in the Metropolis Project, 1997) revealed inconsistencies in public attitudes toward official multiculturalism. *Awareness* of multiculturalism policy had increased from 41 percent in 1976 to 69 percent in 1997. Approval for it, which had dropped from 63 percent in 1989 to 50 percent in 1995, had climbed back to 62 percent by 1997. It is interesting that 41 percent of respondents looked on tolerance and respect for others as key multicultural goals, but far fewer felt that multiculturalism should encourage cultural retention (26 percent) or help immigrants adapt (18 percent).

What can we infer from these national surveys? *First*, that support is not the same as acceptance. Canadians seem to accept multiculturalism as a reality to be tolerated rather than an ideal to be embraced. The *idea* of multicultural tolerance is widely supported, inasmuch as a mix of cultures is perceived as making Canada a more interesting place. Yet there seems to be no passion behind that tolerance, no deep commitment to it. Public approval depends on keeping costs low and demands reasonable (Gwyn, 1996: 203). In short, support for multiculturalism is a kilometre wide but a centimetre thick.

Second, that support is conditional and selective—in other words, people are prepared to accept the superficial dimensions of official multiculturalism as long as cultural differences are "nice." Official multiculturalism is acceptable when it involves learning about other cultures, fostering tolerance (even acceptance) of diversity, and eliminating discriminatory barriers to improve minority access and participation. Support falls off when official multiculturalism is seen as promoting a variety of cultures at the expense of national unity and identity. Resistance mounts when official multiculturalism is seen as eroding Canada's national identity; challenging authority, national symbols, or core values; encouraging separation or division; or fixating on flaws in the mainstream. Multiculturalism is rejected if it means seeing Canada as a mishmash of different but equal cultures, with no centre of gravity for sorting out who's in control. In other words, a pretend pluralism is tolerable under official multiculturalism, but only if everybody is different in the same kind of way, and only if the majority remains in control.

Third, that people often use the term multiculturalism without distinguishing between policy and principle. This is unfortunate: support for multiculturalism as an idea or ideal is not at all the same as support for a government's policies and programs. Failure to distinguish between the formal (i.e., state) and the informal (i.e., society) invites people to "talk past each other."

Fourth, that there may be a tendency to overestimate how much opposition there really is to official multiculturalism because it is so easy to associate it with other, less popular government initiatives. Public resentment over multiculturalism may actually be aimed at immigration or equity policies. The words of Haroon Siddiqui (1999: A18) seem appropriate: "It is not a coincidence that the once-touted multiculturalism has become a dirty word in direct proportion to immigration becoming more coloured, Asian, and African. Now multiculturalism and its public policy cousin, immigration, serve as handy scapegoats for our ills, real or imagined."

Official multiculturalism seems to have evolved into a kind of national lightning rod for a host of discontent. The debate tends to dwell on official multiculturalism as a problem to be managed rather than as an opportunity to be explored. It may be accurate enough to criticize official multiculturalism as a flawed experiment in social engineering. At the same time, it seems unfair to criticize it for failing to meet expectations that were unreasonable in the first place.

MULTICULTURALISM AND ITS DISCONTENTS

Many observers have criticized the Canadian government's multicultural programs (Peter, 1978; Kallen, 1982; Burnet, 1984; Bibby, 1990; Thobani, 1995; Das Gupta, 1994; Bissoondath, 1994; Falding, 1995; Kobayashi, 1999; Sugunasiri, 1999; Bannerji, 2000). Criticism of official multiculturalism is widespread and often intense. It has been denounced as expensive, illogical, unnatural, contradictory, and counterproductive; as expedient and superficial; as a smokescreen; as "oracular hot air"; and as full of sound and fury but signifying nothing. Public opinion has been equally scathing of multiculturalism:

- "There exists a system much like apartheid. Under it, the government segregates individuals according to race and ancestry. They live in separate areas according to race. The majority of the population is governed under the tyranny of the minority, with intimidation and outright persecution of those who dare challenge the establishment and so on. Sound familiar? It's not what you think. The system is multiculturalism" (J.A. "Opinion," *Silhouette*, November 21, 1999).

- "The massive multiculturalization now taking place is the antithesis of nation-building. If it is allowed to accelerate through the further abandonment of traditional immigration standards, we shall soon face insoluable social and economic problems and ultimately the disintegration of the country as we know it" (letter to *The Globe and Mail*, August 14, 1999).

- "Pluralism, the side-by-side existence of many forms of human association, is an essential quality of modern life. Official multiculturalism, the automatic classification of citizens according to race and ancestry, was a bad idea in the beginning, and in time will probably be seen as one of the gigantic mistakes of recent public policy in Canada" (Fulford, 1997).

- "Although the drive to honour diversity through official multiculturalism was originally undertaken in order to promote tolerance, it is accomplishing the opposite. By setting Canadians against one another and emphasizing our differences rather than the many things we have in common, diversity has, in fact, gone too far" (Mallet, 1997: D2).

- "Multiculturalism, for instance, is actually an attempt to prevent the evolution of a common Canadian identity. It wants to preserve immigrants in the aspic of their original culture and ethnicity ... It used to be said that a Canadian defined himself [sic] negatively; he was 'not an American.' Under multiculturalism, a true Canadian asserts his identity by declaring that he is 'not a Canadian.' This is hardly a promising basis for secure nationhood" (*National Post* editorial, July 1, 1999).

Scholarly opinion has been equally dismissive of official multiculturalism. Some academics deplore official multiculturalism as a device that denies, demeans, and disillusions; others revile it for bolstering state interests at the expense of minorities; still others see it as an innovative but flawed social experiment for living together; for yet others, multiculturalism is irrelevant in a society facing more pressing challenges, and is best treated with indifference or complacency.

Multiculturalism has been criticized from both the left and the right. Critics on the left have declared it useless for eliminating social inequities, and denounce it as empty symbolism that papers over the structural roots of inequality (Novo, 2000). Or they have denounced it as a colossal hoax resorted to by vested interests to keep minorities in their place (Duncan and Cronin, 1997–98). Official multiculturalism as it has been practised has succeeded in alienating both aboriginal peoples and the Québécois, many of whom see themselves as basically autonomous political communities rather than as threads in Canada's multicultural fabric (Ignace and Ignace, 1998; Adam, 1998). Critics on the right have been just as rabid in rejecting official multiculturalism; to them it is a severe drain on the nation's resources and a threat to national identity. Instead of promoting sharing and cooperation, it has divided Canadians by making nationalism, separatism, tribalism, and ethnocentrism all the more acceptable.

Critics in the centre concede the double-edged character of official multiculturalism. That is, it certainly has transformative properties, but it tends to be compromised in practice by political manipulations. Too often it is used for conflict resolution and damage control; or for "impression management" and public relations; or to "contain" minorities in the name of consensus; or to defend the status quo; or to assimilate minorities in slow motion. Those in positions of power or privelege don't see it as a threat, which suggests that it serves their purposes more than those of minority groups, especially at election time (see Mackey, 1999).

Neil Bissoondath (1994) is one of the sharper critics of official multiculturalism. He deplores it as the very opposite of what Canada is or should stand for. He regards it as a sacred cow that has been shamelessly abused by politicians and other opportunists. He considers multiculturalism a form of racism, in that it defines minorities solely on the basis of race or ethnicity. At the same time, he argues that Canada's obsession with accommodating diversity under official multiculturalism has emboldened minorities. Their demands that Canada adapt to *their* customs and languages, rather than the other way around, has fanned hatred and tribalism at the expense of Canadian unity, identity, and culture. In short, official multiculturalism impedes what it is most meant to accomplish—the full and equal acceptance of immigrants into society. It fosters a social divisiveness that prevents minorities from participating fully and equally. It also trivializes minorities' contributions, stigmatizes them as outsiders, and patronizes them as incapable of achieving anything on their own. Finally, official multiculturalism can be accused of making a fetish out of cultural differences by fostering ties to "anywhere else but Canada." Many of Bissoondath's arguments can be rebutted. Even so, the popularity of his book suggests that he has struck a chord with Canadians. How valid, then, are his criticisms and those of others?

PUTTING MULTICULTURALISM TO THE CRITICAL TEST

There is no end to the carping about official multiculturalism. It has been attacked as a good policy gone bad; it has also been attacked as a bad policy that, unfortunately, has lived up to its lowly expectations. Some see it as too much of an essentially bad thing; others see it as not enough of a basically good thing. Still others have mixed views, seeing it as more than is necessary to foster a strong society, yet not enough to ensure advantages for Canada in this increasingly interconnected world. Some people perceive Canada as thoroughly multicultural after thirty years of social engineering; others dismiss multiculturalism as little more than platitudes with little substance. For some, official multiculturalism calls for too much national unity at the expense of diversity; for others, Canadian society is a "coexistence without vision" as a direct result of its mindless devotion to endless diversity (Bibby, 1990).

Two points should be clear by now. *First*, criticism of multiculturalism ranges from the mild and inoffensive, to out-and-out diatribes that rattle the very foundations of Canada. *Second*, most criticisms tend to be contradictory. For example, multiculturalism has been criticized both as too inclusive and as not inclusive enough. It has been condemned both as too radical and as too weak. In brief, official multiculturalism has been placed in a no-win situation—"damned if it does, damned if it doesn't"—regardless of its effects or lack of them.

Is it possible to make sense of these often conflicting criticisms? Is there any pattern to the controversies surrounding official multiculturalism? For the sake of analysis, we can classify criticisms of official multiculturalism under five distinct but related headings:

* Multiculturalism is *divisive*, in that it undermines Canadian society.
* It's *marginalizing*, in that it ghettoizes minority aspirations.
* It's *essentializing*, in that it fossilizes differences.
* It's a *hoax*, in that it doesn't address the root causes of inequality.
* It's *hegemonic*, in that it doesn't empower minorities, but rather contains them.

Each of these criticisms is valid up to a point. Each is also misplaced, exaggerated, or outdated. Furthermore, each tends to reflect unrealistic expectations and ignore obvious benefits. In the final analysis, official multiculturalism is neither entirely positive nor entirely negative. In securing the middle ground of the "in between," it has involved making tradeoffs among diverse publics with conflicting demands.

Whether official multiculturalism has been good or bad for this country depends on one's vision of Canada. My intention in the following sections is not to criticize multiculturalism, but rather to organize other people's criticisms of it. To this end, I have recast each of the main criticisms as a yes-or-no question, and then presented the arguments for both answers. I take no sides on any of the questions; I merely wish to demonstrate the range of possible answers. This exercise will show multiculturalism for what it actually is: an imperfect social experiment that has transformed Canada but without compromising its national interests (Fleras, 1994).

Controversy #1: Is multiculturalism divisive?

YES—Multiculturalism works against national unity and identity. Official multiculturalism is balkanizing Canada by corralling minority women and men into distinct enclaves, thereby creating a multitude of solitudes without a centre (Sugunasiri, 1999). The proliferation of ethnically diverse groups fosters an inward-looking mentality that drives a wedge between Canadians (Gagnon, 2000). A national identity is almost impossible to construct when people are encouraged to pursue ethnic tribalism at the expense of their duties as citizens (Bissoondath, 1994). Official multiculturalism places too much emphasis on Canada as a mosaic of culturally distinct groups, and not enough on what holds the tiles in place. According to Rex Nettleford, vice-chancellor of the University of the West Indies, Canada's multiculturalism has erected walls instead of building bridges, and has frozen cultures instead of emphasizing how "different elements now coalescing, now separating, now being assimilated, now resisting, now counter-resisting in a dynamic contradictory relationship [have] produced agony but ... also produced new life" (in Vassell Jr., 1999: 1).

NO—By definition, official multiculturalism is a government policy, and its main concerns are inseparable from the national interest. Its purpose is to craft a functioning society by depoliticizing ethnicity and by encouraging minorities to become full and equal participants in society building (Kymlicka, 1998). Its intent is not to isolate ethnic groups into separate power bases, but rather to protect the right of individuals to identify with the cultural tradition of their choice. Official multiculturalism rejects an "anything goes" mentality. It tolerates diversity only to the extent that such diversity does not violate the laws of the land, does not interfere with the rights of others, and does not discredit Canada's political and economic institutions. It certainly does endorse diversity, but extends equal status and treatment to all differences, and declares that the state has the right to decide which differences are permissible (see Johnson, 1994). Reducing all differences to the same level by "neutering" them may sully multiculturalism's reputation as a progressive force. But this is precisely what accounts for the political popularity of official multiculturalism.

In short, official multiculturalism does not at all promote divisiveness. Policies based on segregation, exclusion, and discrimination existed long before official multiculturalism came into effect. Far from being separatist, and far from sealing minorities into ethnic enclaves, multiculturalism relentlessly promotes integration (see Stam, 1997). It pursues a cohesive and ordered society; it tries to embrace diversity without weakening either the whole or its parts (Fleras and Elliott, 1999). A multiculturalism policy, of course, carries some risks: it may not set out to separate and divide people, but in practice it sometimes has an exclusionary effect. Even well-meaning multicultural initiatives such as intercultural sharing can foster tribal animosities (Hutcheon, 2001). But it is unfair to criticize official multiculturalism for its unintended effects, especially in cases where politicians or minority group leaders manipulate it in the service of goals it was not intended to achieve (Harris, 1995).

Furthermore, it is highly doubtful that multiculturalism divides people by creating special entitlements. Extending preferential treatment to the historically disadvantaged is not the same thing as offering special privileges or encouraging social conflict. Official multiculturalism is meant to promote the national interest by breaking down social and cultural barriers. Clearly, then, multiculturalism does not undermine Canadian identity; in fact, it strengthens that identity by binding Canadians into a single moral community (Jamieson, 1993).

Controversy #2: Is multiculturalism marginalizing?

YES—Official multiculturalism is thought to be regressive, in the sense that it marginalizes minorities and blocks their access to power and resources. By promising much but delivering little, it has shunted minority women and men into occupational and residential ghettos behind a slick veneer of cultural tolerance (Porter, 1965; Bissoondath, 1994). "Hyphenated" labels tend to emphasize the ethnicity of minorities rather than their status as fully fledged Canadians. When we focus too much on celebrating differences, we become fixated on the superficial and lose sight of the power differentials that distort ethnic relations (Bullivant, 1983; Grillo, 1998). Multicultural solutions seem incapable of dealing with structural problems of unequal power.

Minorities are marginalized in two ways. *First*, multiculturalism is meant to combat discrimination and preserve cultural identity. Minority group members appreciate this as far as it goes, but many are suspicious of any policy that could turn them into permanent outsiders (Bissoondath, 1994; Harles, 1998). *Second*, official multiculturalism endorses inclusiveness, but only within the framework of existing institutions. Relative to the dominant culture, all ethnic cultures are multicultural (Mackey, 1999). Other cultures are fine, even "nice," but only when "approved" by the dominant group (Henry and Tator, 1999). But diversity under multiculturalism should never be a default option that segregates, as demonstrated by Rosemary Brown:

> Multiculturalism should not, and must not, be a situation where ethnic groups retain their cultural identities because they are alienated, isolated, oppressed, ostracised, categorized, and manipulated on account of a particular cultural background. In other words, what we must ensure and protect ourselves against is multiculturalism becoming a fancy word for ghettoisation. (in Rees, 1986)

In short, multiculturalism is about containment rather than transformation, about consensus rather than challenge and change, about accommodation rather than inclusion. Tolerance is simply a social veneer, through which the project of assimilation is always visible (Henry and Tator, 1999). To the extent that official multiculturalism is little more than a new twist on an old idea—namely, exclusion through divide and rule in defence of the status quo—there is plenty of truth to the adage that the more things change, the more they stay the same.

NO—Official multiculturalism does not necessarily marginalize people (Fleras, 1994). In fact, it aims quite openly to abolish exclusion by promoting the inclusion of minority women and men (Kymlicka, 1998; Annual Report, 2000). Since 1971, multiculturalism policy has been attempting to dismantle the cultural fences that prevent minorities from participating fully in Canadian society (admittedly, it has done so without rocking the dominant culture's boat). In the 1980s, equity multiculturalism focused on institutional rather than cultural barriers with the goal of ending structural discrimination. Official multiculturalism is still committed to inclusiveness—to the idea that all Canadians should have an equal chance to participate in society by ensuring their race or ethnicity does not deny involvement or citizenship.

Admittedly, there is no clear proof that official multiculturalism has improved the socioeconomic status of minority women and men. Income gaps do persist, especially for visible minorities (Kunz et al., 2001; Galabuzi,

2001). Nevertheless, official multiculturalism provides minorities with the means to articulate their grievances, and to hold governments to account when their actions are at odds with multicultural principles. Perhaps the greatest strength of official multiculturalism is found in its commitment to an inclusive society that values diversity without reneging on inequality. A society is constructed in which diversity can be engaged without public backlash or political turmoil. If multiculturalism does not always succeed, this may have more to do with raw politics than with the shortcomings of multiculturalism itself.

Controversy #3: Is multiculturalism essentializing?

YES—Multiculturalism "essentializes" diversity (Grillo, 1998). That is, it approaches society as a mosaic of distinct ethnic groups that lack diversity within themselves. All individuals are thereby reduced to stereotypes, as if everything about them can be determined by their membership in a group—whether they wish it or not (Shepard, 2000). Pnina Werbner (1997: 228) puts it well:

> To essentialise is to impute a fundamental, basic, absolutely necessary constitutive thinking and acting to a person, social category, ethnic group, religious community or nation. It is to posit falsely a timeless continuity, a discreteness or boundedness in space, and an organic unity. It is to imply an internal sameness and an external difference or otherness.

Under an essentialized ethnicity, all families are extended, all children respect elders, all traditions are revered, all women are dutifully subordinate, religious faith is all-powerful, and ethnic identities dictate all thoughts and actions (Grillo, 1998). The powers-that-be approve of all this because it helps them control minorities. After all, it is much easier to deliver services when clients are organized into distinct groups with separate concerns and needs. Furthermore, this crafty exercise in indirect rule tends to empower the most conservative members of ethnic communities (Grillo, 1998: 198–99). The result is a form of cultural apartheid (Bissoondath, 1994) that freezes cultures in place without any attempt to link them to society at large (Gagnon, 2000).

The essentializing process under official multiculturalism is counterproductive because it reduces culture to mere "saris, somosas, and steel bands." This focus not only diminishes the contributions of minorities, it also makes it harder to establish an inclusive society, writes Jeff Derkson (1997, in Gunew, 1999: 21):

Multiculturalism ... has remained merely symbolic, reducing ethnic and radicalised cultures to folklore and sponsoring celebrations of "red boot" ethnicity while never actually alleviating the real inequalities within Canadian society. This criticism of multiculturalism charges that it cannot forcefully address racism ... precisely because, as a policy and law, multiculturalism fails to recognize race and ethnicity as socially constructed and, rather, deals with them as natural.

Official multiculturalism has commodified cultures, and this is no less essentializing. In international commerce, multiculturalism is being used as a marketing tool (Pedalty, 1998; Gilroy, 2000). This has social costs: differences are taken out of context and repackaged to meet consumer stereotypes; cultures are suspended in time or romanticized as exotic. All of this easily degenerates into a corporate-managed "United Colours of Benetton" pluralism that diminishes differences to lifestyle statements (Stam, 1997). Minorities are compartmentalized into commercial ghettos; attention is diverted from real issues such as racism, unemployment, discrimination, and the shredded social safety net (Philip, 1995). Diversity in these conditions is more apparent than real. This confirms yet again that in multiculturalism, what you see is the opposite of what you actually get (Zizek, 1997).

NO—In its original form, official multiculturalism *was* somewhat essentializing. It was widely seen as promoting a vision of Canada in which separate cultural tiles would be held together by centralizing grout. But it soon rejected the notion of privileging ethnic cultures; ever since, its objective has been to break down exclusionary barriers between cultures. Under multiculturalism, individuals have the right to identify with the culture of their choice. They can affiliate with any culture as long as this affiliation does not interfere with the rights of others, violate laws, or challenge core values. Ethnicity is situational, in the sense that people are identified with the symbols of their culture at appropriate times, and are not locked into permanent ethnic structures. In this sense, ethnicity under official multiculturalism is really more about encouraging hybrid cultures. Individuals travel back and forth in the space between two "fixed" identities: mainstream and ethnic. By emphasizing dialogue and exchange, sharing and movement, official multiculturalism provides a basis for living together (Wieviorka, 1997).

Controversy #4: Is multiculturalism a hoax?

YES—Official multiculturalism promises much but delivers little. It is little more than a frivolous political diversion—all symbols, no substance.

Alternatively, it is a public relations swindle, a form of impression management, and suggests that something is being done when actually nothing is. According to Bolaria and Li (1983), official multiculturalism is not a good policy that has been mismanged but rather a policy that was fundamentally flawed from the outset, because it offered no solutions to structural inequalities:

> Most ethnic groups in Canada do not have the structural resources to promote their cultural heritage, and the policy of multiculturalism simply reinforces the concept of "'symbolic ethnicity" which provides the appearance of pluralism. Simply put, the irony of multiculturalism is that it furnishes Canada with a great hope without having to change the fundamental structures of society. Multiculturalism is the failure of an illusion, not of a policy.

As a symbol without substance, official multiculturalism has distracted Canadians from the real issues. It is a form of pretend pluralism that stops short of challenging the status quo, and only requires the mainstream to make slight adjustments, and always on its own terms (Gonick, 2000). Promises to promote minority cultures and social equality are shallow when the focus is on identity, rights, and diversity rather than on racism and structural discrimination (Kobayashi, 1999). In a particularly subversive reading of official multiculturalism, Zizek (1997) destroys the contemporary myth of coexistence, which he sees as little more than a thinly veiled white supremacist swindle:

> Multiculturalism ... a racism with a distance—it respects the Other's identity, conceiving the Other as a self-enclosed "authentic" community towards which he, the multiculturalist, maintains a distance rendered possible by his privileged universal position ... The multiculturalist respect for the Other's specificity is the very form of asserting one's own superiority.

Multiculturalism camouflages the racism and white supremacism that have always existed in Canada (and still do). It endorses diversity, but only symbolically and in a way that disguises inequalities. Official multiculturalism, by incorporating ethnicity into Canadian society's symbolic fabric, glosses over unequal power relations (Karnoouh, 1998).

NO—There is no question that an official multiculturalism has always delivered less than promised. This compels us to compare original goals with contemporary realities. Official multiculturalism was never intended to promote or preserve the substance of ethnic cultures. Imagine a state in which autonomous minority groups were entitled to entrench themselves! Each with its own independent institutions and separate power base! Nor was official multiculturalism ever about promoting differences; what it meant to do was remove barriers that precluded full and equal participation of minority women and men. Furthermore, official multiculturalism was never intended to be transformative; rather, it sought to adjust core institutions and values to new social, political, and demographic realities (see Povinelli, 1998). Official multiculturalism was never intended to topple Canada's social system; rather, its objective was to adjust the system around a new set of demographics. As Manoly Lupul (1989: 0) writes: "The federal policy of multiculturalism was not intended to change the socioeconomic structure of Canada, enabling cultural minorities equal access to economic and political opportunity without paying the price of assimilation." To the extent that official multiculturalism has always been meant to serve national interests and promote society building, it will always be seen a form of "ethnic appeasement."

Yet official multiculturalism has been more transformative than it is given credit for. Consider that differences were once rejected as inferior or as irrelevant to society building. In hindsight, multiculturalism endorsed the then-radical principle that diverse groups ought to be accommodated provided that:

- their differences do not revoke any individual's claim to recognition or reward,
- racial or cultural divergence from the mainstream does not affect entitlement, and
- differences are nested into a unifying vision of how to live together with differences.

Critics may scold multiculturalism for focusing on symbols rather than substance. And there is evidence that minority interests are being sold out. Yet these critics are chiding multiculturalism for doing what it never set out to do. Moreover, symbols are not empty: they have the power to move mountains, as the saying goes. The symbol of Canada as a multicultural nation equips it with the power to challenge and change.

Controversy #5: Is multiculturalism disempowering?

YES—Official multiculturalism secures national unity by increasing power differentials between groups. It shores up the interests of those who have at the expense of those who have not. It does this partly by legitimizing state-approved differences as integral to society, and partly by denying the validity of unapproved differences, and also by organizing society around the principles of profit, private property, competitive individualism, and insatiable consumerism.

According to Mackey (1999), official tolerance of diversity functions as a kind of add-on to the still dominant Anglo-Canadian core. Official multiculturalism draws on notions of ethnicity to co-opt minority cultures into the service of Canadian society building. It "racializes" differences while subverting minority demands for equality and inclusiveness (Gunew, 1999; Bannerji, 2000). The end result? A model of ethnic relations whereby minorities orbit around a mainstream centre and are valued according to how they contribute to that centre. Mackey concludes (1999: 67) that "dominant cultures exist, whereas minority cultures 'exist for the latter.'" But this raises a question, as Bharucha (2000: 19) points out: "Why should minorities be 'othered' for the enrichment of their assumed bene-factors?" Naomi Klein (1999: A17) writes to this effect:

> The true flaw of multiculturalism is not that it encourages segregation, but that it helps disguise it by allowing our political elites to point to colourful displays of officially sponsored ethnicity as evidence that we, as a nation, have outgrown our colonial mindset. Multiculturalism is not "paying people to maintain their foreign roots" as its critics suggest; it is a payoff: paying ethnic groups to stay out of the way. By encouraging the creation of walled-off ethnic theme parks, the gatekeepers of Canada keep the competition occupied and protect their turf ... As a result, multiculturalism in Canada is little more than marketing.

Official multiculturalism is hardly a threat to the social order. "No voice shall predominate in creating a community of communities under multicul-turalism," the saying goes, "except the voice that says no voices shall pre-dominate" (James, 1997). In the sense that it has the power to define which differences count, and what counts as difference, multiculturalism advances the status quo. Admittedly, Canada's official multiculturalism does not set out to control. Nevertheless, it has a controlling effect in practice—that is, in terms of doling out entitlements. When it comes to that function, official multiculturalism is the only game in town. In effect, this sort of *multi*cultur-alism is merely an elaborate version of *mono*culturalism. As Sneja Gunew (1993: 207) wisely observes in castigating Canada's multiculturalism: "Multiculturalism is a rhetoric of inclusion which can't deal with the politics of exclusion."

NO—Official multiculturalism was established as a political tool for solving political problems, and there is little doubt that it is hegemonic in conse-quence if not always in intent. Yet official multiculturalism has turned out to be counter-hegemonic in two ways. *First*, it has evolved in directions never anticipated by its architects. Its original focus on breaking down exclusionary barriers has "morphed" into a commitment to inclusiveness. This commitment to inclusiveness has resulted in diverse initiatives: ethnic voices are being promoted, tolerance toward diversity is being fostered, prejudice is being reduced, discriminatory barriers are being broken down, cultural ethnocentrism is being eliminated, access to services is being enhanced, institutional inclusiveness is being expanded, and intergroup encounters are being improved. *Second*, minority women and men are using official multiculturalism increasingly as a tool for securing access to symbolic and material resources (Pearson, 1995). They are also using it to challenge social inequality by holding governments accountable for veering from multicultural ideals (Vasta and Castles, 1996). Or as Marlene Nourbese Philip (1995) writes in her critique of Bissoondath's *Selling Illusions*:

> Multiculturalism may have been a cynical ploy by Liberal politicians to address the balance of power in Canada, but the creativity and inventiveness of the people in being able to turn to their own advantage policies that may not have their interests at heart can never be underestimated. Throughout the former British Empire black and brown subjects would use the very precepts employed in governing them against the rulers to gain independence.

In other words, multiculturalism may have originated as a calculated ploy for securing what the dominant group considered the national interest. Yet no one should ever underestimate the power of ideas or the ability of people to take advantage of policies that may not have had their interests at heart (Philip, 1995). Nor should the counter-hegemonic properties of multiculturalism be underestimated. The powerless and the dispossessed are capable of converting the tools used for controlling them into levers of resistance and change (Pearson, 1994).

To sum up: Official multiculturalism has both supporters and detractors. Critics see it as divisive, marginalizing, essentializing, and hegemonizing, and generally as a hoax, and all these criticisms are somewhat accurate as far as they go. But there is another side to the debate. Official multiculturalism may be potentially divisive, but it has also been a unifying force. It has the potential to marginalize groups, but this is offset by its commitment to empowerment through inclusiveness and participation. Yes, official multiculturalism is essentializing, but it also promotes hybridized identities. Far from being merely a hoax that distracts as it diverts, official multiculturalism has helped create an inclusive social climate. And its hegemonic role does not stop minorities from using it to resist and challenge the powers-that-be. Table 4.1 summarizes the preceding sections by indicating how benefits and costs are simply opposite sides of the same coin.

TABLE 4.1

The Dialectics of Multiculturalism

Costs	Benefits
Divisive: undermines Canadian identity and coherence by promoting cultural diversity at the expense of national unity	*Unifying*: promotes unity by depoliticizing diversity without eroding a commitment to participation and equity
Essentializing: envisions Canada as a collection of autonomous ethnic groups that are self-contained, determining, and controlling	*Hybridizing*: promotes the right of individuals to choose their level of involvement without being locked into an ethnoculture
Marginalizing: ghettoizes minorities and commodifies culture by invoking cultural solutions to structural problems	*Inclusive*: an instrument that challenges the exclusion of minority women and men to ensure integration and full participation
Hoax: symbol without substance that promises much but delivers little except to delude, conceal, evade, or distort	*Catalyst*: symbols can "move mountains" by legitimizing diversity as integral while furnishing a platform for minority grievances
Hegemony: instrument of control that achieves consensus by manipulating people's consent without their awareness	*Counter-hegemony*: a lever for advancing minority interests by challenging and transforming the social contract

---

THE GOOD, THE BAD, THE IN BETWEEN

The Politics of the In Between

Everyone agrees that there are enough loopholes in federal multiculturalism to dishearten even the most optimistic. As the self-appointed catalyst for social engineering, multiculturalism has been criticized for conceding too much or not enough, for doing too much or not enough, for proceeding too quickly or not quickly enough, and for being too inclusive or not inclusive enough. For some, official multiculturalism is too broad a policy to solve Canada's small problems but too narrow a policy to solve its larger problems for living together. Few would deny that it is easily manipulated by politicians and minority leaders, many of whom are happy to use multicultural principles for ends different from those intended. Fewer still would dismiss its potential to deter, divide, and diminish Canada-building. People tend to have unrealistically high expectations of official multiculturalism; yet they are woefully ignorant of what it *can* do under the circumstances and of what it is actually *supposed* to do under legislation and according to the Constitution.

The demands placed on multiculturalism are staggering: as policy and practice, official multiculturalism is under pressure to be everything to everybody, from elected officials and central authorities to minority women and men and commercial interests. Official multiculturalism is also saddled with a host of unrelated obligations: to eliminate discrimination, to foster identity, to promote unity, to equalize involvement, and so on. The conclusion seems inescapable: official multiculturalism is in trouble. No special insight is required to conclude that at times, official multiculturalism has been divisive, marginalizing, essentializing, and hegemonizing, as well as basically a hoax. Canadians have much to be grateful for because of official multiculturalism, yet this gratitude should not obscure its flaws and costs. Multiculturalism may sound good in theory, at both ideological and policy levels, but its practice has created problems that resist quick solutions. This means that any critique of multiculturalism must acknowledge how difficult it is to engage diversity in a complex, changing, diverse, and interconnected society. It must also acknowledge that the popular ideals of multiculturalism may clash with the realities of an official multiculturalism.

But much of this criticism glosses over the multidimensional nature of multiculturalism. Multiculturalism can be liberating but also marginalizing, unifying but also divisive, inclusive but also exclusive (Vasta, 1993). Also, Canadians tend to focus entirely on its benefits and strengths, or entirely on its costs and weaknesses, to the exclusion of intermediate positions. Official multiculturalism is neither all good nor an all-consuming evil, neither the problem nor a solution. More to the point, it is both good and bad depending on how you look at it and what one expects of it. Positive and negative effects coexist uneasily in a highly fluid social climate. Official multiculturalism challenges the compulsory assimilation of minorities, and that is a good thing. But it is also a problem because it may prevent individuals from breaking out of their ethnic shells to participate fully and equally in society (Keohane, 1997).

Some Canadians celebrate its society-transforming capacity, noting that it has hastened Canada's transformation from a largely English-speaking colonial outpost into a remarkably cosmopolitan society. Others reject multiculturalism as an affront to Canadian identity. Multiculturalism provides minorities with a platform for participating in society without the imposition of heavy-handed government tactics. At the same time, however, it lures minorities into the dominant culture, in the sense that measures to improve access or participation often have assimilationist consequences. When minorities resist assimilation, they often find their efforts counterproductive—that is, they find themselves absorbed even more quickly into the very system they attempted to reject (Pearson, 1993). Not surprisingly, the balance between unity and diversity is constantly being tested:

> In navigating between two diametrically opposed dynamics, namely, confinement of minorities to ghettoes or dissolution by assimilation, multiculturalism has endured pressure to balance the articulation between respect for differences and a commitment to universal rights. (Wieviorka, 1998: 895)

Navigating between these conflicting demands has had unexpected consequences: official multiculturalism winds up emphasizing differences despite its lofty intentions to focus on similarities; in contrast, it may tout the virtues of diversity yet end up reinforcing conformity and consensus.

Canadian society has long been constructed around a series of working compromises. Multiculturalism is an excellent mediator between national interests and competing ethnicities—between the pull of particularism ("differences must be taken seriously") and the push of universalism ("nobody should be treated differently, because of our commonalities"). As the "compromise of compromises," multiculturalism promotes diversity without ever losing sight of disadvantage and inclusiveness; it advocates national interests but does not ignore the concerns of minorities; it endorses differences but stays focused on unity. This capacity for speaking the language of compromise has enabled official multiculturalism to protect the whole without destroying the parts. Multiculturalism also provides a philosophical rationale for holding together what otherwise would succumb into conformity or collapse into chaos. Its role in society building has been bolstered even further by its capacity to steer a compromise between the conflicting demands of state conformity and ethnic tribalism.

Canada Is Multiculturalism/Multiculturalism Is Canada

Those who defend multiculturalism at all costs are as biased as those who disparage it as utterly valueless. A sense of perspective is useful. Multiculturalism is not the cause of Canada's problems, any more than it can be the definitive solution. Canada's multiculturalism may not be perfect, yet compared to the carnage of Kosovo and Chechnya, it seems positively utopian. The fact that Canada has avoided much of the ethnic strife that is currently convulsing many countries speaks volumes to multiculturalism's capacity for settling differences. There is little risk that Canada will unravel because of multiculturalism: the politics of ethnic nationalism will see to that first. Nor is there much point in getting worked up that Canada lacks a distinct culture; multiculturalism could not have destroyed what Canada may never have had. Perhaps Canada's defining feature is its absence of an explicit common culture and its constant search for identity. Haroon Siddiqui (1999: A18) points out:

> One of the chief strengths of immigrant, democratic Canada is that its identity keeps evolving. If it didn't we would be an intellectually dead society. Only a fascist or fossilized state can offer the conceit and false comfort of fixed values.

Yet shared values can be discerned: a commitment to diversity is one thing Canadians have in common; we also share a basic decency, a respect for the rule of law, and a commitment to individual equality (see Sajoo, 1994). Diversity is one of Canada's strengths; it has to be, considering the heterogeneity of our society (Kaplan, 1993; Kymlicka, 1994; Djikstra et al., 2001). Disagreement and conflict are inevitable in such a context. Shared ethnicity does not automatically lead to unanimity of vision, as Bissoondath (1994) reminds us—albeit in a different sense. By the same token, a multicultural society can survive despite a multiplicity of voices and visions, provided that—within limits—its members can agree to disagree.

Discarding multiculturalism is hardly an option, given the dearth of acceptable alternatives. In seeking to make Canada safe *for* diversity, yet safe *from* diversity, Canadians have little choice except to tap into multiculturalism as an innovative though imperfect approach to engaging diversity in fair and progressive ways. What alternative policies or arrangements can possibly answer Canada's central challenge? Which is, of course, to forge unity from diversity without destroying either. John Harles (1998: 238–39) points to this question:

> Canada possesses neither the ethnic and cultural homogeneity nor the ideological consensus that typically serve as foci of integration in other democratic political systems. Absent a clear sense of Canadian national identity, political assimilation, in the sense of being socialized to the defining beliefs and values of a cohesive policy, is a difficult prospect. Consequently, as a means of incorporating ethnic minorities into a unified Canadian political community, multiculturalism and the ethos of integration without assimilation with which it is twinned are understandable alternatives to a strong consolidative notion of Canadian identity.

A Riddle, a Mystery, an Enigma

Canada may well deserve its global reputation. Our commitment to multiculturalism has contributed to our image as an open, secular, and largely tolerant society. Various United Nations panels have lauded Canada as a socially progressive society with an enviable standard of living. Multiculturalism has proven itself to be a beacon of tolerance in a world inundated with hate. We have developed a social framework that balances diversity and unity, though admittedly, that balancing act is not to everyone's liking. Most Canadians, especially the younger and the better educated, are relatively comfortable with diversity and proud of Canada's multicultural heritage, despite undercurrents of resentment toward certain newcomers.

Yet none of this should be taken as an excuse to overlook Canada's imperfections. Official multiculturalism is riddled with inconsistencies. This should come as no surprise: Canada is a multilayered society of very different minorities with diverse and competing agendas. Basically all the state can do is manage this diversity as best it can by balancing competing interests. Not unexpectedly, multicultural initiatives continue to be second-guessed and endlessly criticized. All of this reminds us that the accidental consequences of official multiculturalism can derail even the best of intentions while yielding a raft of paradoxes.

Multiculturalism is very much double-edged. Those who embrace multiculturalism are both as right and as wrong as those who loathe it. Its capacity to strengthen Canadian unity is as strong as its capacity to tear apart. Diversity has the potential to improve Canada's quality of life; it also has the potential to unravel all that binds Canadians together.

CASE STUDY (Continued)
Multicultural Facts/Multicultural Fictions

DEBUNKING MULTICULTURAL FALLACIES

The case study at the beginning of the chapter listed common (mis)perceptions about official multiculturalism. Below I revisit these perceptions by applying a reality check to them.

Fallacy—Official multiculturalism is not working.
Reality check—What exactly is meant by "not working"? Who says so? Why? On what basis? And compared to what? Multiculturalism possesses neither the power nor the resources to make sweeping changes. It cannot eliminate discrimination or racism on its own, nor can it automatically improve minority opportunities and life chances. It is effective when it fosters an inclusive social climate that promotes full participation yet is responsive to diversity.

Fallacy—Diversity is divisive and disruptive.
Reality check—Diversity only becomes disruptive or divisive when there is no common vision—no overarching set of values—to integrate disparate elements into a cohesive whole. Canada's official multiculturalism provides this coherent framework for living together with differences, even if not everyone is pleased with its goals, processes, or outcomes.

Fallacy—Multiculturalism is about celebrating differences at the expense of national unity.
Reality check—Multiculturalism does not encourage diversity. More accurately, it tries to depoliticize diversity by channelling potentially messy ethnic entanglements into relatively harmless avenues. It also tries to defuse any political and ethnic issues that immigrants bring to Canada with them. Differences are further defused when all differences are treated the same way, when limits of acceptability are placed around differences, and when only superficial differences are endorsed. All of this serves to emphasize disadvantage (rather than differences) as a basis for recognition or reward.

Fallacy—Official multiculturalism is only for "ethnics."
Reality check—Official multiculturalism is not just for ethnic minorities. Paradoxically, perhaps, it is also aimed at mainstream structures and values. Multiculturalism sets out to transform the mainstream by modifying public perceptions of diversity, by removing discriminatory barriers, both attitudinal and structural, and by creating a positive social climate in which equality and diversity can coexist. To date, however, the mainstream has exempted itself from the debate on multiculturalism, having preferred to award itself honorary status as the tacitly assumed standard from which other cultures must take their cue.

Fallacy—Multiculturalism is about multicultures.
Reality check—Multiculturalism does not promote the cultures of ethnic groups as distinctive and coherent lifestyles within specific social communities (i.e., for each identifiable group, there is a single homogeneous and fixed culture). Nor does it favour promoting ethnocultures as unique and fixed (the "essentialist" approach) (Modood, 1997). Rather, multiculturalism is more likely to acknowledge the multicultural rights of individuals who are comfortable with plural and fluid identities, who define themselves more in terms of multiple attachments in this world of transnational cultural connections, and who are aware of their own hybrid natures.

Fallacy—Multiculturalism is about promoting ethnic groups.
Reality check—Multiculturalism is still seen as encouraging each ethnic group to retain its ideology and behavioural uniqueness—with substantial government funding (see Jantzen, 2000). But it is doubtful whether any modern society could survive as a mosaic of autonomous and self-sufficient enclaves. Official multiculturalism is not about retaining culturally different and self-sufficient communities. The only sorts of diversity encouraged by official multiculturalism are the symbolic and the situational. Every individual is permitted to identify with the cultural tradition of his or her choice, provided that tradition falls within acceptable limits and contributes to Canadian society.

Fallacy—Multiculturalism is a problem.
Reality check—Official multiculturalism is neither a problem nor a solution. It is both a problem *and* solution, and a particular evaluation depends on the criteria employed in the assessment. Moreover, many of the problems confronting Canada don't stem from too much multiculturalism, but rather from not enough of it!

Fallacy—Multiculturalism is irrelevant.
Reality check—Whether multiculturalism is relevant or not depends on what you expect it to do. If official multiculturalism is meant to take differences seriously, it may well be perceived as irrelevant or dangerous. If its objective is to make Canada safe *for* diversity and safe *from* diversity, the relevance of official multiculturalism is obvious. In a Canada that is becoming increasingly pluralistic in this increasingly interconnected world, official multiculturalism will assume even greater relevance.

Fallacy—Multiculturalism tolerates an "anything goes" mentality because it embraces cultural relativism.

Reality check—Multiculturalism does not endorse a mindless relativism in which "anything goes" in the name of tolerance. Multiculturalism is clear about what is permissible in Canada. It rejects any customs that violate Canadian laws, interfere with the rights of others, offend the moral sensibilities of most Canadians, or disturb central institutions or core values.

Fallacy—Multiculturalism is experiencing a backlash.

Reality check—Criticisms of multiculturalism are real and valid. But that in its own right does not signal a backlash, any more than public or political silence is proof of growing support. The disgruntlement we hear may be arising from the already disenchanted rather than a new legion of critics. Also, to the extent there is a backlash, it seems to be driven by indifference or complacency; this suggests that official multiculturalism may be a victim of its own success. Finally, it is difficult to determine what people dislike about multiculturalism. Many may agree with its principles but be irked by its status as formal government policy, by the public funds its programs receive, or by its linkage to employment equity and immigration policies. Multiculturalism thus becomes guilty by association.

Fallacy—Multiculturalism promotes collective rights in lieu of individual rights.

Reality check—Canada's official multiculturalism is embedded in a liberal-pluralist society. Under liberal pluralism, what individuals have in common is more important than what divides them as members of groups. Liberal states such as Canada do *not* grant special group rights to immigrants; all they are obligated to do is remove discriminatory barriers to ensure full participation. A liberal state does not demand that minorities abandon their cultures; by the same token, it is not obligated to protect these cultures except to redress historical wrongs. Liberal states endorse individual rights only—that is, equal rights for all.

Fallacy—Multiculturalism is an expensive luxury during times of fiscal prudence.

Reality check—Multiculturalism is not expensive: federal spending on multiculturalism stands at around $15 to $20 million per year—about 50 cents per person—and most of this is directed at antiracism campaigns, settlement and integration, and cultural sharing. Compare this with the $600 to $700 million expended for official bilingualism according to the

1999/2000 annual report from the Office of the Commissioner of Official Languages. To put it in another perspective: multiculturalism in 1992–93 received less than 1 percent of the spending allocated by governments (both federal and provincial) for arts and culture.

Why do all of the above fallacies persist? And who is responsible for perpetuating them? Plenty of people are to blame. Politicians, for engaging in hyperbole. Bureaucrats, for hyping multiculturalism, if only to "cool out" troublesome constituents and protect the status quo. Minority leaders, for circulating misleading claims in the competitive struggle for resources. Opponents of multiculturalism, for making irresponsible statements about impending social calamities. And even proponents of multiculturalism, for making extravagant and unrealistic claims with scant regard for the practical realities of this complex and contradictory world.

Chapter Highlights

- Canadians remain poorly informed about official multiculturalism—about its goals, underlying premises, means, and outcomes. There is even less consensus regarding what multiculturalism is, what it does, what it is trying to do, and what is should be doing.
- Official multiculturalism is not meant to celebrate differences or promote diversity. However, it endorses diversity to the extent that it allows individuals to identify with the cultural tradition of their choice, provided this affilation does not violate human rights or laws of the land.
- Official multiculturalism focuses on depoliticizing diversity by channelling it into harmless outlets, thus short-circuiting its potential for disruption. This underscores the idea that multiculturalism is basically a strategy for society building rather than for ethnic promotion.
- Multiculturalism has been regarded as both an asset and a hindrance to Canada, as both a source of social tension and an innovative means for managing conflicts between minorities. Multiculturalism cannot be blamed for all of Canada's social problems, and it is not the solution to all our ills. It is not a magical formula for success, but it *is* one component—however imperfect—for managing diversity in a complex society in which power is unevenly distributed.

- Most people don't understand what multiculturalism is supposed to do, nor are they clear about what it is actually doing. There is a wide gap between principles and practice, and it keeps shifting.
- Multiculturalism is usually criticized for being divisive, marginalizing, essentializing, hegemonic, and a hoax. It is also praised for being unifying, progressive, hybridizing, a catalyst, and counter-hegemonic. The degree of criticism or praise may vary with a person's vision of Canadian society, and the role of multiculturalism in fostering this vision.
- Multiculturalism is about compromises. Multicultural initiatives must balance the imperatives of the state and of majorities with the rights of minorities, and balance both of those with the citizenship rights of individuals.
- Those who exaggerate the benefits of official multiculturalism are just as guilty of distortion as those who obsess over its flaws. In fact, the costs and benefits of official multiculturalism are inseparable. A relentless emphasis on multiculturalism's costs and weaknesses glosses over the benefits of official multiculturalism.
- Official multiculturalism is associated with many fallacies that impede its functioning. Many of these fallacies reflect inconsistencies between official and popular forms of multiculturalism. They also reflect discrepancies between people's expectations and multiculturalism's actual capacities.

Review Questions

1. What are the major criticisms directed at official multiculturalism? Are these criticisms valid? Explain.
2. What are the benefits of official multiculturalism at the individual, institutional, national, and international levels? Do these benefits stand up to scrutiny?
3. How would you describe the attitudes of Canadians toward multiculturalism, both popular and official?
4. Which statement do you agree with? (a) Official multiculturalism is nothing more than a "sheep in wolf's clothing." (b) Official multiculturalism is little more than a "wolf in sheep's clothing." Or do you agree with both? Explain.
5. Much of the debate over multiculturalism reflects the disparities between what people think it *is* doing or *should* do and what it *can* do. Elaborate.

6. "Official multiculturalism is experiencing a crisis of identity that has transformed it into a contested and unsettled site of hidden agendas and competing priorities." Explain.
7. Multiculturalism has been interpreted as a "riddle wrapped in a mystery inside an enigma." Explain, focusing on official multiculturalism in terms of the good, the bad, and the in between.

Recommended Reading

Australian–Canadian Studies. 2000. Special issue devoted to multiculturalism. 17, no. 2.

Hamani Bannerji. 2000. *The Dark Side of the Moon*. Toronto: Canadian Scholars Press.

Canadian Woman Studies Journal. 2000. Special issue on multiculturalism and immigration. 20. no. 2.

Peter S. Li, ed. 1999. *Race and Ethnic Relations in Canada*. Toronto: Oxford University Press.

Suwanda Sugunasiri. 1999. *How to Kick Multiculturalism in the Teeth*. Toronto: Vintage Publishing.

Ellie Vasta and Stephen Castles, eds. 1996. *The Teeth Are Smiling: The Persistence of Racism in Multicultural Australia*. Sydney: Allen and Unwin.

PART 2 | Putting Multiculturalism to Work

It is one thing to encourage the principles of diversity of Canada. It has proven quite a different challenge to transform these principles into practices that foster inclusiveness. Canada's mainstream institutions for many decades endorsed a monoculturalism based on exclusion and inequity: minority women and men were routinely denied services or opportunities because of their skin colour or cultural practices; they were also treated negatively, defined as inferior or irrelevant, and subjected to direct harassment and indirect violence. Even when they were accepted, this acceptance often had conditions attached, and minorities were expected to do all the compromising.

But changes in the social and political climate have eroded this exclusiveness. Minorities have been asserting themselves, and government policies have changed, and as a result, many institutions have had to become more responsive, more inclusive, and more equitable. Also, institutions are being forced by demographic change to adjust their monocultural practices. Public and private institutions are attempting to enhance their effectiveness in three ways: by capitalizing on the talents and connections of new Canadians; by creating workplaces where people can work productively together despite their cultural differences; and by ensuring that services are delivered in a user-friendly and cost-effective manner.

Whether the public likes it or not, institutions can no longer avoid becoming more inclusive. Canada's institutions no longer have the luxury of remaining aloof from demographic and cultural change. Old ways of managing workplaces and delivering services are becoming more and more irrelevant or unacceptable; inclusiveness is increasingly being endorsed as an approach to working together despite differences. To be sure, the principle of inclusiveness generates its own tensions and conflicts, and barriers continue to hinder responsiveness. Those in positions of privilege often try to avoid relinquishing

119

power or sharing space, especially with those once considered inferior or irrelevant. Also, institutions have their own subcultures and organizational procedures, and both can inhibit inclusiveness. Finally, even the best intentions can be derailed by weak approaches to managing differences.

The benefits of inclusiveness cannot be dismissed. In this rapidly changing and increasingly diverse world, organizations can reap many benefits from a formal commitment to inclusiveness. Such a commitment can ease workplace tensions, foster creativity, strengthen community ties, broaden market appeal, and improve the quality of services. It can help businesses meet the multicultural needs of ethnically driven niche markets, both in Canada and abroad. Organizations are beginning to depend on their diverse workforces to promote a positive corporate image and to strengthen ties to diverse communities. These ties often turn out to be a competitive advantage in international business.

DEFINING INCLUSIVENESS

Under official multiculturalism, all federally regulated organizations are facing pressure to deliver culturally sensitive services based on the principles of inclusiveness. But at the level of organizations, what does inclusiveness mean? For our purposes, it is a process by which organizations engage with minority women and men as different yet equal. It is about responding to diversity by ensuring full and equal participation for historically excluded workers or "clients." Differences are no longer marginalized ("side-streamed"), as they were with monocultural institutions. Instead, diversity is "mainstreamed" as normal and necessary for improving effectiveness or efficiency. Inclusiveness goes beyond celebrating diversity and promoting minorities; it also is concerned with removing disadvantages that accompany minority differences. All of this requires a triple-focus: institutions must be responsive to minority concerns for access, equity, and involvement; they must adjust their structures to accommodate the world-views of minorities; and they must embrace relationships with minorities both within the organization (i.e., in the work environment) and outside it (i.e., with clients).

Put bluntly, inclusiveness is not about being nice to minorities, nor is it about offering special treatment to some at the expense of others. Rather, inclusiveness recognizes that fundamental human rights are essential to a democratic society, and that all people have the right to be treated fairly when goods and services are being portioned out (Tinglin, 1998). Furthermore, inclusiveness is not just about bringing minorities into mainstream institutions; if this is all it was, organizations would never change (Nunan et al., 2000). Rather, it is about organizations transforming themselves and their value systems by taking into account the needs and concerns of the historically excluded (Mittler, 2000).

Obviously, inclusiveness is difficult to bring about. The process is fraught with ambiguity and stress as competing groups protect their interests, resist intrusions, and conceal agendas. Consider the following dilemmas:

- Is inclusiveness about colour blindness or colour consciousness? Does an inclusive institution strive for "neutrality" by eliminating all references to cultural differences? Or does it strive to incorporate as many cultural differences as possible?

- Is inclusiveness about reform or transformation? Some see Canada's institutions as fundamentally sound and as needing only minor adjustments. According to this perspective, any organizational failures can be pinned on individuals. For others (the more radical theorists), Canada's institutions are fundamentally exploitative and unstable, and only structural transformation will bring about true inclusiveness.

- Is inclusiveness about differences or similarities? For some, inclusiveness brings people closer together by emphasizing what they have in common. For others, the purpose of inclusiveness is to emphasize people's differences and then bring them together as different yet equal.

- Is inclusiveness about diversity or disadvantage? Should differences automatically be a basis for rewarding or recognizing people? Or should special treatment be based solely on disadvantage that *arises from* differences?

- What form should Canada's commitment to inclusiveness take? Should strategies focus on removing discriminatory barriers? On "ethnicizing" institutions by hiring minority personnel and embracing their beliefs and values? On creating parallel institutions that are modelled on the mainstream but that cater to minority interests? Or on establishing separate institutions that reflect minority experiences and aspirations?

These questions rarely inspire consensus. There is no "one size fits all" formula for inclusiveness, since every organization faces its own unique diversity issues. In some situations, similar treatment is the best approach; in others, differences will need to be taken into account. Overemphasizing differences can be just as discriminatory as underemphasizing them. Also, too much emphasis on diversity and not enough on disadvantage can be exclusionary. Diversity is a *relationship*, not a *thing*; it is something that evolves within its own context. Failure to understand this can easily torpedo even the best intentions.

INDICATORS OF INCLUSIVENESS

What constitutes an inclusive organization in a multicultural society? Responses vary: some believe that any consideration of diversity runs against the principles of equality; others believe that differences need to be taken seriously to ensure true inclusiveness. These philosophical differences make consensus difficult. Even so, it is possible to establish a broad definition of an inclusive and multicultural organization.

- *First*, an organization's workforce should reflect its region's labour pool. This should apply at all levels, from entry level to senior management. Of course, perfection may not be possible, because of social and cultural factors. Still, some correspondence is vital to ensure at least the appearance of inclusiveness. Canada's employment equity program requires federally regulated workplaces to hire workers of colour in proportions consistent with their presence in the labour force (Beeby, 1998).

- *Second*, employers must end systemic bias in their organizations when it comes to recruiting, selecting, training, promoting, and retaining minority personnel. They must carefully scrutinize their corporate policies and procedures with the goal of ending inadvertent forms of discrimination. The emphasis here is on transforming the workplace so that all workers act in a nondiscriminatory way when discharging their obligations to colleagues and customers.
- *Third*, employers must foster a working climate that accepts minorities as beneficial to the organization's health. At a minimum, harassment must not be tolerated in any form. A shift from monoculturalism to multiculturalism involves more than sensitizing employees to cultural differences; it means actively promoting diversity (Nancoo, 2000) with the goal of improving employees' attitudes toward differences.
- *Fourth*, an inclusive organization is one which ensures that service delivery is community-based and culturally sensitive. Culturally sensitive services are based on close consultation with the community at hand; they cannot be imposed unilaterally. Furthermore, decisions relating to service delivery must be transparent, especially as they relate to representation, access, and equity.
- *Fifth*, service delivery organizations cannot operate in a social or political vacuum; they must always be publicly accountable. This means that communications with stakeholders must be open and productive.

BARRIERS TO INCLUSION

References to inclusiveness have a reassuring ring. Unfortunately, there are many barriers to inclusion. Some of these are so obvious that they are relatively easy to challenge. Others are so subtle and so deeply entrenched that they are taken for granted (Wicks and Bradshaw, 2000). Below, I review some of these barriers.

Self-interest—People in organizations respond to diversity in highly predictable ways. It is widely assumed that around 20 percent are receptive to it, around 50 percent can be converted to it by coaxing or threats, and the remaining 30 percent will resist it at all times. Resistance to inclusiveness is sharpened when people perceive a threat to their self-interest. This should come as no surprise; few people relinquish power or privileges unless they have to—especially to those once perceived as inferior or irrelevant.

Hierarchy—Initiatives on inclusiveness are often long on platitudes but short on practice and implementation. Senior managers may support it strongly for various reasons, ranging from genuine concern to public relations to economic expediency. Middle and lower managers may be less enthusiastic about inclusiveness and prefer to cling to traditional authority patterns. Those at the bottom of the employment pecking order may be the least receptive to diversity, and may in fact sabotage diversity directives that clash with self-interest.

Bureaucratic structures—Organizations love hierarchy. They pride themselves on being rational, objective, and value-neutral. They tend to praise their own efficiency. They like to be predictable. All these things are harder to achieve when the workforce is a diverse one. This works against inclusiveness, especially if that paradigm interferes with a strong desire for "business as usual."

Corporate cultures—Institutions have a tendency to satisfy only themselves. They are sensitive to threats to "the way we do things around here." This runs counter to inclusiveness, especially when the organization's culture was established in the past by white males. Such organizations tend to prefer hiring people "like us" over anyone who might not "fit in."

Occupational subcultures—In all organizations there are informal groups that exercise control over their members' behaviour. These groups are strongly placed to derail diversity initiatives.

The following table provides a brief overview of indicators and barriers.

Institutional Inclusivenes

Indicators	Barriers
Workforce representation	Self-interest
Organizational rules and procedures	Hierarchy
Workplace culture	Bureaucracy
Service delivery	Corporate cultures
Community relations	Occupational subcultures

Clearly, even when inclusion is timely and overdue, efforts to achieve it can easily be derailed. Mainstream institutions remain stuck in Victorian-era foundational principles of "do as you are told or else" because "we are in charge and know what is best for you." Institutions are full of people who resolutely oppose change at all costs because of prejudice, nepotism, patronage, and the "old boys network" (Travis, 1998). Also, structural and systemic barriers make a mockery of the notion of moving over to make space (see Kanter, 1977).

Moves toward inclusiveness are further complicated by those who advocate change without much thought to the complexities involved. Implementing institutional change is not like installing a new computer system. Institutions are complex, often baffling things. They are about domination and control; they both invite and resist change. Conservatives and progressives struggle for power and privilege, and those in the middle cast their lot with whichever trend promises a payoff. Conventional views remain firmly entrenched; vested interests hesitate to discard the tried and true. Newer visions are compelling, yet they lack the resolve and the critical mass to scuttle conventional patterns of "doing business." All of this can be disruptive as the politics of inclusiveness transform institutions into battlefields of clashing agendas.

The theme of inclusiveness is central to this part of the book, in which I focus on how organizations put multiculturalism to work. I emphasize how the media and the education and justice systems are engaging diversity. I explore programs and policies that try to foster inclusiveness, both internally and externally. I also analyze the institutional barriers that must be surmounted in order to foster inclusiveness. Each of the three above-mentioned systems is analyzed in terms of the following criteria: what it has accomplished to date; what it should do to promote more inclusiveness; and what *can* be done in the circumstances.

All three institutions are under pressure. The police and the criminal justice system are doing better at accepting multiculturalism but are having to do more with less at a time when more is especially required. The mainstream media are becoming more responsive to minority concerns, yet their initiatives are often compromised by bottom-line demands and organizational inertia. The education system is exploring innovative multicultural scenarios, but has found itself stymied by powerful conservative agendas. A commitment to inclusiveness is especially important among service-oriented institutions. Because they are mandated to be agencies of socialization and social control, they are held to greater account and subject to more criticism, especially when they fail to match expectations. Finally, I put the principles of inclusiveness to the test where it matters most: at the level of interpersonal relations. In any organizational setting, coexistence between cultures depends heavily on a commitment to inclusiveness. In turn, inclusiveness depends heavily on individuals' skills at dealing with one another across minority fences. Let's call this "multicultural competence." It depends on two factors: a willingness to interact with other cultures, and a willingness to learn how. In this context, the success of multiculturalism in Canada is going to come down to one individual at a time.

CHAPTER 5

Diversifying Criminal Justice: Cops, Courts, Corrections

CHAPTER OBJECTIVES

- To explore inclusiveness issues as they apply to mainstream institutions such as criminal justice, education, and the media.
- To show how broad a concept inclusiveness is and how hard it is to define because of this.
- To point out the components of inclusiveness and the barriers to it.
- To show that Canada's criminal justice system is in crisis as a result of its failure to embrace multiculturalism and inclusiveness.
- To demonstrate how the components of the criminal justice system—namely, the police, the courts, and the prisons—have taken steps toward multicultural responsiveness despite mounting resentment and resistance.
- To describe the crisis confronting relations between urban police and minority youth.
- To discuss how community-based, multicultural policing sounds good in theory but is difficult to implement.
- To explain how the criminal justice system has betrayed aboriginal people.
- To indicate how the principles of aboriginal justice differ from those of Canada's criminal justice system.

CASE STUDY
Putting Aboriginality Back into the Justice System

Jail doesn't help anyone. A lot of our people could have been healed a long time ago if it weren't for jail. Jail hurts them more and then they come out really bitter. In jail all they learn is "hurt and bitter."

Yukon elder, cited in Green (1998: 18)

The debate over "one law for all Canadians" has assumed a new twist with a controversial ruling involving an aboriginal woman. The central question in the debate is this: Should the criminal justice system take into account the cultural context of unlawful actions? A second question, almost as important, relates to the costs of incarceration. These costs are rising. What can be done when one part of the population is disproportionately involved, and no appreciable reduction is in sight?

In 1997, in the B.C. Supreme Court, a twenty-eight-year-old Métis woman, Deanna Emard, received a conditional sentence of two years less a day after stabbing her common law partner to death. Also, she was ordered to perform 240 hours of community service and to stop drinking. The defence counsel, Peter Wilson, had argued that Ms. Emard should receive a lighter sentence because of her "Indianness." There was no documentation of domestic abuse in the relationship. Even so, Wilson argued that Ms. Emard suffered from the systemic problems that plague Canada's First Peoples, including substance abuse, racism, and poverty. The presiding judge agreed: although her aboriginal background did not absolve her of blame for the crime—she was, after all, found guilty of manslaughter—she had endured an unhappy life through "no fault of her own."

This ruling did not appear out of the blue. Rather, it reflected sentencing guidelines introduced in 1995 to the Criminal Code (s. 718.2(e)). According to the new guidelines, "all available sanctions other than imprisonment, that are reasonable in the circumstances, should be considered for *all* offenders, with particular attention to the circumstances of aboriginal offenders." When arriving at sentencing, judges are now required to take into account the social, cultural, and historical background of offenders. They are also expected to seek alternatives to imprisonment—provided, of course, the resulting arrangement does not pose a risk to the public.

The reaction to this ruling was largely negative. Some disparaged the conditional discharge as amounting to a "Get Out of Jail Free" card for aboriginal offenders. This degree of leniency was seen as posing a risk to society, in that it condoned crimes by aboriginals by striking down the principle of deterrence. Others suggested that Emard's sentence amounted to a racial slur, in implying that aboriginal people had diminished capacity simply *because* they were native people. Still others, including columnist Lisa Birnie, dismissed the ruling as a clumsy and racist attempt to assuage white guilt through political correctness. The victim's family accused the system of bending to political correctness because the accused was Métis and a woman. As to the accused's intoxicated state at the time of the crime, the victim's sister said, "Alcohol is not an excuse, and neither is being a native. There should be justice for everyone—not one system for Indian and Métis people and one for white people." Still others expressed concern over the effects of the amendment on the constitutional principle of equality before the law. According to Mike Scott, Native Affairs critic for the Reform (now Alliance) Party, "You can't right historical wrongs by creating new injustices. When you move away from the principle that we're all entitled to the same treatment in the eyes of the law, you're going down a slippery slope."

Even thoughtful Canadians were uncomfortable with the Emard ruling. This unease was intensified when a thirty-seven-year-old Saskatchewan Métis with a long history of violent crimes was spared life imprisonment for an armed robbery that included a sexual assault. According to the assailant, his aboriginal background was the cause of his crime (Mickleburgh, 1999). In another incident, two Haitian males convicted of sexually assaulting a Haitian-Canadian woman were given reduced sentences (with no jail time) on the grounds of "mitigating circumstances." Their lack of remorse for the assault was taken as proof that such actions must be culturally embedded (Fleras and Elliott, 1999: 291–93). So what is going on, multiculturally speaking? To what extent should cultural defences be acceptable in a multicultural society? Is this what is meant by an "inclusive" criminal justice system? I will return to this issue at the end of this chapter.

CRISIS IN CRIMINAL (IN)JUSTICE

Canada's commitment to official multiculturalism has been widely acclaimed, for reasons both good and weak. This praise reflects Canada's success at accepting minority women and men at the level of institutions. Inclusiveness at that level is no longer an option or a luxury: social, political, and demo-graphic changes have made it a necessity. Suggestions that Canada is a mul-ticultural society would reek of hypocrisy without responsive and inclusive institutions. Yet this kind of inclusiveness is not a straightforward thing: How can we make the system more responsive to minorities' needs and concerns without eroding the identity and integrity of the country's institutions? These institutions have found innovative ways to carve out social and cultural space for minorities. Even so, inclusiveness is stiffly resisted in some quarters; every step forward is matched by another one backward.

Canada's criminal justice system is part of this debate over institutional inclusiveness. Its critics declare that the system is ineffective and counter-productive, and the data seem to bear them out. Minority women and men are disportionately represented at all points of the system, and prejudice, dis-crimination, and systemic racism embedded throughout all levels (La Prairie, 1999; Neugebauer, 2000; CCJA, 2000). Consider policing: aboriginal com-munities are underpoliced because of entrenched cultural stereotypes and power imbalances (Turpel/Aki-Kwe, 2000). At the same time, young people of colour are *over*policed because police forces equate skin colour with crime (Neugebauer, 2000: xv). The same sorts of patterns are found in the correc-tions system. Aboriginal people and minority males are vastly overrepre-sented in Canada's prisons. Partly as a result of this, the human and monetary costs of incarceration are escalating.

Not surprisingly, the criminal justice system has come under pressure to deliver services that reflect the new realities of a multicultural society. Changes have been made to apply the principles of inclusiveness to crime problems (La Prairie, 1999). Yet success has been elusive. Alternatives to a "cops–courts–corrections" approach to crime rarely reverse negative trends or reduce crime rates. Some see the present system as too lenient when it comes to sentencing young people and aboriginal offenders; others see the system as too rigid because it refuses to take differences seriously enough; for still others, the system's benefits don't justify its costs. Criminal justice pro-grams are getting more and more expensive, and the resources at their dis-posal are often misdirected or misplaced, and rarely do much to help minority communities solve their most pressing problems (La Prairie, 2000).

So far, the criminal justice system has had mixed success at embracing multiculturalism. Some parts of it have warmed to the task of inclusiveness. With the shift toward community policing and wider recruiting, police–minority relations have improved. The courts and the prison system have incorporated culturally sensitive alternatives for minority and aboriginal offenders. All of that is to the good. But at the same time, efforts to diversify the criminal justice system have encountered both resistance and resentment. Multicultural concessions tend to rankle those who believe in a one-size-fits-all criminal justice system (see Weitzer, 2000). Critics question the authenticity behind alternatives: initiatives such as community-oriented policing may have more to do with public relations and political expediency than with improving community relations. Efforts to divert aboriginal offenders from jails may reflect cost-cutting instead of a commitment to social justice.

More damning still, reforms by courts and corrections have not reduced rates of imprisonment and recidivism among high-offending groups. This has led some to call for even stronger measures to quell crime. Every anticrime measure that has ever been attempted has been attacked from both sides of the debate, as both "too soft" and "too hard," as both "too much" and "not enough." Any shift toward either toughness or leniency is met by a chorus of concern and condemnation. And through it all, no one can even agree on how crime should be measured.

The justice system has become the acid test for Canadian multiculturalism. If there is any social endeavour of which it can be said that multiculturalism *must* work, it is the justice system. In this chapter I consider the problems inherent in applying multiculturalism to that system. I emphasize policing as the sharp end of the stick, in the sense that the police are the most regular and important contact minorities have with the justice system. Community-oriented, multicultural policing has promise but still faces formidable hurdles before it can revitalize relations between police and minority youth. I also consider recent changes related to the courts and the corrections system. Alternative sentencing has done much to highlight the inequities of the Eurocentric criminal justice system. Unfortunately, ideals rarely match realities. The newer models of aboriginal justice suggest that it is possible for native offenders to escape from the revolving door of the justice system without undermining institutional integrity. But there is no guarantee that alternative sentencing will improve the situation.

Structural barriers can undermine even the strongest commitment to inclusiveness. But it is important to make the effort to bring diversity into the justice system. If we fail in the attempt, Canada's reputation as a beacon of inclusiveness will be tarnished.

MIS-POLICING DIVERSITY

Police–minority relations are undergoing a profound reassessment because of changes in public expectations. Especially disturbing has been the rash of seemingly unprovoked killings by police in the United States, often of unarmed men. Agencies such as Amnesty International have criticized the United States for widespread police brutality, especially for police abuse of racial minorities, much of which goes unpunished (Koring, 1999).

But other countries can be criticized for the same reasons (Chan, 1996). In Britain in 1995, only one-quarter of victims of racial assaults reported those attacks to the police. Only half of those who did report were satisfied with the police response. Most respondents perceived the police as uninterested in minorities' complainants and as more sympathetic to the perpetrators (Modood and Berthoud, 1997). Amid accusations of institutional racism, confidence in the British police has plummeted.

Police in Canada are no less subject to harsh criticism for their indiscretions. They have been reproached by critics and supporters alike for mispolicing minority communities—for either overpolicing or underpolicing them, depending on the circumstances (Neugebauer, 2000). In Montreal a coroner's jury castigated the police for their callously racist indifference to human life after they shot an unarmed Black male by mistake. Montreal's police shot and killed ten people between 1988 and 1993: five were Black, three were Hispanic. The Toronto police have also been accused of being trigger-happy—of tending to shoot first, talk later. Their relationship with minority youth is especially difficult (Neugebauer, 2000). Their harassment of young African-Canadian males has sometimes resulted in violence (Henry et al., 2000). The police have also been accused of using strip searches to humiliate the uncooperatively loud or to punish the "deserved." And Canadians cringed in embarrassment on learning that some Saskatoon police officers punished intoxicated aboriginal men by abandoning them to near-certain death on the edge of town in the dead of winter (Koperis, 2000).

These "misadventures" and others similar have created a crisis in police–minority relations. Minorities increasingly distrust and dislike the police. The police, for their part, circle the wagons against minorities' criticisms, and this reinforces the spiral of mutual contempt. All of this negativity is eroding the legitimacy of the police in some multicultural communities (Baker, 1994). It is also raising some disturbing questions: Is the mispolicing of minorities a random coincidence or part of a pattern? Do police–minority relations reflect the harsher realities of minority crime? Or are police "racial profiling" some minorities as dangerous?

According to some minority parents and community leaders, police misconduct is not about the isolated actions of "bad cops"; rather, it amounts to oppression of one group by another. In their view, minority youth are being harassed, and a double-standard is to blame. Minority youth are charged, arrested, convicted, and jailed at a rate far out of proportion to their numbers in the community, in part because of racial stereotypes that have deeply infiltrated the police subculture. The belief that certain races are criminally predisposed has a powerful influence on how police make decisions, select options, and generally go about their work (Neugebauer, 2000). Besides being accused of "overpolicing" profiled communities, the police seem slow to respond to minority requests for help ("underpolicing") (Henry et al., 1995).

The police have their own perspective on all this. They deny that they are racist as an institution. They also dispute whether minorities in targeted communities despise them as much as is commonly believed. They contend that shootings involving minority males are isolated events and a reflection of the growing menace of guns and drugs. They concede that some police officers' actions are racially motivated, but they attribute these excesses to a small number of "rogue" officers rather than to institutionalized racism. Their arrests of minority youths do not amount to discriminatory policing, they argue; rather, they are a legitimate response to street crime. To the extent that the police are excessive in any way, it is a result of the irresponsible behaviour of dissaffected minority youth. In other words, minority communities have only themselves to blame if misguided allegations of police brutality discourage members of the community from seeking police protection.

The polarization could not be clearer: minority youth condemn the police as racist and trigger-happy; the police accuse minority youth of deliberate provocation. This gap in perceptions leads to strained mutual avoidance at best, and mutual contempt at worst. Minority youth deny the legitimacy of the police as tools of the white establishment (Kivel, 1996); the police, in turn, circle their wagons even more securely against what they perceive as unwarranted attacks by stroppy youths, community activists, an unsympathetic press, opportunistic politicians, and the forces of political correctness. This fortress mentality ensures that police remain insensitive to outside criticism. It also underscores the importance of a working environment that encourages cooperation rather than paranoia (Eng, 2000). Who is in the right in all of this, and who is wrong? Or is each side both right and wrong, depending on one's point of view? The following "Thinking Outside the Box" considers these questions.

Thinking Outside the Box

Crime with Colour

If nothing else, the O.J. Simpson trial and acquittal exposed a cultural rift that separates whites from Blacks. Because of different experiences arising from social group membership and social status, Blacks see the world differently from whites (Orbe and Harris, 2001). Perceptions of the criminal justice system are a reflection of the notion that what you see depends on where you stand.

Consider the contrasts. Whites tend to endorse the criminal justice system as a pillar of a civilized society. It's obvious why: the criminal justice system tends to reflect and reinforce mainstream values. Also, whites have generally been satisfied with their experiences with the law, despite occasional miscarriages that have tarnished the image of police. In contrast, Black experiences with the criminal justice system have mainly been a string of disasters. There is plenty of evidence for police misconduct, unsympathetic courts, and correctional institutes that do more harm than good. For example, police in Ontario are twice as likely to stop young Black males than young white ones, according to a 1995 study, *Systemic Racism in Ontario's Criminal Justice System*. Blacks are also more likely to be jailed overnight or denied bail. Not surprisingly, "uppity" Blacks who challenge and resist the "white man's law" tend to be valourized by other Blacks. Those who are "cheeky" enough to beat the system are often accorded hero status, to the dismay of a bewildered mainstream.

That urban police and certain sectors of the minority community do not mix well is an established fact (Ungerleider, 1993; Chan, 1997; Neugebauer, 2000). Neither side can understand the other—much less engage in cooperative actions—and this increases the likelihood of confrontation. To some extent, conflict is inevitable. In societies where race and inequality are closely linked, minorities tend to view police as the local embodiment of state power and privilege (Jain et al., 2000). Many new Canadians expect the police here to act like the ones in the countries they just left—that is, like corrupt and rascist goons at the behest of their repressive masters (Cryderman et al., 1998). Those without power in society condemn the police for obstructing the "safe" delivery of services (Ramsden, 1995). This is backed up by the statistics measuring violence and death: crimes by the poor are more likely to attract police attention, relative to white-collar crimes (which are not as visible or as easily detected, though they are just as damaging and costly). The end result? Police are perceived as criminalizing people on the basis of colour (intentionally or not), and as racializing "them" as the criminal "other" (Ungerleider and McGregor, 1995; Holdaway, 1996). In sum, minorities are not more criminal; however, they are more likely to be criminalized because of their visibility, and because of the stereotypes that attach to them.

TYPECASTING THE OTHER

Police–minority encounters tend to reinforce stereotypes and prejudices on both sides. By the way they communicate, both verbally and nonverbally, the police inadvertently reinforce the notion among Blacks that they are aggressive defenders of white privilege. At the same time, young Black males come across to police as needlessly provocative—as surly, defiant, uncooperative, disrespectful, deceptive, deviant, and deserving of increased surveillance. Considering all this, who can be surprised that police–minority relations are now virtually in crisis, with each side barely able to conceal its contempt for the other?

At the core of this communication breakdown are stereotypes, none of which flatter the other side (Forcese, 2000). Black youth accuse police of racism, and as proof of this point to how the police enforce the law in a discriminatory and insensitive manner. They accuse the police of applying a double-standard, and perceive themselves as harassed, charged, arrested, and convicted more often than whites—when they aren't actually being shot at and killed. Disadvantaged minorities believe that police work relies on stereotypes that reflect wider social conditioning, institutionally sanctioned police practices, and informal occupational subcultures. The police reject these accusations as unwarranted and unfair. As far as they are concerned, their job is to enforce the law evenly and without prejudice. Blacks are charged more often because they commit more crimes, and that in turn is why they receive more attention from police. Blacks deny that as a group they commit more crimes, and contend that the higher crime rates in their community are the result of (unfair) racial profiling and their greater visibility.

Ironically, then, the police are "criminalized" by minorities as the "enemy," as a Toronto race relations consultant once told a shocked audience. The status of the police as an "occupying army" has made cooperation impossible even when the community's concerns coincide with those of the police (see also Modood and Berthoud, 1997). Minority youth perceive their dealings with police as inseparable from race and racism (Britton, 2000). They see the police as overzealous in policing them, and as happy to taunt and bait minorities as part of a "cops 'n' robbers" game. They view police actions as part of a broader institutional pattern of racism and discrimination toward a criminalized "race." Too often minorities find themselves in a no-win situation. An African–Caribbean put it well:

> Any normal reaction is taken as an over-reaction, any quietness of temperament is taken to be arrogance. You see a black person as being, for lack of a better term, "cool" under the circumstances, it's taken to be arrogance. So you can't win. You either say something and be termed violent or you say nothing and be termed arrogant. (cited in Britton, 2000: 704)

Minority youth reject the notion that police excesses are isolated or random. Instead they perceive police misconduct as institutionalized and systemic and as meant to perpetuate white privilege and power. Not surprisingly, they liken the police to just another gang in the city, complete with uniforms, patches, weapons, and an internal code of ethics. Only the legal right to use force in staking out their "turf" distinguishes police from the " 'hood."

Police stereotypes are equally one-sided. The police see Blacks as problem people who must be contained so that chaos doesn't break out. They rarely view Blacks as normal and adjusted. They label most Blacks as criminals, drug pushers, pimps, welfare cheats, or malcontents, even when evidence shows that only a small proportion of Black youth can rightly be described this way. In effect, they are demonizing an entire community because of the actions of a few (Henry, 1994). The police judge minority youth by different standards and place them under constant scrutiny, and as a result, mistakes or problems are greatly magnified. They see Black youth as criminally inclined, as predisposed toward guns, gangs, and drugs, and as having a taste for violence—a taste imported to some extent from the violent street cultures of the Caribbean and the United States. They rarely perceive Black youth as alienated and underprivileged, or as having so little stake in the system that few seem to care if they live or die. They denounce Black activists as self-serving malcontents whose grandstanding rhetoric only widens the chasm. They criminalize the public behaviour of minority youth, and this makes it all the easier to label them as troublemakers. By racializing crime, they are perpetuating the criminal injustice cycle.

SUBCULTURES IN COLLISION

Many of the stereotypes that police and minority youth have of each other are subculturally driven. Minority youth often define themselves in opposition to white society and everything it symbolizes (Henry, 1994). In male Black youth subculture, toughness and assertiveness are core values, and animosity toward the police is part of identity (Neugebauer-Visano, 1996). Theirs is an "oppositional" culture (Elijah Anderson, 1994) that reflects the code of the street, with its pursuit of respect, power, and bravado. Few young Black males are willing to back down from a challenge, especially when personal dignity and individual honour are at stake. This assertiveness is given a menacing edge by the presence of guns and drugs. Further complicating the relationship between police and minorities is the fatalistic perception on the part of the latter that life may be cheap, and even disposable if it isn't lived to the hilt. In sum, Black youth's craving for respect often feeds directly but unintentionally into actions that bring them into conflict with the law (Gillborn, 1998).

Police occupational subcultures also make virtues out of toughness, assertiveness, and control. These virtues, or values, are further strengthened by the notion that the police are the "thin blue line" that protects the civilized from the barbarians. As a result, the police subculture has developed the following norms: deference to police authority and control, respect for the badge, a dislike of uncertainty or disorder, an acceptance of extreme police tactics if they are seen as necessary, limited tolerance for deviance, relatively rigid definitions of right and wrong, a distinction between those who police do things *for* and those they do things *to*, and a suspicion of those who criticize police authority (Ungerleider, 1995). The police deeply resent those segments of the community that defy their authority or resist arrest (whatever the offence), because in doing so they are rejecting their subcultural code of ethics. According to Holdaway (1996), those who challenge a police officer are violating the sanctity of the uniform. A lack of respect for the badge may invite physical retaliation.

The need to look efficient and in control at all times is central to police work (James and Warren, 1995). Police are employed by the state to exercise control by enforcing laws. Yet enforcement can happen only when police are in control of the situation. Police overreaction is more likely in situations where control is difficult because of hostile audiences, uncooperative victims, abusive offenders, or intoxicated patrons (Ungerleider, 1995). Overreaction is also likely in situations where police conceptions of normalcy and order are contested; where the advice of police is disre-spected; where police are denied their status as legitimate authority; and where police are dealing with those whom they have typecast as deviant, dangerous, complaining, and discredited (James and Warren, 1995). When a controlling authority confronts an increasingly uncontrollable force, the potential for confrontation is only too real.

"WHAT YOU SEE DEPENDS ON WHERE YOU STAND"

It should now be quite obvious that police and minority youth hold strong stereotypes of each other. However inaccurate or distorted these stereo-types are, they are decidedly real in terms of their consequences. Where stereotypes are involved, perception *is* reality, and this has serious reper-cussions. Regarding the police, stereotyping can reduce morale and drive officers out of the force; it has also been linked to suicide. Regarding minorities, stereotypes can easily damage lives and life chances. Both sides need to rethink their attitudes. That being said, the onus falls on the police to identify and eliminate barriers to improved service rather than on those who have no choice but to deal with the police (Ramsden, 1995).

Law enforcement is based on a simple principle: the police have certain powers over the rest of society, and people are expected to defer to those powers (*New York Times*, February 27, 2000). But at the same time, demo-cratic societies expect their law enforcement agents to be answerable to the community. To date, police have been moderately successful at improving communication with the public. Unfortunately, positive reforms in policing are being stymied by entrenched subcultural values that revere a "kick ass" style of policing based on an "us against them" mentality (Eng, 2000). The police as an institution seem reluctant to involve the community; except in the most superficial way, they prefer to remain a closed shop. The police per-ceive criticisms of their work as unwarranted, meddlesome, or inaccurate. Not surprisingly, they respond like any other group—by becoming even more defensive and inward-looking (Forcese, 2000). This mixture of defensiveness and suspicion, paranoia and hostility, only widens the gap between police and public.

Today's urban police work in a pressure-cooker. They are required to make split-second decisions in life-or-death situations, and those decisions can always be second-guessed. They are accused of brutality, harassment, double-standards, intimidation, abuse, corruption, and racism. In this more and more diverse society, their effectiveness and efficiency are increasingly being questioned. Put bluntly, parts of the public are losing confidence in them, and raising questions in the process. Is police misconduct a matter of isolated acts, or is it pervasive and structurally rooted? Is policing marred by a few bad apples, or is the system rotten at the core? What is it about policing that creates bad police officers? Is it the recruitment and selection process? The nature of police work? The organizational framework of policing? Negative work experiences? Or is it that certain personality types gravitate toward policing? Community-oriented policing is seen as one way of defusing the growing crisis in police legitimacy and of restoring the public's confidence in the police.

PROFESSIONAL CRIME-FIGHTERS

Canada's police are an agency of the state within the criminal justice system (McDougall, 1988). They are an expression of the state's power and have a monopoly on the use of coercive force. They are empowered to fight crime and enforce the law within the framework of Canadian democratic traditions. The police have many functions, but most of these relate to two activities: protection and service. In terms of protection, they have the primary responsibility for enforcing laws and maintaining public order. To this end, they solve crimes and arrest the perpetrators. They have perfected ways to respond quickly to serious crimes, to allay public anxieties about crime, and to soften political pressure. The police lose some of their effectiveness unless concerned citizens report crimes quickly and provide relevant information about them, and cooperate with the police in prosecuting and sentencing offenders.

At all levels—federal, provincial, and municipal—Canada's police have relied mainly on a professional crime-fighting model (Cryderman et al., 1998). This model was first developed in the United States as a means of reforming a system in which corruption was widespread, services were delivered selectively, and political interference at the precinct level was a fact of life. A commitment to professionalism kept politicians and the community at arm's length from the police. It also defined the police as a highly trained force with a shared identity and code of ethics. Police were judged by how visible they were on the street (i.e., as a deterrent); by how quickly they responded to calls for service; by their arrest, conviction, and "clearance" rates; and by how satisfied the public was. An "incident-driven" approach predominated (Eck, 1986), and this gave rise to "complaint-reactive" or "crime-fighting" models of policing.

One result of all this was that administrators set out to bureaucratize policing. Police departments were organized as paramilitary bureaucracies: chains of command and control were strictly top-down; law enforcement was by the book; internal rules and regulations developed into a compulsion; and checks and balances were established to deter corruption, enhance control, and monitor activities. To some extent, rewards and promotions were allocated on the basis of the "big catch." Promotion became largely a matter of time served.

Under this professional crime-fighting model, certain assumptions about the community came to prevail. The police saw themselves as a "thin blue line" between the community and chaos, and their role in terms of keeping disorder at bay. At the same time, they began discouraging community involvement. Citizens were expected to report crimes to the police by way of the 911 system, to provide information on possible criminal activities, and to help police arrest and convict lawbreakers (Tomovich and Loree, 1989). Beyond that, however, police involvement with the community was minimal, and reluctant at best. This estrangement was captured by Sergeant Friday of the TV series *Dragnet*: in his immortal words, "Nothing but the facts, ma'am."

In other words, police–community relations were typified by exclusion. Crime control is perceived as the function of a distant albeit professional bureaucracy. Community participation was dismissed as irrelevant to the social control process. Only by distancing themselves from the community could the police discharge their duties in a professional manner.

Under this regime, the police and the community drifted apart. Of course, not all police services subscribed to this model; for example, small-town forces could afford a more personal style. But many urban forces embraced it in the mistaken belief that it marked them as professionals. This professional crime-fighting model continues to inform the values and visions of urban policing.

C*O*P*S: Community-Oriented Policing

Recent changes in the social, political, and demographic environment have challenged the very foundations of Canadian policing and created a crisis of confidence. Debates are evolving in many directions. "What are police *for*?" "What mandate do the police have, and what is their underlying philosophy?" "What should the public expect of the police?" "How should the police be organized?" "How should officers actually go about their work?" "What is the optimum relationship between the police and the community?" Clearly, a new approach toward policing is required to meet the demands of an increasingly diverse and demanding population. In particular, police forces must be weaned away from the exclusionary models that for many years have shaped their relations with the community.

Community-oriented policing (C*O*P*S) is now seen as a valid approach to reforming police work (Fleras, 1998). Community policing allows for variations in policing styles (Bayley, 1994). Its objective is to create police services that are responsive to the needs and concerns of diverse and demanding communities. It sets out to establish more meaningful working relationships with local communities; the goal in this is to *prevent* crime by solving problems before they generate crime. This necessarily involves the police sharing at least some of their power with communities, while accepting communities as active participants in crime prevention (Cole, 1998). The police, for their part, are expected to shed their "crimebuster" approach and show willingness to cooperate with those they are supposedly serving and protecting (see Shusta et al., 1995).

To date, no generally accepted definition of community policing exists. Is community policing a paradigm? a philosophy? a strategy? a program? Broadly speaking, community policing involves fostering a more responsive relationship between the police and the communities they serve and protect (Jain et al., 2000). More specifically, community-oriented policing is a commitment by the police to prevent crime by collaborating with an interested public (see Moir and Moir, 1993). Four principles underpin this commitment to community-oriented policing:

Partnership: A partnership is committed to the ideal of police working with the community to prevent crime. It involves the police adjusting their perceptions of the community. It rejects the notion that the police are the experts and that only they have the credentials to control crime. Instead, the police are seen as "facilitators" and "resource personnel" who work cooperatively alongside citizens.

Prevention: Arguably, all policing is about crime prevention. Conventional policing endorses the idea that law enforcement is the main deterrent to crime. In contrast, community policing promotes prevention through community partnership. Proactive approaches confront problems before they arise by putting police and the community in touch with each other.

Problem solving: Problem solving is central to community policing. Many have pointed out the futility of responding over and over to the actions of a small number of offenders in a given area. An approach is required that diagnoses the causes instead of simply treating the symptoms (Saville and Rossmo, 1995). Under a problem-solving strategy, the causes of recurrent problems are isolated and identified, alternative solutions are evaluated, one or more solutions are applied, impacts are monitored, and solutions are redesigned if the first ones don't work.

Power sharing: In community policing, the police must share their power with the community (Doone, 1989). Otherwise, community policing is simply tokenism or a publicity stunt that simply offloads responsibilities for burdensome tasks. Police are facing pressure to share their power by loosening up their organizational structures, by transferring their authority and resources to communities, and by implementing mutually agreed-upon goals. Without meaningful power sharing, creative solutions to crime cannot be found and implemented.

In Canada, community-oriented policing has already been very successful—up to a point. Almost every police service in the country now accepts the principles of community-oriented policing and has enshrined those principles in a mission statement. It has been proved in many cities and towns, including Edmonton, Victoria, and Oakville, that community-oriented policing can work.

But in most municipalities, principles are one thing and implementation and practice have been something else. In this regard, the reality gap is broad (Fleras, 1998). Community policing is a profound change in *thinking* about policing, but its actual effects have been weakened by debates over goals and implementation (Cardarelli et al., 1998). It is often neutralized by police cultures that challenge and resist it (Neugebauer, 1999); it is further weakened by police bureaucracies that endorse conservatism, distance from the community, hierarchy, division of labour, and a paramilitary chain of command. Improvements in police–minority relations are hampered by the realities of incident-driven policing, which focuses on charges and arrests, and by ineffective training in diversity awareness. Typically, the training most officers receive in community policing is conducted by poorly prepared instructors who may lack knowledge or commitment. Training in cultural sensitivity often reinforces the stereotypes it is meant to eradicate (Ungerleider, 1992). Educating police officers about different cultures too often reinforces the idea of minorities as removed, remote, and irrelevant (Holdaway, 1996). Not surprisingly, the drive for community-oriented policing has sputtered and stalled in many jurisdictions.

Toward Multicultural Policing

Multicultural policing is a natural outgrowth of community-based policing. The two are similar in aims and philosophy, in that they share a commitment to prevention, power sharing, partnership, and problem solving. Any differences tend to be of emphasis rather than content or outcomes. In both the objective is foster policing that minority groups perceive as "safe."

Multicultural policing is a variation of community policing that applies the principles of multiculturalism throughout the law enforcement process. Community policing considers the community at large; in contrast, multicultural policing applies the principles of inclusiveness to the policing of minority communities. There are two key points to be made here. *First*, the professional crime control model with its one-size-fits-all mentality cannot possibly be acceptable to minority women and men (see La Prairie, 1992). Multicultural policing focuses instead on customizing services to meet community needs. *Second*, multicultural policing is firmly committed to inclusiveness and is responsive to differences. This involves more than hiring minorities, and more than building good working relationships with the civilian population. Multiculturally inclusive policing must be willing to reinvent the structure and process of police services.

Multicultural policing takes differences seriously as a basis for "smart policing." As a style of policing, it is keenly sensitive to minority values, in contrast to the past, when monocultural values dominated police–minority encounters. Multicultural policing accepts diversity in both principle and practice. It is about policing *of* the multicultural community, *in* the multicultural community, *for* the multicultural community, and *by* the multicultural community. This commitment to diversity is reflected in a police service's procedures for hiring, training, and promoting officers, in its workplace climate, and in its communications with the minority groups it is serving. Multicultural policing is critical if the police are to close the cultural gaps that distance them from minority women and men, and that prevent strong communication (see also McNeill, 1994).

To be effective, multicultural policing must reflect the communities it serves (Jain et al., 2000). New recruitment, selection, and promotion strategies are increasing the number of minority officers. For example, 8.7 percent of Metro Toronto's police are visible minorities; this is much less than the percentage in the population as a whole, but the force is heading in the right direction—28 percent of new hires since 1997 have been officers of colour (Duncanson, 1999). The recruitment of minority police officers is generally considered the necessary first step toward restoring the confidence of communities in law enforcement. Most forces now have specific policies ensuring that new hires will reflect the local population. Various recruitment strategies are being employed: openings are advertised heavily in the ethnic media; police forces take booths at job fairs and career days at local high schools; and police services appeal directly to minority organizations within the community. Also, visible minority police officers are encouraged to recruit within their own communities.

Finally, the police are loosening their weight and height restrictions, which for decades discriminated against minority applicants. The RCMP now allows turbans as head coverings so that Sikhs can join the force; the Peel Regional Police permit Sikh officers to carry the *kirpan*, the Sikhs' ceremonial sword; and the Calgary police and the RCMP now permit First Nations officers to wear their hair in braids. All of these rule adjustments, however modest or symbolic, signify a growing willingness by the police to accept diversity.

To sum up: The police can no longer afford to take diversity lightly. Canada is in the midst of a demographic revolution, and multicultural policing models are eventually going to be imposed. Police at all levels must become better acquainted with the multicultural community in terms of its various needs, entitlements, demands, and expectations. The police must become more inclusive if they are to improve their public image in certain minority communities and to attract more aboriginal people and racialized minorities into the service. The best route to achieving this progress is a variation on community policing. The old model, with its emphasis on more police, more arrests, and more prosecutions is not going to work. Policing is going to have to focus on prevention, on community relations, and on involving the community in punishment and rehabilitation (Cole, 1998).

Of course, it is going to be difficult to transform multicultural rhetoric into practice in light of political and economic constraints. Radical changes will be necessary if the police are to embrace diversity, and police bureaucracies, being so conservative and inward-looking, are hardly eager to make them. Nonetheless, the police are slowly beginning to accept that their work must be community-based, culturally sensitive, and racially aware. Improvements in police–minority relations are noticeable. But until the police fully accept multicultural communities as partners in preventing crime, genuinely multicultural policing is likely to remain elusive.

RETHINKING ABORIGINAL JUSTICE

Justice or Travesty?

Consider what passes for justice in parts of Canada. Sitting at the front of a threadbare community centre room is a white judge, 3 white lawyers, a Crown prosecutor, 2 legal aid lawyers, and 4 burly white RCMP officers. In a line at the back of the room sits a row of grim-faced aboriginal youth in ski jackets and sneakers. Over the next three days, upwards to a 150 people will be shuffled through the court room, most of whom will be charged with assaults, break and enters, and domestic abuse, usually under the influence and drinking at the time. Most of the youth who are charged rarely do damage or steal anything: Many prefer to break into stores and eat chips and drink pop—just for something to do or to be caught. The objective is to "book" into an urban jail where they can escape from a desperate combination of boredom, hopelessness, and despair.

Court is held once every other month when the judge and a court reporter fly in from Yellowknife, spend a few days in sessions, then fly out with the lawyers to other outposts in Northern Canada. Sessions are assembled in a gym or community centre, on plain folding tables, with most of the town turning up to watch. Unlike the glacial-like speed of court trials in southern Canada, the court moves at a bewildering pace to accommodate a packed docket of backlogged cases. The legal aid workers spend only minutes with the accused before cases are called. Stock arguments are aired about the defendant taking anger management counselling. Community reaction is muted when a judge sentences a 16 year old with a text book thick criminal record. Most youth appear only vaguely aware of their legal rights; nor do they take any interest in the functions of the court or court procedures such as legal aid. Many plead guilty because they either do not understand the concept of legal guilt and innocence or are fearful of exercising their rights (CCJA, 2000). Those who are sentenced to jail fly out with the judge to Yellowknife or to a juvenile detention centre in Hay River. (from Stephanie Nolen, "Where Jail is Sometimes the Only Way Out of Town." *The Globe and Mail*, March 21, 2000)

Aboriginal peoples have high expectations of the criminal justice system. They believe that the system should prevent crime, resolve disputes, protect individuals and communities from disorder and disruption, and rehabilitate offenders (La Prairie, 2000). Yet the criminal justice system seems to have betrayed aboriginal peoples, who are disproportionately represented at all levels of criminal justice, from police encounters to incarceration in federal prisons and provincial jails. As a result, the call is going out for more responsive justice that reflects aboriginal people's unique needs and aspirations. This has resulted in various initiatives: aboriginal values and personnel are being incorporated into the criminal justice system; parallel justice systems are being developed, such as band policing on reserves; spiritual therapies are being introduced into prisons (Waldrom, 1997); and community-based, non-incarcerative alternatives to jail—such as sentencing circles and healing lodges—are coming into favour (Cunningham, 1998; CCJA, 2000).

Yet concerns continue to mount. Aboriginal people are still alienated from the criminal justice system, which is often indifferent to them, or discriminates against them, or is simply incompetent to deal fairly with them. Any long-lasting solution to the problems of aboriginal justice must go beyond superficial add-ons. But justice for aboriginal people is easier to talk about than to do. Mainstream criminal justice tends to be punitive, to resist change and prefer conformity. It is not going to be easy to return to aboriginal people control over the justice that applies to them.

Crisis in Aboriginal Communities

Nearly four hundred years of colonial contact have been a disaster for aboriginal peoples (Alfred, 1999). In some cases, government policies set out deliberately to divest aboriginal peoples of their land, culture, and tribal authority. In other cases, aboriginal peoples were subdued through less direct but equally powerful measures—specifically, the education and missionary systems. In still other cases, government policies were well intentioned but ultimately misguided; for example, residential schools did a great deal to marginalize aboriginal peoples (Miller, 1996; Adams, 1998).

By any measure used, aboriginal peoples are among the most disadvantaged in Canada. Their communities suffer badly from overcrowding, poor housing, dirty water, and inadequate waste systems (CCJA, 2000). Their unemployment rate is three times the national average, and this is a direct cause of poor housing, poor health, cultural disintegration, and social decay (Drost et al., 1995). On some reserves 95 percent of the people are on welfare or related programs. Many reserves are geographically isolated and have limited resources and so have difficulty attracting development money. Yet many aboriginal people are reluctant to abandon reserves for fear of losing their entitlements. The end result is dispiriting, as Carol La Prairie points out:

> Socially stratified communities where limited resources and resource distribution create large groups of disadvantaged people, a growing youth subculture with few legitimate outlets or opportunities, decontextualized exposure to the mass media, and the lack of cultural and social resources to assist in identity formation which support pro-social values. (La Prairie, 1996: 63)

Conditions are often just as grim for those who have drifted into Canada's cities. Urban aboriginal people experience high unemployment; they also tend to have few skills, live in derelict housing, and survive on inadequate services; yet at the same time they are cut off from federal funding or reserve benefits. Only 20 percent of aboriginal students finish secondary school. Aboriginal people have long been disenchanted with the European education system, though admittedly this is changing: in the 1960s there were only 200 native students in Canada's postsecondary schools; by 1997 there were 27,487 (Simpson, 1998). With a birthrate that is 70 percent higher than that of the general population, aboriginal communities are getting younger, and as a result, band resources are being stretched. Aboriginal youth on reserves suffer badly from powerlessness, alienation, and irrelevance (Shkilnyk, 1985). As noted by a former president of the Manitoba Indian Brotherhood:

> One hundred years of submission and servitude, of protectionism and paternalism, have created psychological barriers for Indian people that are far more difficult to break down and conquer than the problems of economic and social poverty. (David Courchene, cited in Buckley, 1992: 24)

This powerlessness is reflected in high rates of alcohol abuse; each year, as many as 20 percent of aboriginal people are admitted to hospital for an alcohol-related illness (CCJA, 2000). White people's racism and indifference are also reflected in aboriginal people's feelings of self-hatred. Aboriginal people are nearly four times more likely than other Canadians to die violently; domestic and sexual abuse are rampant in their communities; and among some age groups, aboriginal suicide rates are as much as six times the national average. Sadly, Canada's aboriginal peoples are among the most self-destructive in the world—this even though Canada as a society is widely perceived as among the world's best.

A Criminal *In*justice System

Aboriginal peoples have had a troubled relationship with the criminal justice system (CCJA, 2000). That system has always miscalculated their social realities and cultural needs in imposing Eurocentric mechanisms of social control. Accused who are aboriginals are more likely to be denied bail. They also spend more time in pretrial detention, are less likely to have legal representation, are more than twice as likely to be incarcerated, and are more likely to plead guilty as a result of intimidation or indifference. A 1996 report concluded that aboriginals were eleven times more likely than nonaboriginals to be in provincial jails, and five times more likely to be in federal penitentiaries. Aboriginal people are about 3 percent of Canada's population but 17 percent

147

of its prison and jail population. According to Statistics Canada, in Western Canada 64 percent of federal prisoners are aboriginal, even though they are only 12 percent of that region's population. Nearly three-quarters of aboriginal males have spent time in a correctional centre by the age of twenty-five.

Aboriginal crime differs in kind from mainstream crime. Aboriginal offenders tend toward violent and social disorder offences; these are often alcohol-related and directed at family members or other aboriginals. They also commit fewer property crimes and "crimes for profit" such as embezzlement and drug trafficking (CCJA, 2000). Admittedly, these statistics may be misleading, since offenders may be convicted for petty offences and serve time for offences that require only a fine. Also, the figures may be inflated by a small number of individuals who repeatedly get into trouble with the law (Buckley, 1992). Nevertheless, the revolving door of incarceration and recidivism has stripped many aboriginal peoples of their self-esteem; in turn this has generated cycles of despair and decay.

Aboriginals have entered the criminal justice system in disproportionate numbers for various historical and socioeconomic reasons. Their values conflict with those of the dominant culture; colonialism and capitalism have resulted in their social and economic deprivation; the justice system discriminates against them; social control has weakened within their own communities as a result of cultural unravelling; and poverty and isolation have weakened them in their dealings with the state (Hartnagel, 2000). Years of oppression and neglect have marginalized aboriginal communities. The end result? Unacceptably high crime rates, weak or nonexistent skills for surviving in white society, dysfunctional families, substance abuse problems, and limited access to educational, recreational, or employment opportunities (CCJA, 2000). For all these reasons, aboriginal crime is less a crime problem than a social problem.

Competing Justice Systems

To say that Canada's criminal justice system has had a profoundly troubled relationship with aboriginal peoples is an understatement (Royal Commission, 1996; Green, 1998). For some native people, prisons are intimidating and terrifying. Incarceration severely damages those aboriginal offenders for whom confinement is embarrassing or awkward (CCJA, 2000). Other native people are indifferent to mainstream justice, and perceive jail time as a badge of honour rather than a stigma, so it does no good to imprison them (Waldram, 1997). For still others, the court process is an alien process that inflicts more harm than it does good.

Aboriginal peoples are now seeking an alternative criminal justice system. The contrasts with the Eurocentric model could not be more striking. The mainstream criminal justice system emphasizes punishing the deviant to ensure future conformity and to protect other members of society. The aboriginal system emphasizes healing and reconciliation, the restoration of peace and equilibrium to the community, the avoidance of confrontation, and the preservation of relationships in a spirit of generosity and sharing. In aboriginal justice the restoration of harmony is the main objective; the punishment and the determination of guilt are secondary. Aboriginal justice rejects abstract principles as contrary to the holistic nature of justice. It focuses on reconciling the individual with other individuals, with the family, and with the community, and on integrating the spiritual with the social, cultural, and economic (see Green, 1998, for additional information). In short, the aboriginal justice system is far more conciliatory, the Eurocentric model far more punitive and adversarial (but see Daly, 2000). Table 5.1 compares the two systems.

TABLE 5.1

Criminal Justice System vs. Aboriginal Justice

Mainstream	Aboriginal
Crime is a transgression against the state.	Crime reflects a rupture in the relationship between victim and wrongdoer against the backdrop of the community.
Criminal justice system is the primary source of social control.	Community is the primary source of social control.
Crime is framed in legal terms, with emphasis on abstract principles of right and wrong. The accused has the right to plead not guilty even if he or she has committed the offence.	Crime is framed in terms of how it affects victims and the community, especially when public peace is threatened. Emphasis is on context and consequences of the action. The social, cultural, and spiritual are taken into account.
Process is adversarial, and outcomes are passive.	Process is nonconfrontational, conciliatory, and cooperative. Offender involvement is encouraged in healing the breach.
Restitution for wrongdoing is to the state.	Restitution is to victim and to community in hopes of restoring social order.
Punishment focus.	Focus on healing and rehabilitation.

149

TABLE 5.1 (continued)

Mainstream	Aboriginal
Victim is ignored.	Victims are foregrounded by restoring a sense of control over their lives. Offender is encouraged to take responsibility for his or her actions.
Focus on mental state of offender to determine guilt and assign punishment.	Holistic focus on the social and spiritual needs of offender to determine what went wrong, what can be done to ease the suffering, and how to deter future occurrences.
Benefits reflect the principle that the criminal justice system is a law unto itself.	Benefits are to capitalize on the transformative potential of restorative justice to create a more just society.
Function of justice is to ensure conformity, punish deviant behaviour, rehabilitate offender, and protect society.	Function is to heal offender, restore community harmony, reconcile offender with victim/family; punishment is of secondary emphasis.

However appealing aboriginal justice may be in principle, no one should underestimate the challenges involved in merging it with the Eurocetric system. Legal principles are not "neutral"; neither are criminal justice principles (1999, Law Commissioner of Canada, Discussion Paper, *From Restorative Justice to Transformative Justice*: Ottawa). Both are "loaded" with ideological assumptions that endorse certain values and marginalize others. The criminal justice system is strongly political, in that struggles take place within it regarding who controls whom. This makes it difficult for the system to incorporate alternative systems with clashing ideological bases.

Aboriginal Justice as Restorative Justice

Aboriginal justice closely resembles restorative justice, and both differ from the criminal justice system with respect to crime, corrections, and punishment. Canada's criminal justice system revolves around determining blame and administrating pain; also, it amounts to a procedural contest between a lawyer and the state (Blumenthal, 1999). It is an adversarial system in which offenders are coaxed to distance themselves from the consequences of their actions. Throughout this process, the victim and the community are largely ignored. The result is a no-win situation for many: victims and their families are deeply scarred, the offender's family is left in turmoil, and the community is angered and frightened.

In contrast, restorative justice focuses on restoring the relationships in the community that have been disrupted by crime. This approach has many benefits: it draws attention to victims; it makes offenders accountable; it fosters responsibility, which in turn promotes healing and ensures reparations; and it provides a means for reintegrating victims with offenders and thereby rebuilding the community. Restorative justice, when it works, repairs the wrong that was done, and also negotiates an outcome that restores harmony and avoids a repetition of the crime (Cayley, 1999). Those who have been injured are consoled, and are helped to reclaim their personal power. Prisons remain an option rather than a main objective. The victims feel less forgotten, and the offenders are shamed yet also reintegrated. And of course restorative justice is less expensive than sending people to prison (Layton, 1999).

In short, the differences between restorative and retributive justice could not be more striking, in theory if not in practice (Daly, 2000). The retributive justice system asks three basic questions of a criminal act: "What law was broken? Who did it? What penalty should be handed out?" A restorative approach asks these three: "Who was harmed? What harm was done? Whose responsibility is it to make things right?"

Aboriginal justice has much in common with the restorative model. The victim is brought into the process, the offenders take responsibility for their actions, and the community is involved in negotiating and implementing a solution. A punitive, adversarial style gives way to a holistic approach based on the principles of community, relationships, healing, recovery, reparations, and atonement. Community participation is encouraged in the sentencing, and aboriginal offenders are supervised through alternative measures that do not include prison or jail time (Green, 1998). The goal is to reduce incarceration rates by diverting offenders toward community-based mediation committees. Sentencing circles include the accused, his or her family, the victim, and members of the community. The goals are varied, but generally, they include looking for ways to change the offender's circumstances, bringing together community resources, restoring harmony, and promoting law-abiding behaviour; they do not include punishing the criminal act (CCJA, 2000).

These initiatives have been both praised and disparaged (Daly, 2000). Critics typically point to the lack of effectiveness of these programs. Put bluntly, there are still far too many aboriginal people in correctional institutions, especially in the West (La Prairie, 1999). Alternative initiatives are also criticized as political strategies that do nothing to diminish state control over criminal justice—as a form of neocolonialism that further disempowers aboriginal people (Tauri, 1996, 1999). And it is suggested that alternatives for aboriginal justice won't work without broader changes to society (La Prairie, 1999). Moreover, without adequate resources, justice programs can't be any better than quick fixes, and may do more harm than good.

TOWARD INCLUSIVENESS

Efforts to improve relations between the criminal justice system and aboriginal peoples have taken several approaches. These range from the modest to the radical, and fall into four categories:

- *Responsiveness*: Modify the existing system to ensure equal treatment by removing discriminatory barriers and prejudicial attitudes.
- *Indigenization*: Foster a more indigenized criminal justice system by including aboriginal values and personnel where appropriate.
- *Parallel*: Create a parallel system of criminal justice for aboriginal peoples that replicates the conventional system but is run entirely by aboriginal people. For example, since 1991 a First Nations Policing Policy has provided aboriginal communities with access to police services that are both culturally appropriate and accountable to the communities they serve (CCJA, 2000).
- *Separate*: Establish an indigenous criminal justice system run *by* aboriginal people *for* aboriginal people that reflects the needs and advances the aspirations of aboriginal people. Proposals for a separate system cannot be divorced from aboriginal models of self-government (CCJA, 2000; Fleras, 2000). To be sure, a separate justice system within a self-governing arrangement is unlikely to solve all problems. Even so, it should be regarded as a positive step and as an improvement over the current quagmire.

Time will tell whether inclusive justice principles will advance the healing process for aboriginal peoples. Questions remain: What should be the relationship between aboriginal peoples and the criminal justice system? Should there be one set of rules for all Canadians, or should justice be customized to reflect the diverse realities of aboriginal peoples? Should individuals take full responsibility for their actions, or must historical and social circumstances be incorporated in any assessment of wrongdoing? Should all crime be punished equally, or is it better to ensure that differences are taken into account when decisions are made? Is it racist and paternalistic to imply that racial or ethnic background should be a factor in sentencing? Or does such a concession acknowledge the importance of social and cultural factors in securing a truly multicultural society? Most important, can any substantial change occur without transforming the still colonialist foundational principles that govern aboriginal peoples–state relations (Maaka and Fleras, 2000)?

CASE STUDY (Continued)
Putting Aboriginality Back into the Justice System
Inclusiveness or Political Correctness?

The Emard ruling has inspired a range of negative comments. It has also been a fertile source of misunderstanding regarding the "inclusivizing" of criminal justice. It has also raised a number of key issues regarding the changing relationship between Canada and its citizens—but especially its aboriginal peoples. Any failure to appreciate the underlying dynamics behind this ruling will only hinder the advance of a multicultural Canada.

First the misunderstandings. The ruling does not single out certain ethnic groups or categories of people for differential treatment. Rather, all Canadians now have the multicultural right to have their social and cultural circumstances considered during sentencing. This is consistent with other "cultural" defences such as "Black rage," and acknowledges the importance of social context and historical factors in shaping states of mind that may culminate in criminal actions.

Nor does the Emard ruling undermine the concept that everyone is equal before the law. It does, however, advance the still radical notion that true equality before the law requires us to take differences into account. A one-size-fits-all approach may sound good in theory. In reality, this sort of uniformity may have the unintended effect of freezing an unequal status quo. The Young Offenders Act is merely one example of a vulnerable minority receiving customized treatment.

Equally incorrect is the perception that the Emard ruling absolves aboriginal people of guilt or responsibility. In the case of Ms. Emard, the issue was not "guilty or no?" but rather the appropriate level of punishment. In other words, individuals are still to be held responsible for their actions. Nevertheless, criminal actions do not occur in a social void; rather, they reflect options and choices in contexts that constrain and influence.

Second the context. The Emard ruling was hardly based on race. It was not designed to excuse the criminal act of an aboriginal person or to keep her out of jail because she was aboriginal. Rather, the issue was one of aboriginal rights. In terms of status, aboriginal peoples are not ethnic minorities or ordinary citizens. More accurately, they are fundamentally autonomous political communities, both sovereign and sharing sovereignty with Canada (Asch, 1997; Alfred, 1999; Fleras, 2000). As descendants of the original inhabitants, they hold rights related to culture, land, and political voice that have yet to be extinguished. These rights not only articulate a special relationship with the Crown and the Canadian state, but also provide a rationale for differential treatment.

Third the reality. Initiatives to keep aboriginal people out of jail may have nothing to do with aboriginal rights and everything to do with reducing the grossly disproportional number of aboriginal people kept in expensive and overcrowded jails. The Supreme Court has urged judges to find alternatives to jail for aboriginal offenders, given that they are imprisoned at rates disproportionate to their numbers. Amendments to the Criminal Code in 1996 encouraged judges to consider both the offender's background and alternatives to prison. Prisons hardly rehabilitate aboriginal inmates; instead they are little more than "barbwire" universities that confer degrees in criminality. At a time when community-based alternatives to traditional imprisonment are gaining in popularity, decisions to postpone jailing aboriginal offenders are enlightened. Decisions like *Emard* concede the obvious: the criminal justice system is not working for all Canadians, and something needs to be done before the system collapses.

Finally the broader context. In a multicultural society such as Canada, two sets of rights prevail. (A) Everyone has the right to be treated equally by the law. (B) Everyone also has the right to have his or her cultural differences taken into account by the law. Neither of these "rights" is more "right" than the other; they are fundamentally opposed because they are equally valid. The Emard case has tried to reconcile this tension.

How much diversity can be tolerated in a multicultural criminal justice system? Is there a distinction between multicultural criminal justice and a criminal justice system based on the principles of multiculturalism? How do we reconstruct a system that is safe *for* diversity, as well as safe *from* ethnicity? Where do we draw the line in a rapidly changing and increasingly diverse society? Answers to these questions are elusive, but the essence of being Canadian may lie in constantly adjusting to different levels of ambiguity and compromise as a basis for living together with differences.

Sources: Cori Howard, "Racial Background Key Part of Argument at Sentencing Hearing," *The Globe and Mail*, January 11, 1999; Lisa Birnie,

"An Ill-Advised Native Rider," *The Globe and Mail*, January 15, 1999; Editorial, "Crime, Time, and Race," *The Globe and Mail*, January 16, 1999; Jonathan Rudin, "Aboriginal Offenders and the Criminal Code," *The Globe and Mail*, February 9, 1999.

Chapter Highlights

- The criminal justice system is experiencing a crisis because of its failure to cope with the demands and challenges of an increasingly multicultural society. This country's institutions are failing to respond to requirements for more inclusiveness.
- The criminal justice system is moving slowly toward multicultural inclusiveness, against resistance at both personal and systemic levels.
- Police and minorities continue to distrust each other. Minority youth tend to see themselves as victims of mispolicing. Police tend to see themselves as responding to a minority youth subculture of guns, drugs, and lawbreaking.
- Police and minorities have stereotyped each other, with plenty of negative consequences. For example, neither knows how to "decode" each other's communication styles, nor do they know how to understand each other's subcultural values.
- Canada's police have long relied on a professional crime-fighting model. With a commitment to community-oriented policing, this will change: policing will become more responsive, and be based on the principles of community partnership, power sharing, prevention, and proactivity.
- Multicultural policing resembles C*O*P*S with respect to basic principles. Differences tend to reflect a commitment to a policing *of* the multicultural community, *for* the multicultural community, *in* the multicultural community, and *by* the multicultural community.
- For many structural and cultural reasons, Canada's aboriginal peoples are disproportionately represented in the criminal justice system.
- Canada's criminal justice system seems to be at odds with the needs, values, and aspirations of aboriginal people. Many are proposing a system of aboriginal justice based on restorative principles.
- Efforts to provide alternative sentencing for aboriginal people sound good in theory. In reality, there is some resentment toward any treatment that is perceived as taking differences seriously and providing some Canadians with special rights and privileges.

Review Questions

1. Describe the crisis that confronts the criminal justice system in Canada's multicultural society.
2. What reforms would create a more inclusive criminal justice system that is consistent with the principles of multiculturalism?
3. There is a growing crisis in police–minority relations. Describe this crisis. What measures are police in Canada taking to improve their relations with aboriginal and minority communities?
4. Compare community and multicultural policing with conventional styles of policing in terms of objectives, styles, and outcomes. In what ways do community and multicultural policing result in more inclusive responses to diversity and change?
5. Describe the crisis in criminal justice as it applies to Canada's aboriginal peoples. Why are aboriginal people overrepresented in the criminal justice system?
6. Compare aboriginal justice with Eurocentric-style justice under these four headings: goals, underlying assumptions, methods, and expected outcomes.
7. Is it possible to construct a criminal justice system that takes differences seriously? Or is criminal justice in Canada best served by treating everyone as equal before the law? Explain.

Recommended Reading

Aboriginal Peoples and the Criminal Justice System. Special Issue of the Bulletin. 2000. Ottawa: Canadian Criminal Justice Association.

Janet Chan. 1997. *Changing Police Culture: Policing in a Multicultural Society.* Cambridge: Cambridge University Press.

Brian Cryderman, Chris O'Toole, and Augie Fleras. 1998. *Police, Race, and Ethnicity: A Guide for Police Services*, 3rd ed. Toronto: Butterworths.

Simon Holdaway. 1996. *The Racialisation of British Policing.* New York: St. Martin's Press.

Robin Neugebauer, ed. 2000. *Criminal Injustice: Racism and the Criminal Justice System.* Toronto: Canadian Scholars Press.

"The New Justice and Settler States: Crime, Justice, and Indigenous Peoples." 1999. *Australian and New Zealand Journal of Sociology.* Special Issue.

CHAPTER 6

Miscasting Minorities: Multiculturalism and the Mass Media

CHAPTER OBJECTIVES

- To draw attention to the complex issues surrounding media–minority relations.
- To explain how and why mainstream media continue to *mis*represent minority women and men at the level of newscasting, advertising, TV programming, and filmmaking.
- To show how media *mis*representations of minorities and aboriginal peoples tend to reflect the categories of the ghettoized (or invisible), the stigmatized (or stereotyped), the demonized (or problem people), the whitewashed, and the ornamentalized (or tokens).
- To demonstrate how media miscasting of minorities reflects a variety of factors, both individual and structural, both conscious and unconscious.
- To explain how media images of minorities continue to be shaped and compromised by media logic and dynamics.
- To expose the many factors that undermine media and minority efforts to improve inclusiveness in terms of verbal and visual images.
- To explain how the media defend ideology by way of systemic propaganda.
- To explore approaches to establishing inclusive and multicultural media.

CASE STUDY
Empowering the Arctic

Canada's media have long been perceived as key contributors to society building. This is especially true when it comes to public broadcasting. The CBC, and the federal acts that oversee it, have always had the mandate to include all Canadians. But this commitment to Canada as a community of communities has encountered difficulties when it comes to isolated and sparsely populated areas. Without access to the media, indigenous Canadians have difficulty establishing a sense of national identity within Canada. Nowhere is this more the case than with Canada's northernmost Canadians (Quasser, 1998; Marcus, 1995). Today, many Inuit communities are served by media that reflect their interests and priorities rather than those of the south, and this is encouraging. Canada's reputation as a world leader in northern and aboriginal communications is deserved. Yet each step forward is matched by reversals, as this case study demonstrates (Alia, 1999).

The CBC began operating a northern television service as far back as 1958 (radio broadcasting arrived in the North in the 1930s). It is part of the CBC's mandate to reflect, reinforce, and advance the experiences of all Canadians (McKie and Singer, 2001). To succeed at this it must produce high-quality programming that embraces Canada's diversity, secures its social and cultural fabric, and provides employment for Canadian artists. Yet however hard it tries, the CBC has found it difficult to escape a largely Toronto-centric interpretation of Canada.

The objectives of the CBC's northern service have long reflected a southern perspective (Raboy, 1990). The south's political and economic interests have prevailed. When the northern service began, Canada was intent on establishing its sovereignty in the North—a reflection of Cold War politics and of industrial expansion through mineral extraction. Yet because of distance barriers and isolation, the service turned out to be commercially unfeasible. Satellite technology changed this. With the Telsat Act of 1969, Canada was the first country to establish a domestic satellite transmission policy (Roth, 1995). Soon after the 1973 launch of Anik B, Canada's first domestic satellite, most Inuit communities were connected by satellite through radio, telephone, and TV. For example, the 4,000 inhabitants of Iqaluit on the southern tip of Baffin Island can now subscribe to twenty channels from mainland Canada and the United States (Quasser, 1998).

Northern aboriginal peoples enjoyed their commercial entertainment. Yet they faced this important question: How were they to reconcile traditional values with the modern images conveyed by television? Many feared that television would cut deeply into time-honoured pursuits and social interactions. Fears of a widening generation gap made it even more imperative for the Inuit to gain control over television messages and images. They accepted television as a powerful tool for ensuring their cultural survival, but the programming it carried had to mirror the social, cultural, and linguistic realities of the Far North.

The Inuit Broadcasting Corporation (IBC) was established in 1981 specifically to load the airwaves with Inuit-produced programs about themselves (Meadows, 1996). The IBC promised to balance CBC programming with Inuit programming that reflected the realities and concerns of local communities. It also promised significant funds to create programs in Inuit language ("Inuktitut") about Inuit culture and society (Kulchyski, 1989).

The IBC currently produces five hours of original programming per week that is nonviolent, family oriented, and respectful of Inuit traditions. "Real time" programming lacks much of the slickness of southern television but reflects a high degree of authenticity, in part because of the interaction between the producer and the community, thus allowing the community to "speak its own language" (Kulchyski, 1989). Surveys indicate that 90 percent of Inuit watch one to three hours a week of IBC programming, including *Takuginai* ("Look Here"), a kind of Inuit *Sesame Street*, and *Kippinguijautit* ("Things to Pass Time By") for showcasing Inuit talent and storytelling (Bergman, 1996; Hannon, 1999). Funds have also been set aside to redub CBC programming into Inuktitut, the language of the Inuit. Clearly, modern technology can help preserve indigenous language and culture when the service is locally owned, community based, and culturally sensitive. But there are problems, as the continuation of this case study will reveal.

A CRISIS IN REPRESENTATION

Canada has been widely proclaimed as a multicultural pacesetter in engaging diversity. Central to Canadian multiculturalism is our commitment to improving the responsiveness of our institutions to minority needs and concerns. Canada's intentions are good, and the praise we have received is often deserved, but we aren't perfect: there is a gap between the official rhetoric and institutional realities. Our mainstream institutions have been slow in responding to the multicultural commitments we have made (Fleras and Kunz, 2001).

Few institutions, except perhaps urban police forces, have been criticized as heavily as the mainstream media for failing to "inclusivize." The media's treatment of Canada's aboriginal people, people of colour, and immigrants and refugees is mixed at best, and deplorable at worst (Fleras, 1994; Henry and Tator, 2000). Minority women and men are still being victimized by questionable coverage on television and in print. This miscasting seems to have fallen into a pattern: minorities have been trivialized as irrelevant or inferior, *or* demonized as a social menace and threat to society, *or* scapegoated as problem people creating social problems, *or* ridiculed for being too different or not different enough, *or* "projected" through the prism of Eurocentric fears and fantasies, *or* subjected to double-standards that lampoon minorities regardless of what they do or don't do. Mainstream media continue to insult and caricaturize minority women and men through demeaning images and patronizing assessments (Shaheen, 2001). The impact of these negative depictions cannot be measured precisely. We *can* say that this miscasting has "othered" minorities as not quite Canadian (Fleras, 2001).

The mainstream media have been singled out as obviously negligent in engaging diversity (Siddiqui, 2001a, b). The contention that media are acting irresponsibly toward minorities is not to be taken lightly in view of Canada's multicultural commitments. The mainstream media are often the first and only point of contact in shaping public perceptions of minority women and men (Orbe and Harris, 2001). As defenders of ideology, the media constitute "machineries of meaning" in the sense that they convey powerful albeit coded messages about what is acceptable or not (Hannerz, 1992). The media also play an important role in defining what it means to be a Canadian (Bullock and Jafri, 2000).

It is only fair to note that the mainstream media have been experimenting with inclusiveness and are doing a better job nowadays at depicting minorities. Yet the progress toward inclusiveness has been ragged. Systemic bias and barriers in the media continue to whitewash minorities and to "other" them as invisible, as stereotypes, as problem people, and as cultural "decoration." In the media, minority women and men are accepted and neglected in turn, embraced and belittled at the same time.

This miscasting of minorities in the media is not random or accidental. Nor is it something out of the ordinary—a departure from an otherwise inclusive norm. Rather, it is deeply embedded in the media's structures and processes, which in turn are deeply influenced by the imperatives of free market capitalism. Furthermore, the miscasting of minorities is a key element in the mainstream media's defence of the dominant ideology (see Jakubowicz et al., 1994). Before we decide whether this is all too harsh and pessimistic, we must closely analyze the relationship between media power and minority disempowerment. Specifically, we must ask these questions about media miscasting:

- Are there problems in how the media represent minorities? Who says so, and on what grounds? How do these problems manifest themselves in news broadcasts, TV programming, advertising, and film?
- Who/what has caused this disjuncture between multicultural commitments and media realities? Why are media depictions of minorities so negative? Is racism inherent in the media, or does it arise merely from a few "bad apples"?
- Why does media miscasting persist? How much of the miscasting is systemic and institutionalized, and how much is personal and intentional? How hard would it be to foster inclusiveness in the media?
- Can the mainstream media ever take differences seriously, or are they permanently chained to the superficialities of a "pretend pluralism"?
- What would an inclusive media system actually look like? What steps have been taken so far to "inclusivize" the media? Do the solutions involve working within the mainstream media, or breaking away from it?

All of these questions are hard if not impossible to answer. All the more reason to ask them. When we do, we find that we cannot consider media–minority relations in isolation from the culture of which they are part (Sabo and Jansen, 1998).

In this chapter I consider the complex relationship between the mainstream media and Canada's multicultural minorities as it is reflected in symbols, images, and texts. I show that media representations of minority women and men are "couched in compromise," and, in reflecting both progress and regress, are both confusing and controversial. I pursue three major themes:

- How minority women and men are portrayed visually and verbally in the media.
- What the miscasting of minorities in the media tells us about the organization of power in society, and where the mainstream media are located in that power structure.
- What inclusive mainstream media would look like, and why we don't enjoy them yet.

I begin by looking at media–minority relations in newscasting, TV programming, advertising, and filmmaking as they now stand. The miscasting of minority women and men has clear patterns to it. These patterns are not as strong as they once were; that being said, changes have been uneven—a reflection of the shifting status of media–minority relations. I also consider precisely how minorities are mistreated in the media. My emphasis here is on the systemic biases that still exert a negative and controlling effect. I conclude this chapter by looking at recent initiatives in media inclusiveness, especially at attempts to reform the mainstream media and to promote indigenous and ethnic media.

PATTERNS IN MISCASTING

Canada's mainstream media have been accused of harbouring a love–loathe relationship with minority women and men. The media rely on minorities for many things: as content for narratives, as angles for spicing up a story, as catalysts for driving plot lines, as foils to main characters, and as dashes of colour to otherwise pallid cultural packages. At the same time, minorities are often disliked by the mainstream media *because* they are "others." Their marginality is reinforced by repeated visual and verbal references to them as irrelevant, inferior, dangerous, or unmarketable. Typically, the media (mis)cast minority women and men by ghettoizing them, or stigmatizing them, or demonizing them, or whitewashing them, or ornamentalizing them. All media do this—including films, news broadcasts, TV programs, and advertising—which suggests that the problem is structural rather than restricted in specific personnel or situations (Jakubowicz et al., 1994; Wilson and Gutierrez, 1995; Pearson, 1999; Fleras and Spoonley, 1999; Orbe and Harris, 2001).

Ghettoizing Minorities

Many studies have pointed out what many people regard as obvious: Canada's multicultural diversity is poorly reflected in almost all sectors of the media. Visible minorities are ghettoized when they are made visible in domains that don't count (crime), and at the same time made invisible in those that do count (success). News broadcasts ignore minority women and men unless they are involved in crime or conflict. Advertisers has long worked under the maxim that "white sells," and TV programs still haven't provided a full complement of roles for minorities to emulate. Film continues to rely on stereotypes, both conventional and new, as might be expected of a medium whose story lines are conflict driven. Certain ethnic groups, such as South Asians, are blatantly invisibilized. Others, such as East Asians, are subjected to "model minority" visibilizing in the sense that they are slotted into business or work (see Orbe and Harris, 2001). Still others, such as aboriginal peoples, are ignored unless they threaten existing patterns of power and privilege.

Of course, the media are not entirely guilty of ghettoizing minorities: improvements are inevitable as they scramble to take advantage of ethnic market shares. Yet even strong representation in the media can be misleading. Not much is gained if minority women and men are pigeon-holed into a relatively small number of sectors such as children's programming, or reduced to playing victims or assailants in reality-based programming. Nor is there much sign of improvement. In 1989 Robert MacGregor acknowledged that visible minority women were largely absent from Canada's national newsmagazine (*Maclean's*), measured by the number and kind of their appearances over thirty years. There is a self-fulfilling prophecy in all this: white content attracts white consumers, which in turn encourages more white-based coverage, and the vicious circle continues its exclusionary spiral.

The pattern is similar in the United States (Steinhorn and Diggs-Brown, 1998), where Hispanics, Asians, and Native Americans are still underrepresented relative to their numbers in real life (Kamalipour and Carilli, 1998). Blacks on television are locked into roles as entertainers, criminals, or athletes. Their intellectual or professional prowess is rarely emphasized (Siddiqui, 1999). Programs with Black casts are common enough, but except as they reflect workplaces, most TV sitcoms are still segregrated (Children Now, 2001). Very few dramas are built around Black families or protagonists, the belief being that no market exists for such programming (MacDonald, 1992). The presumption that integrated TV programs lack crossover appeal has resulted in an electronic colour bar (Steinhorn and Diggs-Brown, 1999). Not surprisingly, Blacks on prime time are usually ghettoized—that is, seen in roles that are clownish and demeaning, or that showcase their prowess in sports or entertainment, or that portray their lives as "nasty, brutish, and short." Audiences themselves seem to be racially segregated with respect to programming preferences: the programs that white audiences enjoy (*Friends*) are often disliked by Blacks, and vice versa.

Despite all this, it would be incorrect to say that the mainstream media ignore minorities; more accurately, they give them a "shallows and rapids" treatment. That is, minorities are rendered irrelevant by the mainstream press (the "shallows"); when they are covered, it is in the context of natural catastrophes, civil wars, and colourful insurgents (the "rapids"). According to Susan Moeller, author of *Compassion Fatigue: How the Media Cover War, Famine, and Death*, the mainstream news media only want graphic footage

163

of emaciated children and rotting cattle carcasses. Sadly, she concludes, many aid agencies are often happy to provide it. But attention spans are short in the media. When the crisis subsides or the story stales, they cast about for the next eye-popping debacle. Conflicts and calamities are common enough, of course. But minority concerns are compromised when the coverage does not provide a historical or social context (Steward and Fleras, n.d.). They are further compromised by collapsing developing world events, both spatial and temporal, into easily digested video clips and sound bites (Molnar and Meadows, 2001). The media highlight the flamboyant and sensational to satisfy audience needs and sell copy, without much regard for the impact on the lives of those sensationalized. This distortion may not be deliberately engineered; rather, the misrepresentation may reflect the media's preoccupation with audience ratings and advertising revenues.

The media tend to shun responsibility for their discriminatory impact, and to argue that they are merely reporting what is news. But in the absence of positive role models, this exclusive focus ends up portraying minorities as unworthy of sympathy or fair treatment. When presented without a context, actions seem to reflect personal choices, This serves to gloss over root causes and structural solutions (*We Interrupt the News*, 2001). By alternately denying and exaggerating the presence of minorities in Canada and abroad, the media are circulating mixed messages that racialize antisocial behaviour and at the same time criminalize ethnicity.

Stigmatizing Minorities

Minorities have long complained about stereotyping. Historically, people of colour were stigmatized by unfounded generalizations that emphasized the comical or grotesque. Whites minimized their interactions with minorities unless the latter conformed to stereotypical behaviours associated with ethnicity. Thus, Blacks on prime-time were portrayed as superhero-athletes or as sex-obsessed buffoons when they weren't being typecast in secondary roles such as the hipster and the outlaw (Azam, 2000). Slotting minorities into easy-to-manage stereotypes made it easy to dismiss their importance and significance.

This pattern continues. The sports media still stigmatize Black athletes as "naturally gifted" but lacking "intellect," "a sense of teamwork," and "control" on or off the field (Davis and Harris, 1998). Asian athletes are typecast as compulsively disciplined, and Russian athletes are stereotyped as dishonest and robotic. Arabs are still scripted as terrorists and subversives, as fabulously wealthy, barbaric, and uncultured, or as sex maniacs with a penchant for white slavery (Shaheen, 1984). As noted by Stam and Miller (2000: 664),

Latinos are typically stereotyped as the bandito, the greaser, the revolutionary, or the bullfighter; Latinas are typecast as hot-blooded spitfires. News broadcasts are just as guilty of stereotyping: both Vietnamese and Blacks—especially Jamaicans—are typecast as criminals in a racist discourse that over-reports problems and underreports successes, except in the fields of sport and entertainment (Henry, 1999; Wortley, cited in Hiddiqui, 1999).

In recent years Muslims have displaced other minorities as the most heavily stigmatized. The Islamic world is rarely portrayed as a valid expression of the human experience, or as even worthy of respect in a multicultural Canada. Media coverage concentrates heavily on those differences which clash with the West. Muslim women are portrayed as the antithesis of Canadian women—as repressed, shackled, and dependent. Stories about their activities in Canada resonate with the language of backwardness, repression, or gun-toting militancy (Bullock and Jafri, 2000). At the same time, Muslim men are typecast as ruthless and greedy tyrants whose actions are beyond the pale—as politically and culturally irrational, as religious fanatics without regard for human life and freedom (Canadian Islamic Congress, 1999). Films such as *The Siege* and *True Lies* reinforce the stereotype that Muslims are warlike and "pig-headed," and link Islam with terrorism (Waxman, 1998; Kutty and Youseff, 1998; Elmasry, 1999). As Jack Shaheen (2001: 354) writes about American culture's favourite whipping boy:

> Hollywood producers must have an instant Ali Baba kit that contains scimitars, veils, sunglasses and such Arab clothing as chadors and kufiyahs. In the mythical "Ay-rabland," oil wells, tents, mosques, goats, and shepherds prevail. Between the sand dunes, the camera focuses on a mock-up of a palace from "Arabian Nights"—on a military air base. Recent movies suggest that Americans are at war with Arabs, forgetting the fact that of 21 Arab nations, America is friendly with 19 of them.

The typecasting of Muslims as sleazy bullies or tyrannical patriarchs seems to have intensified discrimination against Muslims, according to a six-month study by the Media Watch group of the Canadian Islamic Congress. An entire people and civilization have been vilified because of the actions of a handful whose deeds contravene the Koran's own teachings. Few Canadians encounter Muslims in daily life on a meaningful basis, so the little they do know is derived from mainstream media messages (Ali, 2000).

The mainstream media have always stigmatized Canada's aboriginal peoples. Stereotypes of them as the "other" offer perhaps the best of all examples of Eurocentricism. Aboriginal peoples have been eulogized as "noble savages" and "quixotic romantics"; they have also been debased as "villains" or "victims" (Smith, 1997). Sandwiched in between these stereotypes are perceptions that aboriginal peoples are "problem people" or irrelevant (see also Blythe, 1994; Wall, 1997). Attached to all these images are various sub-images, such as the "spiritual mystic" and "guardian of the Earth" (see also Jakubowicz et al., 1994). Many portrayals of native people mythologize an imaginary warrior prowling the plains between 1825 and 1880 (Frances, 1992; Beier, 1999). Berton (1975) constructed an "Indian Identity Kit" around the following items, few of which were even part of aboriginal culture before European settlement: a wig with hair parted in the middle into hanging plaits; a feathered war bonnet; a headband (a white man's invention to keep the actor's wig from slipping off); buckskin leggings; moccasins; painted skin teepee; and a tomahawk or a bow and arrows. This "one size fits all" image applied to all First Peoples, whether they were Cree or Salish or Ojibwa or Blackfoot. These images were further broken down into a series of recurring stereotypes; this essentialized "Indianess" in effect reinforcing the stereotype that "seen one Indian, seen 'em all."

Collectively, these images portray aboriginal peoples as primitives remote in time and removed in place, as once-flourishing peoples that vanished with the bison and open prairie. Mainstream media see them as complex humans with an ancient past; they are not seen as existing outside the context of European colonialism (Churchill, 2000). Media programming has forgotten—if it ever knew—that aboriginal peoples collectively resisted European colonization, though some individual acts of protest are remembered and valourized. All of this has served to downplay aboriginal contributions to Canada and to weaken their position as First Peoples in two ways: *first*, by denying they have a past, the colonizers have found it easier to control native people and to continue colonizing them (Churchill, 1999); and *second*, this cultural and social "emasculation" has ensured that aboriginal peoples continue to be perceived as "safe, exotic, and somewhere else" (as Philip Hayward writes with respect to Australian aboriginal artists). The "whiting out of aboriginality" has had the effect of compromising the aspirations of Canada's aboriginal peoples (Switzer, 1997; Bannerjee and Osuri, 2000).

Demonizing Minorities

Minority women and men are routinely demonized by the news media as social problems. As a group they are seen as having problems or creating problems in need of political attention or costly solutions. The media take them to task as problem people who are making demands that could imperil Canada's unity and prosperity. Positive stories are rarely encountered.

Instead, Canadians are fed a steady diet of negativity and conflict. This negativity is reinforced when stories are framed as challenging conventional assumptions about who is entitled to power and privilege (Jiwani, 2000).

Media coverage of Canada's aboriginal peoples provides a good example. Too often they are portrayed as groups whose relationship to Canada is mediated by conflict, welfare dependency, disruption and militancy, social pathologies, and excessive demands. Aboriginal people are routinely defined as:

- a threat to Canada's territorial integrity or national interests (consider here the debate over Nisga'a self-government);
- a threat to Canada's social order (consider the violence between native peoples and lobster fishers at Burnt Church, New Brunswick);
- an economic liability (consider the costs associated with land claims settlements and other forms of restitution such as the residential school redress);
- a thorn in the side of the criminal justice system (consider the wrongful imprisonment of Donald Marshall Jr. and the shooting by the police of Dudley George at Ipperwash, Ontario);
- unscrupulous con artists who happily break the law (consider cigarette smuggling and immigration scams); or
- as "un-Canadians" who "rip off" the system while hiding behind the smokescreen of aboriginal rights (witness reports of nepotism and graft in First Nations communities).

Aboriginal people are portrayed as pathologically reliant on welfare, as chronic abusers of alcohol, glue, and gasoline, as lazy and unambitious, and as poor managers of what little they do have. The mainstream media paint aboriginal communities as insoluble nightmares of self-inflicted crime, pain, failure, or protest (Ziervogel, 1999). The combined impact of all this negative coverage reinforces a "demonic" picture of Canada's First Peoples. Success stories are rarely reported, and those which are are cast as exceptions to the rule.

Attempts by aboriginal peoples to improve their relationship with non-aboriginals are also negatively framed. Time and again, aboriginal people come across as "troublesome constituents" whose demands for self-determination and self-government run contrary to Canada's liberal-democratic tradition. Aboriginal activism tends to be framed at all times as a departure from established norms. Aboriginal protestors are often labelled as dangerous or irrational. All of this has trivialized aboriginal dissent, and thereby marginalized it; it has also distracted audiences from the issues at hand by criminalizing both the actors and their actions. Many news stories about aboriginal assertiveness are framed around a conflict between the forces of disarray (aboriginal peoples) and those of order, reason, and stability (mainstream society) (Abel, 1997). The mainstream ("us") is portrayed as the voice of reason, authority, and compromise; the marginalized "others" come across as demanding extremists with no regard for national interests (Jiwani, 2000).

Nonaboriginal minorities are also demonized by the news media. People of colour, both foreign- and native-born, are subjected to negative coverage that dwells on their costs or threats to Canada. As individuals or in groups, minority women and men are seen as hassling the police, as stumping the immigration authorities, as cheating on welfare, or as battling among themselves for control of turf. Media reports dwell on illegal immigration and the costs of processing and integration, and question refugees' right to their status. Immigrants are routinely cast as potential troublemakers who steal jobs from Canadians, bleed the welfare system, manipulate educational opportunities, buy their way into the country and then refuse to commit themselves to Canada, engage in illegal activities such as drug smuggling, disrupt society by rekindling ancient vendettas and feuds, and imperil Canada's unity and identity by refusing to discard their cultures. This negativity is coded in various ways: some stories are longer than others, some are placed differently, some have taller headlines and more prominent "kickers" (the phrases immediately after the headline), some resort to coded or inflammatory language, and some abuse quotes, statistics, and references to racial origin (Henry and Tator, 2000).

Admittedly, the mainstream media are always willing to problematize anyone: the media by nature are conflict driven. But not everyone is affected in the same way. Generally speaking, mainstream Canadians are at least partly protected from media excesses by their proximity to society's institutionalized power. Minorities are not, and this increases their vulnerability, especially when any negative behaviour is generalized as typical of the minority community (Stam, 2000). This reinforces the wedge between "minority them" and "mainstream us," and too often demonizes an entire community for the sins of a few.

Whitewashing Minorities

The mainstream media are reluctant to include people of colour in any meaningful fashion. Typically, minorities have to be "scrubbed" before they are accepted. This whitewashing of minorities is especially obvious in consumer advertising. Advertisers insist that their products be sanitized and bleached of colour to ensure they don't alienate primary (i.e., white) consumers. Whiteness and beauty are so closely linked that people of colour are rarely encountered in beauty care and personal hygiene products without extensive airbrushing (Bledsloe, 1989). Advertising tends to connect mundane products with minorities. Conversely, high-priced items and luxury goods tend to be marketed with whites in mind. Admittedly, all of this isn't as true as it used to be, but the pattern is persistent.

Many of the most recognizable faces in the world today belong to athletes of colour such as Tiger Woods (Black-Native-Chinese-Thai) and Michael Jordan (Black), and Black media personalities such as Bill Cosby, and Oprah. Yet their acceptance must be approved by the mainstream media and can always be revoked. Consider the now infamous O.J. Simpson, who rose to celebrity status in the 1970s and 1980s by finding acceptance in the white corporate culture (Sabo and Jansen, 1998). With his looks, athletic gifts, congenial personality, and strong family values, Simpson represented the acceptable face of Blackness in the United States—one that allowed everyone to feel good about race relations. But this acceptance turned out to be conditional. Having been accused of murder, he played the "race card" to gain an acquittal, and this "re-raced" him in terms of his identity. A similar situation arose in the case of sprinter Ben Johnson, who underwent a shift in status from Canadian to Jamaican after he was stripped of an Olympic gold medal. In short, minorities must submit to whitewashing before they can be deemed acceptable. And they lose white status if they violate the unspoken agreement.

The mainstream is more accommodative than it used to be. Inclusion is more acceptable, but often only when visible minorities are airbrushed in some way. For example, minority models regularly appear in print advertising and in fashion spreads. However, their appearance must conform to standards of race-neutral beauty (Kunz and Fleras, 1998). The persistence of media "whitewashing" should come as no surprise. According to Paul Farli, a *Washington Post* columnist (1995), 98 percent of TV writers and producers in Hollywood are middle-aged white men. Images of "others" are filtered through their "pale male" preconceptions; this process accentuates mainstream hostilities, fantasies, and fears. Minorities are defined more by what they are not ("nonwhite") than by what they are (Artiles, 1998). This alone reminds us that media minority representations say more about those who construct these images than they do about the "others."

Miniaturizing Minorities

The mainstream media tend to portray minority women and men as ornamental or decorative. Rarely do they appear as average, normal, tax-paying Canadians with a broad range of opinions that go beyond their race or community. Instead, they tend to be trivialized ("miniaturized") as tokens in sorting out who gets what in society. This effect is achieved by casting minorities in roles that are meant only to amuse or embellish. Minorities are coupled with the exotic and sensual, invoked as congenial hosts for faraway destinations, enlisted as superstar boosters for athletics and sporting goods, or slotted into marketing segments related to "rap" and "hip hop." For example, travel brochures tend to portray minority women and men as equivalent to the flora and fauna of the locale—as a soothing visual backdrop that reinforces deference to whiteness (Hoeschmann, 1999).

On TV, minorities tend to be confined to bit parts. As Canadian pianist Oscar Peterson once explained, this kind of "walking away from the camera" diminishes their value to society. Casting minorities as comics panders to mainstream audiences who historically have enjoyed laughing at Black comics or buffoons. The "playing 'em for laughs" angle depoliticizes minorities in society and belittles their contributions; it also neuters differences and thus minimizes their political potency. Depoliticizing Blacks by turning them into "emasculated" cartoons also reassures nervous audiences that minorities still "know their place" (Alia, 1999).

Media relations with minority women are even more controversial (Jiwani, 1992; Bullock and Jafri, 2000). All people of colour are vulnerable to misrepresentation, but minority women are doubly subject to it by virtue of their gender. Gender is superimposed on ethnicity and class to create overlapping exclusions that relegate aboriginal women, women of colour, and immigrant women to the status of decorative props. Minority women are turned into commodities to be controlled and consumed; they are also sexualized in a way that equates fulfillment with "snaring" or "stroking" a man to the exclusion of anything else. This sexualization infantilizes women by casting them as silly or childlike, as obsessed with appearances, and not to be taken seriously. Minority women are also racialized in a way that draws inordinate attention to their status as "other." Their bodies are gratuitously paraded to sell everything from esoteric fashions and sensuous perfumes to a host of exotic vacation destinations (Graydon, 1995). Aboriginal women are increasingly recast in the image of a shapely Indian princess with perfect white woman features—a kind of Barbie in buckskins (Jiwani, 1992). Finally, women of colour are portrayed as dangerous or evil, and as having the potential to destroy the moral basis of civilized society.

THE IMPACT OF "OTHERING" MINORITIES

Media misrepresentations of minorities border on the unacceptable. This applies to *all* media, including advertising, newscasting, TV programming, and filmmaking; each of these has negativized minorities either intentionally or unintentionally (i.e., systemically). The media may not be overtly ethnocentric, and may not actively promote white superiority; but they accept, reflect, and do little to work against the ethnocentric assumptions of white superiority that are deeply ingrained in Western culture. There is no specific conspiracy to sabotage minority women and men, but there doesn't have to be: the largely one-sided images of them *amount* to a conspiracy by the negative effect they have on minorities. All of the strongly negative coverage cannot be considered accidental or unfortunate. What it is, is *systemic*. It reflects processes that are central to how the media function. Admittedly, media images of whites are equally unflattering: What else could be expected from a ratings-driven commitment to sensationalize or trivialize? But miscasting does not damage members of the mainstream nearly as much as it diminishes minorities. Mainstream culture is protected from serious damage by institutional power. Minorities have no such protection because they are already marginalized and lack access to that power.

Media miscasting is a threat to Canada. As a result of rhetoric that "others" minorities as different and as undeserving of equal treatment, minority women and men have been marginalized. This has simplified the process of exerting control and at the same time has minimized the complicating emotions of guilt and remorse (Riggins, 1997). The mainstream is portrayed as the standard by which to judge or accept. In contrast, minority women and men come across as "beings" beyond the pale of normalcy, with lives that seem to be defined by their ethnicity and religion. In the process, other attributes are excluded. For example, the linking of religion with suspected terrorist acts is insulting to Canadian Muslims. It also endangers their physical and social being and violates the core Canadian precept that hatred must not be incited against an identifiable religious and ethnic group (Elmasry, 1999). Public resentment over unpopular social changes has been channelled in a way that scapegoats minorities as dangerous or inferior. Differences that are threatening or dangerous are "contained, controlled, normalized, stereotyped, idealized, marginalized, and reified" (Mackey, 1999). This miscasting drives a psychological wedge between minorities and Canadians at large. Or as Ward Churchill (2000: 702) writes in describing the impact of Hollywood's stereotyping of aboriginal peoples:

> It is elementary logic to realize that when the cultural identity of a people is symbollically demolished, the achievements and very humanity of the people must also be disregarded. The people, as such, disappear, usually to the benefit—both material and psychic—of those performing the symbolic demolition. There are accurate and appropriate terms which describe this:

dehumanization, obliteration or appropriation of identity, political subordination, and material colonization are all elements of a common process of imperialism.

Churchill concludes that in order to quell any potential misgivings over colonization, mainstream audiences are led to believe that their ancestors destroyed a barbaric people. An alternative rendering—that European colonists systematically annihilated entire societies of intelligent and culture-bearing humans who wanted only to be left in peace—would be awkward and disruptive.

What messages are conveyed by these negative depictions? What difference does it make? Imagine if the only information foreigners received about Canadians consisted of news clips about Paul Bernardo or Canadian soldiers in Somalia or the death by beating of Reena Virk. On the basis of such skimpy and selective coverage, Canadians would come across as violent and barbaric and as having a callous disregard for human life. Such a portrayal hardly squares with the realities experienced by most Canadians. Nor is such an indictment consistent with Canada's reputation as one of the world's best countries—in the UN's view, in recent years, the very best (St. Lewis, 1996).

A similar line of reasoning should be applied to media representations of Canada's minorities. Negative images and coded messages reinforce the notion that differences falling outside white middle-class culture are inferior, deviant, irrelevant, or threatening. When minorities are portrayed in an openly demeaning way and media coverage is not balanced, minorities—and especially minority children—develop an inferiority complex. Their self-hatred becomes internalized and negatively affects their opportunities and choices (Spector, 1998). Jack Shaheen (2001: 354) writes:

> To a child, the world is simple: good versus evil. But my children and others with Arab roots grew up without ever having seen a humane Arab on the silver screen, someone to pattern their lives after. Is it easier for a camel to go through the eye of the needle than for a screen Arab to appear as a genuine human being?

Sadly, Muslim children are growing up ashamed of their heritage because of derogatory typecasting. A spokesperson for the American Islamic Association commented on the film *Alladin* (Giroux, 1996: 40):

> All of the bad guys have beards and large, bulbous noses, sinister eyes and heavy accents, and they're wielding swords constantly. Alladin doesn't have a big nose; he has a small nose. He doesn't have a beard or a turban. He doesn't have an accent. What makes him nice is they've given him this

American character ... I have a daughter who says she's ashamed to call herself an Arab, and it's because of things like this.

In short, no one should underestimate the damage that media mistreatment can do to minorities' lives and life chances. Media coverage is based on certain assumptions about race and gender that are consistent with the notion that white males are superior (Corino, 2000). Minority women and men are excluded from full Canadianness, and seen as "others" to be pitied, despised, or shunned depending on the context. This is a symbolic and psychological form of violence.

SILENCES OF THE MEDIA: ACCOUNTING FOR THE MISCASTING

In this supposedly progressive and multicultural society, our mainstream media have stumbled in constructively engaging diversity. Why are the media failing in the inclusiveness sweepstakes? There are number of possible reasons:

- Hard-boiled business reasons that have to do with market forces.
- A lack of cultural awareness.
- Deep-seated prejudice among media personnel.
- Bias so systemic that it escapes detection or scrutiny.

Is the media's mistreatment of minorities a result of personal prejudice, or is it overt discrimination? Is it a case of unwittingly cramming minority realities into Eurocentric categories for the sake of convenience (Shohat and Stam, 1994)? Or is it a matter of self-interest—of pandering to market forces? Or is it the effect of a "white boys'" network?

It isn't clear how Canadians of colour can be brought into the media system without inviting accusations of paternalism, cultural theft, and tokenism. Advertising professionals may be reluctant to incorporate diversity for fear of tripping over cultural landmines, with all the bad publicity and economic losses that entails. Consider the lose–lose situation confronting the mainstream media. Critics pounce on them for focusing on the negative and the confrontational, yet are equally critical of stories that are unrealistically upbeat. Positive minority role models are encouraged, yet the media come under fire for highlighting their successes, which few other minority individuals can hope to achieve (think of *The Cosby Show*). It is considered racist to exclude minority women and men, but attempts to include them are then dismissed as tokenism, berated for oversimplifying complex problems, and criticized as controlling by situating minorities within the social space of white power (see Stam and Miller, 2000: 244). Networks that devote one night a week to Black programming are accused of ghettoizing, yet at the same time, separate radio stations for Blacks or aboriginal people are rebuked as anti-multicultural (Bauder, 2000; Bourette, 2000). The media are applauded when they try to take differences seriously, yet after they do, they are criticized for essentializing differences (Fleras and Kunz, 2001).

No one, including minorities themselves, has yet figured out how diversity ought to be depicted. Should differences be highlighted to draw attention to disadvantages? Or is it better to ignore differences in the hope of conveying a message of commonality "under the skin"? Responses vary. Some believe that ethnicity ("diversity") should not be an issue, since everyone is the same and should be treated accordingly. Others believe that ignoring ethnicity ("diversity") is irresponsible because differences matter. Paradoxically, more problems may arise from treating everyone the same than from acknowledging differences. Put another way, one-size-fits-all casting may not be the fairest approach in situations where people don't start out on equal footing. Equally contested are minority roles. Some prefer minorities to be presented in high-status positions, in other words, as role models. Others want minority women and men to be portrayed as an ordinary part of the mainstream, to reflect the real lives of ordinary minority women and men. Still others would prefer that minorities be depicted in a way that reflects the reality of minority experiences. J. Fred MacDonald (1992) expresses the conundrum at the heart of media minority representations:

> Should blacks be shown only as middle class and assimilated, as are most whites, or is this a denial of racial authenticity? Should blacks be portrayed in terms of the urban underclass, especially when such imagery might appear crude or unaccomplished? Should the folk images of rural blacks ... be propagated now as authentic, or should they be buried as anachronistic and self-defeating?

Can historically disadvantaged minorities *afford* a full range of racial images? There is no consensus to this. In white societies, minorities' differences tend to be devalued. In societies that racialize diversity—that is, in societies that practise discrimination—negative portrayals may reinforce stereotypes and serve to justify continued discrimination. Conversely, in societies that believe that everyone can make it if they try, too many minority professionals may foster false impressions or unrealistic expectations (Jhally and Lewis, 1992).

Bewildered by the criticism hurled at them no matter what they do, the mainstream media have been cautious about engaging diversity. Their reluctance to jump aboard the diversity bandwagon may reflect institutional forces that are beyond any individual's control. Below, I consider some of these forces.

Money Talks

The mainstream private media are commercial enterprises whose main responsibility is to the bottom line. They don't see their purpose as to inform or entertain. Nor do they see themselves as agents of social change—which is not to suggest that they don't have a sense of social responsibility. They exist to generate advertising revenues by attracting the largest possible audiences. When asked to account for media whitewashing, veteran TV producer Aaron Spelling did not mince words: "Our industry is not about black or white. It's about money ... the only color that matters in TV is green" (cited in *The National Post*, July 26, 1999: B7).

This preoccupation with audience ratings and ad revenues influences the quality and quantity of media representations (Gray, 1995). Hollywood is usually interested only in white people's stories; minorities are grafted on as supporting casts for white heroes, or are inserted as obstacles to progress (Stam and Miller, 2000: 244). Fears of bad publicity or negative backlash to minority advertising are real, however unfounded or exaggerated. Programs that deal with complex issues or painful experiences do not suit the happy-face subliminalities conveyed by advertising. TV programs provide sponsors with the least jarring entertainment, and if this means ignoring references to minority women and men that might strike a discordant chord, so be it. The stakes being so high, the medium of television is understandably cautious about unsettling its audience. In a business renowned for its conservatism and caution, moving too quickly can backfire. Minority women and men can easily read this conservatism as racism in disguise.

Stereotyping as a Staple

There is little doubt that minority images in the media were once tainted by overt prejudice, open discrimination, and racialized discourses. Media miscasting of minorities reflected a dislike of "others." It was widely believed that audiences resented minority casting. Overt expressions of prejudice, discrimination, and racism are ill-advised today. Nevertheless, covert or polite displays of these persist.

Prejudice literally means *prejudging*. A prejudice is a set of irrational beliefs that run counter to hard evidence. At the heart of all prejudices are ethnocentrism (a belief in cultural superiority) and Eurocentrism (a tendency to filter reality through Western "gazes"). These two dimensions intersect in such a way that "pale male perspectives" are interpreted as natural, normal, and superior—and not just by white males, since the victims can end up embracing the same perspective. Other perspectives are dismissed as inferior or irrelevant. Prejudice is not necessarily the same as racism. However, when others are denied or excluded as a result of prejudice, racism can easily be the consequence, because prejudice reinforces a racialized social order. At the heart of all prejudices is the notion of stereotyping.

Stereotypes pervade the media. Stereotyping can be defined as a process for understanding the world that involves oversimplifying it, typically by explaining all members of a category in the same way regardless of any individual differences. Stereotypes enable us to overlook the differences within categories of people; they thus make it easier to explain and predict—albeit inaccurately—the behaviour of others (Davis and Harris, 1998). Stereotypes are indispensable as a means of processing everyday information; in a world of bewildering complexity, they reduce reality to manageable proportions. But stereotypes can easily be used to justify behaviour that denies or excludes others on the basis of irrelevant characteristics (James and Shadd, 2001). For example, stereotyping aboriginal people as remote and removed has the effect of keeping them in their place and out of sight; it also assuages white guilt over the theft of aboriginal lands (Churchill, 1994).

People depend on stereotyping to process everyday information; in the same way, the media rely on stereotypes to codify reality. Stereotypes in the media of minority women and men are not necessarily a result of personal prejudices. Rather, media stereotyping is basic to how the industry works: the media must simplify information by tapping into a collective portfolio of popular and unconscious images. Time and space limitations make it difficult for the mainstream media to develop complex interpretations of reality that capture the spectrum of human emotion, conflict, and contradiction. TV programming must be sanitized; it must be kept "safe," "simple," and "familiar," so that audiences and advertisers aren't alienated. Distortions through simplification are inevitable within the constraints of a twenty-six-inch screen and a twenty-two-minute time slot (Fleras, 2001).

The same with the news. All news media, whether print or electronic, transform events "out there" into sound or word bites that are intense, unambiguous, familiar, and marketable (Czerny et al., 1994). News is routinely cast as conflict, with clearly defined protagonists and clearly articulated positions. Conflict appeals to mainstream audiences, but it also oversimplifies the realities faced by minorities (*We Interrupt the News*, 2001). And advertising simply couldn't be done without preconceived and identifiable images for subliminally linking products with consumers.

Stereotyping in the media is systemic; that is, it is basic to how the media operate. Media stereotypes are not conscious or intentional, nor are they random errors in perception; rather, they are the logical consequence of how the media run themselves. The mainstream media do not set out to control or stereotype minority women and men, but in practice they have had a controlling effect. We must not underestimate the cumulative effect of systemic stereotyping, which further marginalizes minority women and men by neutralizing their presence in society. The point here is that stereotypes may not be "real" in the conventional sense, but they are decidedly real in their social consequences.

Systemic Bias: "It's the Way We Do Things Around Here"

There is another type of bias that is just as destructive. Because it is unconscious it is difficult to detect, let alone isolate and combat. *Systemic bias* can be defined as discrimination that is built into the structures, functions, and procedures of organizations. Individuals within the organization may be free of prejudice or act in a nonprejudicial manner. Organizations may not be inherently racist or deliberately discriminatory—that is, they may not go out of their way to exclude or deprive minorities. But with systemic bias, they do just these things in practice, by inadvertently excluding or penalizing those who are different or disadvantaged. With systemic bias, it is not the intent that counts but rather the consequences. When people are treated equally even though differential treatment is required, the status quo is often frozen in place.

The news media have long claimed to be free of bias, but according to Henry and Tator (2000), they are not. Systemic bias pervades the media; this is reflected in how they reinforce assumptions that minorities are outsiders or problem makers. Consider the coverage we see of "minorities" in the developing world. Developing world people find themselves miscast as a result of media preoccupations with style over substance, visuals over depth, adversity over cooperation. The mainstream media generally ignore minorities in the developing world unless they are being victimized (e.g., by natural catastrophes or civil wars) (Steward and Fleras, n.d.). The media are feeding the audience's craving for the flamboyant and the sensational, for the sordid or the outrageous. This obsession with "coups," "quakes," and "body counts" effectively "frames" minority peoples (especially in developing countries) as volatile and prone to mindless violence.

Of course, violence occurs in the developing world, and it deserves coverage and criticism. But the absence of balanced coverage results in distortions of

minority needs and aspirations. Minorities' concerns are trivialized as patho-
logical or impulsive, yet these same concerns are divorced from their causes
(hooks, 1995). Audiences are rarely provided with the social and historical
background to the mayhem. This one-sided coverage perpetuates negative
images; it also contributes to the exploitation of indigenous peoples and
peasant populations. The mainstream media often argue that they are only
doing their job. But in effect, they are distorting minority realities for the sake
of providing information as entertainment ("infotainment"). That in turn contributes to an increasingly unequal global order.

Media Logic: "Discourses in Defence of Ideology"

Few would dispute that the media have the power to shape the way people
relate to the world. Our society is dominated by the media, and we have
tended to endow them with the privilege of defining right and wrong. The
mainstream media set the parameters of discourse by telling audiences what
is acceptable or desirable. In doing so they may suppress information that is
at odds with powerful interests, and in the process perpetuate stereotypes
and ethnocentric value judgments. The elite, agenda-setting media play a key
role in legitimizing dominant values and practices that favour corporate rule
and political interests (Herman and Chomsky, 1988). They frame people's
experiences of social reality, and in the process send out a clear message
about who is normal and what is desirable in society (Abel, 1997).

People depend on the media to construct reality for them—in effect, the
media experience the world for their audience. This is an important point.
News coverage is always filtered. Without necessarily impugning the integrity
of the media, does anyone *really* know what happened? Or do we only know
what the press thinks happened, or what the press wants us to think happened? Whose interpretation made it through the filter? The opportunities
for propagandizing are real, especially in situations where the media are the
preliminary or sole point of contact with the world (Innis, 1951; Ellul, 1965).

The mainstream media constitute a system of persuasion; they are anything but neutral or passive. They have a number of hidden agendas and
dominant ideologies; they advance vested interests, not common ones. The
mainstream media are loaded with ideological assumptions that shore up the
dominant discourse at the expense of those who challenge convention (Abel,
1997). But the media rarely show their ideological hand to audiences, who
are often unaware of how the media produce their products (Abercrombie,
1995). The media naturalize contemporary social arrangements as normal
and necessary, and hide the social constructedness of those arrangements
(Maracle, 1997). In the sense that they conceal as much as they reveal, the

mainstream media serve as defenders of the dominant ideology. They do so by representing dominant interests as universal and progressive rather than particular and parochial; by denying the existence of contradictions such as those related to capitalist production and distribution; by naturalizing the present distribution of power and privilege as "common sense"; and by securing control through consent rather than coercion (Apple, 1996).

The media are ideological in a second way. Besides securing dominant ideologies, they have their own, which influence how they frame news stories. They routinely frame incidents and issues around conflict, and give a racial or gender "spin" to stories (i.e., the "race card" or "gender wars"). This framing is neither neutral nor objective. By offering preferred ways of reading events, the media are serving commerical interests. Other perspectives are dismissed or ignored. For example, many Canadians embrace the ideals of consensus and conformity and see the world as essentially sound and good. Those who challenge these notions through protest or civil disobedience are labelled problems and framed accordingly—that is, as deviations from the norm who must be crushed for the common good. When the media frame protesters as criminal others, they are setting up a clear dichotomy of good versus evil. In doing so, they are distorting minority groups' messages, many of which are far too subtle, complex, or spiritual to fit into the crude guidelines of a conflict-driven and image-obsessed mainstream media (Mander, 1991). The next "Thinking Outside the Box" points out the implications of the media's role as defender of dominant ideologies.

Thinking Outside the Box

Systemic Propaganda

The mainstream media in Canada and the United States function as systems of propaganda (Ellul, 1965; Herman and Chomsky, 1988). This assessment sounds accurate enough—after all:

- The media are often controlled by big business.
- They are in business to make a profit and to defend systems of profit making.
- They have an aversion to those who do not fit into the system.
- Their personnel tend to share the same liberal outlook on life and reality.
- They tend to condone certain ways of doing and thinking.

A neutral or objective media are impossible under these conditions. Instead, we have a system of persuasion that reflects, reinforces, and advances one way of looking at reality over others. The media reflect and reinforce one perspective of reality as superior or inevitable, and discredit other perspectives as inferior or irrelevent. The unintended result is a powerful systemic bias.

To be sure, the mainstream media do not set out to do propaganda. More to the point, propaganda is the inevitable consequence of what they do, which is create messages that support one point of view (the "natural" and "superior" one) over others (the "inferior" or "irrelevant" ones). Furthermore, systemic propaganda is not necessarily deliberate. It is as natural to the media as breathing is to us, just as systemic discrimination is natural to even well-intentioned organizations. A loose definition of systemic bias is simply "the way things are done around here." Systemic bias is so hard to isolate and remove simply because is is so routine.

How is systemic propaganda expressed? Minorities are routinely portrayed in the mainstream media as problem people—as *having* problems or *making* problems—and this is a form of systemic propaganda. Minority women and men are stereotyped as the "other," and their differences are diverted into harmless channels, and this is another form of systemic propaganda. Minority inequality is invariably portrayed on TV not as socially constructed and a result of power differences, but rather as natural and normal, and this is still another form of it. To the extent that minority individuals are blamed for making problems, and to the extent that the media pay little attention to society's structural faults, this is yet one more form of systemic propaganda. A one-sided interpretation of reality that normalizes the dominant culture and marginalizes the rest is systemic propaganda at its most basic.

RETHINKING THE RELATIONSHIP

The relationship between minorities and the mainstream media is difficult at best, counterproductive at worst. Minority representations in the media are not some fantasy entertainment with no discernible impact. Ultimately, image reflect relationships of inequality. This is why we must understand how these inequities work. The world we inhabit is transformed by media images in at least three ways:

- The media often provide our first and only point of contact with the world out there.
- The media tell their audience what is culturally acceptable and desirable.
- The media serve as defenders of ideology and thus are critical in the social construction of reality.

Angus and Jhally (1989) have contended that media images have proliferated to the point that it is no longer possible to distinguish fantasy from reality. They add that the "real" is so thoroughly "media-ted" that any attempt to separate reality from fantasy is basically futile. And the media not only define reality for us, they also "authenticate" it. Put another way: to be seen on TV or in the news is to have one's worth, or that of one's group, validated. As Nicole Kidman's character said in the film *To Die For*, "You are nobody unless you are on TV. Being on TV makes you a better person."

No one should forget how much power the media have to make powerful statements about majority–minority relations. For both minorities and the mainstream, media images are central in the construction of social identity. These images help us identify ourselves and construct ourselves as social beings. They also serve as "windows" that suggest to us why people get what they do. As Yasmin Jiwani (2000) points out, technologies of communication are a vital means of producing and reproducing the social knowledge on which the social order is based. Imagine, then, the power of those who control knowledge and its dissemination.

Images are powerful, and minority women and men well know it. To escape the "psychic prisons" that deny or exclude them, they are seeking to gain control over how they are portrayed in the media (Riggins, 1992; Husband, 1994). Knowledge is empowerment, or so we are told, and by gaining control over how they are represented, minorities will be doing much to counter the privileged discourses that presently control or contain them. Yet the situation isn't quite as simple as all of this suggests. Tokenism, or a "splash of colour," isn't going to change how the media operates. Minorities must be able to control their own images if they are to be perceived as subjects in the world rather than as objects to be manipulated for mainstream society's amusement (Hanamoto, 1995). This means that minority women and men will have to challenge society's dominant forces by uncovering what is hidden, resisting that which is powerful, and channelling their resistance into progressive change.

All representations are socially constructed, and are shaped by those who construct and consume them (Bottomley et al., 1991; Beverley, 1999). If we fail to unmask the ideologies that underpin representations, we will be further marginalizing the people those representations exclude. Visibility may not be the same as power; that being said, invisibility is decidedly disempowering. Until society sorts out who has power, and how it is used, and why it is used that way, and whose values will dominate, biases in representation will continue.

MULTICULTURALIZING THE MEDIA

The mainstream media are powerful agencies with the capacity to dominate and control. Sometimes they exercise their power quite blatantly; other times, their power is sustained by illusions of impartiality, objectivity, and balance. The media are able to frame issues and set agendas in ways that bolster the status quo; this suggests that in democratic societies, the media amount to a mechanism for thought control in the service of a dominant ideology. Yet the mainstream media do not constitute a single, monolithic thing. As a group of institutions, they are too fractured to foment a conspiracy, and they are not impervious to change. It is more useful to think of the media as an ideological battleground on which various interests struggle for control over agendas. It is this quality of the media—a contested site—that makes an inclusive and multicultural media possible.

At one time, Canada's mainstream media were clearly indifferent toward differences. This was reflected in both the amount and the kind of coverage that minorities received. The media diminished and disparaged minorities, stereotyped them, problematized them, whitewashed them, ornamentalized them, and rendered them invisible. Minorities were portrayed as peoples remote in time and place. All of this ensured their marginal status; it also neutralized them politically.

Is this still the case? Some suggest that the media have obviously become more inclusive of minority women and men since the days when soap ads portrayed Black children being scrubbed in a tub while proclaiming, "If you can get this skin clean, think what our products can do for your white complexion" (Jones, 1995). Others are more doubtful, admitting that while there has been some improvement in how minorities are depicted, further changes are going to encounter much stiffer resistance. This latter assessment should surprise no one. Resistance to change is the norm in the mainstream media. Miscasting will continue until there is the balance of power shifts.

Reforms in media–minority relations have followed two paths. One has focused on mainstreaming minority women and men, the other on establishing separate media institutions operated by and for minorities. The challenge is formidable. The mainstream media do not see themselves as in the business of promoting progressive change or minority rights. They have embraced a business model whose operating logic is amorally simple: to make money by connecting audiences to advertisers. Conversely, minority media may not have the financial resources to bring about fundamental change. Next we look at changes that have come about in the relationship between the media and minorities as a result of increasing pressure to multiculturize.

Two Steps Forward ...

Demographic shifts and shifts in intellectual fashion have ignited a broader commitment to diversity. Advertisers are increasingly responsive to diversity as something to be positively marketed (consider here the ads for Benetton) (Steinhorn and Diggs-Brown, 1999). Similarly, TV programming is more inclined to portray minorities in a positive light by acknowledging people of colour across a broad socioeconomic spectrum. While the proof is inconclusive, these shifts seem to be shattering stereotypes; fostering increasing interracial familiarity—including romance; broadening the comfort zone of mainstream Canadians; and expanding the number of minority role models. Similarly, shows such as *North of 60* have shown aboriginal peoples in a positive light, by portraying them as individuals living in a community where problems are explored and solutions negotiated; by offering insights into the sources of social and personal problems, thus putting issues in context; by showing aboriginal culture as anchored in history but not stuck in the past; and by offering a glimpse into the lives of enterprising aboriginal people— although the lack of humour and the perpetual crisis mentality is seen by some as inaccurate (Worley, 1998; Alia, 1999).

Newscasting is also trying to avoid blatant racism. There seem to be fewer disparaging references to minorities—for example, race is no longer "tagged" in crime stories, unless it is important in tracking suspects. But it is films that are doing the most to challenge stereotypes. Interracial buddy films are common enough, even if the Black partner is typically divorced from his community and the white guys still are in charge (Nelson, 1998; Orbe and Harris, 2001). Black male actors are commonplace, Black female actors are among the leading moneymakers in Hollywood, and the Latino/Latina element is primed to break out. The mainstream media are "drooling" over the prospect of attractive young actors with olive complexions (from Jennifer Lopez to Ricky Martin), whose wholesomeness is easy to market (Jones, 2000). Similarly, the portrayal of aboriginal peoples has improved following the success of the epic *Dances with Wolves* (1990); there is much greater emphasis on the courage and tenacity of the indigenous people, especially relative to the colonizers.

... One Step Back

Despite these changes, there is much to the adage that the more things change, the more they stay the same. Improvements in some areas are undermined by indecision in others. Consider the plight of minorities on television. Of the twenty-six new shows scheduled by the four major American networks in 1999, not one featured a minority lead, despite Black and Hispanic demographics that show viewing levels at nearly seventy hours of TV per week (Orbe and Harris, 2001). And according to Children Now, a San Francisco advocacy group, prime-time TV continues to be overwhelmingly white, despite an industrywide promise to increase minority images (Braxton, 2001).

Films are no less ambiguous. Black actors in lead roles are now common, and Wesley Snipes, Will Smith, Eddie Murphy, Denzel Washington, and Samuel L. Jackson have all become major stars. Yet questions persist about which is worse: films that show Blacks only as bad guys, or action pictures that deny Blacks their humanity by not allowing them the luxury of flaws (Cremen, 2000). The rise of positive images is undercut by continued emphasis on Blacks as victims, or as villains to be feared and loathed by white audiences (Steinhorn and Diggs-Brown, 1999).

Newscasting still treats minorities negatively, by framing them as problem people making impertinent, un-Canadian demands. Newscasting agendas have been revamped in such a way that minority women and men are cast as visual "fodder." TV programming is no less ambivalent. The failure by the four major American networks in 1999 to include minority main characters does not bode well for multiculturalizing television. TV programming remains segregated into predominantly white casts or predominantly minority casts, especially in sitcoms set outside a workplace. Not unexpectedly, sitcoms are still rigidly separated, just as they were in the colour-coded days of *Amos 'n' Andy* (Jhally and Lewis, 1992). Finally, advertising and TV programming may both be exploring new dimensions, but neither is averse to capitalizing on minority stereotypes to connect with audiences.

Disney films capture some of the ambiguities in this crisis of representation, as Spector (1998) points out in his article "Disney Does Diversity" (see also Giroux, 1995; Byrne and McQuillan, 1999). Disney films have long had a problem with race. Early Disney cartoons were notorious for clumsily celebrating imperialism, empire, and white supremacy (Newsinger, 2000). Many of these efforts revolved around denigrating images of native people and other minorities. Blacks were routinely infantilized and emasculated by being portrayed as harmless. More recent Disney films seem to be actively engaged with questions about race and identity (*The Lion King*) and tolerance for diversity (*Pocahontas* and *The Hunchback of Notre Dame*). Portrayals of indigenous people have evolved as well, as Byrne and McQuillan (1999) remind us. The "red-skinned Injuns" of old are now eulogized as copper-toned defenders of the ecosystem and guardians of a lost spirituality. Yet mixed messages continue: Pocahontas is praised by some as a goodwill ambassador for multicultural coexistence, despite an excess of "cute" and "curvaceous." But neither her intelligence nor her courage is sufficient for the narrative to escape criticism as airbrushed and sugar-coated imperialism. Clearly, Disney can't win regardless of what it does or doesn't do.

Minorities are criticized for being too different yet may be chided for not being different enough. They are taken to task for aspiring to be the same yet are vilified when they falter or refuse. They are expected to pick up the slack in making a contribution to society yet are criticized as pushy if too successful (Stam, 1993; Root, 1993). Paradoxically, the mainstream media are critical of other institutions for not living up to their multicultural obligations, yet they seem reluctant to admit that their own practices contribute to aboriginal miscasting and media racism (Henry and Tator, 2000). Or as Brian Maracle (1996) puts it, the mainstream media are so steeped in Eurocentric values (including liberal pluralism and universalism) that they may not even be aware of their own biases. The fact that media bias exists is not the problem; after all, all social constructions reflect the values, agendas, and priorities of those who create them. Rather, the difficulties arise from a refusal to admit this bias by hiding behind false claims of neutrality, fairness, and objectivity.

Mainstreaming Diversity

Media institutions have explored the possibility of internal reform in a way that ensures a level playing field with equal starting blocks. Responsible coverage of minority interests and concerns is predicated on the need to stop the following:

- Selective and sensationalistic accounts.
- Images and words that demean and malign.
- Portrayals that are biased and unbalanced and that lack context.
- Stereotyping that inflames hatred and fear (Abel, 1997).

Proposed changes include incorporating minority perspectives into media operations, expanding multicultural programming, removing discriminatory barriers, ensuring balanced and impartial newscasting, and providing journalists and decision makers with sensitivity and antiracist training. The point is not simply to improve portrayals of minority women and men, or increase the raw numbers of them; it is just as important to harness power so that minority women and men can determine what is shown and how. Yet conflicts of interest will persist unless reforms like these are consistent with the economic imperatives of the media business.

Some progress has been made. Minority women and men are being portrayed more positively and realistically. At the CBC, program and production staff are taking sensitivity training; language guidelines have been put in place to reduce race and role stereotypes; and on-air representations of racial minorities are being monitored. Abusive representations of individuals on the basis of race, ethnicity, age, gender, religion, or disability are no longer openly tolerated. The Broadcasting Act of 1991 firmly entrenched the concept of "cultural expression" by expanding air time for ethnic communities. As well, the Canadian Radio and Telecomunications Commission (CRTC) has made it known that when it comes to licence renewals, broadcasters will be evaluated on the basis of their hiring practices. The CBC and Global TV have promised a series of diversity initiatives to reach out to minorities (Siddiqui, 2001b). These initiatives will be consistent with the principles of the Multiculturalism Act. Under that act, all government departments and Crown agencies must improve their practices as they relate to minority access, equity, and representation. Also, the Employment Equity Act of 1986/1995 requires all federally regulated agencies to provide annual progress reports on minority hiring and equity. However, formal sanctions for noncompliance are so far largely symbolic.

The concept of mainstreaming is critical to institutional inclusiveness. Inclusiveness makes good business sense in view of the increasing economic clout of minority women and men. In southern Ontario, CFMT-TV serves eighteen cultural groups in fifteen languages, and produces twenty-three hours of original diversity programming each week. Nearly 60 percent of its programming is non-French or non-English (Quill, 1996). Vision TV is home to around thirty programs about different religious faiths and practices. CHIN radio airs in thirty languages.

Inroads have also been made in the private sector. Specific markets are being served by specialty channels, including Fairchild (Cantonese and Mandarin), Telelatino (Spanish and Italian), and Asian Television Network (English and several languages of India) (Siddiqui, 2001b). Toronto's CITY-TV has addressed multicultural issues since 1984 through two large blocks of non-English, non-French programming. On-air programming such as the critically acclaimed (but now cancelled) series *North of Sixty* and *The Rez* have pushed the envelope of acceptance. In advertising, minorities are appearing more often across a broader range of products and services.

Companies that utilize diversity are now perceived as sophisticated and cosmopolitan relative to their white-bread counterparts, who come across as staid and outdated. Demographics may be pushing the changes: people of colour are over 30 percent of the population in both Vancouver and Toronto; as a result, the media have little choice but to improve the quantity and quality of representation (Fleras and Kunz, 2001).

Aboriginal and Ethnic Media

How well does the present broadcasting system serve Canada's minority communities? This question is critical in light of demographic changes. Nearly 80 percent of the immigrants who arrived in Canada between 1991 and 1996 spoke a mother tongue that wasn't French or English (Zerbisias, 1999). Ethnic minorities and aboriginal peoples have long felt that mainstream media images are racist, negative, and offensive. Yet minorities do not necessarily identify themselves as prisoners of mainstream media, but find space to produce insider viewpoints, in large part by appropriating modern technology for community-based communication. For that reason they have created their own independent media (Meadows, 1995). In the Greater Toronto Area, ethnicity is well served: there are six radio stations, one Black-owned FM station, two closed-circuit audio services, one ethnic TV station, three ethnic specialty channels, and six SCMOs (specialized audio services that work on FM frequencies) (Howard, 1999; Zerbisias, 1999).

The ethnic press is important to Canada's minorities. According to Haroon Siddiqui (2001b), there are around 150 such publications in Canada, about half of these in Toronto. There are at least eight non-English dailies in Toronto: three in Chinese, two in Korean, and one each in Italian, Polish, and Spanish. Each of these reports on news from "home" as well as on current affairs in Canada. The evidence suggests that the ethnically owned media perform several important functions. They create safe havens in which ethnic cultures can flourish; at the same time, they help newcomers adapt to their new environment by serving as agents of socialization. Some contend that ethnic newspapers isolate ethnic communities by emphasizing heritage-culture values and links with the home country (Black and Leihtner, 1988). Also, the growth in ethnic broadcasting may make it easier for the mainstream media to forget their commitments to foster inclusiveness.

Canada is the world leader in aboriginal media: there are several hundred local aboriginal radio stations, eleven regional radio networks, and six television production outlets including Television Northern Canada. There are also lively if uneven print media (Alia, 1999). One of the more successful initiatives has been the Aboriginal Peoples Television Network, founded in 1999.

187

The rationale behind APTV was a good one—to counteract the miscasting of aboriginal peoples on TV and in film:

> Throughout the '50s and '60s, when westerns were at their peak, Indians were routinely depicted as bloodthirsty savages to be gunned down by singing cowboys in white stetsons. Only Jay Silverheels, from the Six Nations reserve in southern Ontario, maintained some dignity as the Lone Ranger's stoic sidekick (Brioux 1999).

APTV is one of the world's first national public TV network for aboriginal peoples. At present, it picks up most of its content from Television Northern Canada, an aboriginal network that has been broadcasting in the North since 1991. In time, APTV will provide a full range of services.

The CRTC established Canada's current Aboriginal Broadcasting Policy in 1990 (see Roth and Valaskakis, 1989). Aboriginal peoples were demanding programming that reflected their own expectations and experiences. Aboriginal programming is defined by present policy as any program about some aspect of aboriginal life directed toward an aboriginal audience, or a program involving one of the indigenous languages. The rationale for the policy is straightforward: if aboriginal societies are to survive, they must share ideas and experiences among themselves.

With the advent of satellite technology in the early 1990s, the means were at hand for northern aboriginal communities to blunt the electronic wedge of southern radio and TV programming. TV Northern Canada, a transarctic aboriginal TV network (which is also a consortium of government and private interests) was established in 1992 and quickly secured firm access to northern airwaves while also reducing its audience's dependence on the CBC (Meadows, 1995; Alia, 1999). TVNC is mainly an aboriginal network and has an audience base of 100,000. It proposes to produce 100 hours per week of programming for 94 communities in 13 different indigenous languages. Aboriginal-owned media are now in a position to assert their own cultural values in ways that reflect their needs, concerns, and aspirations. This is in contrast to "Westocentric" constructions of aboriginality, which have institutionalized racism and differences in power, technology, and ideology and in doing so have effectively "silenced" aboriginal people (Cohen, 1996). Being plugged into the world has enabled northern communities to break out of their isolation and to align themselves with the politics of indigenous peoples elsewhere. TVNC's strongest impact may turn out to be that it exposed Canada's aboriginal peoples to other indigenous movements.

CASE STUDY (Continued)
Empowering the Arctic

IBC: EMPOWERMENT OR DOMINATION?

The case study at the start of the chapter explained how the Inuit took control over northern media away from southerners by appropriating satellite technology. This exercise in local self-determination enhanced Inuit pride and identity; it also empowered Inuit communities by filtering southern realities through Inuit sensibilities. As Valerie Alia (1999) reminds us, the importance of the IBC lies not in *how* it conveys messages, but rather in the *kind* of messages it sends. In the final analysis, local efforts will fail unless indigenous peoples assume ownership and control over programming, with strong community involvement.

The IBC has altered Inuit perceptions of the media (Meadows, 1995). Commodity-driven mass media tend to obliterate identity in an avalanche of American-style programming. Local programming, in contrast, may advance Inuit language and culture. The popularity of shows related to Inuit society points to a bright future for IBC. The station is focusing most of its attention on indigenous youth; the programming concentrates on skills enhancement, language and culture preservation, and entertainment (including music videos by aboriginal artists). There are also magazine-style programs for young people, and talk-back shows hosted by them. Indigenous broadcasting has politicized northern peoples by drawing their attention to human rights issues. The knowledge that the concerns and challenges confronting them are similar to those of other indigenous peoples has united otherwise disparate Inuit communities and fostered a progressive and more globally aware northern society.

Yet the IBC still faces difficulties. Cutbacks in funding have led to uncertainty. Too much reliance on the government has the potential to compromise the integrity of indigenous cultures. For example, the federal government cut the IBC's budget by 36 percent between 1990 and 1995, at a time when almost two-thirds of its budget was provided by Ottawa (Bergman, 1996). The Northern Native Broadcasting Access Program saw its budget slashed from $13.2 million in 1989 to around $9 million by the mid-1990s. Increased reliance on advertising as a primary souce of income could make Inuit and aboriginal programming indistinguishable from mainstream programs (Brisebois, 1990). Equally dismaying is that young Inuit are continuing to drift away from Inuit social and cultural life.

Perilously high rates of suicide and domestic abuse are but one indicator of persistent social problems that even indigenous media cannot solve alone. But none of this suggests that the Inuit will be deterred from establishing their rightful place in the Canadian communication network. The dangers of not doing so are fatal. As put by Rosemarie Kuptana, a former president of IBC, the effects of southern television are devastating: "we might liken the onslaught of southern television and absence of native television to the neutron bomb. This is the bomb that kills the people but leaves the buildings standing" (Brisebois, 1983: 107).

Chapter Highlights

- Minorities are reaping the benefits of media that increasingly concede the importance of inclusiveness to the bottom line.
- Mainstream institutions have been slow in putting the principles of inclusiveness into practice. The mainstream media have been singled out as especially negligent in constructively engaging with diversity.
- As "factories" of meaning, the mainstream media play a powerful role in defining desirability and acceptability, and who is a Canadian and what it means to be Canadian, and in shaping public perceptions of minorities in society.
- Minorities are badly misrepresented in the media, which include television, newscasting, film, and advertising.
- Media miscasting of minority women and men tends to fall into certain patterns: trivialized (made invisible), demonized (made problem people), stereotyped (as scapegoats), whitewashed, and ornamentalized (as inferior or irrelevant).
- The media may not set out to demean or diminish minorities, but have that effect by the logical consequences of how they operate.
- Anti-Islamic bias in the media has created the public perception that Muslims are intolerant, fanatical, antimodern, and a threat to civil society.
- Media miscasting is not accidental or random, nor is it uncommon. Rather, it is systemic and institutionalized within the framework of doing business, and reflects deeply entrenched values, structures, procedures, and commitments.

- Media miscasting can be traced to profit-seeking mentalities, to systemic stereotyping, to systemic bias in the media business, and to media defences of ideologies.
- The media may not set out to demean or marginalize minorities, but the cumulative effect of media depictions may have a denigrating effect.
- Open discrimination is no longer advocated in the media, but systemic bias ensures that discrimination will continue in somewhat muted form.
- The mainstream media are being forced by demographic pressures to rethink their relations with minorities.
- Minorities are enjoying more clout in the media for two reasons: mainstream outlets are becoming more responsive, and they are developing their own separate media.
- Ethnic media are enjoying a boom in Canada with respect to TV programming and newscasting. Aboriginal media are also showing strength.
- Aboriginal media are turning out to be a positive force in securing identity, power, and culture.

Review Questions

1. As defenders of the dominant ideology, the mainstream media serve as systems of propaganda for mainstream cultures. Elaborate.
2. The mainstream media are being challenged increasingly over their treatment of minority women and men. Discuss.
3. The media's treatment of minorities is widely seen as inconsistent with Canada's multicultural principles. Indicate how and why this is the case. Who says so and on what grounds?
4. Why do the media portray minorities so negatively? Why haven't they stopped?
5. What are the five basic patterns of media depictions of minorities? Provide an example of each. Can you think of any other relevant patterns?
6. What constitutes an inclusive media? To what extent can this be accomplished by way of (a) media mainstreaming or (b) ethnic and aboriginal media?
7. As many have noted, the media are criticized regardless of what they do or don't do in portraying minorities. Explain how this is true with reference to the representation of minority women and men in Canada's mainstream media.

Recommended Reading

Sue Abel. 1997. *Shaping the News: Waitangi Day on Television*. Auckland: Auckland University Press.

Valeria Alia. 1999. *Un/Covering the North. News, Media, and Aboriginal Peoples*. Vancouver: UBC Press.

Augie Fleras and Jean Lock Kunz. 2001. *Media and Minorities: Representing Minorities in a Multicultural Society*. Toronto: Thompson Publishing.

Andrew Jakubowicz et al. 1994. *Racism, Ethnicity, and the Media*. Sydney: Allen and Unwin.

Y.R. Kamalipour and T. Carilli, eds. 1998. *Cultural Diversity in the U.S. Media*. New York: State University of New York.

Ella Shohat and Robert Stam. 1994. *Unthinking Eurocentrism: Multiculturalism and the Media*. New York: Routledge.

Clint Wilson III and Felix Gutierrez. 1995. *Race, Multiculturalism, and the Media: From Mass to Class Communication*. Thousand Oaks: Sage.

CHAPTER

7

Multicultural and Antiracist Education

CHAPTER OBJECTIVES

- To indicate that both multiculturalism and multicultural education are increasingly about race and social relations, disadvantage and inclusiveness, rather than about ethnicity, cultural diversity, and sharing.
- To emphasize that multicultural education is not about promoting differences, but rather about creating an inclusive education system in which students of colour can participate fully and equally and express their identity without fear of reprisals.
- To appreciate the differences between monocultural and multicultural education.
- To point out that in the debate over multicultural education, the question at hand is: Should differences be taken seriously in the education system, or is it better to emphasize similarities?
- To show how education is suffering an identity crisis because of difficulties in reforming our predominantly monocultural system.
- To compare and contrast the enrichment, enlightenment, and empowerment models of multicultural education.
- To discuss what antiracism education is and does.
- To explain how multicultural education has trouble coping with the demands of religious pluralism.

CASE STUDY

Campus Racism

It almost goes without saying that racism is pervasive in Canadian institutions (Fleras, 2001; Henry et al., 2000; Satzewich, 1998; Alladin, 1996). The education system is not an exception to this. Primary and secondary schools have been criticized as sites of racism and discrimination. As a result, Canada's reputation as a pacesetter in social change has been sullied (Mukherjee, 1993). In an attempt to address the challenge of diversity, governments at various levels have put considerable energy into progressive education policies. For example, since the early 1990s school boards in Ontario have made multicultural and ethnocultural equity programs an everyday practice. To be sure, theory has not always lived up to reality, nor has rhetoric always reflected practice. Even so, these programs are progressive enough to merit support.

Canada's universities and community colleges have been slower to adjust to social and demographic change. Their student bodies are far more diverse than they were even recently. As a result, course content is increasingly contested, faculty of colour are increasing in sheer numbers and growing more assertive, traditional teaching methods are being challenged, and business-as-usual mindsets are no longer tenable (Price, 1993; Schuman and Olufs, 1995; Henry et al., 1995). But measures to promote inclusiveness have been inconsistent at best, where they exist at all. Typically, multicultural and antiracism initiatives are seen as a form of crisis management rather than an imperative of social justice. Public relations has counted more than doing the right thing.

This should come as no surprise. The common perception of universities is that they are ivory towers, out of touch with business realities and immune from the forces of globalization. They are perceived as long on the principle of diversity, but short on the practice. This footdragging has tarnished the reputation of postsecondary institutions as beacons of enlightenment. How accurate are charges of campus racism?

THE PROBLEM: UNI-VERSITY IN A MULTI-CULTURAL SOCIETY?

Surveys provide some insight into campus racism (Ramcharan, 1991). The results of these studies have been published elsewhere (Fleras, 1995). Generally, they have found the following: the number of *reported* race-related incidents on postsecondary campuses is not especially high—between 20 and 120 incidents per year at Canadian universities and community colleges that keep records on such things. Most of the incidents that come to the attention of authorities do not involve open physical confrontation; rather, they involve verbal slurs (from innuendo to stereotyping) and ethnic jokes. Racist graffiti are common especially in washroom stalls, but these have not yet been analyzed for frequency. By virtue of their numbers, students are the usual instigators of racial encounters. Most incidents occur in residences, pubs, cafeterias, and classrooms.

Some tentative conclusions can be drawn from these surveys. *First*, the numbers themselves may say more about the survey instruments than about campus racism. An incident *recorded* as racial is not necessarily a racist incident. Rather, it may reflect an interpersonal conflict in which people of different backgrounds happen to be involved. Also, any increase in reported incidents may simply mean that people are more willing to report them than they used to be. *Second*, there may be a strong tendency to underreport racial incidents. Victims and targets may be unsure of the procedure for reporting an incident. In some cases they may prefer simply to confide in their friends. Some may fear reprisals, for being branded a malcontent or hypersensitive. Minority women and men worry that their complaints could be dismissed as frivolous (McGill, 1994). International students rarely report racial incidents for fear of losing their visa status or compromising their academic standing (Ramcharan, 1991).

But there is more to campus racism than the obvious. It goes beyond washroom graffiti, a pubcrawl brawl between ethnically different pugilists, and professors who make disparaging remarks about ethnic minorities. Campus racism is neither sporadic nor randomly restricted to the deranged actions of a few social misfits. Nor is it about what happens; rather, it's about what *doesn't* happen because of the system that is in place (Ballard, 1999). Campus racism is systemic in the sense that exclusion is built into the system and is invisible to those who perpetrate it. It privileges some members of the community by way of tacit assumptions, mission statements, cultural and subcultural values, power relations, organizational structures, operating principles, reward systems, and intended outcomes (Chesler and Crowfoot, 1989; McIntyre, 1993; Schuman and Olufs, 1995). Others are disprivileged for the very same reasons.

College and university campuses are racist, in other words, but not because these places are crawling with racists (Blauner, 1972). Rather, they are racist because they exclude minority stakeholders from full and equal participation, and fail to provide an education experience that reflects the realities and needs of minority students. They are profoundly Anglocentric with respect to course content and grading, and are strongly inclined to evaluate the world from a white, "male-stream" perspective. They assume that the Western curriculum is natural and normal. This exclusiveness can be interpreted as systemically racist because it silences minority voices. According to Blauner:

> For the liberal professor ... racism connotes conscious acts, where there is an intent to hurt or degrade or disadvantage others because of their color or ethnicity ... He (sic) does not consider the all-white or predominantly white character of an occupation or institution in itself to be racism ... acts of omission, indifference, and failure to change the status quo.

In the continuation of this case study at the end of the chapter I will look at what *has* been done and what *can* be done to reduce campus racism.

MULTICULTURAL EDUCATION/EDUCATING MULTICULTURALLY

Canada's education system endorses the idea of nurturing the potential in each student. This nurturing process is committed to recognizing individual worth and encouraging participation and equality. Yet this same system has dismissed diversity as irrelevant. It has rejected special curricula and the recognition of diversity as contrary to the imperatives of Canadian society building. Instead, it remains fundamentally committed to monocultural principles and exclusionary practices. From teachers and textbooks to policy and curriculum, all aspects of schooling act to strengthen conformity. Anything that veers outside this Anglocentric framework is dismissed as irrelevant or inferior, and punished accordingly. Not surprisingly, education has become a site for reinforcing social inequality and cultural uniformity. In this way equal opportunity is denied for some Canadians; national interests are privileged.

None of this is explicit anymore. The system is no longer openly monocultural; in fact, it has floated a raft of pluralist initiatives, all of which claim to be fostering a more inclusive education system. More and more, the education system claims to be taking advantage of diversity as a basis for enrichment, enlightenment, or empowerment. It has endorsed a learning environment that acknowledges the value of diversity. Yet in practice, schools have done little to reform their approaches to diversity. They continue to follow monocultural practices and promote hidden agendas, the end result of which is to foster assimilation (Banks and Banks, 1997; May, 1999). Because of all this, schools have been transformed into contested spaces where different interests struggle with each other to advance or repudiate a multicultural agenda (Giroux, 1994).

In theory, multicultural education should be a departure from conventional practices. In reality, there is wide variation in how multicultural education is actually done. "Softer" options in multicultural education wrap themselves around the reassuring discourses of cross-cultural communication, racial awareness, and healthy identity formation. More critical versions do more than expose students to diversity or empathy; they apply themselves to all dimensions of schooling. They analyze diversity and disadvantage and use their findings as catalysts for challenging the system (Turner, 1994; Dei, 2000). They also propose direct actions for yanking out the roots of inequality, in both the education system and the social system as a whole (Giroux, 1994). These "radical" expressions of multicultural education reflect an antiracist orientation that challenges the conventions of schooling and education.

Canada's commitment to educational inclusiveness has much to recommend it. The education system has come a long way since the days when differences were punished. Yet concerns continue to mount. Multicultural education is criticized as a superficial add-on. Or it is damned for not being inclusive enough, or for being too inclusive to do its job. Or it is criticized for being top-heavy with critical theory but light on everyday realities. Or it is rebuked for promising much, but delivering little because it is so deeply embedded in a monocultural framework (May, 1999). Multicultural education may not be accomplishing what it has set out to do, despite good intentions and soothing rhetoric. This in turn may reflect a lack of political will to "go against the grain" by questioning old educational practices.

How, then, do we approach the elusive concept of multicultural education? Many agree that it's the right way to go, at least in principle if not in practice. Yet there is little agreement on what it is, what it is trying to do, and why and how it should be done. There is even greater confusion over what it realistically can accomplish and how far it should go. Opinions on this last point range from the modestly banal to the radically transformative. All stakeholders—parents, teachers, students, minorities, administrators, politicians, and business—have their own take on these questions. But amid all this confusion, one question regularly asks itself: What principles should guide multicultural education? The following questions draw attention to these principles:

What is multicultural education? Is multicultural education about diversity or disadvantage? About culture or social relations? About differences or similarities? About awareness or transformation? And is it for minorities or the mainstream? Is multicultural education about bringing together students from many cultures without their differences getting in the way of full and equal participation? Or does it involve a process of inclusion that takes differences seriously as bases for recognition and reward? In other words, is multicultural education about the uniqueness of cultures or a confirming of our connectedness (Arrighi, 2001)?

What is multicultural education supposed to do? For some, cultural awareness is the main goal. For others, this goal is to dismantle structural racism. For yet others, it is simply to bring racism out of hiding. For yet others still, it is to teach students how to prosper and prevail in a multicultural society. This lack of consensus may prove beneficial, since all these goals are worthy in some way.

What does inclusive multicultural education actually entail? Reform? Minority-ization? Separate but equal structures? At a minimum, multicultural education involves incorporating diversity to foster educational success. At maximum, it is a comprehensive plan for challenging and transforming policies and programs in all aspects of the education environment. From almost everyone's perspective, it includes a commitment to responsiveness. Initiatives are introduced to make schooling and education more reflective of minority needs and aspirations; at the same time, students are encouraged to think hard about ethnic and cultural differences, including their own (May, 1999).

What are the objectives of multicultural education? What should they be? Should multicultural education focus on self-affirming issues related to identity and culture? Or should it focus instead on cultivating marketable skills so that minorities will succeed in the outside world? Should the emphasis be on modifying the behaviour of both minority and mainstream students? Or should it be on challenging and transforming institutional structures? Is there too much emphasis on changing curricula and not enough on challenging structural racism?

What are the limits of multicultural education? What can multicultural education realistically accomplish in light of prevailing constraints, vested interests, hidden agendas, and competing demands? How much and what kind of diversity can we incorporate into Canada's school system without robbing it of core cultural values, a sense of purpose and integrity, and institutional coherence? Can differences be taken seriously by a bureaucratic complex better known for its monoculturalism and resistance to change? Can multicultural solutions cope with the root causes of society's problems?

Should diverse religious practices be included within a multicultural curriculum? The relationship between religion and multiculturalism is highly charged. Canada's "pretend pluralism" is highly secular, and clashes with those groups that are religiously devout. Should diverse religions and religious practices be ignored to ensure separation of church and state? Or should they be tolerated within the school system but not supported? Or should they be promoted as an integral part of the mainstream curriculum? Or should they be conferred publicly funded status?

Who should be targeted under multicultural education programs? Are minority pupils the appropriate targets for multicultural education? Should the principles of multiculturalism be applied to all stakeholders, from the general student body and teachers to resource personnel and administrators? Is the objective to sensitize mainstream students, or is it to empower minority students, or is it to transform the education system? What level of education—primary, secondary, or tertiary—responds best to multicultural initiatives?

What is the appropriate strategy for multicultural education? Strategies vary according to goals. Should multicultural education ignore diversity by treating everyone the same whatever their cultural differences? Or is multicultural education mainly about taking differences into account to ensure that no one is denied because of ethnicity? Should multicultural education be bringing us closer together by assuming that everyone is the same? Or should it be fostering a healthy distance by insisting that everyone is fundamentally different?

Is multicultural education doing its job? Responses to this question will depend on how we define the goals of multicultural education. Also, how do we define effectiveness? Who gets to define it? And how do we measure it?

Multicultural education is an enormously complicated issue. The lack of consensus can easily lead to sharp disagreements and undermine reform. Yet its very complexities provide opportunities to explore, experience, and experiment with multicultural schooling. In this chapter I explore multicultural education as an institutional response to a rapidly changing and increasingly diverse society. I demonstrate how multicultural education can mean different things in different contexts. I begin by looking at how multicultural education differs from monocultural education—at least in theory if not in practice. I then compare three different styles of multicultural education: enrichment, empowerment, and enlightenment. I compare antiracist education with multicultural education, and provide a case study on the politics of inclusiveness in postsecondary education. Finally, I discuss the thorny issue of religious pluralism in schools in terms of its implications for a society with multiple religions.

CONTESTING SCHOOLING

All societies must socialize their children for participation in adult life—for getting a job, raising a family, complying with the obligations of citizenship, conforming with the laws of the land, and contributing to social progress and prosperity. The means for achieving these goals are both formal and informal, and the specific strategies vary across time and place. Pre-industrial societies survived without formal education and schooling, relying instead on informal approaches such as parental or peer instruction. In urban–industrial systems, education and schooling have become much more formal, and revolve around institutionalized rules, roles, and relationships. Educational institutions share a number of characteristics: they have standardized norms, values, and practices; they employ teams of specialists, both in the classrooms and outside them; and they use specific locations and equipment (Robertson, 1987). Formal education is still widely endorsed because a literate population is considered necessary for progressive development.

Education, like the media, is regarded as a *secondary* agent of socialization, in the sense that its social control functions may not correspond with its formal mandates or with the perceptions the public has of it. It is widely agreed that education has three explicit functions:

- To impart knowledge and skills.
- To prepare individuals for citizenship and employment.
- To foster intellectual development.

The specific goals of education include the following:

- Socialization, or the transmission of culture.
- Self-actualization and individual self-development.
- Preparation for the workplace, for consumerism, and for citizenship.
- Improvement in Canada's competitive edge.

The implicit functions of education are no less real, and include reproducing the social order. The education system is committed to consensus and conformity and, it follows, to maintaining the existing distribution of power and resources in society (Mukherjee, 1992). Hence, education is neither culturally neutral nor politically aloof. Rather, it is a defender of ideology:

> Its intellectual content and orientation is permeated by the world-view characteristic of the dominant culture. It cultivates specific attitudes and values. In so far as these assist and conduce to the maintenance of a particular type of social and political order, it is also a political activity. All this means that although an educational system may avow the ideals of freedom, objectivity, independent thought, universality of knowledge, intellectual curiosity and so on, in actual practice it often does little more than initiate and even indoctrinate its pupils into the dominant culture. (Bhikhu Parekh, cited in Gay, 1997: 157)

Monoculturalism is central to an assimilationist educational agenda. Monocultural education has various goals: to ensure uniformity, to homogenize identity and culture, and to foster loyalty to the state (Kalantzis and Cope, 1999). Not surprisingly, public education evolved in tandem with the modern Canadian state. As many historians have noted, the educational system's earliest objective was to forge social cohesion according to the standards of nineteenth-century elites. A single nation-state was to be created by eliminating cultural diversity and promoting identification with a state-endorsed national culture (Dijkstra et al., 2001). Schooling in English-speaking Canada promoted a pan-Canadian, Anglo-conformist world-view (CES, 2000: 40). Also advocated was a Protestant Christian morality superimposed on a British parliamentary tradition. At the same time, Roman Catholic demands for separate institutions were met.

This largely assimilationist monoculturalism persisted well into the twentieth century. Pluralism and multicultural education have taken hold only since the 1970s. Inclusiveness has also been embraced as a guiding principle, the hope being to incorporate all students as equal yet different. Regrettably, education and schooling seem incapable of taking differences seriously. Canada's schools have evolved into complex bureaucracies serving the needs of the state. They are designed to perpetuate existing power structures by securing a docile and stratified workforce. They also are organized to indoctrinate the populace so as not to disturb existing cultural hierarchies and social stratification (Sleeter, 1992).

Canada's schools accomplish all of this in different ways. *First*, directly, by openly reflecting mainstream experiences and values—for example, through course content and textbook selection. *Second*, indirectly, by privileging whiteness as the standard by which all cultures are to be judged. Largely invisible measures are also employed. The school system in its decision-making processes and daily routines projects certain views of the world as necessary and normal, and others as irrelevant and inferior. In other words, through schooling the ideological and social order is reproduced almost without the public being aware of it, let alone debating the results. Power and culture are thereby linked, and as a result, the very inequities that education promises to purge are in fact perpetuated.

Identity Crisis

The education system is in a state of crisis. Controversies and contradictions abound regarding what schools should be doing, and how. Public confidence in the formal education system is being eroded. All of this is largely because people hold widely diverse perceptions about the role of education in society. Some believe that contemporary education is losing its humanism, and that creativity and the capacity for criticism are being dampened by the harsh realities of authority, dogma, routine, conformity, cost-cutting, depleted resources, and credentials at all costs. For these people, education is no longer about creativity, or about personal growth or social progress; instead it has become an inflexible and bureaucratic process that destroys critical judgment. A sociologist, Ian Robertson (1987: 383), confirms what many students already know: "Not all schooling is educational. Much of it is mere qualification earning ... ritualistic, tedious, suffused with anxieties, destructive of curiosities, and imagination; in short, anti-educational."

Then there are others who see modern education as too market-oriented to perform its proper functions. Neil Postman (1995) has written that schools were once expected to forge a coherent, stable, and unified culture out of diverse students; in contrast, the present system is based on economic utility and career prospects, on consumerism as an inescapable lifestyle, on reliance on technology and technological solutions as opposed to critical judgment, and on information rather than knowledge and wisdom. Countering this point of view are critics who believe that modern education is out of touch with reality. For them, much of what now passes for education is being driven by the dictates of an earlier, print-based industrial era. As a result, the realities of the digitally driven, knowledge-based, post-industrial economy are glossed over, to the detriment of students and society (Spender, 1997). Finally, there are those who believe that the education system has "lost the plot." Parents are growing more and more worried about declining educational standards, deteriorating performance levels, lax discipline, and learning without the "basics." There is increased concern that children aren't learning fundamental literacy skills and instead are drowning in pedagogical mumbo-jumbo about self-esteem and personal creativity. Child-centred education is fine up to a point, they argue, but how is it relevant to the knowledge-based economy? Is it sufficiently market-oriented?

Amid all this argument over priorities, the education system is suffering an identity crisis. The system is no longer certain of its role and responsibilities, and can do little more than plod along as best it can with shrinking resources. Schools have become strongly diverse places as a result of immigration, yet the system is still based on an assimilationist logic that undermines any multicultural agenda. Where monoculturalism prevails, commitments to diversity are severely compromised (Kalantzis and Cope, 1999). Multiculturalism has had hardly any effect on curriculum, language, and culture programs; on placement and assessment; on employment and promotion; on teacher training; or on relations with the community (McAndrew, 1992). The reforms that have been carried out are often cosmetic, and change little about how decisions are made, agendas are set, and power is shared. All of this should warn us not to expect too much of multicultural education.

In the education system, progressive and reactionary forces have become two opposing camps. Yet neither side has been strong enough to impose its agenda on the other. Ambiguity and paradox are inevitable in a fragmented and contradictory system within which debate is always raging (see Stone, 1993). By nature, schools are both conservative and progressive: they support democratic values in theory even as they oppose them in everyday practice. They encourage learning, but do so from within structures that *inhibit* learning (Sleeter, 1991). They take pride in promoting equality, until it comes time to actually implement equity initiatives. Instead of taking differences seriously, schools embrace diversity while it is politically expedient, and then discard it when priorities shift or costs are too high.

In sociological parlance, the education system is a "contested site" involving a struggle of opposing interests for control of the agenda. But in general terms, that system tilts toward conformity rather than change, toward consensus rather than disagreement, toward the reproduction of the status quo rather than the reconstruction of social reality, and toward fitting in rather than resistance. To expect multicultural principles to take root in such an environment is either optimistic or naive. So how does all this jell with the fact that diversity has become an inescapable fact of Canadian society?

MODELS OF MULTICULTURAL EDUCATION

It is surprisingly difficult to define multicultural education, mainly because the concept embraces so many different activities. For many people, multicultural education is little more than mandatory workshops in sensitivity training or prejudice reduction, with—perhaps—separate modules on interesting ethnic customs. For others, multicultural education is about enhancing inner-city schools in the hope of improving the life chances of disadvantaged minorities. For still others, it is about overhauling the entire education system for the purpose of transforming society along pluralistic lines. For others still, it involves learning about other people, nurturing positive attitudes, and developing skills for living together with differences (van Driel, 2000). With such a spectrum of meanings, who can be surprised that multicultural education is constantly second-guessed?

Not surprisingly, definitions of multicultural education vary with the activities they are attached to and the mindsets of the people involved in those activities (Grant and Sleeter, 1997). Multicultural education can mean the study of many cultures. Or it can mean learning to understand the world from diverse perspectives. Or it can involve analyzing how power and politics are linked with unequal group relations (see Schuman and Olufs, 1995). Some definitions are more radical than others. For example, multicultural education can mean celebrating differences and improving students' interactional skills (van Driel, 2000; Moodley, 1999), or it can mean advancing inclusiveness by unmasking racism and politicizing students (Banks and Banks, 1997).

In short, multicultural education encompasses a variety of policies, programs, and practices for "learning together with differences." Such a range makes it difficult to define multicultural education. A useful definition is by Banks and Banks (1997), who contend that multicultural education is three things—an idea, a reform movement, and a process—and that its purpose is to redesign the education system to ensure the inclusion of all minority students. This definition allows for a broad range of approaches to multicultural education. For purposes of argument, we can key on three: *enrichment, enlightenment,* and *empowerment.* A fourth, *antiracism,* is also useful.

Enrichment Multicultural Education

The enrichment model is perhaps the most popular. It aims to enrich all students by celebrating differences. Students are exposed to a variety of different cultures with the goal of enhancing their knowledge of and appreciation for cultural diversity. The curriculum is based on various "add-ons." Special days are set aside for multicultural awareness; projects are assigned that reflect multicultural themes; and specific cultures are singled out for intensive classroom study. The emphasis is on healthy identity formation, cultural preservation, intercultural sensitivity, awareness of stereotyping, and cross-cultural communication. Equally important is a commitment to inclusiveness. The following box provides a list of enrichment ideals espoused by New Zealand's Education Review Office (cited by Rivers, 2000: 10).

FYI: Multicultural Ideals

- Mission statement, charter, policies acknowledge significance of other cultures.
- Membership in Board of Trustees reflects cultural diversity.
- Teaching, clerical, and cleaning staff are made up of different cultures.
- Close connections with community.
- Positive role models from different cultures are present in school.
- School processes reflect the individuality of students.
- Barriers to learning are identified.
- Where possible, students are taught in their own language.
- The school actively supports non-English-speaking students.
- Perspectives from other cultures permeate the curriculum.
- Career guidance is responsive to different cultures.
- Cultural differences are recognized and celebrated.
- Students are encouraged to take pride in their culture and maintain it.
- Schools signs and art reflect other cultures and languages.
- Library contains books of other cultures.
- Students are enriched by a range of cultural experiences.
- An atmosphere of inclusion.

It is interesting that the easiest goals to achieve (e.g., "Mission statement, charter, policies acknowledge significance of other cultures") may do the least to foster a multiculturalized school environment. Conversely, those which are most difficult to achieve (e.g., "Cultural differences are recognized and celebrated") typically have the most impact.

Enrichment models tend to be widely accepted because they are nonthreatening. Students can be enriched without fundamental changes to classroom procedures. This superficiality is in fact the source of most criticisms of enrichment. Greater tolerance, enhanced sensitivity, and more harmonious intercultural relations are all good things, but they don't change patterns of denial or exclusion. In that sense, enrichment is a highly static and restrictive approach.

It focuses too much on the exotic components of cultures that everyone can relate to, rather than on substantive issues such as values and beliefs. Diverse societies are studied at the level of material culture, stripped of their historical context, and compared implicitly to the mainstream culture, and this can actually strengthen stereotypes (Mukherjee, 1992). Enrichment also threatens to overromanticize minorities by focusing on a timeless past, or to "demonize" them as present-day social problems.

Presentations on diversity, even carefully considered ones, must grapple with various dilemmas. How can we discuss differences without "othering" minorities as exotic or inferior? Is it possible to emphasize the positive features of minority life without ignoring the problems that many confront? Can we present cultural differences without reinforcing stereotypes or out-group hostility? The effectiveness of an enrichment-through-exposure approach is weakened because we haven't yet answered these questions.

Enlightenment Multicultural Education

The enlightenment model is similar to the enrichment one in the sense that both hope to modify people's attitudes by changing how they think about diversity. However, enlightenment models focus less on cultural enrichment and more on the impact of race relations. These "enlightenment by analysis" models approach diversity not as a "thing" but rather as a relationship. Attention is directed at how minority–mainstream relations develop and are expressed and maintained, and on how unequal relationships can be challenged and transformed (Fleras and Elliott, 1999).

The enlightenment approach can be quite radical. Students are taught about Anglo-European complicity in crimes against humanity, including racism, dispossession, imperialism, and genocide. Specific cases of group victimization are often included—for example, genocide against First Peoples. Achievements of indigenous and immigrant peoples are often noted to provide a corrective to their marginalization in history, society, and culture (see Dinesh, 1996). One objective of the enlightenment approach is to show how, intentionally or not, minority students have been given a rough ride in schools. The aim of all this is straightforward enough: to transform unequal power relations by informing students of the social power that oppresses some and privileges others (Sleeter and Grant, 1992).

Empowerment Multicultural Education

The enrichment and enlightenment models tend to concentrate on mainstream students. In contrast, the empowerment model focuses on the needs of minority students. Students of colour do poorly in school for a variety of reasons, including a lack of adequate school resources, low expectations on the part of teachers, an alienating school environment, and inappropriate social and academic codes (Gay, 1997). Furthermore, a "Westocentric" curriculum rarely acknowledges minorities' achievements and contributions to society. Minorities' voices are often muted because of the overwhelming attention paid to mainstream authors, scientists, and explorers. Minorities' strengths and learning styles are dismissed by mainstream education.

Empowerment education has two main variations: The *first* is a compensatory approach that capitalizes on the cultural differences of students to help them "fit" into the system. This approach does not promote diversity per se; rather, it uses differences as a means for fostering integration.

The *second* type is known as "minority focus": this model assumes that monocultural mainstream schools are failing minority pupils. Even schools that take inclusiveness to heart may fail in their efforts unless they enhance the collective lives of groups that constitute society, take seriously the claims of disenfranchised groups, accept that group membership is an important basis for participating in society, and incorporate different knowledge bases (Banks and Banks, 1997). For minority students who feel disengaged from the Eurocentric education system, a minority-focus school offers a "safe" place to develop self-esteem and to affirm identities (van Driel, 2000). Students recover their own voices by telling their own stories; this provides them with space to compare the history they are told with the lives they have lived (Giroux, 1994). This empowerment model—exemplified by Black focus schools—has been controversial. Not everyone agrees that separate but equal is the appropriate multicultural path to take (Dei, 1996; also Smith and Smith, 1996).

An example of empowerment education is found in Canada's aboriginal communities (see also Fleras and Spoonley, 1999, for similar developments in New Zealand). Since the early 1970s, aboriginal peoples have been trying to implement a variety of reforms. These include decentralizing education, transferring funding control to local authorities, devolving power from the centre to the communities, and empowering parents to direct their own children's education. Aboriginal peoples have good reason to feel aggrieved about their children's schooling. For many decades the government used education as a tool for assimilating aboriginal children. The goal was to disrupt the cultural patterns of aboriginal children, then indoctrinate them to Western values. This often involved removing them from their families and communities and placing them in off-reserve schools. The abuses they suffered in residential schools have been widely documented (Miller, 1999). Some of the resulting damage was no less real for being less direct. According to a Métis scholar, Paul Chartrand (1992: 8–9), "It is easy to assert power over others if they are made to feel they have no identity, they have no past, or at least no past that matters." Only a relatively separate education system controlled by aboriginal people for aboriginal people may reverse the damage.

Aboriginal-controlled education has two aims. The *first* is to impart skills that aboriginal children will need to succeed in the outside world. The *second* is to immerse them in an environment that is unmistakably aboriginal in content. Aboriginal education is meant to develop children with a resilient sense of identity and with the skills to become whatever they choose. The results have been mixed. Nearly 60 percent of aboriginal children are enrolled in reserve schools (Simpson, 2000). More and more aboriginal youth are graduating from high school. Also, over 27,000 are attending some form of postsecondary education, up from the 200 or so in the mid-1960s. But aboriginal students are still underrepresented in Canada's education system; specifically, they are more likely to drop out of high school. Aboriginal-focus schooling has come under fire. The idea of fostering aboriginal youth's self-esteem by exposing them to traditional languages and culture sounds good on the surface. But, as critics remind us, "feel good" schooling can leave aboriginal people illiterate in English, poorly prepared for the "real" world, and consigned to a life of material poverty (Rubenstein, 2000).

Schooling with a Difference

Multicultural education has been criticized from all angles. According to critics on the right, it is potentially divisive because it emphasizes oppositional and even dangerous knowledge, because it celebrates other cultures excessively and uncritically, and because it focuses on groups rather than on individuals—this, in a society that is based on rewarding individual achievement (Nieto, 1997). According to critics on the left, multiculturalism is too optimistic in an almost romantic way; it also ignores chronic inequalities, which require radical restructuring rather than sensitivity training.

Both sets of criticisms may be accurate, but each also tends to ignore a fundamental fact: multicultural education may be flawed in philosophy and practice, but it still has enormous potential to shift the very foundations of the present-day education system (Gay, 1997). Under multicultural education, groups that were once marginalized are moving to the centre, where they are challenging historic monopolies over the educational agenda (Kalantzis and Cope, 1992).

Multicultural education comes in so many shapes and sizes that a pattern is nearly impossible to detect. That being said, multicultural education is always, ultimately, about fostering inclusiveness. This, of course, forces questions about how inclusiveness should be defined, who should be included, how to achieve inclusiveness, and what the point of inclusiveness is. In Table 7.1, I provide an overview of multicultural education by comparing the three modes discussed earlier: "enrichment through exposure," "enlightenment by analysis," and "minority-focused empowerment." It goes without saying that these models are ideals; they also overlap to some extent and are not necessarily internally consistent.

TABLE 7.1

Models of Multicultural Education

	Enrichment	Enlightenment	Empowerment
Focus	celebrate	analyze	empower
Objectives	ban prejudice	ban discrimination	enhance success
Goals	diversity	disparity	achievement
Outcome	lifestyle ("heritage")	life chances	biculturalism
Means	attitude change	behavioural modification	"whole" person
Style	experience	understand	enhance
Target	student	institution	minority students
Scope	individual	interpersonal	community

ANTIRACISM EDUCATION

Multicultural education often centres on changing attitudes. It often consists of activities that highlight diversity's value to minorities and to society at large (Ministry of Education and Training, 1993). It sets out to enhance sensitivity by improving students' knowledge of cultural differences (enrichment) and ethnic relations (enlightenment). Yet there is no evidence that enriched or enlightened attitudes lead to changes in behaviour. At best, people simply learn to act "correctly"; at worst, prejudices and stereotypes are reinforced.

In contrast, antiracism education focuses on modifying behaviour—that is, on identifying and removing discriminatory barriers at the interpersonal and institutional levels. It begins with the assumption that minority under-achievement is caused by systemic factors, not cultural differences or individual failure. Cultural solutions cannot solve structural problems; it follows that improving minority status must focus on removing the behavioural and structural roots of racial inequality (Kivel, 1996). Sweeping changes in the education system are proposed, rather than cosmetic tinkering with multicultural concessions. On the assumption that racism is the problem and antiracism education is the solution, Carole Tator (1987/1988: 8) has written: "The goal of anti-racist education is to change institutional, organizational policies and practices which have a discriminatory impact; and to change individual behaviours and attitudes that reinforce racism."

Antiracism education sets out to transform those aspects of the education system that exclude minority women and men, intentionally or not. In particular, it contests the power structures—the institutional policies, practices, and procedures—that sustain racism. This effort has at least five dimensions:

- Analyzing the differences that students and teachers bring into the classroom.
- Treating race and racism as "issues of power and inequality rather than matters of cultural difference."
- Questioning existing school practices to uncover the structural roots of monoculturalism and inequality.
- Shifting minorities to the centre of the curriculum by providing a platform for them to tell their own stories in their own voices, and by rejecting the notion that "white" knowledge is the only legitimate knowledge (Allingham, 1992; Mukherjee, 1992; McCaskill, 1995).
- Challenging and rupturing the status quo—rather than layering reforms over the existing system—by encouraging political and social activism (Dei, 1996).

References to "critical pedagogy" are central to antiracism education. A critical pedagogy challenges students and teachers to empower themselves for social change by adopting an ideological stance. Giroux points out that pedagogy becomes critical when it attacks old ways of producing knowledge, social identities, and social relations. Students and teachers are offered an opportunity to see how culture is organized, how some people become authorized to speak about different forms of culture, and how some cultures come to be seen as "worthy" of public esteem. The emphasis here is on understanding how power operates in the interests of the socially dominant, and how existing relations can be challenged and transformed (Giroux, 1994). Sleeter and McLaren (1997: 7) define critical pedagogy this way:

[An] arena of schooling insurgent, resistant, and insurrectional modes of interpretation and classroom practices which set out to imperil the familiar, to contest the legitimating norms of mainstream cultural life, and to render problematic the common discursive frames and regimes upon which "proper" behavior, comportment, and social interaction are premised. Together they analyze extant power configurations and unsettle them when such configurations serve to reproduce social relations of domination. Critical and multicultural pedagogy defamiliarize and make remarkable what is often passed off as the ordinary, the mundane, the routine, and the banal.

In brief, a critical pedagogy scrutinizes those conventional wisdoms which are supposedly neutral, ahistorical, and separated from power, and shows that they are none of these. Students and teachers can then begin to understand how they have been situated despite themselves in a politicized arena of unequal power relations.

Antiracism education is organized around a commitment to share power by taking differences seriously (Dei, 1996). It is rooted in the principle that race and racial discrimination are intrinsic to institutions. Because they are, it important to confront institutional structures and the inequalities they encourage.

Two levels can be discerned: at the level of individuals, antiracism education concentrates on modifying behaviour through education and training (Stern, 1992). At the level of schools, antiracism strategies aim at uprooting systemic racism. These systemic biases are most likely to be found in mission statements, in cultures and subcultures, in power and decision-making arrangements, in rules, roles, and relationships, and in how assets (both financial and human) are distributed.

In *Letters to Marcia* (1985), Enid Lee listed the attributes of antiracist education. These are summarized below:

- Antiracism education is a perspective that permeates all subject areas and school practices.
- Antiracism education emerges from an understanding that racism exists in society; therefore, the school, as an institution of society, is influenced by racism.
- Antiracism education attempts to equip both teachers and students with the analytic tools to critically examine the origins of racist ideas and practices.
- It demonstrates the relationship between our personal prejudices and the systemic discrimination that institutions practise on a daily basis.
- It reveals how racism is learned and can be unlearned.
- It exposes those societal structures which have organized people's lives in a way that impoverishes some while enriching others on the basis of their race.

- It exposes inadequate explanations that attempt to justify and account for people's different positions in the society. It does not allow the examiner to dismiss "failures" as the result of bad luck or inherent inferiority. Rather, antiracism education highlights some of the "men"-made social structures and barriers that prevent individuals and groups from improving their chances in life.
- Antiracism education identifies how much value society has placed on people of different racial groups. It exposes the benefits that some derive from these evaluations, and the opportunities others have lost.
- Antiracism education provides a model for a true multicultural society. It moves beyond the material aspects of cultures—the foods, the festivals—to examine the more controversial dimensions of culture that have led to change in the past and can lead to more in the future (Lee, 1985: 8–9).

In short, antiracism education differs sharply from multicultural education. Multicultural education is about learning; antiracism education is about *doing*. Multicultural education is about diversity; antiracism education is about *disadvantage*. Multicultural education is about cultural diversity; antiracism education is about *social relations*. Other differences can be discerned: antiracism education shifts attention away from minority cultures as timeless or exotic. It approaches racism as something that is historically created, symbolically expressed, and institutionally embedded at various levels in society (Giroux, 1994). The focus is on transforming the structural roots of racism and racial discrimination rather than on acknowledging differences or analyzing stereotypes. Table 7.2 provides a quick summary of the differences.

TABLE 7.2

Multicultural and Antiracism Education Compared and Contrasted

	Multicultural Education	Antiracism Education
Focus	culture	structure
Objectives	sensitivity	removing discriminatory barriers
Concerns	diversity	disadvantage
Scope	student	institutions
Styles	accommodative	challenge and transformation
Outcomes	harmony	equality

RELIGIOUS PLURALISM AND MULTICULTURAL EDUCATION

Religious pluralism has always been a fact of Canadian life. The British North America (Constitution) Act affirmed the religious rights of English Protestants and French Catholics. Under the BNA Act, common schools in Upper and Lower Canada would cater to the creed of the majority. Minority education rights for Protestants (in Quebec) and Catholics (in Ontario) were also enshrined. The need for political tranquillity and national unity justified all of this (Callan, 2000). Admittedly, Catholics were routinely denied full involvement or equal protection under the law—a discriminatory situation that persisted until recently. But formal religious affiliation no longer has the importance—or the clout—it once had in public affairs. This ideological shift is proving to be double-edged.

Canada is less religious than it used to be, but at the same time far more religiously complex. According to the 1991 census, Roman Catholicism (46 percent) and Protestantism (36 percent, in the six main denominations) are still the dominant religions among those who state an affiliation. At the same time, other religions such as Hinduism, Islam, Buddhism, Confucianism, Sikhism, and Judaism are increasingly part of Canada's multicultural map. These other religions are tolerated far more than in the past. In these ecumenical times, open criticism of other faiths is routinely denounced as bigotry and backwardness. Tolerance is also reflected in the separation of church and state, in the growing secularization of Canadian society, and in the acceptance of cultural relativism. Canadians ought to be proud of all this. But at the same time as religion has lost its social force, it has been marginalized. For those who take religion seriously, this marginalization is unacceptable.

The importance of religion to people's lives and to group survival should never be underestimated (Uphoff, 1997). In the organizational or personal sense, religion addresses the fundamental question of why we are here and where we are going. It also aids individuals in their search for meaning, self-affirmation, and commitment. For many ethnic and racial minorities, religious affiliation is an important source of identity and continuity, as individuals search for ways to adapt to Canadian society (Herberg, 1989). Religions are neither an option nor a luxury; they are communities of faith within which members embrace beliefs that are beyond criticism or question (Callan, 2000). Not everyone, of course, takes religion seriously. For many, religion is largely symbolic and situational—something that is activated when necessary (at Christmas, for marriages and funerals) but allowed to lapse in the everyday. To the extent that religion is increasingly perceived as an individual matter, it forces this question: Where should Canadians draw the line when religious practices conflict with mainstream values?

Religion and Schools: A Volatile Mix?

One of the more heated debates in present Canadian society involves the relationship between religion and education. Few topics are more emotional than this one. Public schools are becoming more and more secularized, and reject displays of religion as potentially dangerous. The secularization of Christmas festivities is merely one example. Yet religion still matters. Schools are under pressure to take religion into account lest they lose public support and credibility. But organized religion no longer resonates with the same meaning once enjoyed. Because religion has been dislodged from Canada's national agenda, many Canadians find it hard to appreciate how much it matters in other cultures.

In Canada's early decades, religion and schooling were inseparable, notwithstanding they were kept separate under the BNA Act. Protestantism and Catholicism were both strong enough that every child was socialized in a school of his or her faith. But Canada is now a far more diverse country, and various minority groups are beginning to acquire political clout in hopes of securing state funding for schools of their own religion. In the interests of fairness, justice, and human rights, some of those groups are beginning to have their demands met, and for Canada, this is revolutionary (Callan, 2000). Provincial governments find themselves in a bind. Canada's religious mosaic is growing increasingly diverse. Multifaith diversity is a fact of Canadian life. At the same time, there is heartfelt resistance to extending tolerance to the point of funding separate schools along religious lines.

What should this country do when religious practices fall outside Canadian ways? Where should official multiculturalism draw the line when visions collide? A ruling by Ontario's Supreme Court has allowed baptized Sikhs to carry ceremonial daggers (*kirpans*) into the classroom provided that the symbolic replica is well secured under outside garments and that school authorities are informed. Is this concession a valid expression of religious pluralism? Or does it pose a grave risk to Canada's social security? There is no consensus on questions like this, which makes it increasingly important for Canadians to address the politics and paradoxes of religious pluralism in schools. Consider the following questions, which are only a sample from the many that could be asked:

- To what degree can schools (which are ostensibly neutral, notwithstanding their roots in the two founding religions) incorporate religious pluralism without eroding Canada's historic integrity and multicultural commitments?

- How should schools respond to religious beliefs and practices that run counter to core values in education? And how should they respond to fundamentalist sects that are critical of liberal pluralism (i.e., its permissiveness, relativism and tolerance, and secularism) (Kenny, 2000)? What happens when religious traditions promote principles of hierarchy and obedience that are incompatible with core educational values such as individualism, equality, inclusiveness, mutual respect for differences, and critical thinking (Spinner-Halev, 2000)? What can be done when compulsory sex education, which accepts homosexuality as normal, encounters religious traditions that condemn gay and lesbian sex as an abomination (Callan, 2000)?

- Should governments be encouraging religious pluralism? Should funding be allocated to private religious schools that disavow Canada's liberal democratic commitment to social justice, economic fairness, and human rights? By endorsing such schools, are governments splintering the school system, and thereby damaging Canadian identity and national unity?

- Should the government be tolerant of religious faiths that are intolerant of others? How much tolerance ought to be extended to cultural practices that leave some people vulnerable to inequality within their own communities (Shachar, 2000; Saharso, 2000)? Some religious groups condone the mistreatment of individuals within their community—for example, by obligating women to obey their husbands, by hushing up incidents of domestic abuse for fear of dishonouring the family name, and by making divorce and remarriage impossible.

Thinking Outside the Box

Erecting Walls or Building Bridges?

Islamic schools are testing the limits of tolerance in Canada's multicultural school system (see also Sampson, 2000). Islam rejects a number of Canada's mainstream practices. How, then, can Canada's school systems accept Islamic schools without falling into chaos? And how can they not accept them without denying the validity of diversity? To accommodate the religious practices of Muslim students, Canada's schools have already made many policy adjustments: they have acknowledged that these students must dress modestly and cover their heads; they have banned depictions of human and animal figures; they have acknowledged special dietary restrictions; they have respected a prohibition on playing stringed instruments; and they have stopped putting boys and girls in close contact, even on group projects (Scrivener, 2000). Problems arise when moves toward inclusiveness clash with the stricter tenets of Islam. Equity policies on sexual orientation have been a flashpoint for many Muslim parents, who see these policies as encouraging a gay lifestyle that many perceive as contrary to their beliefs.

In short, the public school system may not be inclusive enough to take these differences seriously. At the same time, it may be too accommodating and inclusive in its efforts to incorporate everything and everybody. Islamic schools have been founded in reaction to community concerns; there are eighteen of them in Toronto alone, with an enrollment of 2,240 (Scrivener, 2001). Waiting lists continue to surge even though these schools are short of equipment, staffed by underpaid teachers, and supported by annual fees and voluntary help. As with all independent schools in Ontario (currently there are 725 schools, with nearly two-thirds espousing Christian principles; Scrivener, 2001), these schools must register themselves with the Ministry of Education and Training. However, they are exempt from regulation or inspection (unless they grant high school diplomas), and their teachers do not require teaching certificates. Obviously, they are popular not only because they provide a good education. Rather, they provide a cocoon for Muslim children and a degree of protection from the excessively secular and undisciplined public school system. Islamic schools are not curriculum or child centred. They are prayer centred, with goals anchored in religion, prayer, morality, and discipline.

The conclusions are mixed. Islamic schools reflect multiculturalism at its best; they may also slip between the cracks of official multiculturalism. To the extend that Islamic schools are responding to a need, they exemplify multiculturalism in practice. To the extent that these schools divide rather than unite people, they run counter to the goals of Canada's official multiculturalism.

Schooling Together with Religious Differences

All of the issues surrounding religious pluralism remind us that Canada's schools are contested sites. This country's schools have four basic options: tolerate religions without actively supporting them; promote religion as part of the curriculum; support religion by providing public funds to separate schools; or reject religion in the public realm (with several exceptions) to ensure separation of church and state. These options are worth a closer look.

First, some people want compulsory religious instruction, but only in mainstream Christian faiths. Precedent for this demand has been established by Catholic schools, whose right to provide religious instruction is enshrined in the Constitution and generously interpreted in provinces such as Ontario.

Second, some argue that religion has no place in a secular school system, nor (it follows) does religious instruction. In a truly multicultural society, religion must never be imposed. Religious indoctrination violates the spirit of Canada's multicultural realities. It also interferes with the freedoms of religion and conscience, which are guaranteed in the *Charter of Rights and Freedoms*. Religious instruction can be conducted outside regular school hours, provided all faiths have equal access to space and resources as stipulated by equality-of-treatment provisions.

Moves to take "Christ" out of Christmas celebrations reflect this line of thought. More and more often, Christmas celebrations in urban public schools are discarding overtly religious symbols in an effort to provide a multiculturally inclusive environment. Schools have renamed their annual Christmas assembly a "holiday" celebration and purged all references to Christian theology and to Christ's nativity. The singing of religious Christmas carols is often discouraged for fear of upsetting non-Christian children. When an obvious Christian component is retained, other religious symbols are included to ensure balance.

Third, in between these two poles is a position that rejects religious indoctrination but upholds the right to instruction in a variety of religious traditions. This falls under the rubric of mutual learning and intercultural sharing. Ontario's Ministry of Education and Training has released guidelines that allow multifaith religious instruction in schools as long as no single religion is emphasized (Ministry of Education, December 6, 1990). The Ontario Court of Appeal has ruled that education about (or instruction in) religion and moral values is not a breach of the Charter. The distinction between indoctrination and education is captured in this excerpt from the Ontario Ministry of Education (Policy/Program Memo No. 112, 1990):

— The school may sponsor the study of religion, but NOT the practice of religion.

— The school may expose students to all religious views without endorsing a particular one.

— The school's approach to religion is one of instruction, NOT one of indoctrination.

— The school's function is to educate about all religions, not to convert to any one religion.

— The school's approach is academic, not devotional.

— The school should study what all people believe, but not what a student should believe.

— The school should strive for student awareness of all religions, not acceptance of any one.

A *fourth* position advocates that religious differences be incorporated into the school system, either as part of the curriculum or as separate streams of schooling. A truly multicultural school system takes religions seriously. It acknowledges that a diversity of religious beliefs and practices must be recognized in the daily routines of school life if Canada's multiculturalism is to mean anything. Some have applauded this move to provide equal time to all religions as a useful step toward multiculturalizing the education system. Others have criticized this approach because it makes unnecessary demands on teachers while becoming confusing to young children. A number of alternatives and substitutes have been implemented as gestures of good faith. But school boards acknowledge that difficulties can arise because of staffing problems, resource shortages, and the demands of other religious groups. Jeff Spinner-Halev (2000: 88–99) captures the essence of the dilemma:

> Schools and teachers are in a particularly tough spot. If they teach values, they are bound to anger the parents who have different values. If they refuse, and teach instead that each student should decide for herself what her values are, then schools will be accused of lacking any moral compass and of teaching relativism. If they teach that everyone's perspective is valid, as some multiculturalists advocate, and that we all have our own understanding of reality, then they will again be accused of relativism.

The dilemma is clear. Schools are being criticized for not being inclusive enough in endorsing a pretend religious pluralism. They are also being criticized for being too inclusive in taking religious differences seriously. The end result is confusion over what to do and how.

CASE STUDY (Continued)
Campus Racism

FROM IVORY TOWER TO INSTITUTIONS OF COLOUR

Campus racism exists. Minority students have drawn attention to a chilly campus climate that generates a hostile learning environment (Alladin, 1996). They have complained about harassment from students, the racial biases of faculty, and the exclusionary practices of technical and support staff (Henry et al., 2000). The presence of hate groups, from white supremacists to Holocaust deniers, remains a source of contention. And a predominantly Eurocentric curriculum continues to erode any pretext of a pluralistic and inclusive campus.

Campus racism has elicited a variety of responses, from denial to bandwagon. Most people are willing to concede that there are sporadic and individual acts of racism, and that attempts to combat racism have been ineffective; they are less willing to acknowledge systemic biases. Casual solutions can easily magnify tensions instead of reducing them. Indecisiveness is just as harmful when campus administrators are perceived to be balking at responding to racist acts (Stern, 1992). When they fail to act quickly with zero tolerance, administrators can worsen matters by encouraging the impression that they don't take racism seriously—or as seriously as courting alumni.

There are two basic possible responses to campus racism: reactive and proactive. Campus administrators have *reacted* to the reality of racism by establishing appropriate policies and offices (Fleras, 1996). They have implemented harassment codes and antidiscrimination guidelines in conformity with provincial human rights codes. They have put contingency measures in place to deal with emergencies. They have established committees representing a cross-section of the campus to help formulate policies, as well as procedures for worst-case scenarios. They have developed mechanisms for opening lines of communication and mediating conflicts. They have appointed resource people to advise students in need. They have drafted disciplinary codes as a last resort for punishing the guilty and for deterring potential offenders.

Proactive measures concentrate on prevention. Universities and community colleges across the country have drawn up plans to increase the participation of minority women and men at all levels of decision making. They have introduced equity initiatives to improve their recruiting and hiring practices, and are taking steps to retain minority faculty and staff. They are trying to be more responsive to the needs of minority students (Ford, 1998). They are holding workshops to foster cultural sensitivity and to train people in the skills needed for engaging diversity. They have established race relations offices and human rights committees. And they have denounced campus racism in their mission statements (Queen's University, 1991; University of Western Ontario, 1993; McGill University, 1994; O'Neill and Yelaha, 1994).

Universities and community colleges seem to be moving in the right direction. Admittedly, the effectiveness of their policies is open to question (Henry et al., 1995). Most of their reforms have been moderate ones, and have not done much to challenge entrenched ways of doing things. When policies place too much emphasis on overt, individual acts of racism, individual victims may be helped, but systemic racism can end up being forgotten about (Carniol, 1991; Hick and Santos, 1992; also Bartolome, 1994).

Institutions of higher learning are generally looked up to as bastions of enlightenment. Yet at the same time, they have been saddled with the messy responsibility of spearheading progressive social change. All post-secondary institutions are expected to act in progressive and liberal-minded ways, but without actually subverting the system (McIntyre, 1993). How willing are postsecondary institutions to go the inclusive route, given its potential to provoke or disrupt (Garcia and Baird, 2000)? To meet this challenge, they will require both political will and financial muscle—this, at a time of fiscal restraint and minority assertiveness. Campus staff will require personal courage if they are to withstand charges of "political correctness" in speaking out against racism and sexism (Richer and Weir, 1995). Their commitment to fighting racism will be sorely tested as they attempt to balance quality with equality. In the final analysis, debates about inclusiveness in higher education are really about power and control—who has it, who wants it, and who is going to do something about it (Schuman and Olufs, 1995).

Chapter Highlights

- Canada's education system has had to respond to unprecedented social change. This has led to a crisis of confidence in the system.
- The need to provide more sensitive, relevant, and equitable education for all Canadians has prompted a series of initiatives for fostering multicultural and inclusive schooling.

- Education has become a contested site. The new forces of inclusiveness are clashing with the traditional forces of assimilation and monoculturalism.
- No one is sure what multicultural education is, what it is trying to do, what it should be doing, and what it realistically can do in difficult circumstances.
- Debates about multicultural education confront one overriding question: Is it about transcending differences, or is it about taking differences into account?
- For some, multicultural education is about celebrating diversity. For others, it is about challenging institutional practices as they relate to students, teachers, and administrators.
- There are three basic approaches to multicultural education: enrichment, enhancement, and empowerment. Each makes its own assumptions about what multicultural education is meant to accomplish.
- The enrichment model of multicultural education focuses on changing people's attitudes by exposing them to different cultures. The enlightenment model emphasizes that minority relations are fundamentally unequal. The empowerment model sets out to provide minority students with "space" within the system for their own cultures.
- Those on the left have criticized multicultural education because it avoids real discussions of race, it supports an assimilationist agenda, and it accepts cultural differences too readily. Those on the right tend to criticize multicultural education as divisive.
- Antiracism education emphasizes challenging, resisting, and transforming the status quo in the system itself and in society at large.
- Multifaith diversity is proving an awkward fit within a predominantly secular school system.

Review Questions

1. Contemporary education is a contested site. Explain.
2. What is multicultural education? What is meant by an education that endorses the principles of multiculturalism? What is multicultural education trying to accomplish? How and why?
3. How does a monocultural education system differ from multicultural one?
4. In what sense is the present-day education system undergoing a crisis of identity? Why?

5. Compare and contrast the different types of multicultural education in terms of problems each raises and the solutions each offers.
6. How does antiracism education differ from multicultural education?
7. How does racism manifest itself in universities and community colleges? Do existing institutional responses to racism provide an adequate solution?
8. What are some of the dilemmas associated with incorporating religious pluralism into a multicultural and seemingly secular school system?

Recommended Reading

Michael Apple. 1979. *Ideology and Curriculum*. London: Routledge and Kegan Paul.

James A. Banks and Cheryl A. McGee Banks, eds. 1979. *Multicultural Education: Issues and Perceptions*. Toronto: Allyn and Bacon.

Frances Henry et al. 2000. *The Colour of Democracy: Racism in Canadian Society*, 2nd ed. Toronto: Harcourt.

Stephen May, ed. 1999. *Critical Multiculturalism: Rethinking Multiculturalism and Anti-Racist Education*. London: Falmer Press.

Peter Mittler. 2000. *Working Toward Inclusive Education and Social Contexts*. London: David Fulton Publishers.

Christine Sleeter and G. Grant. 1992. *Making Choices for Multicultural Education*. Columbus: Merrill/Macmillan.

CHAPTER

8

Multicultural Competence: Communications, Mindsets, and Imagination

CHAPTER OBJECTIVES

- To appreciate some of the difficulties and challenges of putting multicultural principles into everyday practice.
- To explore the meaning of multicultural competence in a society that embraces the principles of multiculturalism.
- To discuss multicultural competence as it relates to cross-cultural communication and a "multicultural imagination."
- To demonstrate the differences between a multicultural and a monocultural mentality.
- To explore the barriers to multicultural competence, including prejudice and racism.
- To explain the need to unmask the many faces of racism, at both individual and institutional levels.
- To show the importance of cross-cultural communication for attaining multicultural competence.
- To concede the inevitability of breakdowns in effective cross-cultural communication.
- To acknowledge that the concept of "cultural safety" may improve the delivery of social services to diverse clients.

CASE STUDY
Communication Breakdown

The ability to communicate cross-culturally is vital in a multicultural society (Samover and Porter, 2000). The ability to understand and get along with others who are culturally different is critical to peaceful coexistence. These abilities are becoming especially important with the world's cultures coming into closer and closer contact. Yet communication and interaction skills are easier to talk about than to acquire. Individuals must learn to discard their biases and prejudices; they must also develop more general skills in empathy, openness, and tolerance. More important still, they must learn how to apply general principles to specific situations. Failure to do so can create cross-cultural calamities—as the next scenario demonstrates.

A police officer stops a motorist on a routine search. The motorist avoids looking at the officer when questioned. Her culture forbids her to make direct eye contact with social superiors or in stressful situations. The police officer is puzzled by this lack of eye contact and assumes that the motorist is being evasive. Assuming that the motorist has done something wrong, the police officer responds with a flurry of questions in the hope of getting at the truth. The fixed stare of a police officer intimidates the motorist, who interprets it as a challenge or threat. The situation rapidly escalates out of control.

Most Canadians are taught to look people in the eye when communicating. Not too directly, of course, since too much eye contact or staring is often interpreted as rude or aggressive. And not too indirectly either, as this can easily be perceived as a sign of evasiveness or deceit. Rather, each person must maintain a kind of intermittent eye contact that looks without staring—what Erving Goffman calls "civil inattention." Not everyone practises the same eye management, however. Canadians from other cultures often manage their eyes differently when communicating. When they avert their gaze they are not being shifty; if anything, a direct gaze would signal that they are feeling guilty or remorseful. In other words, an averted gaze signals different things in different cultures: anything from aggression to deferrence (Fleras, 1998).

What we have, then, is a clear case of poor communication because of cultural differences (Sue and Sue, 1990). The driver's avoidance of eye contact matches the officer's cultural expectations of how wrongdoers behave, and the officer proceeds on that basis. The officer draws false and insulting conclusions about the motorist as a person. The motorist picks up on these and responds accordingly, first by averting her gaze and then by reacting verbally and physically to this "intrusion." The purpose of this case study is not to blame anyone, but rather to highlight a number of important questions: Was the officer acting in a multiculturally competent way? How would a multicultural mindset have dealt with the situation? Is it possible for the officer to act in a culturally safe manner? At the end of this chapter we will explore this issue more carefully.

"WALKING THE TALK"

Canada has been widely acclaimed as a multicultural success story. Yet our high reputation isn't totally deserved, and how much it is deserved depends greatly on how you define multiculturalism and what you think its goals should be. Canada's official multiculturalism has rarely been an agent of radical change; it is neither equipped nor designed to challenge, resist, and transform. Yet official multiculturalism has all the same turned out to be transformative, in that it has dismantled the Britishness that once defined English-speaking Canada. Equally transformative have been Canada's moves toward more inclusive institutions. We can only conclude that multiculturalism, as a policy and in practise, is inseparable from Canadian society building.

But all of this represents the "big picture." Now what about the human dimension? When we emphasize the macro side too much, we forget to ask micro yet equally important questions, most of them to do with how multiculturalism is practised day by day, on the street, between individuals. How are the micro and macro connected? This question has to be asked. Official multiculturalism is unlikely to do much to foster inclusiveness unless Canadians learn to "walk the talk."

A microsociological analysis asks how Canadians are internalizing multiculturalism as a basis for seeing the world, thinking about the world, experiencing the world, and relating to others. It focuses on the notion of *multicultural competence*. This concept can mean many things. Ultimately, however, it considers people's ability to perform "acceptably" in a society that endorses multicultural principles. There are two basic facets of multicultural competence: people's attitudes, and their actions (i.e., how those attitudes are communicated). Only when Canadians internalize multicultural attitudes and improve their skills in communicating cross-culturally will the prospects for living together be improved.

The benefits of multicultural competence are obvious. Multicultural literacy and competence are vital in today's rapidly changing and highly competitive global business environment (Bennett et al., 2000). Those who are multiculturally competent enjoy a competitive edge in coping with the demands of a diverse and changing Canada. The same skills also come in handy for navigating the sometimes treacherous shoals of interpersonal relations. To the extent that multicultural competence increases the flexibility and resilience of our minds, it provides us with the tools to promote interpersonal harmony to global peace (Annual Report, 2000).

Those who develop multicultural competence will reap many benefits. A multicultural orientation connects people locally, nationally, and internationally (Iyer, 2001). Yet people have found multicultural competence difficult to achieve, despite its importance both to them and to society. What do individuals require if they are to live together with their differences? Consider the following questions:

1. What constitutes multicultural competence? How can we tell whether a person or society has become multiculturally competent?

2. Is a multicultural mindset rooted in taking differences seriously? Or is it really about treating everyone the same (i.e., being "colour blind")? Is it about cultural uniqueness or connectedness?

3. Is multicultural competence about what people think, or is it about what they do? Is it based on a general ability to move between different cultural worlds? Or is it based on the ability to selectively learn cultural customs as needs arise?

4. What constitutes effective cross-cultural communication? To what extent can communication skills be learned? Are some communication barriers simply too formidable to overcome?

5. How great a factor are cultural values in fostering multicultural competence?

There are no cut-and-dried answers to these questions, any more than there is a clear definition of multicultural competence. Yet answers must be found if multiculturalism is to work in practice.

In this chapter I explore the challenges of putting multiculturalism into daily practice. I will be assuming that multicultural competence is neither a luxury nor an option; in this changing and diverse world, we must all be groomed to perform competently to achieve our personal goals and survive as a society. I begin by comparing a multicultural mindset with a monocultural one. I then consider the barriers to attaining multicultural competence, paying special attention to prejudice and racism as major stumbling blocks. I then discuss cross-cultural communication. In a society that endorses living together with differences, the ability to communicate cross-culturally is critical.

THE NOTION OF COMPETENCE

Canadians live in a society that officially extols multicultural principles as a basis for living together with diversity. Yet at everyday levels, there are formidable barriers to multicultural coexistence. Generally speaking, Canadians are of two minds when it comes to diversity. Some believe that we are fundamentally the same, whatever our heritage, and that people should be treated alike for the purposes of defining who gets what. Others believe that we are fundamentally different as a result of our experiences or birthrights, and that these differences must be taken into account to ensure full equality and inclusion.

Some Canadians intuitively dislike diversity and change, and prefer the status quo with its reassuring predictability and prevailing distributions of power and privilege. Other Canadians seem to enjoy the challenges of change and diversity, and embrace them as intrinsically valid and valuable—even if the engagement process is fraught with tensions and disappointments.

This split between multiculturalism and monoculturalism is somewhat artificial; clearly, they are two poles, and most people are closer to the middle. Even so, this distinction offers insights into the challenge of engaging diversity. Too much diversity may undermine cohesiveness; not enough may stifle flexibility. In the final analysis, transforming multicultural principles into everyday practice tends to "go against the grain" of convention.

The practical demands of living together with differences are extremely complex and resist implementation. Central to living together with differences is multicultural competence. What exactly does it mean to be multiculturally competent? What skills do people need to embrace multiculturalism? How do multiculturalistically competent people think, and how does this competence reflect and reinforce a multicultural mindset?

Since there is no secure definition of multicultural competence, the debate over these questions is unlikely to subside anytime soon. This isn't necessarily a bad thing, if it helps people avoid being locked into formulas for living together in a changing and diverse world that shuns the routine and predictable.

Monoculturalism and Multiculturalism

One approach to defining a multicultural mindset involves establishing what it is not. The antithesis of multiculturalism is monoculturalism. A person with a monocultural mentality is judgmental and prone to categorizing others. Such a person allows no exceptions and rejects all nuances, and insists on sharp distinctions and fixed categories. People like this process information in a rigid, moralistic, and often dualistic manner. They dismiss other perspectives as inferior or irrelevant. Central to monoculturalism is unthinking ethnocentrism or *idiocentrism*. Idiocentric people automatically assume that their own perspective of the world is the natural and normal one. They misguidedly assume that others would see it exactly the same way if they somehow knew better.

The monocultural mentality is made even narrower by a refusal to take differences seriously. For example, consider the lingering power of liberal pluralism. Liberal pluralism is often (but not always) opposed to diversity, as a result of its assumption that what people have in common as individuals is more important than differences arising from their membership in a group. Liberal pluralism accepts differences, of course, but only in the context of "pretend pluralism," whereby everyone is different in the same kind of way. The result of this monocultural mentality? Multiculturally incompetent people who are incapable of coping with the complexities and nuances of diversity.

A multicultural mindset is the reverse of all this. People with a multicultural mindset tend to be flexible and nonjudgmental. They are not intimidated by ambiguities and paradoxes, but flourish as a result of them. They accept that humanity is multidimensional, and acknowledge the importance of differences—including their own. They also tend to understand that reality is a fluid thing. All of this suggests that versatility and resilience are central to a multicultural mindset. In a world in which rules are changing and games are constantly shifting, such nimbleness is vitally important.

A multicultural mindset is inseparable from a commitment to taking differences seriously. This openness to diversity as natural and normal results in a distinct way of looking at the world. People with a multicultural mindset examine the world from many different perspectives, and see these different perspectives as equally legitimate; but they do not reject the possibility of universal cultural codes. These people acknowledge the importance of a common vision as grounds for living together. Yet they also concede that such a vision will be subject to compromise. The following table compares monocultural mentalities and multicultural mentalities.

TABLE 8.1

Processing Information: Monoculturalism and Multiculturalism

Monoculturalism	Multiculturalism
Judgmental	Nonjudgmental
Rigid and unbending	Flexible and resilient
Dualistic and polarized ("black and white")	Holistic in approaching ambiguities and paradoxes
Static and categorical	Situational and provisional
Absolutist	Relativistic
Ethnocentric and dismissive	Altrucentric and empathetic
Culturally blinkered	Culturally self-aware
Pretend pluralism	Taking differences seriously

This table clarifies key terms and demonstrates how they relate to each other. Multicultural competence is about developing the skills needed to cope with the demands of living together in a multicultural society. As was noted in the introduction to this chapter, there are two basic facets to multicultural competence: how people think (including their multicultural mindset), and how they communicate based on their thinking. People with multicultural mindsets process information on pluralistic principles. They take differences seriously by nurturing a receptiveness toward diversity (Harris, 1995). They do not approach cultural differences as simply an option or luxury to be discarded when convenient. Rather, they approach these differences as critical in terms of shaping patterns of beliefs and behaviours.

People with multicultural imagination are routinely willing to approach reality from a variety of perspectives. They appreciate that people live in widely different social realities. This cultural relativism makes it doubly important that differences be taken into account to understanding, assessment, and action. Multicultural competence also requires effective cross-cultural communication skills, which are vital to personal and professional relationships.

The path to competence is strewn with perils and pitfalls. The cliché "It's easier said than done" is highly applicable here. Barriers exist that can daunt even the most multiculturally imaginative people. Can anyone transcend idiocentrism and genuinely engage with other cultures on their terms? Or are people doomed to refract reality through the prism of their own truths? Are human experiences too customized by gender and race to bridge the gap?

All of us have been socialized to see, think, experience, and relate to the world in specific ways. As a result, each of us has become "trapped within our truths," whether we are aware of it or not. We fob off other world-views and perspectives not because of bigotry but rather as a result of cultural blinkers and tunnel vision. Clearly, it is hard to develop multicultural competence. Doing so involves "going against the grain" and learning to walk up "down" escalators.

Countdown to Competence

The challenge of multicultural competence faces all Canadians. Those who provide services to Canada's increasingly diverse citizens face even more responsibilities. Service providers, from teachers to the police to social welfare workers, are often the first and only point of contact for new or native-born Canadians. Their skills at relating to minority women and men have a powerful impact on those who are trying to "settle down," "fit in," and "put down roots." But the goal of multicultural competence is an elusive grail for most people. At a minimum, service providers must develop competence in three major areas: appreciation of one's own culture, appreciation of other specific cultures, and interaction skills (Diller, 1999; Lynch and Hanson, 1999).

Awareness and Acceptance: "Taking Differences Seriously"

The first step in developing a multicultural mindset is to learn to take differences seriously. This obviously goes beyond "celebrating cultures" and "live and let live" tolerance. It is equally important to learn to accept, without prejudgment, other cultures' values, perceptions of time, communication styles, and outlooks on reality. Cultural differences shape how people see, think, experience, and relate to others. Only by acknowledging all of this can we situate people's motives and behaviours in a specific cultural context.

Yet caution must be exercised. Cultures are more than grocery lists to be memorized. Individual behaviour is not a simple, robotic reflex to cultural demands and structural constraints. Culturally specific information can explain a great deal, but it is not an absolutely reliable predictor. In fact, more problems are likely to arise when culturally specific information is used as an infallible blueprint for expectations and behaviour.

Self-Cultural Awareness: "Know Yourself, Culturally Speaking"

It is important to understand other cultures. What is less apparent is that people need to understand their own cultures. Members of the mainstream are influenced by their own cultural values; their culture is so tightly linked with daily existence that its impact is seldom acknowledged. Every individual has a cultural inventory that influences his or her perceptions of what is acceptable, normal, expected, and necessary. All people must try to understand how they are a product of their own cultural conditioning, and how this conditioning affects their patterns of communication with others.

Service providers must acknowledge the impact of their own cultural values on culturally diverse clients, especially when providers and recipients come from different cultures. Consider the difficulties that arise when service providers value independence over interdependence, competition over cooperation, permissive childrearing practices over authoritarian styles, and efficiency over interaction, and recipients do not (Lynch and Hanson, 1999). When service providers acknowledge the attitudes and prejudices they bring with them to work, empathy is possible, and attention is drawn to how cultural misunderstandings are a regrettable yet inevitable aspect of all social interactions. Competing values are discussed toward the end of the chapter.

Dynamics of Interaction: "Open Mind/Thick Skin"

It is one thing to appreciate cultural diversity. It is often quite another to understand that these differences invariably lead to confusion. Good interaction involves understanding what can go wrong, conceding that interaction usually *will* go wrong because of divergent perspectives, addressing the communication breakdowns that arise, and shrugging off failures and forging ahead with a renewed determination.

Culture shock is inevitable. It is the result of disorienting encounters between different sets of beliefs and values. The strategies that a person once used to solve problems and interact successfully with others suddenly no longer work. The result can be overwhelming discomfort. Behaviour that was acceptable in one cultural context may be misunderstood, demeaned, laughed at, or even illegal in a new setting (Lynch and Hanson, 1999). Service providers must learn to cope with culture shock in two ways. *First*, they must acknowledge the cultural values that gave rise to it, and introduce or interpret novel cultural practices to Canadians. *Second*, they must respond proactively to their clients' disorientation. This may involve adjusting to the service recipient's patterns of interaction and communication. Or it may simply involve keeping an open mind and a thick skin, on the assumption that such slippages are inevitable, and can't always be anticipated.

To sum up: Understanding multicultural competence is not the same as practising it in daily life. Culture is not always a reliable predictor of behaviour. Embracing multicultural ideals is challenging enough in everyday life. It is even more difficult when it comes to service delivery. Those who ignore the messages of multiculturalism will fumble the challenges of living together with differences.

BARRIERS TO MULTICULTURAL COMPETENCE

It is commonly assumed that Canada is a largely tolerant and open society. Prejudice, to the extent it exists, is found only among a fringe element that just doesn't know any better. Racism is quickly disappearing from Canada's social landscape. A few "rotten apples" such as neo-Nazis are of course spoiling it for everybody, but generally speaking, Canadians have come far in shedding their racist past. Official multiculturalism is perceived as proof of such enlightenment (Allahar and Coté, 1998).

Yet this self-congratulation has little basis in reality. Canadians tend to be in denial about racism, and have no right to see themselves as more progressive than Americans (Allahar and Coté, 1998). Actually, prejudice is endemic among Canadians: even the most open-minded have often prejudged others, at odds with multicultural principles. Contrary to popular belief, there is still racism in this country, and it is reconstituting itself in a variety of forms, interpersonal and institutional and cultural (Henry et al., 2000). Despite a great deal of effort and commitment, ending it is proving to be even more difficult than unmasking it (Fleras and Elliott, 1999). The pervasiveness of racism and prejudice (including ethnocentrism and stereotyping) is a blot on Canadian society and is eroding the possibility of multicultural competence.

Prejudice

Prejudice is typically defined as negative and preconceived notions about others. These notions are often unconscious. They are irrational and unfounded and run counter to existing evidence. A prejudiced individual refuses to modify beliefs when presented with contrary evidence; this is what distinguishes prejudice from ignorance.

As a way of processing information, prejudice involves a set of generalized attitudes and beliefs at odds with objective facts (Holdaway, 1996). It arises from our tendency to prejudge people or situations when defining the world around us. Prejudicial thinking is "normal" and "necessary" in two senses. *First*, it is fundamental to how individuals process information with respect to in-group/out-group relations (Thomas, 1998). *Second*, it is perceived as a deeply rooted psychological phenomenon with a corresponding set of author-itarian personality traits (Adorno, 1950; Allport, 1954). Not surprisingly, the vast majority of Canadians have unconscious prejudices from being exposed to monocultural cultural values and social dynamics (Henry and Tator, 1985; Large, 1998).

At a "practical" level, prejudice is even more sinister. Prejudice involves a deep and visceral dislike of those whose appearances or customs threaten the status quo. For some, prejudice is based on fear of those who are different or who challenge certitudes and values. For others, prejudice is closely linked with feelings of superiority, perceptions that subordinate groups are inferior, a belief in white privilege and power, and a reluctance to share scarce resources (Blumer, 1958). For still others, prejudice is a projection of main-stream fears and fantasies onto the "other" (which reveals more about "us" than about "them") (Curtis, 1997). However it is perceived, prejudice is always a function of group dynamics in society. Prejudices do not materialize out of nowhere; they are just not the byproduct of unhealthy personal devel-opment. The roots of prejudice are always social and historical. Two of its most important dimensions are ethnocentrism and stereotyping.

Ethnocentrism

Every society socializes its members to accept the way of life it offers as the normal and natural one. People grow up believing that what they think and how they act are universally applicable, and that others tend to think or act along the same lines. The term for this is *ethnocentrism*, which has two reper-cussions. *First*, individuals tend to be "trapped within their truths." They rou-tinely and automatically interpret reality from their own cultural point of view, and assume that others are thinking along the same lines (or would if given a chance). Other realities are dismissed as inferior or irrelevant. *Second*, ethnocentrism asserts the superiority of one's own culture over others. It reflects an uncompromising loyalty to and belief in one's own cul-tural values and practices. As a result, other cultural beliefs and practices are dismissed simply because they are different.

Ethnocentrism is not a conscious political stance by people who want to declare their bias. Rather, it is an "implicit positioning" (Stam, 1997: 194) in the sense of being a result of centuries of European domination. There is nothing intrinsically wrong with preferring one's own culture. Difficulties arise when this preference provides a frame of reference for negatively evaluating others as backward, immoral, or irrational in circumstances where power is unequally distributed (Stam and Miller, 2000). The problems are even worse when ethnocentric judgments are used to condone the mistreatment of others. A variant of ethnocentrism, Eurocentrism, assumes the universality and superiority of the "white" perspective (Battiste and Henderson, 2000). Other perspectives are dismissed accordingly. In other words, ethnocentrism is a two-edged social phenomenon: favouritism toward one's group may forge the bonds of cohesion and morale; it may also foster outgroup hostility and intergroup conflict.

Stereotyping

Ethnocentrism often leads to stereotyping. Stereotyping is the universal tendency to assign simple (and simplistic) explanations to complex phenomena, and then generalize those explanations to an entire category in such a way that individual differences are rejected (Isajiw, 1999). Essentially, *stereotypes* are generalizations about others and often reflect first impressions. Like prejudices, they are not supported by available evidence. Stereotypes are a form of conceptual "shorthand"; they allow people to sort through information-rich environments with an economy of effort. Stereotypes are oversimplistic. As statistical approximations, they may have a little truth to them, though never as much as the people doing the stereotyping typically give to them (Seligman, 1999).

Stereotypes, like prejudices, are harmless on their own. They are systems for processing information (Fleras and Kunz, 2001). Problems arise when these preconceived mental images give way to discriminatory practices. For example, consider how stereotypes continue to drive a wedge between Black youth and the police; each side seems willing to believe the worst of the other. According to one youth: "The police perceive me as being a bad person ... they judge me by how I look. Just because I am black, wear baggy jeans, have a gold tooth, and wear a cap or tuque, they won't even talk to me properly" (cited in Moss, 1998: D1).

In short, stereotypes are not errors in perception—at least, no more than prejudices are. More accurately, stereotyping is an expression of social control, a means of preserving existing distributions of power and resources (Stamm, 1993). Stereotypes do not set out to control, yet their cumulative impact has had a controlling effect on those who are stereotyped.

UNMASKING RACISM

Every age has its hierarchy of crimes, and this one is no exception, and at present racism is at or near the very top (Benoist, 1999). Yet racism is not a uniform concept (Fleras and Elliott, 1999). Racism as an ideology ascribes the label "inferior" to physical or cultural differences (Moodley, 1999). As a practice, it perpetuates inequality and privilege in ways that are inadvertent yet real. As dogma, it places people in a hierarchy based on race. Because racism has so many dimensions, it is difficult to isolate and remove. There are even greater difficulties in defining it.

Definitions abound, of course. Is it a thing, a process, or an attribute applied after the fact? Is racism something people think or something they do? For our own purposes, let us define racism as follows:

> Those ideas and ideals that assert the normalcy or superiority of one social group over another because of perceived differences, together with the institutionalized power to put these beliefs into practice in a way that has the intent or effect of denying or excluding. (Fleras and Elliott, 1999)

This definition incorporates key dimensions of racism. It suggests that racism involves both beliefs and practices; it emphasizes the importance of institutionalized power; and it concedes that consequences are as important as intent.

Racism has different dimensions (Winant, 1998); it varies in intent, levels of awareness, magnitude, styles of expression, intensity, and consequences. These variations enable us to unmask the different types of racism—for example, *interpersonal* (both rednecked and polite), *institutional* (both systematic and systemic), and *societal* (both everyday and cultural). Racism can also be expressed in terms of "who people are" (race), and "what they do" (culture), and "where they stand in status" (power).

Racism as Race

Racism as race can mean three things. *First*, a belief that people's behaviour is determined by genes or biology. For example, assuming that Blacks are natural-born athletes while the Japanese are naturally gifted scientists can be regarded as racist. *Second*, the use of biology as a basis for any kind of entitlement, rejection, or evaluation. For example, establishing employment equity targets for visible minorities may be regarded by some as racist regardless of the intent or outcome, because it assigns privilege or preference on the basis of "race" rather than merit. *Third*, racism as biology refers to the classic racial typologies of the nineteenth century. These linked moral differences to racial differences, and constructed a hierarchy of races to justify the dominance of one group over another (Jakubowicz et al., 1994). Under this type of biological racism:

- The human world was partitioned into fixed and discrete populations.
- Each of these populations was assigned distinct, inherited social and biological characteristics.
- These attributes were evaluated as "good" and superior or as "bad" and inferior.
- The categories were arranged in ascending or descending order of importance.
- Unequal treatment, from denial of rights to exposure to hate, was then justified on the grounds of innate differences between races.

Two examples of racism as hate are "rednecked" and "polite." Rednecked racism is linked with the jackbooted hooliganism that most people picture when asked to describe racism. It is the kind of old-fashioned racism that prevailed in the past; it continues to exist today among a handful of the reactionary or defiant. Rednecked racism consists of explicit and highly personal attacks (from verbal abuse to physical assault) toward those who are perceived as culturally or biologically inferior. Nowadays, racist attitudes are more muted than this; they are also expressed obliquely, and are coded in such a way that racism is difficult to prove (Wetherell and Potter, 1993).

Polite racism, in contrast, is a contrived attempt to disguise a dislike of others through behaviour that *seems* nonprejudicial. It is often masked by coded or euphemistic language. This politeness is especially evident when people of colour are being turned down for jobs, promotions, or accommodation (Henry and Ginzberg, 1985). For example, an employer may claim that a job has been filled rather than admit "no Blacks need apply." Polite racism may seem more sophisticated than its rednecked equivalent, but this politeness has no less sting; it is just as powerful in reinforcing patterns of control, exclusion, and exploitation.

Racism as Culture

Cultural racism is more common nowadays than the biological kind. The new racism is rooted in a dislike of the "other," not because of who they *are* ("biology") but because of what they *do* ("culture"). Assertions about the biological endowments of different races are rejected in favour of references to cultural differences. This sort of racism-without-race emphasizes cultural superiority and uniformity beneath the mask of citizenship, patriotism, and heritage (Wievorka, 1998).

Under cultural racism, dominant groups are defined not as racially superior but rather as culturally appropriate. Minorities, in turn, are dismissed not as racially inferior but rather as culturally inappropriate. The "other" is seen as posing a threat to mainstream culture. Differences between cultures are presented as immutable, and as rendering coexistence impossible (Vasta and Castles, 1996). Thus, multicultural societies are unstable and conflict-prone societies. These claims about cultural incompatibility ensure that people, by nature, will prefer to live among their own kind rather than in a multicultural society (Stolcke, 1999).

Cultural racism takes different forms. Sometimes it takes the form of criticizing those who fail to subscribe to liberal-pluralist values. Other times, reactions to cultural differences are ambiguous, are presented in the form of general principles, and convey a unresolved dislike of others. Cultural racists consist of people who in principle abhor racism and discrimination, yet who harbour doubts about the validity of cultural differences. They may endorse progressive attitudes as a matter of principle, yet disapprove of minority assertiveness (Essed, 1991). Subliminal racists often claim that they are committed to the principles of equality, and often express sympathy for the disadvantaged. Nonetheless, they oppose measures that might remedy inequality (see Henry et al., 2000).

Subliminal racism is often expressed in highly ambiguous ways. For example, employment equity programs for historically disadvantaged minorities are often accepted in theory but then disparaged in practice as unfair, divisive, and counterproductive. Government initiatives to protect and promote diversity are tolerated, but only as long as they don't cost money or require the sharing of power or cultural space. Minority cultural differences are fine unless they interfere with the rights of individuals, violate the law of the land, or undermine core Canadian values and institutions. Immigrants are endorsed as industrious contributors to Canadian well-being, yet acceptable only as long as they know their place and act in a way that meets mainstream approval. Refugee claimants are condemned not in blunt racist terms (i.e., "too many from the wrong places"); rather, they are criticized on procedural grounds (i.e., for "jumping the queue"), or they are criminalized for taking unfair advantage of Canada's generosity.

Both cultural and subliminal racism tend to soft-pedal a dislike of what others do. This dislike is camouflaged by a thin veneer of "concerned" opposition to progressive policies and to programs that are seen as "un-Canadian." Criticism of minorities is masked as support of mainstream values, national interests, fair play, equality, and justice. Aversion toward others is not openly hostile or hateful. It more often takes the form of avoidance rather than intentionally destructive behaviour.

Racism as Power

At one time, racism was assumed to be a problem with individuals. This definition has since expanded; it is now recognized that racism, as an expression of privilege and power, is part of the very structure of society (Powell, 2000). Racism as power can be defined as virtually any type of exploitation, or process of exclusion, that institutionalizes and privileges the dominant group at the expense of others (Bonilla-Silva, 1996). Racism in this sense is the power held by one group to dominate and control another—often by establishing what is normal and necessary, desirable and acceptable. bell hooks (1995: 154–55) explains how racism is not about prejudice, but rather about power:

> Why is it so difficult for many white folks to understand that racism is oppressive not because white folks have prejudicial feelings about blacks ... but because it is a system that promotes domination and subjugation. The prejudicial feelings some blacks may express about whites are in no way linked to a system of domination that affords us any power to coercively control the lives and well-being of white folks.

To the extent that racism is about power, not pigmentation (Khayatt, 1994), the pervasiveness of racism is unlikely to diminish as long as those in positions of authority refuse to share power with those once perceived as inferior or irrelevant.

Reference to racism as power involves two types of racism: systemic racism is found within institutions that deliberately go out of their way to deny or exploit minorities. *Systemic racism* is the name usually given to an impersonal and largely unconscious form of bias. As the term suggests, it is typically encountered at institutional levels. It is built into systems without people being aware of its processes and consequences. It has also been described as the unintended result of applying seemingly neutral rules in unequal contexts. The standards, rules, and expectations may be universal and ostensibly colour-blind, and there may not be any deliberate attempt to exclude others, since standards are equally applied. Yet this "abstract" equality may unintentionally exclude people with specific vulnerabilities. Under systemic racism it is not intent or motive that counts, but *context* and *consequences*.

Consider the plight of foreign-born professionals such as doctors and engineers. Once in Canada, their credentials and experience are of little use to them (Carey, 1999). Most have trouble getting even low-paying entry-level jobs in their chosen profession. As a result, they end up washing dishes, driving cabs, keeping house, or working security. Perhaps Canada's immigration policies were drawn up by well-meaning people. And perhaps professional bodies have good reasons for insisting on retraining or Canadian experience. But the consequences of these seemingly even-handed actions are systemically discriminatory, in the sense that minorities are excluded through no fault of their own. Insistence on Canadian experience as a precondition for employment can easily be interpreted as systemic bias because, intentionally or not, it has a controlling effect. This marginalization is exacerbated when minority experiences and credentials are devaluated, when certain occupations enforce unnecessarily high educational standards, and when the bar is set so high that immigrant professionals cannot qualify for membership in professional bodies.

COMMUNICATING ACROSS DIFFERENCES

The entire world is changing—becoming more uncertain, more diverse, yet at the same time more interconnected. These changes are in turn transforming Canada in unprecedented ways. In the span of a generation this country has pulled out its own Anglocentric roots and transformed itself into a multicultural society that defines itself in terms of equality, respect, and diversity (Annual Report, 2000).

The challenges of living together are most obvious at the level of interpersonal communication. Canada's growing diversity is making cross-cultural communication of vital importance. It is no longer an option or a luxury, but an obligation. Yet necessity has hardly made it easy. Too often, cross-cultural encounters are badly mangled, sometimes to the point where violence results. And tensions and recriminations will continue to mount without a concerted effort to bridge these communication gaps.

Effective cross-cultural communication is an elusive goal even in the best of circumstances. The field is littered with homilies about "empathy" and "when in Rome ..." Routinely invoked are clichés such as "walk a mile in my moccasins." These bromides are well intentioned, and may even be valid in theory, but they are also impossible to implement. Other platitudes such as "meeting of the minds" are of doubtful value. Even references to "effective" are problematic. What exactly constitutes the "effective" in effective cross-cultural communication? Who says so, and on what grounds? And how can we tell?

The challenge is clearly before us. Unless we take steps to improve our cross-cultural communication, Canada's adventure with diversity will fizzle. Canadians are increasingly taking proactive measures to improve their interactions with culturally different others. Those who lack such foresight are risking personal and career failure. They are also derailing positive attempts at living together. The damage that could result from an erosion of Canada's social fabric is too frightening to contemplate in the aftermath of Chechnya and Kosovo. To ensure that these worst-case scenarios never happen here, Canadians must address the principles of cross-cultural communication. But the learning curve is long and steep, and no one can expect to become an expert when we can't even agree on what cross-cultural communication means. That being said, the general principles of effective cross-cultural communication are simple enough for most individuals to grasp if the commitment is there.

CROSS-CULTURAL COMMUNICATION: FALLACIES AND FACTS

Most people perceive communication between individuals as a routine and even mundane activity. When pressed, people readily admit that communication is important in everyday life, but they see no deep mysteries to solve. Yet many aspects of communication baffle even the experts. There are social dimensions to communication that are easy to miss or to misunderstand. The communication process is loaded with fallacies that refuse to disappear. Still, there are certain recognizable communication barriers that routinely occur. Understanding these will cast light on the challenges of communicating across cultures.

The Paradox of Symbolic Communication

Humans cannot communicate directly because it is physically impossible to transfer ("implant") information directly from one mind to another. Biology compels us instead to communicate *in*directly by way of symbols. In our minds, we encode meanings into symbols. We then transmit these symbols through a variety of channels. They are then decoded in the mind of the receiver(s), who assign meanings to the symbols on the basis of social cues and cultural codes.

If a literal meeting of the minds were possible, communication would involve little risk. The potential for miscommunication increases when messages are encoded into one set of defined symbols, then decoded according to another. The risk factor increases substantially when communication symbols are decoded and encoded according to different culture codes (Scollon and Scollon, 1995; Lustig and Koester, 1996). At the heart of all miscommunication is a lack of shared cultural experiences. Those who do not share a common culture live in vastly different realities. It follows that they interpret the world differently and communicate accordingly.

The Social Dimensions of Language

One of the more common assumptions that hampers cross-cultural communication is that we inhabit the same world—that any differences are superficial and generally reflect the use of different languages. Thus any difficulties in communicating across cultures can be resolved by speaking louder or more clearly or by repeating the message more slowly.

These assumptions do not stand up to scrutiny. Language is far from the only barrier to cross-cultural communication. The worlds people inhabit are fundamentally different in terms of how people perceive, experience, think about, and relate to reality. There is nothing natural or normal about these separate realities; they are socially constructed. They are created by individuals who make meaningful choices in contexts that are situational and evolving. They reflect negotiated ways of defining what is right, acceptable, or desirable (see for example Hall, 1976, on high versus low context languages). In sum, differences in language and in the social realities they reflect are real enough that they must be taken seriously.

Communication as Social Activity

Interpersonal communication is an intensely social activity. The meanings people convey reflect their membership in a particular group or social category (Collier, 1995; Herberg, 1993). Conversely, messages that are received are also based on group membership. As a result, communication involves a social act between individuals as social actors.

There is nothing inherently wrong in communicating as a representative of a group. Problems arise when this social dimension interferes with the exchange of information—that is, when preconceived notions ("stereotypes") are introduced into the communication process. Take the case of police–minority communication. In discharging his or her duties, a police officer never communicates solely as an individual; that officer is also a member of the police service. Not surprisingly, minority youth may not see the officer as an individual with a distinct personality and style. They may perceive the officer as inseparably linked with a controlling institution, and judge his or her actions accordingly.

"You Cannot Not Communicate"

It is often assumed that communication is centred on the sender, because it is the sender who is formulating and transmitting the message. The receiver's primary responsibility is to decode the message. For reasons that are perhaps now clear, this assumption is false: communication ultimately depends on the receiver. It is the receiver who determines whether the sender's message has

241

registered, is comprehensible, or is worth responding to. If the receiver does not recognize or respond to the sender, there is no communication.

All of this has several implications. *First*, anything and everything has the potential to be communication. Also, an act that one person considers insignificant, another may perceive as resonating with powerful messages. For example, wearing a uniform is just part of the job for a police officer; yet members of a minority community may perceive the uniform as a powerful symbol of repression. *Second*, it is impossible not to communicate. Others can always apply meanings to words, appearances, and actions, even if none were intended. Conversely, senders cannot impose meaning on receivers, if the latter are unwilling to respond or incapable of responding. In short, we cannot *not* communicate. Furthermore, we cannot predictably control our communication.

Communication as Power and Control

Communication is usually thought of as an exchange of factual information. Actually, communication is as much about power and control as about content. All communication is political, in the sense that there are power differences in all situations. Communication is usually between individuals who are unequal in status and power: for example, this is true in parent–child relations, in friendships, and even in partnerships. According to Martin and Nakayama (1997), those in positions of authority need power to preserve their privilege and status in society, and they can gain it by skillfully manipulating communication. In turn, those with less privilege may resort to communication symbols to challenge the power of others. For example, the use of Black English or "ghetto rap" can be interpreted as a challenge to "the system" rather than a failure to learn proper English. In these terms, communication is an indicator of who controls the power in a relationship. This is especially obvious in exchanges between women and men (Tannen, 1990).

Deception *Is* Communication

Most of us have been led to believe that effective communication is open, candid, and honest. Deception-free communication is widely pitched as the solution to most interpersonal problems. This is true to some extent; honesty in communication *is* quite often appropriate. Yet most of us intuitively know that honesty is not the best policy in some situations—for example, when the truth would hurt. Interpersonal relations thrive on some degree of dishonesty. Concealment is part of social life. Social existence involves a great deal of impression management, which always entails some degree of deceit, concealment, evasion, and distortion. And, of course, people manipulate language when jockeying for power and privilege.

In short, deception is central to communication; it is not a deviation from the norm. The Danish linguist Otto Jesperson once commented that language is used both to inform and to conceal. Thus, what is said "between the lines" is as important as the message itself.

KEYS TO COMMUNICATION COMPETENCE

What do we require to communicate competently cross-culturally? What are the major impediments to gaining this competence? It goes without saying that the first thing people need is the right mindset. Unfortunately, many of us carry around fallacies about communication that interfere with our competence. It follows from this that understanding the basics of interpersonal communication should help in reducing the likelihood of breakdowns (though it can't eliminate them). There are two other bedrocks of effective cross-cultural communication: communicating without words, and acknowledging the role of culture. These two can be collasped to one: the necessity to take differences seriously.

Communicating Without Words

Most people think of language when they think of communication. Yet in some situations, as much as 98 percent of information is conveyed nonverbally (see Hall, 1976). This figure is astonishing, considering how much emphasis the school system places on words and grammar. Communication without words involves much more than embellishments to speech. It is absolutely central to the human experience. It also has its own rules and functions that are independent of language, though related to it.

The relationship between the verbal and the nonverbal is ambivalent. "Body language" can amplify the verbal message, or impart a more nuanced meaning, or openly contradict what the sender is saying. Is is possible that nonverbal communication is actually more reliable than the verbal kind. This is because words are subject to manipulation and bias; in contrast, "silent language" may well be a more "truthful" indicator of a person's attitudes or intentions. In moments of stress or unhappiness, some people resort to nonverbal language to express emotional states that are otherwise difficult to articulate. Nonverbal messages can also be used to establish relations without letting words get in the way. People gain first impressions of others through body language. We make inferences about others from nonverbal gestures as varied as eye expressions, body movements, hand motions, and speech patterns.

Much of what we know and believe about others is derived from their body language—or more precisely, from how we interpret their body language. Thus, Arabs are "pushy," Japanese are "reserved," Chinese are "sly," Jamaicans as "cocky," Americans are "loud," and so on. None of these stereotypes holds up to scrutiny. Yet they have acquired a social currency because of our universal tendency to compartmentalize others. And just as we misinterpret others when we interpret their actions by our standards, they misinterpret us in exactly the same way. Clearly, the likelihood of miscommunication is staggering. For purposes of analysis, let's consider five different types of nonverbal communication: kinesics, proxemics, haptics, vocalics, and chronemics.

Kinesics, or body language, consists of actions such as body movements and postures, hand gestures and placements, and facial expressions. Of particular importance is eye management—that is, how we look at others and how they look at us. Where do they look? When do they look? For how long? Breakdowns in communication often arise from improper eye contact.

Proxemics is about how people use space to convey information or establish relations. All of us have developed techniques for claiming space in our everyday lives. Our fidgeting and evasive movements on crowded elevators and subways attest to our obsession with personal space. We routinely apologize for violating others' space. Spatial management techniques are often deployed deliberately to improve the flow of communication or to confirm hierarchies. People also use space to illustrate a particular relationship or social context.

Haptics is communication by contact. In high-contact cultures, people are encouraged to touch people when they are communicating. In low-contact cultures, contact is generally construed as inappropriate, or even abusive in some contexts.

Vocalics (also called metacommunication or paralanguage) refers to the language "beyond the words." It is the pitch, intonation, stresses, pauses, and emphasis that people employ as accents to their words. Examples: using silence to emphasize a point, or raising one's voice to show indignation.

Chronemics is the application of time to communication. The rules governing time vary from culture to culture. Canadians and Americans tend to be time dependent. They run their lives by the clock, whether the increments are minutes, hours, months, or decades. They count on things to unfold with clockwork precision. In contrast, time in "polychronic" societies is seen as a process in which things happen when they will, in a sequence that while logical, is also beyond social control (Hall, 1976).

Coping with the Culture in X-C Communication

There are no aspects of human existence that are not influenced by culture. People are socialized into a fairly narrow range of beliefs, values, and norms, and this ensures patterns and predictability. Members of a particular culture become conditioned to think and act in certain ways. Other patterns of thought and behaviour are dismissed or devalued as inferior or irrelevant.

Nowhere are the contrasts more evident than in the values that define and shape culture. These values become the unmarked and often unquestioned standards that guide our behaviour. They also provide a basis for us to evaluate the behaviour of others. Yet strangely enough, people—especially those in the mainstream—rarely recognize how their cultural values influence their thoughts and behaviours. Values—the "ought to's" that are the foundations of our behaviour—are typically unacknowledged until challenged (Lynch and Hanson, 1999). Not surprisingly, until we appreciate the importance of values in shaping cross-cultural interaction, we will find it hard to achieve communication competence.

There are two basic types of cultures, with different world-views, activity orientations, time and space orientations, perceptions of self and human nature, and approaches to organizing society (Samovar et al., 1981; Fleras, 1998; Samovar and Porter, 2000). *First*, there are urban–industrial–Western cultures, which are generally committed to the values of liberal-democratic capitalist society. *Second*, there are rural–agricultural–indigenous cultures, whose values are often opposed to the first type, in theory if not in practice. Table 8.2 provides an overview of the differences between the two. Keep in mind that the types being described are two poles on a continuum; in the real world, nothing is ever so simple.

TABLE 8.2

Competing Value Orientations

Value Orientation	Urban/Industrial/ Western Value Orientation	Rural/Agricultural/ Indigenous Value Orientation
World-view	Defiance	Deference
Activity orientation	Optimism/doing/progress	Resignation/being/ fatalism
Time and space orientation	Commodified and linear	Natural and collateral
Human nature	Malleable	Fixed
Perception of self	Possessive individualism	Individual communalism
Social organization	Equality, created, evolving	Hierarchy, ascription, timeless

According to Samovar and colleagues (1981), urban industrial Western societies possess a core of shared values that transcend specific cultures. These core values reflect a commitment to a capitalist, liberal, and democratic society. They also reflect Enlightenment ideals. Collectively, they offer a way of thinking about the natural world and its relationship to the social world. Such societies give primacy to reason, empiricism, science, universalism, progress, individualism, secularism, tolerance, common human nature, and freedom (Hamilton, 1992). They place a high value on controlling the physical world and using it to improve humanity. They make virtues out of action, doing, accomplishment, competition, and practicality. They are boundlessly optimistic that anything can be achieved if people put their minds to it. They are equally committed to progress, and perceive both individuals and societies as moving relentlessly upward and forward into a better future. They consider human nature to be infinitely malleable and perfectible rather than fixed at birth or biologically determined. They assume that both time and space can be measured, commodified, and manipulated to serve human ends. They sanctify the individual as free and morally autonomous, and assume that people are distinguished—to the extent they *can* be distinguished—by their talent, hard work, and merit. They define society as a collection of freedom-seeking individuals in competitive pursuit of self-serving interests, and they see society as ideally egalitarian and as always evolving.

The values of rural agricultural indigenous cultures are opposed to metropolitan values, at least in theory or for the sake of analysis (Samovar and Porter, 2000). The emphasis in such cultures is on deference: the collective well-being is the first priority, with individual rights slotted in accordingly. The focus is not on control or competition, but rather on cooperating with the natural and social worlds. These societies tend toward fatalism or resignation because of the endless cycles that humans are powerless to halt or influence. They view time as a natural unfolding of events rather than an abstract reality that can be controlled. They see the relationship between the individual and society as largely fixed at birth. Thus, each person should know his or her place in the wider scheme of things. If they don't, social retribution or supernatural wrath will follow. Collective conformity overrides individual competition; social relations and obligations take precedence over individual rights. To be sure, individualism is encouraged, but only to the extent that it advances collective interests rather than personal gain. Society is highly stratified, mainly as a function of birth and ancestry. The emphasis is on descent rather than consent; put another way, individuals are judged by who they are rather than by what they do. Core values relating to hierarchy, social standing, and patterns of traditional authority are strongly endorsed as a basis for constructing a harmonious social order.

It is not my intent here to evaluate one set of values as superior to another. Nor do I want to suggest that societies are ever fixed, homogeneous ("essentialized"), or simple to categorize. Also, whatever society they are in, people never stop being individuals with the power to conform or deviate. All people are both at all times, though which dimension will take precedence will change with the context at hand. This broad comparison is meant to reinforce the idea that differences are real, that communication competence is contingent on taking these differences into account, and that miscommunication is likely when other people's behaviour is interpreted according to familiar cultural values.

To sum up: Perfect cross-cultural communication is unattainable for most. Yet people can take certain steps to improve their communication across cultural borders. Shared experiences are key: without them, cross-cultural communication is essentially a series of ad hoc adjustments that rarely connect in a meaningful fashion. But it is just as difficult to share experiences as it is to become competent.

To communicate effectively, it is vital that we confront our ethnocentrism, as well as the idea that mainstream cultural patterns are inevitable, normal, universal, or superior. Instead of ethnocentrism, we ought to embrace *altrucentrism*—that is, we ought to try at all times to interpret reality from the perspective of other people's cultures, and seek out the logic that underpins the world-views of others. To accomplish this will require flexibility and resilience. We will have to replace dogmatic thinking with cultural versatility. Multicultural versatility involves learning to take differences seriously, to see situations from a variety of different perspectives, to reject one's first "cultural take" on a situation, to factor in the importance of other cultural values, and to tolerate ambiguity and uncertainty.

There are no magic formulas for success in this endeavour. Perhaps the best we can hope for is a willingness to concede that miscommunication must always be the norm rather than exception, and a willingness to fix communication breakdowns whenever possible. This is likely all that most people can do. But even this will improve our prospects for living together with differences in a multicultural society.

CASE STUDY (Continued)
Communcation Breakdown

CULTURAL SAFETY: "DECONSTRUCT THYSELF"

The case study at the beginning of the chapter revealed a clear incident of multicultural incompetence. The monocultural mentality of the police officer resulted in a series of communication breakdowns that resulted in social disaster. How could the situation have been avoided?

The concept of cultural safety provides an escape—that is, a workable solution to the challenges of service delivery in multicultural contexts (Ramsden, 1995). "Cultural safety" as an approach was developed initially in New Zealand for health care providers. The principles behind it can be applied to intervention strategies in Canada.

Cultural safety can be best defined by its conceptual opposite. A culturally unsafe service is one that makes recipients feel unsafe. Their unease arises from the tendency of service providers to deny the importance of cultural differences. This rejection of the cultural by service providers has a long history with good intentions. Traditionally, service providers were trained to work with different people by *not* taking their differences into account. The point of this colour-blind approach was to ensure equal treatment for everyone. The mistaken belief was that it was fair and just to treat everyone the same.

Perhaps colour-blindness was a good approach in the past, when minorities were routinely denied equal treatment. But the present situation requires more than a level playing field. Proposed instead is a culture-conscious approach that takes differences seriously. The rules of the game must be adjusted to foster substantive equality—that is, equality that acknowledges difference and disadvantage when necessary. The concept of cultural safety has taken root in the context of creating a culturally safe environment by taking differences into account.

None of this implies that the content of diverse cultures must be internalized. Most service providers would find this impossible, and in attempting to do so, they would often be reinforcing stereotypes. Yes, cultural awareness *is* important, but with cultural safety the focus is on the cultural values and social status of the *service providers*. Cultural safety is about overcoming the cultural beliefs that interfere with the design and delivery of culturally sensitive services. It is about making the service providers responsible for identifying cultural barriers. It involves helping them understand themselves as bearers of a culture whose ethnocentric and Eurocentric biases may put others at risk. Furthermore, cultural safety draws attention to the privileges and powers associated with whiteness, and to the powerful impact that those in positions of authority may have on the less powerful. Cultural safety has five main objectives:

- To educate service providers. Put another way, to help them examine the cultural realities and social status they bring to each encounter. Of particular importance is helping them become aware of the bias in their culture when it comes to shaping interventions.
- To educate service providers on how to be open-minded and flexible toward cultural "others." Culturally diverse clients are influenced by their cultural background but are not fully defined by that background. Moreover, cultural beliefs and behaviours are not static; rather, they are fluid and dynamic, and learning them is a lifelong process. Once this is understood, cultural differences can be used to enhance interaction rather than stereotype others (Lynch and Hanson, 1999).
- To educate service providers about not blaming clients for their predicaments. To be culturally safe is to understand that historical and structural circumstances contribute to people's problems. Many presumed differences do not spring from individuals or from culture, but rather from the socioeconomic and political circumstances that define peoples lives and life chances (see also Lynch and Hanson, 1999).
- To educate service providers on how to provide practices that are culturally safe from the perspective of *those they are serving*. As the Brazilian educator Paulo Friere once noted, the objective is service delivery that responds to recipients' needs and is tailored to life's everyday realities. Recipients of services are the ultimate judges as to whether a service is culturally safe or culturally risky.
- To understand that formal equality and the removal of discriminatory barriers have not eliminated discrimination, but have made it more subtle and difficult to detect. Discrimination involves lack of awareness that (a) one's prejudices are being communicated to clients, (b) cultural differences can lead to miscommunication, (c) theories taught during training are culture bound, and (d) treatment must be adapted to clients' cultural needs (Diller, 1999).

In cultural safety, the focus is that one must know oneself before one can hope to understand others. An understanding of the self begins with a commitment to take differences seriously—especially one's own. This self-understanding extends to recognizing those largely unearned privileges a person has and how they shape interactions (McIntosh, 1988). Cultural safety can be achieved only when the privileged in society acknowledge how their advantages are based on systems that disadvantage others.

Chapter Highlights

- Multicultural principles are one thing. It may be quite another to put these principles into everyday practice.
- The concept of multicultural competence is critical to achieving the goal of living together with differences.
- A multiculturally competent person can perform capably in a society that endorses the principles of multiculturalism.
- The competence concept has two dimensions: a multicultural mindset and cross-cultural communication skills.
- A multicultural mindset is the opposite of a monocultural mentality: it is versatile, flexible, and resilient rather than dogmatic, fixed, and one-dimensional.
- Cultural safety begins with deconstructing oneself as a cultural being. Precautions are then taken to ensure that culturally diverse clients receive services that are culturally appropriate.
- There are many barriers to multicultural competence. Two of the more common are prejudice and racism.
- Prejudice involves prejudging others in such a way that everyone in a particular group is portrayed negatively.
- Prejudice can involve ethnocentrism (a belief in cultural superiority) and/or Eurocentrism (a tendency to see the world from a particular point of view).
- Racism is multidimensional: it can manifest itself as biology (race), as culture, and as power.
- Racism as biology incorporates both rednecked and polite racism. Racism as culture includes subliminal cultural racism. Racism as power is inseparable from systemic racism.

- Cross-cultural communication is central to multicultural competence. An inability to communicate cross-culturally undermines all the good intentions in the world: we must learn how to walk the talk.
- The main barriers to cross-cultural communication are ignorance of the social dimensions of language and of nonverbal communication.
- Cross-cultural communication can be improved by an awareness of culture's role in shaping interaction.

Review Questions

1. What is meant by the terms "multicultural competence" and "multicultural imagination"? What is the relationship between them?
2. Do you know anyone who could be described as multiculturally competent? What is it about that person that makes him or her so? If you don't know anyone, describe a person who would qualify as multiculturally competent.
3. How does the concept of cultural safety reflect, reinforce, and advance the principles and practices of a multicultural mindset?
4. What fallacies stand in the way of effective cross-cultural communication?
5. Explain the importance of nonverbal communication to any understanding of cross-cultural communication.
6. What role does cultural variation play in shaping cross-cultural interaction? Illustrate your answer by demonstrating the differences between urban–metropolitan cultural values and those of rural–indigenous peoples.

Recommended Reading

Dieter Haselbach, ed. 1998. *Multiculturalism in a World of Leaking Boundaries*. New Brunswick: Transaction Publishers.

Carl E. James. 1999. *Seeing Ourselves: Exploring Race, Ethnicity and Culture*, 2nd ed. Toronto: Thomson Education Publishing.

Will Kymlicka. 1998. *Finding Our Way: Rethinking Ethnocultural Relations in Canada*. Toronto: Oxford University Press.

Myron W. Lustig and Jolene Koester. 1996. *Intercultural Competence: Interpersonal Communication Across Cultures*, 2nd ed. New York: HarperCollins.

E.W. Lynch and M.J. Hanson. 2000. *Developing Cross-Cultural Competence*. Sydney: Paul H. Brookes.

Larry Samovar and Richard Porter. 2000. *Intercultural Communication*. Boulder: Wadsworth.

AFTERWORD | This Adventure Called Multiculturalism

MULTICULTURALISM AS CANADA BUILDING

Canada's image as a society eludes any single consensus. Competing visions define Canadian society: Is Canada a contract among provinces? A compact between the French and English? A coalition of communities? For some, there is one Canada that triumphed on the Plains of Abraham in 1759 and must be protected to ensure national coherence and identity. For others, Canada comprises two founding peoples whose priorities and debates constitute the core of its integrity. In recent years, the image of Canada as a three-nation state has incorporated aboriginal peoples as a founding people with self-determining rights. Still others disagree with these assessments. As far as they are concerned, Canada is a mosaic of multicultures whose needs and concerns require an appropriate discourse and a responsive system. The interplay of these opposing views impart much of the dynamic that animates Canada's society-building enterprise.

Official multiculturalism has proven pivotal in reshaping the symbolic landscape of Canadian society. As a model for living together with differences, official multiculturalism has irrevocably transformed both the concepts of "living together" and of "differences." Political discourses once extolled a vision of Canada as a compact (or "covenant") between two founding nations. This dualism was rooted in constitutional law and long-standing political agreement that guaranteed Quebec protection of its status and entitlements as a French-speaking society. For better or worse, the role of official multiculturalism has assisted in eroding the fundamental duality that symbolized Canada's political landscape. Inception of multiculturalism has had a powerful effect in transforming English-speaking perceptions of Canada as a social, political, and cultural space. In its place is a modernist view espoused by Trudeau. A new set of foundational principles have come into play in hopes of reconstitutionalizing Canada along pluralistic lines (McRoberts, 1997). In place of those scripted rigidities that once defined who got what is a multicultural and diverse Canada—a loosely integrated mosaic of pre-existing tiles that are constitutive of Canada as a community of individuals (Weisman, 2000).

In the midst of this profound ambivalence, the challenge is twofold: first, to foster symbols and choices that permit an understanding of how Canada has changed; second, to establish a new social order and political identity so that all Canadians can realize their potential. These challenges should not be underestimated. Liberal-democratic systems exist as exercises of the collective imagination, in part because of people's desire to belong to something they can call their own (Anderson, 1991). Yet minorities' demands for greater representation and inclusion in societies have raised a raft of thorny questions about (a) the legitimacy of minority identity claims, (b) the affiliated notions of minority rights, and (c) the assumptions that historically have undergirded majority-minority relations.

Canada is no different. In the final analysis, Canada is an idea and a set of ideals ("ideology") rather than a nation with roots or history or a people (Iyer, 2001). Canadians have little in common, not even a language, no shared ancestors or genetic pool, no origin myths, and few common rituals except a commitment to public institutions such as universal health care (Hiller, 2000). The onus is on creating a society that comprises a moral community of communities to be nurtured rather than a treasure-trove for individuals to plunder. Of particular importance is the fostering of a political union with a sense of shared core values, a common vision, a sense of belonging and commitment, a workable citizenship, and a singularity of collective purpose. In short, it is misleading to imagine Canada as a mosaic. The image is too rigid and unbending. More accurately, it constitutes a rather complex matrix of defining lines and "decomposable sub-elements" that expand or contract in response to multiple identities and competing sovereignties under a single polity (Doran, 1995).

Of course, Canada is not alone in capitalizing on multiculturalism as a blueprint for living together. Canada sits among a handful of modern countries, including Australia and New Zealand, that are in the vanguard of constructing a coherent yet multicultural society (Vasta and Castles, 1996; Pearson, 1996). Yet Canada's commitments are pioneering. Its multiculturalness confirms how dissimilar peoples can share land, power, and resources while respecting and sustaining their differences, including the right to be treated equally irrespective of ethnicity and the right to be treated differentially because of ethnicity (see Royal Commission on Aboriginal Peoples, 1996). A commitment to cultural identity, social equality, and civic citizenship has ensured a multiculturalism that touches on all bases—albeit not without criticism or backlash. No one is suggesting that Canada is perfect in constructively engaging diversity. But in shifting from a predominantly monocultural system to one consistent with multicultural principles and egalitarian practices, the politics of multiculturalism have put Canada in the enviable position of being the world's least imperfect society.

(CON)TESTING MULTICULTURALISM

On balance, Canada appears to have been relatively successful in balancing society building with minority rights even if the juggling act tends to be wobbly at times. Such an achievement should not be sneered at. The society-building challenge is increasingly and internally undermined when traditional coordinates are contested and spinning beyond control. External pressures also complicate the process. The world we occupy is engulfed by two mutually exclusive yet extremely powerful forces (Nelson and Fleras, 1998). On the one hand are the universalizing (and homogenizing) forces of a freewheeling global market economy. Transnational movements of goods and services, as well as jobs and investments, are conducted with little regard for societal boundaries. Advances in information technology tend to render national borders increasingly porous and difficult to monitor or control. On the other hand, the fragmenting forces of insurgent ethnicities are poised to dismember and destroy. Radical ethnicities and ethnic nationalisms are largely indifferent to the legitimacy of the nation-state, and are often willing to jettison this arrangement for parochial interests (Ignatieff, 1993). This interplay of centrifugal and centripetal forces promises to reconfigure the political landscape of societies large and small. These apparently dichotomous forces may also unravel the prospect of living together with differences.

Two scenarios loom large in light of these opposing forces. The first suggests that a multicultural Canada may collapse for lack of a coherent centre. Yet, one could argue that multiculturalism is not only consistent with Canadian values, but is the quintessential Canadian value (Frideres, 1997). Its creation may be visionary, but its ability to provoke and confuse both critics and supporters confirms its double-edged status as an inclusive yet divisive force. Critics of multiculturalism are skeptical of Canada's prospects (Sugunasiri, 1999). Any policy that encourages diversity, they argue, intensifies or creates social cleavages. Without a unified centre to paper over fissures, Canada may well implode upon itself.

Others disagree with such a gloomy scenario. By virtue of its very "decentredness," Canada stands on the cusp of becoming the world's first postmodernist society (Gwyn, 1994, 1996). In a world that is rapidly changing and increasingly diverse, Richard Gwyn asserts, the lightness of being that constitutes Canada may provide a prototype for the ideal twenty-first-century society. Canada represents a political union born out of compromise and expediency rather than a national spirit forged out of violent struggle (Simpson, 1993; Eisler, 1994). Instead of a definitive centre that categorically defines identity and unity, Canada is constructed around the principle that nothing is absolute and everything is subject to negotiation and compromise. In a postmodern era, weaknesses conceal strengths or "morph" into strengths with changing priorities in response to evolving circumstances. Canada's so-called weaknesses may prove a tower of strength in a world where certainty and authority may clash with a freewheeling global market economy (Erickson, 1997). The decentralization within Canada, long thought a bane of our existence, may hold up well in a world where calls for self-determination threaten to fragment and dismember countries. Resiliency and flexibility are key, not dogma or rigidity. Canada's genius in transforming diversity into a society-building asset may also contribute to its reputation as open and tolerant (Saul, 1998).

This author, too, believes that Canada will survive and prosper despite any conclusive proof of this assertion. Societies that are wired for dealing with diversity will have an enormous competitive edge in coping with an interconnected global marketplace. Canada's advantage stems from precedent and practice in engaging with diversity—from the dynamics of French–English duality to the society-building challenges of immigration. Its fortuitousness may originate from yet another unexpected source. Canadians are frequently accused of lacking shared values or national character. Canada's nationalism is understated. Its sense of peoplehood is fractured along regional and ethnic lines, without any root in history and homeland. This dispassionate, self-effacing nature should not be interpreted as an indifference to Canada, as Gwyn (1994) notes. Recent surveys indicate that a staggering 94 percent of Canadians agree that Canada is the best place in the world to live (the highest ranking among all industrialized societies). The UN has also placed a similar stamp of approval for eight consecutive years—suggesting that Canadian perspectives are not out of line with international perceptions. Other surveys point out that Canadians are among (a) the happiest people in the world, (b) proudest and most confident in their uniqueness, and (c) those inhabitants of a country that is admired most (*Maclean's*, 1997).

Put bluntly, in a world of diversity, uncertainty, and change, Canada's atypicalness may be its strength. Canadians may possess the kind of temperament best suited for the indeterminacies of the twenty-first century, namely, a dedication to pragmatism, a commitment to civility and tolerance, and a willingness to compromise as a way of constructively engaging with diversity. Our multiple and nested identities will allow us to shift or reposition without necessarily experiencing contradiction or dissonance. Our historical experience of muddling through problems rather than having solutions unilaterally imposed by decree may pave the way for living together with differences. Endless debates over power, resources, and jurisdictions have congealed into a kind of glue for binding Canadians by defining who we are (Editorial, *The Globe and Mail*, July 1, 1996). In a world where rules and conventions are being turned inside out, a capacity for uncertainty and tolerance for ambiguity may stand us in good stead. In a world where a passionate attachment to homeland or culture may maim or destroy, our redemption may reside in failing to specify precisely what it means to be a Canadian (MacQueen, 1994). With multiculturalism, moreover, even the notion of citizenship is being contested.

CASE STUDY
Canadian Citizenship: From One Size Fits All to Inclusive

Passage of Canada's first Citizenship Act sharply challenged historical notions of belonging, identity, and entitlements. Prior to 1947, there was no such thing as a Canadian citizen. All recognized persons in Canada were defined as British subjects, with an obligation to conduct themselves in a manner consistent with the language, culture, and identity of England. Interest in a distinctive Canadian citizenship intensified with the proposed entry of immigrants and refugees from war-ravaged Europe. The citizenship rights of previously disenfranchised minorities such as Asian-Canadians were recognized as part of the fight for freedom and against fascism. Yet a move toward inclusiveness was not entirely unproblematic: for central authorities the challenge lay in infusing a largely unconnected peoples into a community with a common sense of purpose and identity.

Canada's citizenship principles are anchored in a fundamental assumption. Citizenship as a universal category transcends particular backgrounds because of race, ethnicity, or nationality. Statutory rights and mutual obligations would be conferred upon all immigrants or their descendants without distinction or favouritism. Compare this inclusiveness with an exclusionary past when immigrants of colour were routinely denied, excluded, or exploited. The universality of Canadian citizenship is twofold. First, it applies to everyone in Canada. Those who are born on Canadian soil receive it automatically. Foreign-born Canadians qualify for citizenship by declaring an oath of allegiance to Canada, loyalty to the Constitution, and obedience to laws (Moodley, 1999). Second, the same rights and obligations apply to all citizens whether native-born or naturalized. The principle of consent not only defines Canadian citizenship but also confers universal rights to full and equal participation for those who agree to abide.

But the dominance of Canada's one-size-fits-all citizenship has been sharply contested. Conventional notions of citizenship have outlived their usefulness. A universal citizenship is being challenged with the emergence of identity politics, the continued politicization of national minorities such as the Québécois and First Nations, and persistence of culturally diverse but historically disadvantaged groups. A postnational world where minorities routinely embrace several transnational affiliations puts pressure on a universal citizenship (Dijkstra et al., 2001). Abstract definitions of universality have come under fire as discourses in defence of the status quo. Unfairness arises from treating all citizens regardless of race or ethnicity as individuals with abstract rights rather than as disadvantaged members of real groups who may need collective rights to protect concerns and promote interests.

Proposed instead is a more "contextual" citizenship rather than one focused on disembodied individual rights and abstract legal status (Bosniak, 2000). A more customized form of citizenship is contemplated that reflects multilayered differences. The rationale is simple enough: for citizenship to mean anything in an increasingly diverse, demanding, and decentred society, it must expand from its universal focus by becoming more inclusive of those who prefer or require a more "customized" belonging to Canada. According to customized citizenship, equality and full citizenship rights can only be fulfilled when differences are taken into account to neutralize barriers or advance interests (Kymlicka, 1995; Schouls, 1997). Of course, the value of universal citizenship rights is widely acknowledged. But however necessary, such rights are simply insufficient in contexts where inequalities and exclusions are chronic, embedded, and systemic. Nor are they sufficient for national minorities whose attachments are rooted in a belonging to societal cultures rather than state citizenship (Kymlicka, 2001). Endorsed instead for historically disadvantaged and national minorities are entitlements commensurate with their distinct identities, evolving aspirations, patterns of belonging, and unique circumstances. Three types of customized citizenship can be discerned: equity, self-determining, and multicultural (Kymlicka, 1992).

Yet this rationale for a multilayered citizenship has not gone unchallenged. Can Canada incorporate radically different ways of belonging without losing its sense of identity and internal integrity? Indeed, how do multilayered yet fundamentally monocultural societies cope with highly politicized demands for recognition of differences as a basis for meaningful citizenship? How does one create a common identity when citizenship is splintered? How are unity and identity fostered when primary membership is anchored in a group rather than through individual citizens? Is it possible to reconcile a universal individual-rights citizenship with customized collective rights? What happens when minority culture rights clash with the egalitarian norms espoused by liberal-democratic societies (Okin, 1999)?

Sorting through these questions will prove difficult. Canadians will have to grapple with the principle of different ways of belonging to Canada without forsaking universal rights. A mindset shift will be required not only to value differences. Differences must be valued in different ways depending on the status of the group, level of needs, relationship to society at large, and nature of the grievances and claims against the state. An inclusive citizenship openly acknowledges a perspective that is both universal and customized in allowing Canadians to be different (differences of tolerances) yet the same (tolerance of difference) (see also Modood, 1997). All Canadians will continue to possess universal rights as part of their citizenship entitlements. They will also be endowed with additional citizenship rights because of social justice and political urgency.

The balancing of the universal with the customized under an inclusive citizenship will prove a challenge to this adventure called Canada. The viability of an inclusive citizenship with its universal yet customized strands serves as a reminder that the new millennium is not about the adjustment of old rules for an old game. The new millennium may be on the threshold of proposing new rules for a new game. The radical notion that sometimes living together with differences may entail a pattern of standing apart is but one indication of the challenges ahead.

CHANGING DIRECTIONS, EMERGENT REALITIES

It is a strength and a not a weakness that we are a permanently incomplete experiment built on a triangular foundation—aboriginal, francophone and anglophone. What we continue to create today, began 450 years ago in a political project ... It is an old experiment, complex, and, in worldly terms, largely successful. Stumbling through darkness and racing through light, we have persisted in the creation of a Canadian civilization. (Adrienne Clarkson, Governor General, October 7, 1999, cited in Canadian Heritage, 2001: 1)

What began as a symbolic and somewhat modest initiative to defuse and promote is now precariously perched at the crossroads of Canadian history. Multiculturalism in the new millennium has the capacity to transform the "management" of Canada's race, ethnic, and aboriginal relations. Conversely, it also has the potential to become increasingly irrelevant in light of convulsive changes, both domestic and international. The unspeakable horrors September 11, 2001, in New York City and Washington attest to that. Not surprisingly, then, Canada's multicultural engagement with diversity has come under fire recently, with the result that the pluralistic umbrella appears in danger of being blown inside out by unsympathetic forces. Yet any inclination toward despondency should be discarded. For whatever else it may be or aspire to be, Canada is a multicultural society whose official commitment to diversity is widely admired but rarely duplicated throughout the world.

As the politics of diversity burrows even more deeply into our collective psyche, three options are possible: official multiculturalism will continue to command respect as a blueprint for living together with our differences; alternatively, it will become an object of scorn or indifference for failure to do what it's supposed to do; or it may languish in oblivion as little more than a public relations stunt for visiting dignitaries. To some extent these concerns are already being answered, albeit not to everyone's satisfaction. The double-edged quality of multiculturalism is apparent: multiculturalism may challenge existing notions of culture and identity, nationality and citizenship. It may also reinforce foundational structures of society while conveying the impression of change and accommodation. Multiculturalism may be an excuse for marginalizing and oppression; it can also serve as a tool of empowerment and emancipation. As an ideology, multiculturalism may endorse the principle of diversity, yet the practice of multiculturalism may reinforce intolerance to secure national interests (Modood, 1997). It is precisely this ambiguity that confirms the status of multiculturalism as an enigma wrapped in a riddle inside a mystery.

Multiculturalism remains the policy of necessity if not of choice for living together in a changing and diverse Canada. With its mixture of compassion and calculation, of empowerment and expediency, it symbolizes an innovative if imperfect social experiment for engaging with diversity in a postmodern era. Multiculturalism has excelled in rescuing Canada from its colonialist past, to its much ballyhooed status as a trailblazer in institutional responsive-ness and inclusion. The Canada of today no longer consists of a British (or French) mainstream with ethnically related tributaries (Burnet and Palmer, 1988). In many parts of urban Canada, minorities *are* the mainstream, and this revolutionary shift holds out the promise and the perils of reshaping our institutions, priorities, and mindsets. And sometime before mid-century, Canada's majority population will no longer be of European origin but of sources from around the world. Canada will then become the first country in the world to "change its colour" from inside out. Multiple national identities and postnational citizenships will be the norm in a postmodern society of intersecting sovereignties, divided loyalties, multiple identities, and the meaninglessness of concepts such as margins and centre (Gwyn, 2000; Dijkstra et al., 2001). The fact that this transition is occurring without exces-sive stress or violence is a testimony to official multiculturalism.

Under the circumstances, it is not a question of whether Canada can afford multiculturalism. More to the point, Canada cannot afford to dismiss multiculturalism in its quest for political unity, social coherence, economic prosperity, and cultural enrichment. And the turmoil of shifting from a monocultural past to multicultural present may reap future dividends, as noted by an Australian Advisory Council: "Canada, having been a multicul-tural society since its earliest days, has the advantage of long experience in what seems bound to become a mandatory 21st century skill: constructive co-existence among culturally and racially diverse communities" (Australian Advisory Council on Languages and Multicultural Education).

MULTICULTURALISM INTO THE MILLENNIUM

What once was seen as a multiculturalism-inspired weakness (lack of a strong, distinct identity) may in fact prove to be a strength in the twenty-first century. According to Michael Adams, president of Environics Research Group and author of *Sex in the Snow*: "Ours is a population that is resigned to, and may even take some pride in, the relatively weak attachments that bind us to each other. It is my feeling that we will continue on much as we have ... forever pragmatic, forever flexible, forever Canadian."

Advances notwithstanding, however, there is a downside that confirms the adage about "appearances being deceiving." The Canada of today is remark-ably similar, structurally speaking, to the one of a generation ago. Surface pat-terns have changed, to be sure. Paradoxically, the deep structure remains intact. The foundational principles and hidden agendas remain anchored around Anglo-Canadian values, institutions, agendas, and structures. The intellectual and institutional inheritance of an Anglocentric enlightenment remains relatively unquestioned: its main tenets (from possessive individualism to "whiteness" as norm) continue to unconsciously shape processes and outcomes. Those claiming Anglo-Canadian identity still exert hegemonic control over Canada's social, cultural, political, and economic life. Conversely, those who differ from the "figure in dominance" remain marginal.

In short, Canadians deserve kudos in advancing the concept of a progressive and tolerant society at the cutting edge of global change. But, there is a long way to go in shedding our monocultural "skin" for a multicultural "wrap." In capturing the enigma and paradox that is official multiculturalism, we are reminded of yet another venerable cliché—"the more things change, the more they stay the same." The impact of official multiculturalism has proven effective in abolishing the most egregious forms of discriminatory bigotry that once divided Canadians. Official multiculturalism has barely made any inroads in contesting the foundational structures of Canada's constitutional order. Nor has it done much to disrupt the norm and normalcy of a "real" Canadian as "white, preferably blond, and articulate in English." A commitment to "pretend pluralism" is acceptable, but deep diversities continue to perplex. Failure to connect with the demands of national minorities for recognition and redistribution will test the mettle of Canadians in the twenty-first century (see Fraser, 1997; also Young, 1997). The conclusion seems inescapable: a commitment to symbolic inclusiveness, notwithstanding, Canada arguably remains a white man's world where multicultural minorities orbit around a "pale male" centre with little choice except to scramble for spaces in a pre-existing script.

With its limitations and strengths clearly before us, a sense of perspective is critical and overdue. Considered by some a revolution in the making, yet reviled by others as another example of Anglocentric cultural hegemony, inception of official multiculturalism helped to redefine an era in which everything seemed possible with dollops of government dollars. Multiculturalism at present no longer commands the kind of attention it once did. Both the public and politicians appear increasingly complacent or indifferent in light of more pressing demands on unity and prosperity.

A cautious optimism is in order when taking stock of a modestly innovative if flawed social experiment. Any assessment of official multiculturalism cannot be reduced to the mutually exclusive categories of either good or bad. To the contrary, any assessment must acknowledge the simultaneity of official multiculturalism as progressive and regressive, both good and bad, with strengths as well as weaknesses, depending on the context or criteria. Official multiculturalism must be accepted for what it is: an evolutionary process whose revolutionary impact may eventually transform a Canada that once routinely denied and excluded. The challenge lies in marrying the political clout of an official multiculturalism with the vitality and vibrancy—even subversiveness—of a critically informed multiculturalism. Only time will tell if another thirty years of official multiculturalism can further advance a revolution in the evolution of "living together" as different yet equal.

Glossary

Affirmative action Affirmative action refers to programs introduced in the United States that since the late 1960s have sought to improve minority status (initially only African-Americans) in the workplace through preferential treatment and special programs. These programs tended to rely on quotas and deadlines as a way of complying with federal laws. Compare this with Canadian employment equity initiatives with their focus on goals, guidelines, and timetables. *See also* employment equity.

Antiracism A commitment to identify, isolate, and challenge racism in all its forms through direct action at individual and institutional levels.

Apartheid Apartheid represented the official race relations policy in South Africa that was formally dismantled in 1993. Derived from the Dutch word meaning "separate," apartheid involved a racialized system of laws and procedures that segregated whites from nonwhites. Central to the notion of apartheid was the creation of semi-autonomous, Black homelands whose primary purpose was to provide cheap and disposable labour for white-owned industry. Also included under apartheid was a powerful belief in the virtues of racial purity and white supremacy.

Assimilation The concept of assimilation is derived literally from the process whereby nutrients are absorbed by a living organism. Sociologically speaking, assimilation also consists of a complex and dynamic process in which minorities begin to lose their distinctiveness through absorption into the ongoing activities and objectives of the dominant society. As policy, assimilation can refer to specific and formal government directives for the transformation and incorporation of minority populations into the mainstream. It can also encompass an overarching political framework for justifying program initiatives by which minorities internalize dominant cultural values with a corresponding diminishment of their own. Finally, assimilation may occur because of the logical consequences of policies or practices, involvement or exposure, that have had an absorptive effect. The impact of assimilation can also vary depending on whether the process of change occurs at the level of culture, social structure, individual, or group. Also known as Anglo-conformity.

Bilingualism Bilingualism entails the coexistence of two official languages, each of which can be expressed at territorial, institutional, or individual levels. Canada is officially bilingual at institutional levels: both French and English are legally and constitutionally entrenched as official and equal languages. Official bilingualism is applied primarily to federal institutions; that is, people have the right to work in either language or to receive services in French or English. Parliament and federally funded organizations (from Air Canada to Parks Canada) are bilingual for public service purposes. Official language minorities are also entitled to certain guarantees to official language services in areas where numbers warrant. Of the ten provinces, only New Brunswick is officially bilingual. Approximately 16 percent of all Canadians regard themselves as bilingual speakers.

Capitalism Capitalism can be defined as an economic (and social) system dedicated to the rational pursuit of profit. It is also characterized by (a) an unequal exchange of labour for wages; (b) the organization of production and distribution of goods at prices determined by the "laws" of supply and demand; (c) the use of modern technology and machinery for bolstering the production process; (d) private ownership of the means of production; and (e) competition as catalyst for economic growth.

Charter groups The French and English comprise the second major force in Canadian society. The 1867 British North America Act acknowledged and enshrined the rights of the French and English settlers/colonizers as the foundational members of Canadian society, with the right to establish agendas and define priorities.

Charter of Rights and Freedoms Canada passed the *Charter of Rights and Freedoms* in 1982. The Charter constitutionally entrenched the right of individuals to be free from discrimination because of irrelevant grounds and unnecessary state intrusion. The government retains the right to impose special measures or to invoke the concept of collective rights as a reasonable limitation on individual rights when used to assist the historically disadvantaged.

Citizenship The reciprocal rights and duties that exist between persons and the state in which they live. Citizenship has historically involved the concept of treating everyone the same through conferral of similar rights and obligations. The concept of "one-size-fits-all" citizenship is currently contested by the notions of a customized citizenship, both differentiated and inclusive. A customized citizenship acknowledges that people can belong to society in different ways (either as individuals or as members of national minority groups) without necessarily eroding a commitment to the whole.

Class An aggregate of persons who occupy a similar status or strata in society because of similarities in power, wealth, or status. Those of a Marxist persuasion prefer to see class as the division of society in terms of people's relationship to the means of production and private property. Those who own productive private property are the ruling class; those who must sell their labour power in an unequal exchange for wages are called the working class. Those of a Weberian bent tend to see class as a complex interplay of factors such as wealth, power, and prestige, not all of which coincide, in effect leading to different class systems, including a division of society into the ever-popular categories of upper, middle, and lower class.

Colonialism Colonialism refers to a specific era of European expansion into overseas territories from the sixteenth to the mid-twentieth centuries. It entailed the process whereby a European power took control and exploited an indigenous sector by appropriating land and resources, extracting wealth, and capitalizing on cheap labour. Racial doctrines that reinforced patterns of superiority were often invoked to justify, explain, and promote the blatant exploitation of indigenous minorities. White settlement often accompanied the colonialist enterprise; that in turn led to the displacement of indigenous populations as barriers to progress.

Conflict theory One of several sociological perspectives that can be applied to a study of race and ethnic relations. Conflict theory takes as its starting point the idea that confrontation and change are critical components of society. Race and ethnic relations are interpreted as competitively different groups that compete for scarce resources in contexts that favour some groups, not others. *See also* internal colonialism.

Constitutionalism Does not refer to specific rules of constitutional law or provisions of the Constitution Act. Rather, constitutionalism refers to the general framework of assumptions and premises that inform our under-standing of public action, that help to justify the distribution of government power within society, and that explain the relationships of groups to each other. Constitutionalisms can also refer to those foundational principles that govern the constitutional order of society in terms of defining what is impor-tant, acceptable, or desirable. These presumptions and foundational princi-ples, according to Jeremy Webber, operate at relatively high levels of generality and often are beyond examination or criticism.

Contested site The concept of contested site suggests that any domain in society may be viewed as a kind of battleground involving a competition for scarce resources. Opposing groups with conflicting visions struggle to impose their agendas and priorities at the expense of others. The end result of this struggle is a social reality that is continually emergent and evolving in response to the contestation.

Cultural relativism Cultural relativism consists of a belief that cultures are relative to the society in which they exist. It also entails the notion that the worth and value of cultural practices are relative to the social context from which meaning and significance are derived. Thus, each culture (or cultural practice) should be assessed on its own terms rather than by some arbitrarily selected external criteria. It is widely (but incorrectly) thought that, in the absence of absolute standards, cultural relativism embraces all cultural practices as good and valid—even when in violation of basic standards of human decency. But cultural relativism is not a blanket endorsement of "anything goes." Proponents of a thoughtful cultural relativism argue instead that cultural practices must be approached *as if* equally good and valid for purposes of understanding and study without necessarily condoning or prejudging them.

Culture Social scientists normally employ the concept of culture in a more comprehensive sense than nonacademics. The concept of culture can be defined as a complex and socially constructed system of rules, meaning, knowledge, artifacts, and symbols that (a) guide human behaviour; (b) account for pattern regularities of thought and action; (c) provide a standard for right or wrong, good or bad; and (d) contribute to human social and physical survival. More specifically, culture can refer to the integrated lifestyle of a particular group of people who differ from others in terms of beliefs, values, world-views, and attitudes.

Deconstruction Deconstruction refers to the process of unpacking the socially constructed. On the assumption that social reality consists of constructs created by individuals who make choices, albeit in contexts not of their making, the process of deconstruction exposes those assumptions and the underlying logic that created the product in the first place. Reality is treated as any kind of text that can be exposed in terms of those biases and premises that went into the construction.

Depoliticize The process of taking something that resonates with the language of danger and subversion, then transforming ("co-opting") this potential potency into something that is relatively harmless, marginalized, and "neutered."

Discourse A conceptual framework with its own internal logic and underlying assumptions that may be readily recognizable to the audience. A discourse involves a distinct way of seeing, thinking, and speaking about the world out there. It also suggests that the item under discussion is not a natural attribute of reality, but socially constructed and defined in deference to the postmodernist notion that there is no such thing as reality, only discourses about reality. As a result, discourses about the world "out there" are constructed in the same way as literary texts, are relative to a particular position rather than reflect "rightness" or "goodness," and in their totality are imbued with more meaning than what might be gleaned from deciphering the constituent elements in isolation from each other.

Discrimination Discrimination represents a denial of equal treatment to some group or member of a group because of race, ethnicity, gender, or disability. Often viewed as the behavioural counterpart of prejudice (attitudes), discrimination consists of actions that have an adverse effect (whether deliberate or not) of denying or excluding someone because of his or her placement in a socially devalued category. Diverse types of discrimination can be discerned, ranging from the personal, intentional, and direct to the impersonal, inadvertent, and systemic. *See also* racism.

Diversity For many, diversity is widely seen as a mixture of items characterized by differences and similarities. But diversity is more than a "thing" or separate state of being in which people are slotted into a pre-existing category. Rather, diversity entails a hierarchical relation of power in which individuals are placed into categories that are undergoing constant evaluation and adjustment because of contexts that are relational and unequal.

Dominant group The collectivity of persons in society with both power and authority to preserve and promote the prevailing distribution of privilege in society. The dominant sector represents that part of society with the capacity to define itself and its culture as the standard or norm by which others are judged and evaluated.

Dominant ideology Those ideas and ideals that are commonly used to justify and rationalize the prevailing patterns of what is acceptable and desirable in society. *See also* ideology.

Employment equity Employment equity is a concept that can be interpreted as a principle, a policy, and a set of practices. As a principle, employment equity embraces the notion of institutional inclusiveness by improving the hiring and treatment of minorities. As law, employment equity refers to official policies such as the Employment Equity Act of 1986/1995, which enshrined equity principles as formal government initiatives. The policy is aimed at providing equitable employment opportunities for all Canadians through removal of discriminatory barriers and implementation of proactive measures to accommodate differences. As practice, employment equity consists of formal programs and procedures by which companies draw up plans to hire and promote targeted minorities (women, people of colour, individuals with disabilities, and aboriginal people) in compliance with federal or provincial laws. *See also* affirmative action.

Engagement Involves a process by which interaction between parties establishes a working relationship. Often entails the notion of a positive and productive partnership.

Entitlement The conferral of certain rights, rewards, and privileges ("who gets what") because of claims by an individual or group.

Equality of outcome A pattern of distribution by which the good things in life (wealth, power, and privilege) are allocated on the basis of people's needs of rights rather than on market skills or ability to generate revenue. Compare this egalitarian pattern of allocation with the concept of equal opportunity and its connotation of individual competition and abstract merit as a basis for sorting out who gets what.

Equity The belief that each individual is entitled to an equitable share of scarce resources. Attainment of equity may entail recognition of collective rights by taking people's differences into account as basis for allocating scarce resources.

Essentialism The belief in unchanging human characteristics that are uniform and stable within a certain category and impervious to social context or historical modification.

Ethnic The largely ascriptive identity of a group of individuals who see themselves as belonging to a certain cultural affiliation because of their identification with a common language, ancestry, homeland, and historical and cultural symbols.

Ethnicity A principle by which people are defined, differentiated, organized, and rewarded on the basis of commonly shared physical or cultural characteristics. Ethnicity embraces an explicit or implicit system of beliefs, values, loyalties, and practices of relevance to group members who regard themselves as different and apart. The salient feature of ethnicity is the notion of a collective awareness of shared commonalities as a basis for engagement or entitlement ("peoplehood"). This shared awareness provides a rationale for organizing these like-minded individuals into activity to protect, preserve, or advance group interests.

Ethnic stratification A hierarchical ranking of racial and ethnic minorities in ascending/descending order on the basis of the criteria of income, education, or social class. Think of Canada as "layered" into "strata" based on how different minorities fare in the competition for scarce resources. Canadians of British or northwestern European background have historically ranked near the top of the hierarchy. Groups such as aboriginal First Nations and racialized minorities occupy the bottom of the stratification system, with others in between.

Ethnocentrism A tendency to see reality from a person's cultural perspective as necessary, normal, and desirable. It also includes a belief in the superiority of one's culture or cultural inventory when compared with other practices or values, with a corresponding inclination to dismiss or denigrate others as inferior or irrelevant. Ethnocentrism can interfere with our capacity to understand or empathize with others, given a belief in the moral superiority of European thoughts and practices as the norm or standard by which others are judged and interpreted.

Everyday racism Racism that is expressed and reinforced in the dynamics of daily life and interaction. Everyday racism can be interpreted as an interplay of actions involving the individual (beliefs), the system (organizational rules and priorities), and culture (social values).

Genocide An orchestrated effort by a segment of society to eradicate members from a devalued group. Genocide can be open, deliberate, and violent; it can also be systemic and nonviolent in process.

Hegemony Strictly speaking, hegemony can be defined as consent without coercion. It consists of a process of "thought control" by which dominant ideas and ideals are reproduced through consent and active involvement, but without peoples's awareness that their attitudes are being changed. Hegemony involves a social process where values pertaining to power and privilege are internalized in such a way that they no longer are questioned, but are assumed to be natural, normal, and inevitable. These beliefs and activities are so ingrained and deeply embedded as to be outside the realm of normal discourse, tacitly assumed, and an article of faith to be defended at all costs.

Ideology Defined in its broadest sense, ideology refers to a complex of ideas that attempt to explain, justify, legitimate, and perpetuate a specific set of circumstances. Ideology can be employed in the Marxian sense as those ideas underlying particular material ("class") interests that distort and falsify an account of the real world. Thus, societies are ideological: they are loaded with ideas and ideals that reflect, reinforce, and advance patterns of power that empower some, disempower others.

Immigrant Refers to any person born outside Canada ("foreign-born") regardless of citizenship or permanent resident status. Immigrants include those who are seeking family reunification or improvement in economic status. Refugees are seen as a special category of immigrants (fleeing because of persecution fears), while visa students would not normally be included, since their status is temporary. With the exception of the First Nations, all Canadians are immigrants or descendants of immigrants. About 17 percent of Canada's population is foreign-born (that is, immigrant), a figure that has remained relatively constant since the early 1950s.

Inclusion In its basic sense, the concept of inclusion refers to the incorporation of minority individuals and differences into a pre-existing institutional framework. A more sophisticated notion of inclusion acknowledges the need to restructure values and systems to ensure full and equal participation for minority women and men.

Institutional inclusiveness The idea that mainstream institutions must move over and make space for the historically disadvantaged if they are to reflect the reality of diversity and take advantage of differences as an asset. At one level, inclusion is about increased minority presence through proactive measures to improve minority representation, treatment, and equity. At another level, however, inclusion is about redesigning institutional structures and priorities to ensure minority differences are taken into account when defining who gets what.

Institutionalized racism Institutionalized racism involves an explicit set of discriminatory policies and practices endorsed by the institution that openly deny and exclude minorities from full and equal participation.

Integration The concept of integration as a technique for managing race and ethnic relations can be used in two ways. First, it involves a set of policy ideals and practices that oppose the principles of segregation or separation. As policy or process, integration is concerned with incorporating once-excluded minorities into the mainstream as formally equal. Second, integration refers to a process of fusion in which differences are melted to create a new entity. Unlike assimilation, which involves a one-way process of minority compliance or conformity with majority beliefs and practices, integration allows the adaptation and acceptance of the minority without sacrifice of their cultural identity. In practice, however, the difference between assimilation and integration in terms of impact is more nominal than real.

Internal colonialism Internal colonialism is a concept applied to explain the process of settler control and domination of indigenous ("aboriginal") groups. Unlike the case of salt-water colonies, internal colonialism involves a process of forcibly incorporating indigenous peoples into the system to ensure access to lands and resources. A colonized indigenous minority is forced to live in a society not of its own accord, but one where (a) political and social involvement is curtailed; (b) the cultural basis of society is undermined; and (c) bureaucratic structures are constructed to regulate movements or aspirations.

Liberal pluralism One of the central values and foundational principles that govern the constitutional order of settler societies. Liberal pluralism is firmly anchored in the concept of universalism: that is, a belief that what we have in common as rights-bearing, equality-seeking, and morally autonomous individuals is more important as a basis for entitlement or engagement than the differences that divide people as members of a group.

Mainstreaming A process whereby minorities are incorporated into institutions as legitimate and integral contributors. The term is employed in opposition to "sidestreaming," with its connotation of relegating minorities to the margins of society. *See also* institutional inclusiveness.

Melting pot A metaphor that is used to describe the preferred ideal in American race and ethnic relations. The concept of a melting pot suggests the fusion of minority differences to create a new and improved national culture. The ideal, however, does not match the reality for many racialized minorities who by choice or circumstances remain unmeltable. *See also* mosaic.

Merit/meritocracy The act of rewarding a person on the basis of credentials or achievement. Three features make a judgment meritocratic: the measurement of achievement against a commonly accepted scale is applied to all candidates; every candidate is measured impersonally, that is, on the basis of performance rather than identity; and a reliance on examiners who are selected on the basis of their excellence and impartiality.

Minority group The concept of minority group does not refer to numbers or statistical proportions. Sociologically, the concept of minority group refers to any group (whether based on race, ethnicity, or gender) that is disadvantaged, underprivileged, excluded, discriminated against, or exploited. More accurately, it refers to a socially defined category of individuals who are perceived as different and treated accordingly by the majority and whose disproportionate share of resources stems from a lack of institutionalized power, discriminatory barriers, and denial of opportunity.

Mosaic A metaphor to describe the ideal arrangement involving various racial and ethnic groups in societies such as Canada. The proposed image is that of a patterned entity comprising disparate and distinct elements arranged into a cohesive whole. Proponents admire the positive images associated with the mosaic; detractors denounce it as a gross distortion that neither fits reality nor escapes the conceptual trap of cultural essentialism.

Multicultural competence Multicultural competence refers to the expertise acquired by individuals for coping with the challenges of a multicultural society. Those who are multiculturally competent possess the capacity to constructively engage diversity without necessarily abandoning their values and principles in the process.

Multicultural imagination Individuals who are multiculturally imaginative possess the ability to take differences seriously and take differences into account when trying to see the world from the perspective of others.

Multiculturalism Multiculturalism is one of those vacuous terms that can be used to mean everything yet mean nothing. For our purposes, multiculturalism can be defined as a set of ideas and practices for engaging diversity as different yet equal for the purposes of "living together with differences." A distinction between popular and official multiculturalism is critical. Popular definitions include multiculturalism as a statement of fact (Canada is ethnically diverse); a set of ideals around celebrating diversity; and a critique or social movement that challenges the cultural status quo. Used in a political or institutional sense, multiculturalism represents a doctrine and a corresponding set of practices that officially acknowledge and promote diversity as legitimate or integral without necessarily undermining the interconnectedness of the whole or the parts that hold it together.

Multicultural minorities One of the three major ethnic categories within Canada's multilayered diversity, multicultural minorities comprise those Canadians who are immigrants or descendants of immigrants. Multicultural minorities have the same citizenship rights as Canadians at large, in addition to special considerations because of inclusion under Canada's official multiculturalism. Both visible minorities and European ethnics are known to possess a distinct set of problems, with a corresponding set of solutions consistent with this problem definition. Their goals are less political than those of aboriginal peoples or Québécois and tend to focus on institutional inclusion, social acceptance, and establishment of cultural space. Also known by racial or ethnic minorities, or as "others."

Multicultural thinking What does it mean to think in multicultural terms? One characteristic would reflect a pattern of thought that is nonjudgmental, altruocentric (non-ethnocentric), and relativistic. Multicultural thinking approaches diversity not as a threat or as irrelevant, but as something to be enjoyed for its own sake and as a way of learning about ourselves and the world at large. In contrast, ethnocentric or stereotyped thinking is judgmental, morally evaluative, rigid and unbending, static, uncritical, and dismissive of alternatives.

Nation A nation consists of a moral community of people who share a common homeland, language, identity, set of grievances, and cultural and historical symbols. Essentially a kinship or descent group, it can also be seen as a fundamentally autonomous political and social community based on symbols of identification and a sense of belonging. Both Quebec and the First Nations prefer to see themselves as "nations" within Canadian federalism.

Nationalism Nationalism entails an ideology about the proper political relation between peoples and their homeland. Under the notion of nationalism the world is divided naturally into identifiable and distinct populations, each with the right to self-determination over territory, institutions, and values. Nationalism evolved into a formidable political force in Europe during the nineteenth century and provided the basis for the creation of nation-states in the twentieth century.

"Nations within" A term normally employed to describe aboriginal ambitions for self-determination in Canada. The "nations within" concept acknowledges the claim that aboriginal peoples are relatively autonomous and self-determining political communities that share sovereignty in society in general and are sovereign in their own right by way of aboriginal models of self-determination.

Official language minorities The Official Languages Acts of Canada (1969/1988) offer protection to Canada's official languages. French-speaking Canadians who live outside Quebec and English-speaking Canadians who reside in Quebec have certain rights that not only allow them access to services in their language, but enable them to exercise control over institutions such as education.

Official Languages Act The Official Languages Act of 1969 officially declared Canada a bilingual society (*see* bilingualism). The act was updated in 1988 to consolidate changes since 1969 as well as to strengthen the rights of official language minorities.

Official multiculturalism Official multiculturalism refers to an institutionalized set of policies and practices for integrating minority women and men into the institutional framework of society. The underlying logic of an official multiculturalism is to acknowledge differences without losing sight of national interests related to unity, identity, and prosperity.

"Other(iz)ing" The process by which minority women and men are portrayed as people who are removed in time, remote in space, marginal to society, and undeserving of equal treatment because of their inferiority or irrelevance. Also known as "othered" or "other."

People of colour Those Canadians who are nonaboriginal, nonwhite, and non-Caucasian in origin, and are defined as such by the government or have agreed to be defined in such a way for employment or census purposes. People of colour share one attribute in common: most lack access to the institutionalized power that defines "who gets what" in society. *See also* visible minorities.

Pluralism Pluralism can be defined as a doctrine extolling the possible coexistence of culturally different groups. This cultural coexistence is achieved through the creation of an overarching set of values or institutions that acknowledges the value and legitimacy of differences without eroding the interconnectedness of the parts or the distinctiveness of the parts in the process. A commitment to multiculturalism represents one variant of a pluralist society.

Policy Policy can be defined as a formal set of specific initiatives (including laws, rules, and practices) designed to solve an acknowledged problem. Policy can also be defined as an ideological framework that justifies the creation and implementation of specific initiatives to solve problems.

Politicization The process by which issues are taken out of the personal or private domain and elevated instead into the public domain in the competition for scarce resources.

Postmodernism A term that does not lend itself to a quick-fix definition. In rejecting the principles of modernism, postmodernism may be defined as a rejection of a unified and organized way of thinking about the world from a fixed and objective point of view. Also rejected is the idea that there is a rational core of meaning at the centre of society with a host of myths and symbols that secures unity and identity. Endorsed instead is a perspective that embraces the notion of reality as a series of discourses, a relativism that embraces diversity as valuable and normal, a perception of identities as fluid and multidimensional, and a critique of conventional patterns as discourses in defence of ideology.

Power Power refers to the capacity of dominant groups (or at least the elites within the dominant sector) to enforce a degree of compliance ("obedience") in accordance with dominant needs and aspirations. Power can be acquired and applied in different ways, ranging from the exercise of physical coercion to the construction of ideologies without people's awareness. Power should not be thought of as a thing, but as inherent to relationships. The relational nature of power shifts from context to context, suggesting that minorities can wield power in certain situations.

Prejudice Prejudice can be defined as a set of biased and generalized pre-judgments about the "other" that are resistant to correction. It represents a dislike of others based on faulty and inflexible generalizations, involving an irrational and unfounded set of assumptions that compromise the treatment of minority groups in an impartial or equitable manner. Prejudice is "framed" as a social construction rather than a purely psychological phenomenon; it originates when the dominant sector invokes negative ideas to justify and entrench its power and privilege over the subordinate sector.

Problematizing Problematizing refers to the process by which the taken-for-granted is scrutinized, questioned, and debated. The objective is to make transparent ("deconstruct") the socially constructed nature of this taken-for-granted reality. By deconstructing this social construction, sociologists hope to reveal as clearly as possible ("make transparent") the issues, agendas, politics, pressures, and arbitrariness that construct the aspect of reality under study.

Race Race can be employed in two ways: (a) a belief that people's behaviour is determined by biology; (b) a belief that humanity can be classified into categories on the basis of fixed attributes and arranged in an ascending and descending order of superiority or inferiority, and treated accordingly. Race is generally regarded as having no empirical validity or scientific merit. It exists instead as a social construction that is manipulated to define and reinforce the unequal relations—proving again that phenomena do not have to be real to be real in their consequences.

Race and ethnic relations Race and ethnic relations consist of those recurrent and unequal patterns of interaction that evolve between groups who are defined as biologically or culturally different. Race and ethnic relations are inseparable from relationships of inequality, and this puts the onus on sociologists to determine how these inequities are constructed, maintained, challenged, and transformed within contexts of control and exploitation.

Racialization The concept of racialization refers to the assigning of racial connotations to the activities of minority women and men. Racialized can also be used in the sense of describing race relations. That is, there is no such thing as race relations, but only relationships that have been conferred a racial meaning by those in positions of power. Minorities may also be racialized in that they are invested with negative biologically determined attributes that are seen as creating problems, posing a threat to society, and providing unwanted competition for scarce resources.

Racialized minorities The racializing of minorities reflects a process whereby minority groups and their differences are defined largely by race while whites are not, thus reinforcing how race can be manipulated to deny, exclude, or exploit.

Racism The concept of racism no longer has a single meaning, but takes on meanings depending on context, criteria, and consequences of actions. Definitions of racism will also vary depending on the proposed focus: biology, culture, or power. For our purposes, racism refers to a relatively complex and organized set of ideas and ideals ("ideology") that assert natural superiority of one group over another, together with the power to put these beliefs into practice in a way that denies or excludes those because of membership in a devalued category. The components of racism are often summarized in this popular equation: racism = prejudice + discrimination + power. It is important to discern different types of racism, from the personal and direct to the impersonal, institutional, and systemic. Racism also exists at diverse levels, including the individual, the institutional, and ideological.

Representation Representation refers to the way people are signified through words or visual images that often say more about the creators than the object of creation.

Scapegoating A situation in which a particular group is singled out and unjustly blamed for the misfortunes, failures, and shortcomings of another.

Segregation The process and practice of separating groups on the basis of race or culture. This separation can be repressive and occur involuntarily, as was the case in South Africa's apartheid. Conversely, separation may be voluntary, as with the Anabaptists of Canada and the United States, or it may be strategic, as may be the case with the Québécois.

Self-determination A claim to assume control over jurisdictions (or domains) of immediate concern to a particular group of peoples.

Social constructionism Social constructionism represents a distinctive way of looking at the world. According to social constructionists, there is no such thing as reality, but only discourses of reality. Insofar as there is nothing inherently natural or normal about social reality, reality represents a convention created by individuals who make choices within contexts that are not necessarily of their making. That makes it doubly important to determine whose discourses prevail in the social construction of reality: Why? How? On what grounds?

State A political, legal, and administrative unit that exercises political sovereignty over a specific territory, monopolizes the legitimate use of authority, and is ruled by a government that alleges to speak for the inhabitants.

Stereotype A stereotype is a shorthand way of classifying social reality into convenient categories on the basis of common properties. As a generalization, it provides an oversimplification or exaggerated version of the world based on preconceived and unwarranted notions that extend to all members of the devalued group; for example, Germans are "industrious;" Blacks are natural "athletes." Stereotypes become harmful when individuals are judged and evaluated according to the norms of their group rather than on personal merit. They can also be damaging if employed to deny equality of opportunity or participation.

Stratification Every society can be divided into layers or strata that can be hierarchically ranked according to certain criteria in ascending or descending order. This suggests that inequality is not random or fleeting, but is patterned and predictable and tends to cluster around certain devalued categories related to race or ethnicity. *See also* ethnic stratification.

Substantive equity Substantive equity is based on the idea that differences have to be taken into account for achieving genuine rather than formal equivalence. This colour-conscious approach to equality appears to be at variance with colour-blind notions where everyone is treated the same ("mathematical equality"). *See also* equality of outcome.

Symbolic ethnicity Symbolic ethnicity (also situational ethnicity) constitutes a process in which an individual retains a cognitive or emotional affiliation with a cultural past. Involvement in the daily and organizational life of that particular ethnic group is kept to a minimum without necessarily abdicating any sense of belonging or attachment. This type of ethnicity is popular in Canada, reflecting a type of continuity with the past that is voluntary and without the costs and sanctions of primary group participation. Canada's multiculturalism is based on endorsement of symbolic ethnic affiliation. It remains to be seen if Canada can accommodate the "deep" ethnicities at the core of contemporary society-building processes.

Systemic discrimination Systemic discrimination is based on the principle that bias can be built into the institutional system through the even and equal application of rules and procedures that may impact vulnerable minorities in different ways. It can be defined as any action that has a discriminatory effect (rather than intent) of denying or excluding persons regardless of intent or awareness. An action may also be systemically discriminatory because of logical consequences of actions that are predicated on faulty if well-intentioned assumptions.

Systemic racism Systemic racism can be defined as a largely inadvertent bias that is built into the institutional framework of society. In contrast to deliberate and conscious expressions of denial or exclusion, systemic racism refers to the subtle yet powerful form of exclusion that is entrenched within institutional structures, cultures, processes, and outcomes. Institutional standards, rules, and rewards may appear to be univerally applicable and colour-blind; nevertheless, they have had the unintended yet controlling effect of excluding those who fall outside the mainstream while consolidating the pattern of power and privilege of a racialized social order.

Vertical mosaic A twist on the notion of Canada as a multicultural "mosaic," the term originated with publication of the book *The Vertical Mosaic* by John Porter, an eminent Canadian sociologist. According to Porter, Canada's multicultural mosaic is organized and aligned along a system of stratification that has disadvantages for certain racial or ethnic minorities. Any policy or program that involves the promotion of diversity, Porter contends, would only serve to entrench and perpetuate the hierarchical notions of racial or ethnic inequality.

Visible minorities Also "people of colour" or "racialized minorities." The term "visible minority" is used to designate nonwhite, nonaboriginal, non-Caucasian racial minorities in Canada regardless of place of birth. The term "visible minority" refers to an official government category of native- and foreign-born, nonwhite, non-Caucasoid individuals, including Blacks, Chinese, Japanese, Koreans, Filipinos, Indo-Pakistanis, West Asians, Arabs, Southeast Asians, Latin Americans, and Pacific Islanders. This administrative category does not always square with popular perceptions of what constitutes visibility. However unacceptable, the term represents an improvement over other pejorative connotations; it also has the bonus of acknowledging the common problems encountered by members of this category because of their visibility.

References

Adam, B., & Stuart, A. (Eds.). (1995). *Theorizing culture: An interdisciplinary critique after postmodernism*. New York: NYU Press.

Adam, H. (1989). Contemporary state policies to subordinate ethnics. In J. Frideres (Ed.), *Multiculturalism and intergroup relations* (pp. 19–34). Westport, CT: Greenwood Press.

Adam, H. (1998). German and Canadian nationalism and multiculturalism: A comparison of xenophobia, racism, and integration. In D. Haselbach (Ed.), *Multiculturalism in a world of leaking boundaries* (pp. 193–210). New Brunswick, NJ: Transaction Publishers.

Adams, H. (1999). *Tortured people: The politics of colonization*. Penticton, BC: Theytus Books.

Alba, R. (1999). Immigration and the American realities of assimilation and multiculturalism. *Sociological Forum, 14*(1), 3–26.

Alexander, J., & Smelser, N.J. (1997). *Diversity and its discontents: Cultural conflicts and common ground in contemporary North American society*. NJ: Princeton U Press.

Alienikoff, T.A. (2001). American citizenship: An introduction. *Citizenship Studies, 5*(1), 5–15.

Apple, M.W., & Kegan, P. (1979). *Ideology and curriculum*. London: Routledge.

Asbury, K.E. (1989). Innovative policing: Foot patrol in 31 division, Metropolitan Toronto. *Canadian Police College Journal, 13*(3), 165–81.

Aujla, A. (2000). Others in their own land: Second generation South Asian Canadian women, racism, and the persistance of colonial discourse. *Canadian Women Studies, 20*(2), 41–47.

Bagley, C., & Gajendra K.V. (1983). *Multicultural education: Education, ethnicity, and cognitive styles*. London: Gower.

Bailey, R., & Brake, M. (1975). Introduction: Social work in the welfare state. In R. Bailey & M. Brake (Eds.), *Radical social work* (pp. 1–12). New York: Pantheon.

Bak, H. (1993). Introduction. In H. Bak (Ed.), *Multiculturalism and the canon of American culture* (pp. ix–xviii). Amsterdam: Amerika Instituut.

Ballard, R. (1999, Mar. 12). Singular failure to tackle plurality. [Letter to the editor]. *The Times Higher Education*.

Banks, J.A. (1981). *Multiethnic education: Theory and practice*. Boston: Allyn and Bacon.

Banks, J.A. (1984). Multicultural education in the USA: Practices and promises. In T. Corner (Ed.), *Education in multicultural societies* (pp. 68–95). London: Croom Helm.

Banks, J.A. (1997). Multicultural education: Characteristics and goals. In J. Banks & C.A. McGee Banks (Eds.), *Multicultural education: Issues and Perspectives* (pp. 3–31). Toronto: Allyn and Bacon.

Banks, J.A., & McGee Banks, C.A. (Eds.). (1997). *Multicultural education: Issues and perspectives*. Toronto: Allyn and Bacon.

Bannerjee, S.B., & Osuri, G. (2000). Silences of the media: Whiting out aboriginality in making news and making history. *Media, Culture, & Society, 22*, 263–84.

Bannerji, H. (2000). *The dark side of the moon*. Toronto: Canadian Scholars Press.

Bayefsky, A. (2000, Jan 31). We must fund all schools equally. *Toronto Star*.

Beckton, C. (1987). Section 27 and Section 15 of the Charter. In Canadian Human Rights Foundation (Ed.), *Multiculturalism and the Charter: A legal perspective* (pp. 1–14). Toronto: Carswell.

Beier, J.M. (1999). Of cupboards and shelves: Imperialism, objectification, and the fixing of parameters on native North Americans in popular culture. In J.N. Brown &

P.M. Sant (Eds.), *Indigeneity: construction and re/presentation* (pp. 244–56). Commack, NY: Nova Science Publishers.

Bennett, R., Aston, A., & Colquhoun, T. (2000) Cross-cultural training: A critical step in ensuring the success of international assignments. *Human Resource Management, 39*(2/3), 239–50.

Berry, J.W. (1984). Multicultural policy in Canada: A social psychological analysis. *Canadian Journal of Behavioural Science, 16*(4), 353–70.

Berry, J.W. (1989). Costs and benefits of multiculturalism: A psychological analysis. Paper presented at the Canadian Studies Conference, St. John's College, University of Manitoba, Winnipeg, Feb. 28–Mar. 2.

Berry, J.W. (1990). The role of psychology in ethnic studies. *Canadian Ethnic Studies, 22*(1), 8–21.

Berry, J., Kalin, R., & Taylor, D.M. (1977). *Multiculturalism and ethnic attitudes in Canada*. Ottawa: Ministry of Supply and Services.

Bhabha, J. (1999). Belonging in Europe: Citizenship and post-national rights. *International Social Science Journal, 159*, 11–19.

Bharucha, R. (2000). *Interculturalism and its discrimination: Shifting the agendas of the nation, multiculturalism, and the globe* (3rd ed.).

Bibby, R.W. (1990). *Mosaic madness: The potential and poverty of Canadian life*. Toronto: Stoddart.

Blumenthal, H. (1999). Taking a new approach to crime and corrections. *Let's Talk*, Mar. 2–4.

Bolaria, B.S., & Li, P.S. (1988). *Racial oppression in Canada*. (2nd ed.). Toronto: Garamond Press.

Bosniak, L. (2000). Citizenship denationalised. *Indiana Journal of Global Legal Studies, 7*(2), 447–509.

Bottomley, G., de Lepervanche, M., & Martin, J. (1991). *Intersexions: Gender/race/culture/ethnicity*. Sydney: Allen & Unwin.

Bourassa, R. (1975). Objectives to multiculturalism. [Letter to *Le Devoir*, Nov. 17, 1971]. Reprinted in Palmer, H., *Immigration and the rise of multiculturalism*. Toronto: Copp Clark.

Braxton, G. (2001, May 2). TV nets lashed on minority mix. *Toronto Star*.

Breton, E. (2000). Canadian federalism, multiculturalism and the twenty-first century. *International Journal of Canadian Studies, 21*, Spring, 160–75.

Breton, R. (1964). Institutional completeness of ethnic communities and the personal relations of immigrants. *American Journal of Sociology, 70*, 103–205.

Breton, R. (1984). The production and allocation of symbolic resources: An analysis of the linguistic and ethnocultural fields in Canada. *Canadian Review of Sociology and Anthropology, 21*(2), 123–40.

Breton, R. (1989). The vesting of ethnic interests in state institutions. In J. Frideres (Ed.), *Multiculturalism and intergroup relations* (pp. 35–56). Westport, CT: Greenwood Press.

Breton, R. (1990). The ethnic group as a political resource in relation to problems of incorporation: Perceptions and attitudes. In R. Breton, W.I. Isajiw, W. Kalbach, & J. Reitz (Eds.), *Ethnic identity and equality: Varieties of experience in a Canadian city* (pp. 196–255). Toronto: U of Toronto Press.

Breton, R. (1998). Ethnicity and race in social organizations: Recent developments in Canadian society. In R. Helmes-Hayes & J. Curtis (Eds.), *The vertical mosaic revisited*. Toronto: U of Toronto Press.

Breton, R, Isajiw, W.I., Kalbach, W., & Reitz, J. (1990). *Ethnic identity and equality: Varieties of experience in a Canadian city*. Toronto: U of Toronto Press.

Britton, N.J. (2000). Examining police/black relations: What's in a story? *Ethnic and Racial Studies, 23*(4), 692–711.

Broadhurst, R. (1999). Introduction: The "new justice" and settler states: Crime, justice, and indigenous peoples. *Australian and New Zealand Journal of Criminology*. Special issue.

Buenker, J.D., & Ratner, L.A. (Eds.). (1992). *Multiculturalism in the United States: A comparative guide to acculturation and ethnicity*. Westport, CT: Greenwood Press.

Bullivant, B. (1981). Multiculturalism: Pluralist orthodoxy or ethnic hegemony. *Canadian Ethnic Studies, 13*(2), 1–22.

Bullivant, B. (1981a). *The pluralist dilemma in education: Six case studies*. Sydney: Allen & Unwin.

Bullock, K.H , & Jafri, G.J. (2000). Media (mis)representations: Muslim women in the Canadian nation. *Canadian Woman Studies, 20*(2), 35–40.

Bulmer, M., & Solomos, J. (1998) Introduction: Rethinking ethnic and racial studies. *Ethnic and Racial Studies, 21*(5), 819–38.

Burayidi, M.A. (1997) Multicultural nations in a monocultural world: An introduction. In M.A. Burayidi (Ed.), *Multiculturalism in a cross-national perspective* (pp. 1–11). NY: University Press of America.

Burnet, J. (1984). Myths and multiculturalism. In R.L. Samuda, J.W. Berry, & M. Laferriere (Eds.), *Multiculturalism in Canada: Social and educational perspectives* (pp. 18–29). Toronto: Allyn and Bacon.

Burnet, J. (1988). Multiculturalism. In J.H. March (Ed.), *The Canadian Encyclopedia* (p. 1401). Edmonton: Hurtig.

Burnet, J., & Palmer, H. (1988). *Coming Canadians: An introduction to the history of Canada's people*. Toronto: McClelland and Stewart.

Burnet, J., & Palmer, H. (1990). State of the art: Canadian ethnic studies. *Canadian Ethnic Studies, 22*(1), 1–7.

Byrne, E., & McQuillan, M. (1999). *Deconstructing Disney*. Sterling, VA: Pluto Press.

Caglar, A.S. (1997). Hyphenated identities and the limits of culture. In T. Modood & P. Werbner (Eds.), *The politics of multiculturalism in the New Europe* (pp. 169–85). London: Zed Books.

Canadian Criminal Justice Association. (2000, May 15). *Aboriginal peoples and the criminal justice system*. Special issue.

Canadian Heritage. (1997). *Multiculturalism: Respect, equality, and diversity*. Canadian Heritage Program Headlines. Ottawa.

Canadian Heritage. (1997/1998–1999). On the operation of Canada's multiculturalism act. Annual Report. Ottawa: Minister of Public Works and Government Services, Canada.

Canadian Heritage. (2001). *Canadian multiculturalism: An inclusive citizenship*. Retrieved August 13, 2001, from www.pch.gc.ca/multi/what-multi_e.shtml.

Canadian Press. (2000, Jun. 2). Prison population down but costs are up. *Kitchener-Waterloo Record*.

Cardarelli, A.P., McDevitt, J., & Baum, K. (1998). The rhetoric and reality of community policing in small and medium-sized cities and towns. *Policing: An international journal of police strategies and management, 21*(3), 397–415.

Carey, E. (2000, Sept. 1). City's diversity key to olympic sales pitch. *Toronto Star*.

Caws, P. (1994). Identities: Cultural, transcultural, and multicultural. In D.T. Goldberg (Eds.), *Multiculturalism: A critical reader* (pp. 371–87). Oxford, UK: Blackwell Publishers.

Cayley, D. (1999). *The expanding prison: The crisis in crime and punishment and the search for alternatives*. Cleveland: United Church Press.

Charon, J. (1995). *Ten questions: A sociological perspective*. Belmont, CA: Wadsworth.

Children Now. (2001). *Fall colours 2000–01*.

Churchill, W. (1999). *Fantasies of the master race: Literature, cinema, and the colonization of North American Indians*. Winnipeg: Arbeiter Ring.

Chwialkowska, L. (2000, May 8). Canada tougher on youth crime than U.S. *National Post*.

Clause, C. (1999). Nostalgia, freedom, and the end of cultures. *Queen's Quarterly 106*(2), 233–43.

Cole, D. (1998). *Race and class in the American criminal justice system*. New York: NY Press.

Conlogue, B. (2000, Oct. 10). Hero of English Canada. *The Globe and Mail*.

Copeman, P., & Scollen, R. (2000). Of training, tokenism, and productive misinterpretation: Reflections on *After China* Project. *Journal of Australian Studies and Australian Cultural History*, 35–43. Special joint issue.

Cowen, T. (1999, Apr. 24). Cashing in on cultural free trade. *National Post*.

Cowlishaw, G.K., (2000). Censoring race in "post-colonial" anthropology. Critique of *Anthropology, 20*(2), 101–23.

Crean, S. (1986). Cracks in the mosaic. *Border Crossings, 5*(4), 9–11.

Cremen, C. (2000, Oct. 28–29). That old black magic. *The Weekend Australian*.

Crossette, B. (1999). Balancing immigrant customs with human rights. *National Post*. Reprinted from the *New York Times*.

Cryderman, B., O'Toole, C., & Fleras, A. (1998). *Police, race, and ethnicity: A guide for police service officers*. (3rd ed.). Toronto: Butterworths.

Cummins, J., & Danesi1, M. (1986). Military models of policing: Comparative impressions. *Canadian Police College Journal 10*(4), 267–85.

Cummins, J., & Danesi1, M. (1990). *Heritage languages: The development and denial of Canada's linguistic resources*. Toronto: Garamond Press/Our Schools-Our Selves Education Foundation.

Daly, K. (2000). Restorative justice in diverse and unequal societies. *Criminal Justice in Diverse Communities 17*(2), 167–80.

Das Gupta, T., & Iacovetta, F. (2000). Whose Canada is it? Immigrant women, women of colour, and feminist critiques of multiculturalism. *Atlantis 24*(2), 1–4.

Davis, L.R., & Harris, O. (1998). Race and ethnicity in US sports media. In L.A. Wenner (Ed.), *Mediasport* (pp. 154–69). New York: Routledge.

de Benoist, A. (1999). What is racism? *Telos, 114*, 11–48.

Dei, G.S. (2000). Contesting the future: Antiracism and Canadian diversity. In S. Nancoo (Ed.), *21st century Canadian diversity* (pp. 295–319). Mississauga: Canadian Scholars Press.

Desroches, F.J. (1986). The occupational subculture of the police. In B.K. Cryderman & C.N. O'Toole (Eds.), *Police, race, and ethnicity: A guide for law enforcement officers* (pp. 39–51). Toronto: Butterworths.

Dijkstra, S., Geuijen, K., & De Ruijter, A. (2001). Multiculturalism and social integration in Europe. *International Political Science Review 22*(1), 55–84.

Diller, J. (1999). *Cultural diversity. A primer for the human services*. Toronto: Brooks/Cole.

Dion, S. (2000). Unity in diversity, the Canadian way. In S. Nancoo (Ed.), *21st century Canadian diversity* (pp. 9–101). Mississauga: Canadian Scholars Press.

Diop, A.M. (1997). Negotiating religious differences: The opinions and attitudes of Islam associations in France. In T. Modood & P. Werbner (Eds.), *The politics of multiculturalism in the new Europe* (pp. 111–25). London: Zed Books.

Driedger, L. (Ed.). (1987). *Ethnic Canada: Identities and inequalities*. Toronto: Copp Clark Pitman.

Driedger, L. (1989). *The ethnic factor: Identity in diversity*. Toronto: McGraw-Hill Ryerson.

DuCharme, M. (1986). The coverage of Canadian immigration policy in *The Globe and Mail* (1980–1985). *Currents*, Spring, 6–11.

Duncanson, J. (1999, Mar. 6). Police woo minority recruits. *Toronto Star*.

Dyer, G. (1999). France puts female genital mutilation on trial. *Toronto Star*.

Dyer, G. (2000, Oct. 9). His legacy is our diversity. *Kitchener-Waterloo Record*.

Dyer, G. (2001). Visible majorities. *Canadian Geographer*, Jan/Feb, 45–51.

Eagleton, T. (2000). *The idea of culture*. Oxford, UK: Blackwell Publishers.

Early, G. (1993). American education and the postmodernist impulse. *American Quarterly, 45*(2), 220–41.

Eichstedt, J.L. (1997). Multiculturalism in the arts. In *Reproducing Racial and Class Inequality*.

Eisenstein, Z. (1996). *Hatreds: Racialized and sexualized conflicts in the twenty-first century*. New York: Routledge.

Eller, J.D. (1997). Anti-anti-multiculturalism. *American Anthropologist, 99*(2), 249–60.

Elliott, J.L. (Ed.). (1983). *Two nations: Many cultures: Ethnic groups in Canada*. Scarborough, ON: Prentice Hall Canada.

Elliott, J.L., & Fleras, A. (1990). Immigration and the Canadian ethnic mosaic. In Peter S. Li (Ed.), *Race and ethnic relations in Canada* (pp. 51–76). Toronto: OUP.

Elliott, J.L., & Fleras, A. (1991). *Unequal relations: An introduction to race and ethnic dynamics in Canada*. Scarborough, ON: Prentice Hall Canada.

Eng, S. (2000, Jan. 27). Cop culture: For us or against us? *The Globe and Mail*.

Fish, S. (1997). Boutique multiculturalism, or why liberals are incapable of thinking about hate speech. *Critical Inquiry*, Winter, 378–95.

Fleras, A. (1984). Monoculturalism, multiculturalism, or biculturalism: The politics of Maori policy in New Zealand. *Plural Societies, 15*(1/2), 52–75.

Fleras, A. (1989). Towards a multicultural reconstruction of Canadian society. *The American Review of Canadian Studies, 19*(3), 307–320.

Fleras, A. (1994). Multiculturalism as society-building: Blending what is workable, necessary, and fair. In M. Charleton & P. Baker (Eds.), *Cross-Currents: Contemporary Political Issues* (pp. 26–42). Toronto: Nelson.

Fleras, A. (1998). Working through differences: The politics of isms and posts in New Zealand. *New Zealand Sociology, 13*(2), 56–87.

Fleras, A. (2001). *Social problems in Canada: Conditions, constructions, and challenges*. Toronto: Pearson.

Fleras, A., & Elliott, J.L. (1991). *Multiculturalism in Canada: The challenges of diversity*. Toronto: Nelson.

Fleras, A., & Elliott, J.L. (1992). *The nations within: State-Aboriginal peoples relations in Canada, New Zealand, and the United States*. Toronto: OUP.

Fleras, A., & Elliott, J.L. (1999). *Unequal relations* (3rd ed.). Scarborough, ON: Prentice Hall.

Fleras, A., & Lock Kunz, J. (2001). *Media and minorities: Representing diversity in a multicultural society*. Toronto: Thompson Publishing.

Fleras, A., & Spoonley, P. (1999) *Recalling Aotearoa: Indigenous politics and ethnic relations in New* Zealand. Melbourne: OUP.

Foot, R. (2000, Jan. 28). Canadians are an ethnic group in their own right, professor says. *National Post*.

Frances, M. (2000). The beautiful and the damned. *Journal of Australian Studies, 64*, 154–65.

Fraser, N. (1997). From redistribution to recognition? Dilemmas of justice in a post-socialist age. In C. Willett (Ed.), *Theorizing multiculturalism* (pp. 19–49). Oxford, UK: Blackwell Publishers.

Frederickson, G.M (1999). Mosaics and melting pots. *Dissent*, Summer, 36–43.

Frideres, J.S. (1997). Multiculturalism and public policy in Canada. In M.A. Burayidi (Ed.), *Multiculturalism in a cross-national perspective* (pp. 87–111). NY: University Press of America.

Fry, A.J., & Forceville, C. (Eds.). (1988). *Canadian mosaic: Essays on multiculturalism*. Amsterdam: Free University.

Gagnon, A. (2000). Canada: Unity and diversity. *Parliamentary Affairs*.

Garcia, J.A. (1995). A multicultural America: Living in a sea of diversity. In D.A. Harris (Ed.), *Multiculturalism from the margins* (pp. 29–38). Westport, CT: Greenwood Press

Garcia, M., & Baird, L.L. (2000). The shape of diversity. [Introduction to a special issue of *JHE*]. *The Journal of Higher Education, 71*(2), v–vii.

Gay, G. (1997). Educational equality for students of color. In J. Banks & C.A. McGee Banks (Eds.), *Multicultural education* (pp. 195–228). Toronto: Allyn and Bacon.

Giese, R. (2000, Sept. 28). Anti-gay faith groups target local school board. *Toronto Star*.

Gillespie, M. (1996). *Television, ethnicity, and cultural change*. London: Routledge.

Gilroy, P. (2000). *Between camps: Nations, cultures, and the allure of race*. London: Allen Lane/Penguin Press.

Giroux, H. E. (1994). Insurgent multiculturalism as the promise of pedagogy. In D.T. Goldberg (Ed.), *Multiculturalism: A critical reader* (pp. 325–43). Oxford, UK: Blackwell Publishers.

Glazer, N. (1997). *We are all multiculturalists now*. Cambridge, Mass: CUP.

Goldberg, D.T. (1994). Introduction: Multicultural conditions. In D.T. Goldberg (Ed.), *Multiculturalism: A critical reader* (pp. 1–44). Oxford, UK: Blackwell Publishers.

Goldsmith, A., & Israel, M. (2000). Criminal justice in diverse communities: An introduction. *Criminal Justice in Diverse Communities, 17*(1), 1–14.

Gosine, A. (2000). Presenting Adrienne Clarkson: Gender, nation, and a new governor-general. *Canadian Woman Studies, 20*(2), 6–11.

Grant, C.A., & Slater, C.E. (1997). Race, class, gender, and disability in the classroom. In J. Banks & C.A. McGee Banks (Eds.),

Multicultural education (pp. 61–84). Toronto: Allyn and Bacon.

Grillo, R. (1998). *Pluralism and the politics of difference: State culture and ethnicity in comparative perspective*. Oxford: Clarendon Press.

Gunew, S. (1993). An interview. In G. Rajan & R. Mohahram (Eds.), *Postcolonial discourse and changing cultural contexts: Theory and criticism* (pp. 205–17). Westport, CT: Greenwood Press.

Gunew, S. (1999). Colonial hauntings: The (post) colonialism of multiculturalism in Australia and Canada. *Australian-Canadian Studies, 17*(2), 11–31.

Gwyn, R. (2001, Mar. 21). Old Canada disappearing from scene. *Toronto Star*.

Gwyn, R. (2000, Jan. 1). Globalism. *Toronto Star*.

Ha, T.T. (2000, Aug. 4). Multiculturalism, Canadian-style, lauded. *The Globe and Mail*.

Habermas, J. (1976). *Legitimation crisis*. (T. McCarthy, Trans.). London: Heinemann.

Halka, E. (1996). Madam Justice Bertha Wilson: A "different" voice in the supreme court. *Alberta Law Review, xxxv*(1), 242–65.

Harles, J. (1998). Multiculturalism, national identity, and national integration: The Canadian case. *International Journal of Canadian Studies, 17*, Spring, 80–99.

Harris, F. (1995). *Multiculturalism from the margins*. Westport, CT: Bergin and Harvey.

Hartnagel, T.F. (2000). Correlates of criminal behaviour. In R. Linden (Ed.), *Criminology: A Canadian perspective* (4th ed.) (pp. 94–135). Toronto: Harcourt Brace.

Hellsten, S.K. (1999). Pluralism in multicultural liberal democracy and the justification for female circumcision. *Journal of Applied Philosophy*.

Henry, F., & Tator, C. (1985). Racism in Canada: Social myths and strategies for change. In R.M. Bienvenue &

J.E. Goldstein (Eds.), *Ethnicity and ethnic relations in Canada* (2nd ed.) (pp. 321–35). Toronto: Butterworths.

Henry, F., & Tator, C. (1999). State policy and practices as racialized discourse: Multiculturalism, the charter, and employment equity. In P.S. Li (Ed.), *Race and Ethnic Relations in* Canada (2nd ed.) (pp. 88–115). Toronto: OUP.

Herman, E.S., & Chomsky, N. (1988). *Manufacturing consent: The political economy of the mass media.* New York: Pantheon Books.

Hesse, B. (1997). It's your world: Discrepant multiculturalisms. *Social Identities, 3*(3), 375–94.

Hiebert, D. (2000). Immigration and the changing Canadian city. *The Canadian Geographer, 44*(1), 25–43.

Higham, J. (1993). Multiculturalism and universalism: A history and critique. *American Quarterly, 45*(3), 195–219.

Holland, J., & Gentry, J.W. (1999). Ethnic consumer reaction to targeted marketing: A theory of intercultural accommodation. *The Journal of Advertising, 28*(1), 65–78.

Howard, R.E. (1998). Being Canadian: Citizenship in Canada. *Citizenship Studies, 2*(1), 133–48.

Howard, R.E. (2000). "Canadian" as an ethnic category: Implications for multiculturalism and national unity. *Canadian Public Policy.*

Hughes, R. (2000, Feb. 9). Canadian is an "ethnicity". *The Hamilton Spectator.*

Hughes, R. (2000, Sept. 1). The real Australia. *Time Magazine,* Olympic issue.

Hutcheon, P.D. (2001). Can humanism save the rising tide of tribalism? *Humanist, 136,* 6–11.

Hutchinson, J. (1994). *Modern nationalism.* London: Fontana Press.

Iacovetta, F. (2000). Recipes for democracy? Gender, family, and making female citizens in cold war Canada. *Canadian Woman Studies, 20*(2), 12–21.

Ignace, M.B., & Ignace, R.E. (1998). The old wolf in sheep's clothing: Canadian aboriginal peoples and multiculturalism. In D. Haselbach (Ed.), *Multiculturalism in a world of leaking boundaries* (pp. 101–32). New Brunswick, NJ: Transaction Publishers.

Isajiw, W. (Ed.). (1997). *Multiculturalism in North America and Europe: Comparative perspectives on interethnic relations and social incorporation.* Toronto: Canadian Scholars Press.

Iyer, P. (2001). *Imagining Canada: An outsider's hope for a new global future.* Toronto: Hart House, University of Toronto.

Jackson, S., & Solis, J. (Eds). (1995). *Beyond comfort zones in multiculturalism: Confronting the politics of privilege.* Westport, CT: Greenwood Press.

Jain, H., Singh, C.P., & Agocs, C. (2000). Recruitment, selection, and promotion of visible-minority and aboriginal police officers in selected Canadian police services. *Canadian Public Administration, 42*(3), 46.

Jakubowicz, A. (1994). *Racism, ethnicity, and the media.* Sydney: Allen & Unwin.

Jalsevac, P. (1999, Nov. 20). A class action. *Kitchener-Waterloo Record.*

James, J.B. (1997). What are the social issues involved in focusing on *difference* in the study of gender? *Journal of Social Issues, 53*(2), 213–32.

Jantzen, R. (2000). Five paradigms of ethnic relations. In L. Samover & R. Porter (Eds.), *Intercultural communication: A reader.* Belmont, CA: Wadsworth.

Jiwani, Y. (1998). On the outskirts of empire: Race and gender in Canadian TV News. In V. Strong-Boag (Ed.), *Painting the maple* (pp. 53–68). BC: UBC Press.

Jelloun, T.B. (1999). *French hospitality: Racism and North African immigrants.* New York: Columbia U Press.

Johnson, J. (2000). Why respect culture? *American Journal of Political Science, 44*(3), 405–18.

Johnston, P., & Maringi, G. (1994). Examining a state relationship: "Legitimation and Te Kohanga Reo. *Te Pua, 3*(2), 22–34.

Joppke, C. (1999). How immigration is changing citizenship: A comparative view. *Ethnic and Racial Studies, 22*(4), 629–52.

Jordan, G., & Weedon, C. (1995). The celebration of difference and the cultural politics of racism. In B. Adam & S. Allan (Eds.), *Theorizing culture* (pp. 149–64). New York: NY U Press.

Joseph, J. (2000). A realist theory of hegemony. *Journal for The Theory of Social Behaviour, 30*(2), 179–202.

Jupp, J. (1997). Tacking into the wind: Immigration and multicultural policy in the 1990s. *Journal of Australian Studies, 53*, 29–39.

Kalantzis, M., & Cope, B. (1999). Multicultural education: Transforming the mainstream. In S. May (Ed.), *Critical multiculturalism* (pp. 245–76). Madison: U of Wisconsin Press.

Kallen, E. (1982). Multiculturalism: Ideology, policy, and reality. *Journal of Canadian Studies, 17*, 51–63.

Kallen, E. (1987). Multiculturalism, minorities, and motherhood: A social scientific critique of Section 27. In Canadian Human Rights Foundation (Ed.), *Multiculturalism and the Charter: A legal perspective* (pp. 123–38). Toronto: Carswell.

Kamalipour, Y.R., & Carilli, T. (Eds.). (1998). *Cultural diversity and the U.S. media.* New York: State U of NY Press.

Karnoouh, C. (1998). Logos without ethos. *Telos, 110*, Winter, 119–34.

Kelly, J. (1998). *Under the gaze: Learning to be black in white society.* Halifax: Fernwood Publishing.

Kenny, A. (2000, Apr. 22). One god, three faiths. [Review of Karen Armstrong's *The battle for god*]. *National Post.*

Klein, N. (1999, Jul. 24). Boats, not birthrights. *National Post.*

Kobayashi, A. (1999). Multiculturalism and making difference: Comments on the state of multiculturalism policy in Canada. *Australian-Canadian Studies, 17*(2), 33–39.

Koring, P. (1999, Sept. 22). Human-rights group lashes out at "widespread" police brutality. *The Globe and Mail.*

Kumar, S. (2000, Feb. 21). Why Rushdie is no hero. *The Globe and Mail.*

Kurthen, H. (1997). The Canadian experience with multiculturalism and employment equity: Lessons for Europe. *New Community, 23*(2), 249–70.

Kymlicka, W. (1995). *Multicultural citizenship.* London: OUP.

Kymlicka, W. (1998). *Finding our way: Rethinking ethnocultural relations in Canada.* Toronto: OUP.

Kymlicka, W. (1999). Liberal complacencies. In S.M. Okin (Ed.), *Is multiculturalism bad for women?* (pp. 31–40). NJ: Princeton U Press.

La Prairie, C. (1999). Some reflections on the new criminal justice policies in Canada: Restorative justice, alternative measures, and conditional sentences. *Australian and New Zealand Journal of Criminology.* Special issue.

Landry, K. (1999, Nov. 12). Funding for Ontario's religious schools. *Toronto Star.*

Lawton, V. (2000, May 3). Hard time. *Toronto Star.*

Layton, D. (1999, Aug. 22). [Review of David Cayley's *The expanding prison*]. *Toronto Star.*

Lee, J., & Cardinal, L. (1998). Hegemonic nationalism and the politics of feminism and multiculturalism in Canada. In V. Strong-Boag (Ed.), *Painting the maple* (pp. 215–41). BC: UBC Press.

Li, P.S. (1999). The multiculturalism debate. In P.S. Li (Ed.), *Race and ethnic relations in Canada* (2nd ed.) (pp. 148–77). Toronto: OUP.

Lichbach, M.I., & Zuckerman, A.S. (Eds.). (1997). *Comparative politics: Rationality, culture and structure.* New York: CUP.

Longley, K. (1999). Beyond multiculturalism: Australia and Canada. *Australian-Canadian Studies, 17*(2), 75–83.

Lozoff, B. (1998, Mar.). A nation behind bars. *Shambhala Sun*, pp. 15–16.

Lunt, N. (1999). The discipline of social policy and biculturalism. *Social Policy Journal of New Zealand, 12*, Jul. 1–18.

Lustig, M.W., & Koester, J. (1996). *Intercultural competence: Interpersonal communication across cultures* (2nd ed.). NY: HarperCollins.

Lynch, E.W., & Hanson, M.J. (2000). *Developing cross-cultural competence* (2nd ed.). Sydney: Paul H. Brookes Publishers.

Magsino, R.F. (2000). The Canadian multiculturalism policy: A pluralist ideal revisited. In S. Nancoo (Ed.), *21st century Canadian diversity* (pp. 320–41). Mississauga: Canadian Scholars Press.

Manzo, K.A. (1996). *Creating boundaries: The politics of race and nation*. London: Lynn Rienner Publisher.

Margison, S. (1999). Diversity and convergence in Australian higher education. *Australian University Review, 42*(1), 12–23.

Martiniello, M. (1998). Wieviorka's views on multiculturalism: A critique. *Ethnic and Racial Studies, 21*(5), 911–19.

Matas, R. (1999, May 15). Motorcycle helmet law in B.C. ruled unfair. *The Globe and Mail*.

May, S. (1999). Introduction: Towards a critical multiculturalism. In S. May (Ed.), *Critical multiculturalism: Rethinking multicultural and anti-racist education* (pp. 11–41). London: Falmer Press.

McGovern, M. (2000). Republicanism and pluralism. *Capital & Class, 71*, 134–44.

McLaren, P. (1994). White terror and oppositional agency: Towards a critical multiculturalism. In D.T. Goldberg (Ed.), *Multiculturalism: A critical reader* (pp. 45–74). Oxford, UK: Blackwell Publishers.

McRae, H. (2000). The criminal justice system and the construction of aboriginality. *Criminal Justice in Diverse Communities, 17*(2), 148–66.

Melleuish, G. (1998). *The packaging of Australia: Politics and culture wars*. Sydney: U of NSW Press Ltd.

Miliband, R. (1973). *The state in capitalist society*. London: Quartet Books.

Mittler, P. (2000). *Working toward inclusive education and social contexts*. London: David Fulton Publishers.

Modood, T., & Werbner, P. (Eds.). (1997). *The politics of multiculturalism in the new Europe* (pp. 1–26). London: Zed Books.

Moletsane, R. (1999). Beyond desegregation: Multicultural education in South African schools. *Perspectives in Education, 18*(2), 31–42.

Moodley, K. (1981). Canadian multiculturalism as ideology. *Ethnic and Racial Studies, 6*(3), 320–32.

Moodley, K. (1999). Antiracist education through political literacy: The case of Canada. In S. May (Ed.), *Critical multiculturalism* (pp. 138–52). Madison: U of Wisconsin Press.

Nancoo, R.S., & Nancoo, S.E. (2000). The mass media and Canadian diversity. In S. Nancoo (Ed.), *21st century Canadian diversity* (pp. 36–67). Mississauga: Canadian Scholars Press.

Nancoo, S.E. (2000a). Managing diversity. In S. Nancoo (Ed.), *21st century Canadian diversity* (pp. 102–14). Mississauga: Canadian Scholars Press.

Nancoo, S.E. (2000b). The police and the diverse society. In S. Nancoo (Ed.), *21st century Canadian diversity* (pp. 158–82). Mississauga: Canadian Scholars Press.

National Post. (2000, Feb. 5). Call us Canadian. Editorial.

Neugebauer, R. (1999). First nations people and law enforcement: Community perspectives on police responsiveness. In Corsianos and Train (pp. 247–69). Toronto: Canadian Scholars Press.

Newsinger, J. (2000). Me Disney, you Tarzan. *Race & Class, 42*(1), 78–81.

Normandeau, A., & Leighton, B. (1990). *A vision of the future of policing in Canada: Police-Challenge 2000*. [Background Document]. Policy and Security Branch, Ministry Secretariat, Solicitor-General Canada. Ottawa: Minister of Supply and Services.

Novo, A. (2000). The matter with multiculturalism. *Revolution*, Aug.–Oct. 18–19.

Nunan, T., George, R., & McCausland, H. (2000). Inclusive education in universities: Why it is important and how it may be achieved. *International Journal of Inclusive Education, 4*(1), 63–88.

O'Connor, J. (1973). *The fiscal crisis of the state*. New York: St. Martin's Press.

Oettmeier, T.N., & Brown, L.P. (1988). Role expectations and the concept of neighborhood oriented community policing. In *Developing neighborhood oriented policing in the Houston Police Department*. Houston: The International Association of Police Chiefs.

Offe, C. (1984). *Contradictions of the welfare state*. London: Hutchinson.

Okin, S.M. (Ed). (1999). *Is multiculturalism bad for women?* [with respondents] (pp. 7–26). NJ: Princeton U Press.

Panitch, L. (1975). The role and nature of the Canadian state. In L. Panitch (Ed.), *Canadian state: Political economy and political power* (pp. 3–27). Toronto: U of Toronto Press.

Parekh, B. (1996). The united colours of inequality. *New Statesman*, Dec. 13, 18–19.

Parekh, B. (1999). Political theory and the multicultural society. *Radical Philosophy, 95*, 27–32.

Partington, G. (2000). "Empowered" but impoverished: Multiculturalism and aboriginal education. *Quadrant*, Oct., 33–38.

Patton, C., & Caserio, R.L. (2000). Introduction: Citizenship 2000. *Cultural Studies, 14*(1), 1–14.

Pearson, D. (1994). Canada compared: Multiculturalism and biculturalism in settler societies. *ISER Occasional Paper No 3*.

Pearson, D. (1995). Multi-culturalisms and modernisms: Some comparative thoughts. *Sites, 30*, Autumn, 9–30.

Pearson, D. (1996). Crossing ethnic thresholds: Multiculturalisms in comparative perspective. In N. Patai & P. Spoonley (Eds.) (pp. 247–66). Palmerston North: Dunmore

Pearson, S. (1999). Subversion and ambivalence: Pacific Islanders on New Zealand prime time. *The Contemporary Pacific, 11*(2), 361–88.

Pedalty, M. (1998). Coors world and culture war. *Socialist Review, 92*, 71–99.

Pentney, W.F. (1989). Race relations: The legislative base. In O.P. Dwivedi (Ed.), *Canada 2000: Race relations and public policy* (pp. 53–63). Guelph, ON: U of Guelph.

Peter, K. (1978). Multi-cultural politics, money, and the conduct of Canadian ethnic studies. *Canadian Ethnic Studies Association Bulletin, 5*, 2–3.

Poetica: An International Journal of Linguistic-Literature Study. (1997). Multiculturalism south: Cultural perspectives from Oceania. Editorial.

Pollitt, K. (1999). Whose culture? In S.M. Okin (Ed.), *Is multiculturalism bad for women?* (pp. 27–30). NJ: Princeton U Press.

Poole, R. (1999). *Nation and identity*. London: Routledge.

Porter, J. (1965). *The vertical mosaic*. Toronto: U of Toronto Press.

Porter, J. (1979). *The measure of Canadian society: Education, equality, and opportunity*. Toronto: Gage Publishing.

Poulantzas, N. (1975). *Classes in contemporary society*. London: New Left Review.

Povinelli, E.A. (1998). The state of shame: Australian multiculturalism and the crisis of indigenous citizenship. *Critical Inquiry, 24*, Winter, 575–610.

Powell, R. (2000). Overcoming cultural racism: The promise of multicultural education. *Multicultural Perspectives, 2*(3), 8–14. An Official Journal of the National Association for Muticultural Education (Erlbaum Associates).

Priegert, P. (1991, Jul. 17). Canada's decision to celebrate ethnic diversity has backfired. *Kitchener-Waterloo Record*.

Qualter, T.H. (1991). Propaganda in Canadian society. In B.D. Singer (Ed.), *Communications in Canadian society* (pp. 200–12). Scarborough, ON: Nelson Canada.

Rex, J. (1997). The problematic multinational and multicultural societies. *Ethnic and Racial Studies, 20*(3), 1–15.

Richards, J. (2000, Oct. 6). Divided we stand. *The Globe and Mail*.

Riger, S. (1997). From snapshots to videotape: New directions in research on gender differences. *Journal of Social Issues, 53*(2), 395–408.

Rizvi, F. (1994). The new right and the politics of multiculturalism in Australia. In *Multiculturalism and the State*, Vol 1. (Collected seminar papers no. 47.) U of London: Institute of Commonwealth Studies.

Royal Commission. (1996). *Looking forward, looking backward*. Vol 1. Report of the Royal Commission on Aboriginal Affairs. Ottawa: Minister of Supply and Services.

Rubinstein, H. (2000, Mar. 20). Apartheid is alive and well in Winnipeg. *The Globe and Mail*.

Rukszto, K. (2000). Out of bounds, perverse longings, transgressive desire and the limits of multiculturalism: A reading of *Fall on Your Knees. International Journal of Canadian Studies*, Summer, 19–31.

Samad, Y. (1997). The plural guises of multiculturalism: Conceptualising a fragmented paradigm. In T. Modood & P. Werbner (Eds.), *The politics of multiculturalism in the New Europe* (pp. 240–60). London: Zed Books.

Samover, L., & Porter, R. (2000). *Intercultural communication: A reader*. Belmont, CA: Wadsworth.

Samuel, J., & Schachhuber, D. (2000). Perspectives on Canadian diversity. In S. Nancoo (Ed.), *21st century Canadian diversity* (pp. 14–35). Mississauga: Canadian Scholars Press.

Samuels, B.A. (1997). *Multiculturalism in Canada*. Calgary: Weigl Education Publishers Ltd.

Savard, P., & Vigezzi, B. (1999). *Multiculturalism and the history of international relations from the 18th century up to the present*. Ottawa: Carleton U Press.

Schlesinger, Jr., A.M. (1992). *The disuniting of America: Reflections on a multicultural society*. NY: Norton.

Schwimmer, E. (Ed.), (1968). *The Maori people in the 1960s*. Auckland: Longman Paul.

Scollon, R., & Wong Scollon, S. (1995). *Intercultural communication: A discourse approach*. Oxford, UK: Blackwell Publishers.

Scrivener, L. (2001, Feb. 25). Islamic schools a safe place. *Toronto Star*.

Shephard, D. (2000). *Reframing women*. Auckland: HarperCollins.

Shkilnyk, A.M. (1985). *A poison stronger than love: The destruction of an Ojibwa community*. New Haven, CT: Yale U Press.

Shkilnyk, A.M. (1986). *Progress report— Aboriginal language policy developments*. (Unpublished report for the Assembly of First Nations.)

Siddiqui, H. (1999, Jul. 1). Wave the flag for Canadian mosaic. *Toronto Star*.

Siddiqui, H. (1999, Dec. 30). Canada's challenges can be overcome. *Toronto Star*.

Siddiqui, H. (2000, Oct. 1). Pierre Trudeau's cultural revolution. *Toronto Star*.

Siddiqui, H. (2001, Apr. 29). Media world coverage shallow, often biased. *Toronto Star*.

Siddiqui, H. (2001, May 2). Canadian, U.S. media compared. *Toronto Star*.

Sleeter, C., & Grant, G. (1992). *Making choices for multicultural education* (2nd ed.). Columbus: Merrill/Macmillan.

Smith, M. (1997). Overcoming racial stereotyping through multicultural education: A native American perspective. In

M.A. Burayidi (Ed.), *Multiculturalism in a cross-national perspective* (pp. 265–85). NY: University Press of America.

Stam, R. (1997). Multiculturalism and neocon-servatives. In A. McClintock, A. Mufti, & E. Shohat (Eds.), *Dangerous liaisons: Gender, nation, and postcolonial perspectives* (pp. 173–87). Minneapolis, MN: U of Minnesota Press.

Stam, R. (2000). Introduction: Permutations of difference. In R. Stam & T. Miller (Eds.), *Film and theory: An anthology* (pp. 661–68). Oxford, UK: Blackwell Publishers.

Stam, R., & Miller, T. (2000). Black America cinema. In R. Stam & T. Miller (Eds.), *Film and theory: An anthology* (pp. 236–56). Oxford, UK: Blackwell Publishers.

Steyn, M. (1999, Apr. 1). The Kosovo war on the homefront. *National Post*.

St. Lewis, J. (1996). Identity and black con-sciousness in North America. In J. Littleton (Ed.), *Clash of Identities* (pp. 21–30). Englewood Cliffs, NJ: Prentice Hall.

Stoffman, D. (2001). Some of my best friends. *Maclean's*, Commemorative Issue, 122–23.

Stolcke, V. (1999). New rhetorics of exclusion in Europe. *International Social Science Journal, 159*, 25–32.

Stone, M. (1981). *The education of the black child in Britain: The myth of multicultural education*. London: Fontana Books.

Sugunasiri, S. (1999). *How to kick multicultur-alism in its teeth*. Toronto: Vintage Publishing House.

Tauri, J. (1999). Recent innovation: Empowering Maori or biculturalising the state? *Australian and New Zealand Journal of Criminology*. Special issue.

Taylor, C. (1992). The politics of recognition. In A. Gutman (Ed.), *The politics of recog-nition* (pp. 25–48). NJ: Princeton.

Thobani, S. (1995). Multiculturalism: The politics of containment. In A. Nelson & A. Fleras (Eds.), *Social problems in Canada reader* (pp. 213–16). Scarborough: Prentice Hall.

Tinglin, W. (1998). Making changes: Reflections on police relations in Ontario over two decades. *Currents, 8*(3), 30–34.

Tong, R.P. (1998). Multiculturalism and global feminism. In R.P. Tong, *Feminist thought: A more comprehensive introduction* (2nd ed.). Boulder, CO: Westview Press.

Turner, T. (1994). Anthropology and multicul-turalism: What is anthropology that multi-culturalists should be mindful of it? In D. Goldberg (Ed.), *Multiculturalism: A critical reader* (pp. 406–25). Oxford, UK: Blackwell Publishers.

Ujimoto, K.V. (1999). Studies of ethnic identity, ethnic relations, and citizenship. In P.S. Li (Ed.), *Race and ethnic relations in Canada* (2nd ed.) (pp. 253–90). Toronto: OUP.

Van Driel, B. (2000). Intercultural education. *Outsider* (Newsletter of Minority Rights Group International), *54*, 3.

Vassell, Jr., A. (1999). Caribbean leads world in diversity. *Southwestern Guardian*, Dec.

Vasta, E. (1996). Dialectics of dominion: Racism and multiculturalism. In E. Vasta & S. Castles (Eds.), *The teeth are smiling: The persistence of racism in multicultural Australia* (pp. 46–72). Sydney: Allen & Unwin.

Vasta E., & Castles, S. (Eds.). (1996). *The teeth are smiling: The persistence of racism in multicultural Australia*. Sydney: Allen & Unwin.

Vertovec, S. (1996). Multiculturalism, cultur-alism, and public incorporation. *Ethnic and Racial Studies, 19*(1), 49–68.

Walker, R. (1995). Immigration policy and the political economy in New Zealand. In S.W. Greif (Ed.), *Immigration and national identity in New Zealand* (pp. 282–301). Palmerston North: Dunmore.

Wallace, J. (1999, Mar. 5). The colour blind spot. *The Times Higher Education*, p. 21.

Ward, A. (1999). An unsettled history. [Stout Annual Lecture.] Reprinted in *Stout Annual Review, 9*(2), 21–30.

Warley, L. (1998). The mountie and the nurse: Cross cultural relations *North of 60*. In

V. Strong-Boag (Ed.), *Painting the Maple* (pp. 173–86). BC: UBC Press.

Weinrib, L. (2000, Oct. 5). A giant legal footstep. *The Globe and Mail*.

We Interrupt This Message/Youth Force. (2001). How the *New York Times* frames youth. In *Between the Lines*.

Weitzer, R. (2000). Racialized policing residents' perceptions. In *Three Neighborhoods*.

Werbner, P. (1997). Afterward: Writing, multiculturalism, and politics in the New Europe. In T. Modood & P. Werbner (Eds.), *The politics of multiculturalism in the new Europe: Racism, identity, and community* (pp. 261–67). London: Zed Books.

Wicks, D., & Bradshaw, P. (2000). The oppression of women in Canada: From denial to awareness and resistance. In S. Nancoo (Ed.), *21st century diversity* (pp. 143–51). Mississauga: Canadian Scholars Press.

Wieviorka, M. (1998). Is multiculturalism the solution? *Ethnic and Racial Studies, 21*(5), 881–910.

Wilson, V.S. (1995). Canada's evolving multicultural policy. In C.E.S Franks (Ed.), *Canada's century: Governance in a maturing society* (pp. 165–95). Montreal/Kingston: McGill-Queen's University Press.

Wolf, A. (1999). *One nation, after all.* New York: Viking.

Wrong, D. (2000). Adversarial identities and multiculturalism. *Society, 37*(2), 12–14.

Young, C. (1993). *The rising tide of cultural pluralism: The nation-state at bay?* Madison: U of Wisconsin Press.

Young, I. (1990). *Justice and the politics of difference.* NJ: Princeton U Press.

Young, I. (1997). Unruly categories: A critique of Nancy Fraser's dual systems theory. In C.Willett (Ed.), *Theorizing multiculturalism* (pp. 50–67). Oxford, UK: Blackwell Publishers.

Younkins, E.W. (2000). Why the world is the way it is: Cultural relativism and its descendants. *The Free Radical*, Sept./Oct. 29–33.

Zizek, S. (1997). Multiculturalism, the cultural logic of multinational capitalism. *New Left Review, 225*, 40–52.

Index